The Dilemma of Toxic Substance Regulation

MIT Press Series on the Regulation of Economic Activity

General Editor
Richard Schmalensee, MIT Sloan School of Management

The Dilemma of Toxic Substance Regulation
How Overregulation Causes Underregulation at OSHA

John M. Mendeloff

The MIT Press
Cambridge, Massachusetts
London, England

This book was set in Times Roman by Asco Trade Typesetting Ltd., Hong Kong, and printed and bound by Halliday Lithograph in the United States of America.

Library of Congress Cataloging-in-Publication Data

Mendeloff, John M.
  The dilemma of toxic substance regulation: how overregulation causes underregulation at OSHA/John M. Mendeloff.
    p.   cm.—(MIT Press series on the regulation of economic activity; 17)
  Bibliography: p.
  Includes index.
  ISBN 0-262-13230-3
  1. Hazardous substances—Law and legislation—United States.   2. Administrative procedure—United States.   I. Title.   II. Series.
KF3958.M46 1988
344.73′0472—dc19
[347.304472]   87-21320
                                                                                CIP

For my parents

Contents

III
DIRECTIONS FOR REFORM

Series Foreword

Government regulation of economic activity in the United States has grown dramatically in this century, radically transforming the economic roles of government and business as well as relations between them. Economic regulation of prices and conditions of service was first applied to transportation and public utilities and was later extended to energy, health care, and other sectors. In the early 1970s explosive growth occurred in social regulation, focusing on workplace safety, environmental preservation, consumer protection, and related goals. Regulatory reform has occupied a prominent place on the agendas of recent administrations, and considerable economic deregulation and other reform has occurred, but the aims, methods, and results of many regulatory programs remain controversial.

The purpose of the MIT Press Series on Regulation of Economic Activity is to inform the ongoing debate on regulatory policy by making significant and relevant research available to both scholars and decision makers. Books in this series present new insights into individual agencies, programs, and regulated sectors, as well as the important economic, political, and administrative aspects of the regulatory process that cut across these boundaries.

Since the middle 1970s social regulation has become more important relative to economic regulation, but no corresponding shift has occurred in the allocation of academic resources. John Mendeloff's study of the regulation of toxic substances thus makes a significant contribution to the literature by providing a careful and thorough analysis of the operation and effects of a major social regulatory program. But it does more than this.

Although the economic literature on economic regulation is full of prescriptions, most studies of social regulation are content to show that in practice these programs fail basic cost-benefit tests. In this volume Mendeloff asks why this occurs and goes on to present and defend an explanation of agency behavior in the toxic substances arena. He then explores the implications of this explanation for alternative approaches to regulatory reform. This study should appeal to all who are interested in why social regulation seems to perform poorly and what might be done about it.

Richard Schmalensee

Acknowledgments

It is a pleasure to acknowledge the debts accumulated in the course of preparing this book. My greatest thanks go to the many people who took the time to talk with me about the events described here.

In addition, all or parts of the manuscript were reviewed by Neal Beck, Les Boden, Robert Bohrer, Don Chisholm, Steven Finan, Michael Gough, Gary Jacobson, Carol Jones, David Laitin, Sandy Lakoff, Ben Mintz, Toby Page, Sam Popkin, Jamie Robinson, Martin Shapiro, Gary Schwartz, Kip Viscusi, and David Wegman. John Graham and Gene Bardach gave especially lengthy and helpful comments. Kelly Charter and Lee Dewey provided the human support system for my word processing program, and they were unfailingly gracious.

An outline of the basic argument of this book appeared in "Does Overregulation Cause Underregulation? The Case of Toxic Substances" (*Regulation* 5:47–52, September–October 1981). Parts of chapters 8, 9, and 10 appeared in "Regulatory Reform and OSHA Policy" (*Journal of Policy Analysis and Management* (Spring 1986), 5(3):440–468). That issue also carried commentaries on my article by Kip Viscusi and by Robert Litan and William Nordhaus, all of whom were quite helpful. I would like to thank the editors of both journals.

While I was writing this book, I received financial support from several sources. A contract from the congressional Office of Technology Assessment (OTA) let me learn about many of the data sources cited here. Serving as the special consultant to the OTA's study *Preventing Injury and Illnesses in the Workplace* also proved stimulating and helpful. A contract with OSHA's Office of Policy Analysis allowed me to investigate these data sources further. Most recently, I was able to serve on a National Academy of Sciences panel on occupational safety and health statistics; this opportunity provided some new insights into the data needed for intelligent regulation. My work on the valuation of risk reduction has been supported by the National Science Foundation's Regulation and Policy Analysis Division under grant SES 8420410. NSF also supported a conference at which I was invited to present a paper about the relevance of the OSHA experience to recent theorizing about regulation. Finally, the University of California, San Diego, Academic Senate provided funds on several occasions.

The last debts are personal. My wife, Fay, contributed common sense and clarity to whatever parts of the manuscript she touched. Along with our daughter, Lauren, she also helped keep the book-writing process in perspective.

Introduction

Many observers have pointed out that the level of conflict over health, safety, and environmental regulation in the United States exceeds that found in other nations. In this book I supply a new perspective on what some of the harmful consequences of that conflict have been. By identifying the mechanisms that sustain the conflicts, I try to point the way toward more fruitful resolutions.

Some people argue that the standards that the federal government has established to reduce the workplace risks posed by toxic substances are often so strict that we would have been better off by doing nothing. They are right.

Some people argue that the slow pace at which standards have been set has left us underprotected against a large number of hazards. They too are right. This book makes the normative argument that standard setting for toxic substances in the workplace has been characterized by both overregulation and underregulation. It also makes the positive argument that overregulation is an important cause of underregulation.

I have three objectives. The first is to convince you that these twin dilemmas do indeed exist. The second is to explain what created this socially undesirable situation. The third is to suggest what to do about it. The degree to which the first and third objectives are achieved will be of special importance to those interested in occupational health policy and in the broader issue of the regulation of toxic substances.

Readers interested in the politics of regulation, especially in the role of administrative law and the courts, should find my treatment of the second objective provocative. I think that the argument applies to all standard-setting programs that impose significant costs on well-organized groups. In addition, because my policy recommendations are based in part on this political analysis, their merit depends on its validity.

In 1979 I published a book on OSHA (*Regulating Safety*, MIT Press) that primarily examined why the legislation had been enacted, why it enshrined the enforcement of standards as the regulatory instrument instead of other more efficient approaches, what OSHA's impact on injury rates had been, and how the cost-effectiveness of its safety program could be improved. These subjects are not examined in this book. When research for that book ended in 1977, OSHA had adopted new exposure limits for only three health hazards. Although both the strictness and the slow pace of standard setting were already evident at that time; in that book I did not probe very deeply into those issues. At that time I viewed standard setting as an activity more subject to the discretion of agency leaders. As a result, I lacked sufficient appreciation of the obstacles to developing a rule-making system that regulated more extensively but less strictly.

Policy Analysis and Policy Reform

There are two chief criteria by which policy analysis should be assessed: Does it redefine problems in more interesting and more fruitful ways, and does it invent options that have potential for breaking unproductive policy stalemates? The two criteria are related. One could argue that the test of fruitfulness is precisely whether or not stalemates are broken. This is a practical and demanding criterion. Alternatively, one can view problem redefinition primarily as an intellectual task whose effects on policy changes are rarely direct but work, as James Q. Wilson has argued, through its impact on the terms of debate. The more fundamental the nature of the changes that are contemplated, the more appropriate this latter view becomes. The analyst provides general directions rather than a road map.

In either view the political feasibility of reform proposals is often difficult to gauge precisely. Reformers often appear wishful and naive. This is especially true if they first give a convincing analysis of "why things are the way they are." Even when the dynamics of change can be identified, it is difficult to predict how fast changes will come and how far they will go.

The Organization of This Book

I assert a number of points in this book: that attempts to regulate strictly have generated political opposition to regulating more extensively; that the rules issued have indeed often been too strict; that, as a result of the slow pace of standard setting, there really are things "out there" that could merit further regulation; that most regulatory reforms proposed by economists speak only to the overregulation problem; and that a good strategy would be to adopt new legislation that calls for less strict standards and makes it easier for the agencies to produce more standards by reducing the burden of proof they have to meet in the courts. Because major reforms of this type face formidable obstacles, the contribution that hazard-by-hazard rule making can make will be limited. That limitation is a serious problem because such rule making is a necessary, though not a sufficient, tool for dealing with hazards.

To make this argument convincing, we must get down to cases. Toxic substances present the most relevant case, and in this book I focus on standard setting for toxic substances at OSHA, although EPA programs are also considered. The case of health standard setting at OSHA can illuminate broader problems of regulation and rule making, but solutions to the problems of toxic substances and occupational disease are important in their own right.

In part I of the book (chapters 2 through 4) I address the questions of whether we have, in fact, both overregulated and underregulated. In chapter 2 I present the rudiments of benefit-cost analysis and ask why everyone doesn't agree that this is a proper framework to use and why, even if they do agree to use it, they may disagree about the method to use to value the prevention of death and disease. I also focus on how the particular features of occupational diseases might affect how we value their prevention.

In chapter 3 I review the evidence regarding the cost of OSHA's health standards and then explain the sources of uncertainty in estimates of their health effects. I also examine the policy implications of the scientific assumptions that underlie these estimates. The conclusions support the view that we have overregulated, although perhaps not by as much as some have suggested. Those who agree with this conclusion will probably wonder why the argument has been so long and belabored. Those who disagree will no doubt find it incomplete and unconvincing. Both its length and its incompleteness stem from what I see as the difficulty of resolving how judgments of this sort should be made.

I present the argument that we are underregulating in chapter 4. No one has tried to make this case in a systematic fashion. Although the available information does not allow a definitive conclusion, it strongly suggests that for a substantial number of hazards some degree of further stringency could confer net benefits. The data that are reviewed here also present fresh insights into the nature of the workplace toxics problem.

I take up the problem of explaining the key features of underregulation and overregulation in part II: Why is the pace so slow? Why does OSHA set priorities the way it does? Why are individual standards so strict?

In chapter 5 I take the previous chapter's conclusion that we have underregulated and try to explain why. I show that, despite the high degree of conflict, firms have not taken all possible measures to oppose standards and that their degree of opposition is related to the strictness of the standards. A substantial part of this chapter reviews how judicial review constrains the pace of standard setting. Here, as elsewhere, I argue that the key factor is not the time required to fulfill procedural requirements, but rather OSHA's uncertainty that it can meet the standard of proof that judges will require it to meet in order to justify its strict standards. I show that OSHA's attempts to overcome the slow pace, especially its Cancer Policy, have failed precisely because they attempted to accelerate the pace without changing the policies that generate political opposition. A look at a comparable program at the EPA, the administration of section 112 of the Clean Air Act, shows how strictness leads to slowness there too.

In chapter 6 I show that the choice of which hazards to address takes on added significance in a system characterized by overregulation and underregulation. If OSHA had a good system for setting priorities, the underregulation problem would be eased somewhat. But my review of the main influences on OSHA's priority setting does not give grounds for confidence that the choices maximize either public health or efficiency.

I look in chapter 7 at the underpinnings of strictness with an eye to identifying which of them might be most easily removed. The most direct impact on strictness would come from altering the statutes or the way that the courts have interpreted them. Unions will oppose amending the OSH Act unless they can be convinced that underregulation cannot be solved in any other way. Even then, it will take a difficult legislative compromise to win approval. Other factors that hold protective policies in place— scientific uncertainties, popular mistrust of big business and big government, and the political rewards of speaking out for "people over profits"— are even harder to alter.

In chapter 8 I examine whether some of the most prominent proposals for procedural regulatory reform will help to resolve the overregulation/underregulation problem. I look at proposals for a regulatory budget, regulatory negotiation, and greater use of centralized regulatory analysis.

In chapter 9 I look at substantive "alternatives to regulation," for example, information strategies and expanded use of the tort system. Although there is considerable merit in most of these ideas, the conclusion is that they do not provide adequate means to address both parts of the regulatory dilemma.

And, finally, in chapter 10 I present a strategy that could be used wherever the overregulation/underregulation dilemma exists and tailor it to OSHA's case. I call for a three-part legislative reform: (1) allowing the balancing of benefits and costs, (2) creating a two-track rule-making system that allows standards to be set with a lower standard of proof when the total costs of the rule are small, and (3) adopting en masse all the changes in exposure limits that the ACGIH has recommended since the OSH Act mandated the adoption of the 1968 ACGIH exposure limits.

Support for these changes will depend on the acceptance of the general argument presented in this book, which in turn requires a shift in the way that elites think about the problem of rule making.

The Dilemma of Toxic Substance Regulation

Overregulation, Underregulation, and the Rule-Making Dilemma

The 1960s and 1970s witnessed the enactment of a new wave of federal regulatory programs designed to protect citizens from hazards ranging from automobile accidents and unsafe products to toxic substances in the workplace and in the ambient air. Proponents of these programs believed that existing regulatory agencies, whether at the state or federal level, lacked the political will and the capability to force firms to behave in a socially responsible manner. Underlying this critique of regulatory programs was a body of scholarship that argued that regulatory agencies frequently cater to the interests of the regulated rather than to a broader notion of the public interest. These outcomes were attributed to the domination of the policymaking process by the "iron triangle" of regulated industry, regulatory agency, and the legislative committees that oversee the agency.

Transmitted to a generation of professionals in virtually every college and law school, this critique of regulation was reinforced by increased questioning of business legitimacy and by heightened concern with environmental deterioration and toxic chemicals. Legislators discovered that these popular concerns could be used to their own political advantage. Mistrustful of administrative discretion, reformers tried to write statutory language that precluded sacrificing safety to other objectives. They also sought to mandate procedures allowing outside parties to request action, requiring agencies to respond to them in a timely fashion and requiring agency decisions to be well documented.[1]

To a considerable extent, these statutes, aided by popular support for protective regulation, have prevented the pro-business backsliding that their architects sought to avoid. (Even the Reagan administration, despite some attempts, was largely unable to dismantle the underpinnings of these programs.)[2] However, this accomplishment should be balanced against two other features of our recent regulatory experience.

First, many of the programs have been sharply criticized for their inefficiency. Although this criticism includes complaints that the goals have been pursued through unnecessarily costly methods, it often goes on to argue that the goals themselves have been set too high, beyond the point at which the benefits of reducing hazards justify the costs. For example, staff on the Council of Economic Advisers have complained that the Environmental Protection Agency (EPA) set too low an exposure limit for smog-producing ozone, requiring over $12 billion in annual costs, more than could be justified by the benefits from the resulting drop in smog levels. Economists on the Council on Wage-Price Stability have lambasted the Occupational Safety and Health Administration (OSHA) for promulgating rules on such chemicals as benzene, arsenic, and vinyl chloride that may cost tens of millions of dollars per fatal cancer prevented.[3]

Although many economists and business leaders have protested that regulations have required large outlays for trivial benefits, advocates of strict protection have been disappointed with the slow pace of standard setting. They feel that many serious hazards have simply not been addressed, causing deaths and diseases that we should be preventing (although others question whether the magnitude of the threat from these hazards is significant). Examples include the following.

After fifteen years, despite the urgings of the Natural Resources Defense Council, the EPA has issued final rules for only five toxic substances under section 112 of the Clean Air Act, which addresses hazardous air pollutants such as asbestos and benzene.

After fifteen years, OSHA has established new workplace exposure limits for only ten health hazards. During the same period, the private standard-setting organization, which OSHA was designed to supplant, has recommended lower exposure limits for hundreds of chemicals.

Dissatisfaction with the slow pace of the EPA's reregistration program for existing pesticides led Congress, in 1978, to try to streamline the process by calling for standards for six hundred active ingredients instead of for reregistration of each of the tens of thousands of pesticide products. Although the task was projected to take ten years to complete, by 1985 standards had been set for fewer than a dozen ingredients.

Advocates claimed that the Toxic Substances Control Act (TSCA) of 1976 would provide a comprehensive framework for the regulation of toxic chemicals. By the end of 1984, controls had been placed on only four so-called old chemicals (those on the market before 1979). And although the EPA officials in charge of TSCA had identified forty-one additional chemicals for which additional testing would be required, no testing regulations had been adopted.

In this book I present and examine two arguments drawn from this experience.[4] The first is normative, concerned with what our policy *should* be; the second is positive, attempting to explain *why* policy has developed as it has.

1. For many protective regulatory programs we would be better off setting standards less strictly but more extensively. This prescription de-

parts both from economists who have focused only on "overregulation" and from the environmental and health lobbies who have focused only on "underregulation." Many defenders of regulation dispute the claim that existing standards have been set too strictly, and many economists tend to be skeptical of claims that there are hazards "out there" worth regulating.

2. Setting standards (for example, exposure or emission limits) strictly is a significant cause of the slow pace of the standard-setting process. Although the strictness of standards is not the only influence on the pace of standard setting, a program with stricter standards will, holding all other things constant, tend to have a slower pace.

The normative argument has important implications for how particular regulatory programs should be changed. To examine its validity, we need to see whether individual standards have, in fact, been set too strictly and whether there are, in fact, many other hazards for which stricter standards would be justified. Answers to these questions are elusive because of the uncertainties about the nature of these hazards and disagreements about how to value their reduction. We need to review how, in the face of these difficulties, estimates can be made of the health effects, the costs of standards, and the value placed on reducing them. I address these issues in chapters 2, 3, and 4.

The prescription that we should set standards less strictly but more frequently provides one motivation for examining what the relationship between the strictness and frequency of standard setting actually is. If strict regulation is one cause of the lack of extensiveness, then looser regulation will speed the pace. This argument is also controversial. Based on his study of regulation in the United States and Britain, David Vogel concurs that "the American experience demonstrates that overregulation can readily lead to underregulation";[5] and Lester Lave argues that "if Congress writes ... rigid frameworks into law, inevitably a few substances will arbitrarily be selected for special treatment, while the rest will languish until some real or imagined disaster elevates them to the spotlight."[6] Yet many proponents of strict regulation argue that the pace of rule making would not speed up in response to laxer rules. Even if it is correct, the relevance of my argument for policymaking would still depend on whether a policy of less strict but more extensive regulation is politically feasible. Answering these questions presents a real test for our understanding of the politics of regulation. An answer requires examining the political, legal, administrative, and technical factors affecting the pace and stringency of regulation. I take up that task in chapters 5, 6, and 7.

A Concise Statement of the Normative Argument

Judgments about whether a particular regulation is justified depend on assessments of the value of reducing risks. Valuing the benefits of reducing mortality and morbidity is ethically, politically, and analytically controversial. A major argument in favor of explicit valuation of these benefits is that they will be valued implicitly even if they are not valued explicitly. Thus, for example, a decision to spend $2 million to prevent an estimated two deaths indicates that the policymaker places a value on preventing each of those deaths of at least $1 million. Refusal to acknowledge this valuation explicitly may have several consequences; policymakers may not clarify confusion in their own minds, and valuations across programs are less likely to reflect consistent judgments, with a consequent sacrifice of efficiency. Of course, as I discuss in chapter 2, public distaste for explicit valuations of human lifesaving indicates that explicitness imposes costs as well as benefits.

The current approach to valuation in favor with most economists is to find out how much the people at risk are willing to pay for small reductions in risks. If we assume, for the moment, that the people at risk are also the people who will pay for the program, then it seems reasonable not to require them to spend more for it than they value it.

One method for estimating these values has been to examine the so-called risk premiums paid to workers in more hazardous jobs.[7] These have been estimated in a number of studies to range from only a few hundred thousand dollars to more than $5 million for each accidental death experienced. In chapter 2 we will look at these estimates more critically. For now, I assert that it seems unlikely that workers place a value higher than $3 million on preventing a death that would occur twenty to thirty years in the future, the typical latency period for most occupational cancers.

Although many risk reduction programs have low or moderate costs per fatality prevented, others, especially those dealing with toxic substances, have high costs. For example, one major review found relatively low costs (that is, under $1 million and often much lower) for auto safety standards and relatively high costs ($3 million and up) for most efforts to regulate toxic substances.[8] An estimate of the cost of meeting the EPA's 1980 benzene standard was $6.5 million per death prevented.[9] Looking at standards at OSHA, a team of analysts estimated that the average costs per cancer death averted were $20.2 million for the arsenic standard, $18.9 million for benzene, $4.5 million for coke oven emissions, and $3.5 million for acrylonitrile.[10] For the asbestos standard, however, which accounts for almost 90 percent of the estimated fatal cancers averted by these five standards, the estimated costs were below $200,000.

It is important to keep in mind that these are *average* costs. In the case of acrylonitrile, for example, it is the average cost of moving from the preexisting exposure level of 20 ppm (parts per million) to 2 ppm. With acrylonitrile and probably with most toxic substances, it becomes increasingly expensive to achieve added reductions in exposure. Thus the extra cost per death averted in moving from 3 ppm to 2 ppm was undoubtedly much higher than $3.5 million, probably at least twice as much. It is this higher figure that is the valuation implicit in a decision to adopt a 2 ppm standard. Thus, even if preventing cancer deaths is valued at $3.5 million each, a 2-ppm standard should not be supported unless the only choices are 20 ppm and 2 ppm, with no options in between. Because the same point applies to the standards on arsenic and the others, the overall numbers are clearly high. Although these numbers are subject to major uncertainties, it should be apparent why the overregulation argument has merit.

The finding that overly strict health and safety standards have frequently been set does not preclude the possibility that some more moderate regulatory action is justifiable. The high costs of these standards typically resulted from exposure reductions of 90 to 99.8 percent. But because the cost per death averted is strongly affected by the degree to which exposures are reduced, reductions of 50 percent might have been easily justifiable. By the same token, the finding that past standards have been set too strictly does not preclude the possibility that additional standards are needed. In addition, of course, new hazards may be identified that have not been addressed at all.

The Reagan administration campaigned in 1980 against overregulation and made regulatory relief a major component of its initial economic package (along with budget cuts and tax cuts). It tried, with mixed success, to require agencies to use benefit-cost analyses to guide their decisions. The other leg of the regulatory relief effort was to encourage a slowdown in the generation of new regulations, reflecting a strongly held view of many of its leaders that most rules were, on net, undesirable.

The casual lumping together of the charges that regulation has been both too strict and too extensive is particularly unfortunate because it obscures some important relationships between the two issues and, in so doing, some possible remedies. It is generally agreed that, where markets "fail" (because of inadequate information or externalities), regulation of hazards can *potentially* be beneficial. Yet, if we expect that the regulatory response will be improper—that standards will not reflect the most efficient approach or will be set far too strictly—we may prefer inaction on the grounds that it is the lesser of two evils. In this manner overregulation may cause underegulation. Ironically, the costs of overregulation would include not only the excessive costs of strict regulation but also the potential benefits foregone when we decide that no standard is better than an overly strict one.

An important implication of this view is that, if standards are set more sensibly, with more attention to weighing costs and benefits, we should be willing to regulate more extensively than we would otherwise. For example, suppose that an agency, instead of issuing one new standard a year with a reduction in exposure of 95 percent, issued five new standards with reductions of 50 percent each. It is highly likely that the second approach of regulating more hazards less strictly would be more cost-effective—would lower the average cost for each fatality averted. (As noted, however, critics might still claim that even these less strict standards impose net costs and thus that more extensive regulation should be shunned.) The Reagan administration's regulatory policy comes down hard on the side of weighing costs and benefits but ignores altogether the implications for extensiveness.

The lesson of this book is that a comprehensive plan for regulatory reform of standard-setting programs should simultaneously consider the pace and extent of regulation as well as the the strictness of individual standards.[11]

My emphasis on standard-setting programs is deliberate, for there are important differences between regulatory programs that rely on "screening" new products or processes before they are marketed or used and programs that rely on setting standards to address the hazards of products that are already on the market. Examples of standard-setting programs include the EPA's program for hazardous air pollutants (for example, asbestos), the Food and Drug Administration's (FDA's) regulation of "old" food additives (for example, saccharin), the National Highway Traffic Safety Administration's (NHTSA's) auto safety measures, and OSHA's standards for workplace safety and health. Examples of screening programs include the FDA's approval of new drugs and new food additives, the Nuclear Regulatory Commission's licensing of nuclear power plants, and the EPA's review of premanufacture notices for new chemicals under the Toxic Substances Control Act (TSCA).[12]

The screening programs place the burden of showing that products are "safe" on the firms that produce them. Thus the firms are hurt by delays. In contrast, standard-setting programs place the burden of proof on the regulatory agencies. Until agencies can meet it, products can stay on the market. Thus firms benefit from delays.

Regulators in both types of programs should seek to minimize the sum of the costs imposed by hazards and the costs imposed by hazard prevention. But the "lesson" stated for guiding the reform of standard-setting programs does not fit screening programs because the policy problems that regulators face with screening programs are different. In screening programs there is only one key policy issue: how high to set the standard of proof that firms have to meet to show that their products are not too risky. If the standard of proof is set too high, many worthwhile products (some of which might even reduce risks) will be stillborn. If it is set too low, too many hazardous products will be approved. In standard-setting programs, as we have seen, there are several key policy issues in addition to the proper burden of proof that the agencies should bear: the choice of hazards to address, the number of hazards to address, and the strictness of individual standards.

One great paradox found in many standard-setting agencies is the disparity between their activist rhetoric and their cautions actions. The statutes and regulations emphasize their preventive goals; they should not wait until "the bodies are counted" before taking action. The agencies have adopted rules for interpreting evidence, especially animal bioassay data, that clearly take more pains to avoid false negatives (that is, identifying hazardous chemicals as innocuous) than false positives (identifying innocuous chemicals as hazardous). Yet, if we look at programs with highly protective mandates and potentially broad scope, such as OSHA's health program and the EPA's hazardous air pollutant program, we find that not only have they addressed a paltry number of hazards but also in almost every case they have chosen hazards from the small category for which evidence of disease in humans (as opposed to animals) is available. In these programs regulations based solely on animal evidence have not been attempted, even though they are the quintessential preventive measure.[13]

Several factors help to explain this apparent anomaly, but I need mention only one here. The statutory requirement to set standards stringently makes it more difficult to justify them as sensible public policy. Of course, courts are not supposed to assess regulations in these terms. Yet, faced with standards that they perceive as constituting overregulation, judges sometimes reject them on procedural grounds, arguing that the agency has not amassed enough evidence to show that they are necessary or feasible. In the Supreme Court's benzene decision, for example, the plurality's concern about overregulation led it to argue that OSHA had to show that it was "more likely than not" that exposure at currently allowable limits constituted a "significant risk." Yet such a requirement could easily preclude wise preventive measures. For example, suppose that there is a 20 percent chance that a chemical is hazardous and that, if it is, it will cause $50 million in damage. If the harm could be prevented by a standard costing less than $10 million, then it would confer expected net benefits. However, because 20 percent is less than 51 percent, such a standard would not meet the test of showing that the risk it addressed was "more likely than not" to cause harm.

The regulatory regime envisioned here would be more tolerant of regulations that were precautionary, that is, that accepted a higher level of false positives in order to reduce the number of false negatives. But this change would be tolerable only if the agencies did seek to balance costs and benefits, rather than always trying to achieve the "lowest feasible level" and the "best achievable control technology."

The Positive Argument

The argument that overregulation causes underregulation implies that the initial direction of any policy change—for example, toward less or greater protection—will be at least partially offset by its impact on the pace of that activity. For example, the Supreme Court's 1981 cotton dust decision forbidding the use of cost-benefit analysis in OSHA health standards was hailed as a union victory, but one effect was to strengthen the Reagan administration's resolve to avoid setting new standards. The most obvious alternative model of standard setting views strictness and extensiveness as unrelated. The implication of this alternative view would be that Reagan officials would not have issued rules at a faster pace even if they had been allowed to set less stringent standards.[14]

What analysis underlies the argument that strictness does reduce extensiveness? When regulation of business is involved, a plausible model of profit-maximizing firms suggests that, when the net costs imposed on them by a government program or activity increase, the firms will have a stronger incentive to try to prevent the activity from occurring. Cross-nationally, there is some evidence that industry is more cooperative when regulators show more concern with costs.[15] But because such comparisons always encounter a host of competing explanations, I concentrate on American programs to show that industry responses are related to the degree of strictness.

This simple model of firm behavior comprises an important element of the argument presented here. However, we also need to explain how their responses actually slow the pace of rule making. That requires an understanding of the political and legal institutions through which the responses of firms and other interest groups must be mediated.

Before turning to that task, I must address one other issue briefly. Although it may be obvious that the degree of opposition by a firm to a regulation will increase as the net cost imposed on the firm grows, it is less clear that the same can be said of an industry. In part, the problem is one of defining the "industry" involved. If one chemical is banned, the manufacturers of substitute chemicals will benefit from the ban. More generally, firms within an industry are not homogeneous. Some firms may benefit from a regulation and others will incur differing net costs.[16] With such differential effects, predicting the "industry's" response to a proposed regulation becomes problematic. I discuss how firms may try to use the regulatory process for their own ends in chapter 7. Suffice it to say here that, although these differentials can influence regulatory outcomes, stricter standards still tend to generate stronger overall business opposition than laxer ones. Thus it is difficult to find cases, especially in the area of toxic substances, where firms have sued agencies for issuing standards that were too lax.

Now we can return to the question of the impact of the institutional setting in which regulation takes place.

Although conflict among industry and other interest groups determines the broad patterns of regulatory politics, regulatory policies are less fully determined by interest group pressures than are legislative policies. With regulation, political conflict must be filtered through an unusually large number of analytical and procedural requirements. The American regulatory process requires that decisions be "based upon substantial evidence, affected parties be given the right to participate in the process by submitting evidence and argument in support of their interests, decisions of an agency must be logically derived from its legislative mandate, and decisions are subject to judicial review should any affected party believe that these requirements have not been satisfied."[17]

The slow pace of standard setting has four interrelated causes: (1) Political conflict between health or environmental lobbies and industry groups will generally lead standards to be appealed to the courts; (2) the effects of the standards are complex and uncertain; (3) the burden of proof to demonstrate that standards are needed is on the agencies; and (4) agency resources are quite limited. These four causes interact in the following manner: Because of the political conflict, agencies must assume that rules will be reviewed in court. Because they bear the burden of proof and because the evidence is rarely clear-cut, agencies face a time-consuming task; often the evidence is suggestive of a hazard but far from clear-cut, and agencies will be uncertain about whether or not courts will uphold the rule. Because agency resources are limited, it is difficult to carry on many standard-setting activities at the same time. In turn, their limited resources are due in part to the impact of the political conflict on the appropriations process. Similarly, the legislative choice of the standard of proof was influenced by the relative power of the interests when the statute was enacted.

Again it is important to point out that this analysis applies to standard-setting programs and not to screening programs. Among standard-setting programs it is most relevant to those that confront a large number of potential candidates for regulatory attention. With over 50,000 chemicals in commerce, attempts to regulate toxic substances are the prime examples.[18] However, even for agencies like the NHTSA, where the number of potential auto safety standards is quite limited, an underlying conflict between the strictness and the pace of standard setting is evident.[19]

The actual mechanisms by which stricter standards generate delays include the following.

1. Court appeals by industry become more likely and better funded. Of course, less strict standards increase the threat of appeals by pro-regulatory groups. This threat is probably not fully offsetting. Defenders of strict regulation have smaller resources than industry groups. More important, their objective is to reduce delay, which will sometimes preclude challenging rules that they view as too lax.

2. Strict standards face a higher probability of failing judicial scrutiny. Again, lax standards also face a higher probability of being overturned. Thus the relationship between strictness and reversals is U-shaped. My assumption is that we are usually operating on the upward-sloping side of the U so that increases in strictness increase the probability of reversal.

3. The information that an agency needs to justify a standard is more likely to be withheld by industry groups if they believe that the agency will behave unreasonably.

4. Both White House economists and political operatives are more likely to try to delay rules that they (or industry) perceive as particularly inefficient or burdensome.

5. In the larger ideological arena it also seems likely that there are long-run trade-offs between strictness and pace. Industry complaints about overregulation are less likely to elicit sympathy from the attentive public

our earlier lists of the causes of the slow pace and the mechanisms through which they work.

If political conflict between pro- and anti-regulation groups could be reduced, court appeals would be less frequent and less serious. In turn, *if* agencies could be assured freedom from litigation, the degree of proof they would have to amass would decline and rule making could be hastened. But this assurance would be lacking for any particular standard, unless industry on the one hand and labor or environmentalists on the other could reach some overarching agreement to sue only if certain bounds have been exceeded. And such agreements would be difficult to reach because they would be difficult to enforce. On industry's side especially, any maverick firm could afford litigation that would upset any bargains.

Because agencies tend, when confronted by scientific uncertainties, to overestimate risks, the elimination of uncertainty would make it easier to justify less strict standards. However, reducing the complexity and uncertainty surrounding the effects of standards is an unlikely prospect, at least in the near term. Some of the issues (for example, the existence of thresholds below which exposures are not harmful) have been labeled "trans-scientific"—beyond the foreseeable ability of science to resolve.[25] In any event, a heavy burden of proof will probably be placed on those who want to use less protective assumptions.

In the late 1970s some agencies tried to speed rule-making proceedings by foreclosing debate about the protective assumptions that they were using to identify carcinogens (for example, that positive findings in animals always outweigh nonpositive findings in humans). Even if they had been fully implemented, these "generic carcinogen policies" would probably not have succeeded in speeding the pace. The use of an overinclusive criterion for identifying hazards, combined with draconian regulatory response, would heighten fears of overregulation and force the political system to respond.

Although the strict substantive provisions of the statutes and their rigid procedural requirements contributed to the agencies' heavy burden of proof, independent factors were making the rule-making process much more cumbersome as the 1970s wore on. Agencies that issued rules in the early 1970s put two or three pages in the *Federal Register* to justify their actions. By the end of the decade, 100 pages of justification—the equivalent of a 320-page book—were no longer startling. White House requirements for regulatory analysis, introduced in the 1970s and elaborated in the 1980s, sought to deter inefficient rules while adding to the overall rule-making burden.

The central actor in this process, however, has been the judiciary. The repeated appeal of agency rules to the courts lets them, over time, fill in many of the blanks that Congress left. Beginning in the 1960s, judges dropped the New Deal assumption that they should defer to technically expert agencies.[26] Responding to the intellectual themes of pluralism and group access, they reinforced the congressional reformers' efforts to make the process accessible to outsiders' scrutiny and participation. "Agencies were increasingly required to respond to and rebut critical comments, to compile more and more data, and to make findings that increasingly resembled those in adjudicatory cases if they wished their rules to withstand challenges."[27] Most of the new regulatory statutes required rules to be backed by "substantial evidence," the presence of which, of course, is in the eye of the beholder. The emphasis on procedures sometimes masked more substantive concerns: "Even when a court was really intent on reversing what it saw as bad policy rather than on improving group access, it typically did so by inventing some new procedural hurdle, noting that the agency had not jumped over it, and then reversing the agency on those grounds."[28] Nor have courts refrained from striking down rules on the explicitly substantive grounds that they were not in accord with the courts' interpretation of such statutory terms as "unreasonable risk," "practicable," and "ample margin of safety." The burgeoning requirements of rule making led several agencies to begin seeking alternative methods of carrying out their mandates. In what may be an extreme case, a 1984 analysis of the Consumer Product Safety Commission reports that "the informal consensus in the agency is that rule making is dead; it simply takes too much effort."[29]

Although Congress could amend statutes to require courts to allow agencies to meet a less stringent burden of proof for their standards, the de facto determination of the standard of proof appears to lie in the hands of the judges themselves. If judicial faith in the legitimacy and competence of rule making waxes or if new appointees on the crucial courts feel their policy views are congruent with those of the agencies, then the "hard look" with which rules have been scrutinized may ease. If the signals from the courts sharply shifted, agencies would worry less about the evidentiary burden. Predicting such shifts is difficult. The judiciary is the most ideological branch of government, the least constrained by "interests," the most swayed by ideas. Because fashions in ideas wax and wane more quickly than political clout does, it is more difficult to predict judicial policy changes than legislative policy changes.

As for agency resources, the White House could try to shrink or expand their budgets for rule making depending on the reasonableness of each agency's rules, but Congress would obviously have a say in any strategy relying on appropriations.

Congress appears again and again in these considerations, perhaps not surprisingly, given that it initiated most of the proposals for protective regulation. Indeed, a central issue is the proper role for Congress. In only a few statutes has Congress itself explicitly made trade-offs between costs and protection by mandating specific standards. This delegation of substantive rule-making authority to the agencies has been justified on the grounds that Congress lacks the necessary expertise.[30] Those standards that were written by Congress have been so roundly criticized that, whether one believes that congressional shortcomings stem from lack of expertise or from lack of incentives to use it properly, it is hard to argue for a larger legislative role in writing standards.

However, Congress does have a vital role to play in reform. Encouraging steps toward a regulatory budget and endorsing the practice of "negotiating regulations" would be helpful. At least as important, especially for addressing underregulation, are specific legislative measures to require both more balancing of costs and benefits and more flexibility in establishing the burden of proof that agencies are required to carry. Precautionary measures should be accepted with relatively little evidence so long as the stringency of the measures seems reasonable.

Achieving this legislative trade-off will be difficult because of the mistrust that prevails among the central parties in these disputes, the scientific uncertainties that make it unclear what one is getting or giving up, and the media attention that gives a premium to grandstanding rather than to serious efforts at compromise. Yet regulation in the United States does not have the option of relying as fully on deference to experts, as in Britain, or as fully on corporatist bargaining, as in much of Europe. Several writers have noted the paradox that, although business values and influence are probably greater here than in other countries, business and government have traditionally viewed each other with relatively large doses of suspicion and hostility.[31] The last wave of regulation reflected an intensification of this hostility and, in turn, reinforced it, at least temporarily. Nevertheless, moves in either of these two "foreign" directions do represent reform strategies that may have at least limited promise. The concept of a "science court" to resolve scientific controversies is one embodiment of the first approach; the idea of "negotiating standards" among the interested parties is representative of the second.[32]

However, adoption of these approaches remains difficult so long as policy views on regulation are highly polarized. Therefore, unless Congress proves willing to set up the framework required to implement a less strict and more extensive system of rule making, the best alternative may be to adopt strategies that are not so reliant on rule making. One such strategy is to provide more information to individuals so that they can better assess the risks that they face. Another is to reform tort law so that firms will be more likely to bear the full costs of their hazardous products, activities, and effluents.[33] The government would continue to set the rules of the game, but it would let the game be played out in the markets and in the courts rather than impose solutions directly. Again, however, despite the attraction of these options (especially information strategies), they would not be able to fully substitute for an intelligent standard-setting program.

The conclusion must be that a failure to address directly the over-regulation/underregulation dilemma in current rule-making programs cannot be looked on with equanimity. Other reforms may reduce the damage that this unfortunate combination causes, but none of them can eliminate its baleful effects.

Social Science and Regulatory Reform

Assessments of particular risk regulations clearly depend on our having the scientific, technical, and behavioral knowledge to predict their consequences. Similarly, assessments of regulatory reform strategies should be based on an understanding of political institutions that would allow us to predict the consequences of altering policies or institutional arrangements. As in so many other areas, however, social science rarely provides the kind of specific predictions that analysts need to assess proposals. We have a better sense of the role of basic institutional features—electing legislators by majority rule in single member districts in a weak party system where legislative committee assignments are not made randomly—but none of these "root causes" are open to policy manipulation in the short run or probably even in the long run. Similarly, the "national styles of regulation" that David Vogel identifies cannot easily be changed.[34] The proposals that are feasible tend to be much more incremental. Contrary to the hoary label, when it comes to policy analysis, it is political science, not economics, that deserves to be called "dismal." Economists can dream up all kinds of reform proposals; it is usually up to the political scientist to shoot them down. The scarce resources are political. The creative task becomes how to leverage those resources for maximum policy impact.

More concretely, a crucial weakness for policy purposes is that, even when we can plausibly predict the *direction* of the impact of a particular policy, theory provides almost no help in predicting its *magnitude*. Yet the magnitudes are essential because, although the theories apply holding all other things constant, other things are rarely constant. This flux causes special trouble when two conflicting policy changes are being considered. Suppose that a trade association or environmental group is considering whether to endorse a measure predicted to speed the pace of regulation in exchange for one predicted to reduce its strictness. We can be reasonably confident that the new policy combination would lead to a more cost-effective program (that is, a lower cost per disease prevented). However, the parties care more about the likely impacts on the *total* costs and the *total* diseases prevented. But these impacts will depend, in part, on how the regulatory agencies will behave: how much faster they will promulgate new rules, which hazards they will choose to address, and how strict those rules will be.

Social scientists can provide only limited insights into these issues. In this book I try to investigate what policy implications can be drawn from this limited knowledge.

I

THE NORMATIVE ISSUES

Are We Overregulating? How Should We Value
Preventing a Death?

Spending $1 trillion to prevent a single death is going too far; the benefits of prevention are not worth what we would have to give up to get them. Conversely, we underregulate when we fail to adopt measures for which the added benefits would exceed the added costs. If a death could be prevented for a penny, failing to spend it constitutes a case of underregulation.

Of course, few if any cases have such extreme costs or can be classified so easily. Instead, society faces hard choices about how to resolve the conflict between values that hold life precious and the need to ration scarce resources.[1] Table 2.1 presents estimates of the costs, deaths prevented, and costs per death prevented for the standards in which OSHA lowered a permissible exposure limit (PEL). Great uncertainty pervades the estimates on which the figures in the table are based, but they are the best estimates that can be made. Are these amounts excessive?

This chapter and the next attempt to provide an answer to that question. In this chapter I examine both how we should decide how much to spend and what the appropriate levels of spending should be. Although any specific figures are inescapably subjective, analysis can help to bound the most reasonable range. In chapter 3 I back up to explore the factual underpinnings of table 2.1. Along with an investigation of the firmness of these estimates, I also examine several of the political issues that arise in the course of quantitative risk assessments.

Can We Sidestep the Issue of Valuing "Lifesaving"?

Even economists who have been highly critical of OSHA's inefficiency have usually been reluctant to assert that spending $10 million, or even $20 million, to prevent a death is more than society should spend.[2] In part, this reluctance reflects their awareness that explicit valuation of lifesaving is viewed by many as unsavory. In part, it also reflects awareness that judgments about what society should be willing to pay involve ethical issues to which economic analysis has little to contribute.

In addition, analysts often believe that they can employ cost-effectiveness analysis as a useful and less controversial alternative to cost-benefit analysis. Cost-effectiveness analysis, in contrast to cost-benefit analysis, does not require placing a value on the health effects. It takes the

Table 2.1 Estimates of the Cost per Death Prevented by New OSHA Health Standards[a]

Agent	Date of promulgation	New OSHA PEL	Annual cancer deaths prevented	Total annual cost (millions of dollars)	Cost per cancer prevented (millions of dollars)
Asbestos	June 1972	2 fibers in 4 years	396	173	0.4
Vinyl chloride	October 1974	1 ppm	1	40	40
Coke oven emissions	October 1976	0.15 mg	8–36	200–400	6–50
Benzene	February 1978	1 ppm	6–21	94–188	4.5–32
DBCP	March 1978	1 ppb	?	6	?
Arsenic	May 1978	0.01 mg	5–20	95–190	4.8–38
Cotton dust	June 1978	0.2–0.75 mg depending on process	NA	95	NA
Acrylonitrile	October 1978	2 ppm	7	18–37	2.6–5.2
Lead	November 1978	0.05 mg	NA	460–690	NA
Ethylene oxide	June 1984	1 ppm	4–16	18–36	1.1–9

a. Costs are in 1985 dollars. The figures in this table are based on calculations by John Morrall, III, and Ivy Broder; however, when new data were available, I adjusted the figures to take account of them. Chapter 3 presents the basis for the adjustments. See Ivy Broader and John Morrall, III, "The Economic Basis for OSHA's and EPA's Generic Carcinogen Regulations," in *What Role for Government?* Richard Zeckhauser and Derek Leebaert, eds. (Durham, N.C.: Duke University Press, 1983), pp. 242–254. See also John Morrall, III, "OSHA after Ten Years," paper prepared for Conference on Health, Saftey, and Environmental Regulation, Washington, D.C., November 18–19, 1981, Tables V-7 and V-8.

Table 2.2 Most Federal Risk Reduction Measures Prevent Deaths at a Lower Cost than OSHA's New Health Standards

Agency	Measure	Net cost of measure per death prevented[a]
NHTSA	Roadside hazard removal versus status quo	0
CPSC	Clothing flammability law versus status quo	0
CPSC	Mandatory smoke detectors versus status quo	85,000
EPA	Stationary source provisions of 1970 Clean Air Act versus pre-1970 conditions	70,000
HHS	Pertussis vaccine immunization versus no program	424,000
NHTSA	Mandatory air bags versus no passive restraints	528,000
NHTSA	55 mph speed limit versus earlier limits	1,700,000
EPA	Mobile source provisions of 1970 Clean Air Act versus pre-1970 conditions	2,700,000

a. Costs are in 1985 dollars. John D. Graham and James W. Vaupel reviewed thirty-seven studies, including the eight listed, in "The Value of a Life: What Difference Does It Make?" *Risk Analysis* (1981), 1(1):89–95. These eight are typical of the non-OSHA measures they review. The net cost subtracts benefits (other than for fatality prevention) for which dollar values have been calculated (for example, property damage and nonfatal accidents prevented). For some measures, they reviewed more than one study; I have included the figure with the highest cost.

objective of preventing a certain number of deaths as given and looks at ways to achieve it at a lower cost (or it takes a given cost as a constraint and looks at ways to prevent more deaths for that cost). We know that some government programs (including OSHA) spend much more to prevent a death than others (such as highway safety programs), sometimes ten to a hundred times as much, as table 2.2 shows. These differences would be greater still if we chose to discount those deaths that would not have been prevented immediately. Most of the more cost-effective programs prevent accidental deaths. Most of the OSHA standards prevent cancer deaths that would have occurred several decades after the initial exposures. We could prevent many more deaths for our current cost by reallocating funds to those programs where deaths can be prevented more cheaply.

But this conclusion sidesteps the issue of whether it is *worth* spending the money to prevent the high-cost deaths. Perhaps we are not spending too much on the costly programs but spending too little on the inexpensive ones. Underlying this point is the reality that the budget for preventing deaths is not necessarily fixed. As a result, it is hardly evident that less money for OSHA would actually mean more money for highway safety. Finally, even if the budget were fixed, perhaps society values preventing some deaths more than it values others; thus the higher spending for the deaths prevented by OSHA standards might be justified.[3]

Although these objections raise serious questions about the inferences that can be drawn from cost-effectiveness comparisons, they do not vitiate the value of comparing the value of expenditures with the value that would be gained by alternative uses, including uses outside the health field. Indeed, there is really no way of thinking about what something is worth without considering what you would be willing to sacrifice to get it. In addition, although resources for a given societal objective can potentially be expanded, *total* societal resources do pose an ultimate constraint that may help to place spending in perspective. For example, occupational disease is often described as entirely preventable. Some have claimed that it causes 100,000 deaths a year in the United States, 5 percent of all deaths. If that were true and if we were to spend $10 million per death prevented to eliminate it, then the task would require $1 trillion per year, well over 20 percent of the gross national product. At that price the elimination of occupational disease, or even any major reduction in its toll, would be a pyrrhic victory for society.[4]

Benefit-Cost Analysis: A Graphical Analysis

Before turning to the substantive problems of valuing risk reduction, I find it helpful to become more precise in defining overregulation and under-regulation. In figure 2.1, the marginal benefit curve is flat, based on the assumption that the prevention of each additional disease or death is equally valuable. The marginal cost curve is increasing, based on the assumption that some diseases or deaths can be prevented easily but that more costly measures are required to address the remaining ones. (More plausibly, the marginal cost curve not only slopes upward but does so at an increasing rate so that the curve approaches a vertical line.) We should spend money up to the point (S^*), where the marginal benefit and marginal cost curves intersect. Up to that point each increment in spending brings more benefits than costs to society; beyond that point more spending brings more costs than benefits. Therefore net benefits to society are greatest at point S^*. (The area under the marginal benefits curve measures the total benefits; the area under the marginal cost curve, the total costs.)

It is important to note that the desirability of a particular choice almost always depends on the available alternatives. S^* is always the best level, but if the choice is limited to only S_0 or S_1, we should choose S_1. We can treat S_0, the option of doing nothing, as having neither costs nor benefits; so its net benefits are zero. S_1, however, has net benefits equal to area A − B, which is clearly greater than zero. Compared to S^*, an exposure level of S_1 consti-

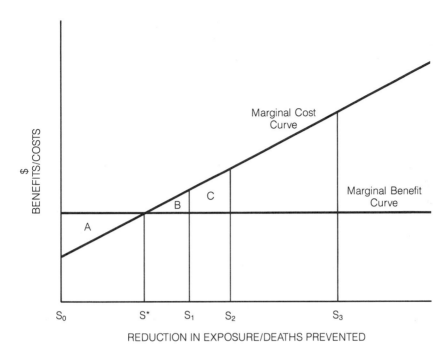

Figure 2.1   A representation of overregulation and underregulation.

tutes overregulation, going past the point that maximizes net benefits. But because the net benefits at S_1 are positive, it is better than S_0, which represents a clear case of underregulation.

The underregulation of S_0 is as undesirable as the overregulation of S_2. At S_0 society forgoes the net benefits equal to area A, but at S_2 that gain is exactly wiped out by incurring the net cost equal to area B + C. A regulation that took us all the way to S_3 would have total costs that exceeded the total benefits (the net benefits would be negative). In other words, it would be worse than doing nothing.

Thus we can distinguish two degrees of overregulation. In the more severe case we would have been better off doing nothing. In the less severe case the standard is an improvement over the status quo but still requires measures that are not justified by the costs.

The implication of much of the economists' criticism of OSHA's new health standards is that they have been set at a level like S_3—the total costs have exceeded the total benefits and thus society is worse off as a result.[5] That conclusion has to rest on a judgment about how much the prevention of disease is worth. As we will see, most of the estimates that have been offered are in the range of $500,000 to $4.3 million (in 1985 dollars). Thus we could say that the marginal benefit curve in figure 2.1 is anywhere between those figures. For now, call it $2 million. Then, for any given standard, OSHA would be justified in ordering further reductions in exposures so long as the cost of the last death prevented was less than $2 million.

Although the estimates in table 2.1 are subject to major uncertainties, they suggest why the overregulation theme has credibility. These estimates are the *average* cost per death prevented, that is, the total cost divided by the number of deaths prevented. If the estimate is below $2 million, we know that it is better to have adopted the standard than to have accepted the status quo (S_0). But note that, in terms of figure 2.1, a standard with an average cost of $2 million results from an exposure level of S_2. At that point the total benefits and total costs are equal; net benefits are zero, just as they would be if we had done nothing. Yet at that point the *marginal* costs (the cost of the last death prevented) are well above $2 million. Thus a decision to adopt a standard almost as strict as S_2 would be justified only if we decided to value the prevention of a death at much more than $2 million.

To make the point more concretely, consider the acrylonitrile standard, which lowered the permissible exposure limit (PEL) from 20 ppm (parts per million) to 2 ppm. By the criterion of a $2 million cutoff, the average cost of $2.6 to $5.2 million (in 1985 dollars) implies that we would have been better off doing nothing. Moreover, we can be sure that the marginal cost for the lives saved by going from 3 ppm to 2 ppm was much higher. We do not know how much higher, but we can make a rough guess by using estimates of what the costs would have been to reach exposure limits below 2 ppm. Each extra death prevented by going from 2 ppm to 1 ppm would have cost an average of between $21.5 and $43 million. Based on this figure, it is likely that the marginal cost of going from 3 ppm to 2 ppm was in the neighborhood of $10 million. Thus this was the valuation implied by a decision to adopt a 2-ppm PEL.

Measuring Benefits in Practice

The preceding discussion talked glibly about the benefits of preventing morbidity and early death. But how, in fact, can we develop measures of benefits to compare with the costs? Until the 1970s the usual method for valuing health improvements was to calculate the wealth that society gains from the changes—chiefly in greater productivity and reduced medical costs. Labeled the "human capital" approach, this method has been pilloried on ethical grounds for treating the lives of infants, the elderly, and (often) housewives as having little or no value. More fundamental, the human capital approach operates on the assumption that the dominant social goal is maximizing the gross national product. Although economic growth is obviously one important social goal, economists reflected that their usual criterion for assessing a policy change was whether it made the individuals in society better off. And the appropriate measure of the value of something to people is how much they are willing to pay or sacrifice to get it. In concept, measurements of willingness to pay (WTP) can be used to study not only how much people value tastier tomatoes and drier deodorants but also how much they value living in a more beautiful, safer, or more just society. Thus the research question became how to measure how much individuals were willing to give up for reductions in risk or how much they demanded for accepting higher risk levels.

It is important to realize that the WTP approach does not address the issue of how much a given individual would pay to avoid or accept certain death. Instead, the effort is based on the observation that individuals constantly make decisions in which they make trade-offs between risk reduction and other good things, including money. A ladder, a lawn mower, tires, the car itself—safer models are available at a higher price. Skiing is fun but risky. Sweets, meat, and eggs all have their pleasures and their cholesterol. The trick is to examine these choices to derive an estimate of how much people value a given reduction in risk. This valuation of risk reduction can be translated into the value of preventing a "statistical" death. For example, if each of 1000 people would give $500 to eliminate a one in a thousand risk of dying faced by each person, then the group as a whole is willing to spend $500,000 to prevent one death among its members. By far the most common source of these estimates has been the labor market, where researchers have examined whether workers in more risky jobs get paid higher wages, controlling for other factors that affect wages, such as experience and education.

Table 2.3 summarizes the results of many of the studies that have been carried out. All but the first four and last two were based on labor market studies. The four consumer market studies were based on studying purchases of risk-reducing products (for example, smoke alarms). The contingent valuation studies were based on asking people to respond to hypothetical questions about their spending for risk reduction, rather than on studies of their actual behavior.

Table 2.3   Estimates of the Marginal Willingness to Pay for Reductions in Risks

Study	Mean risk level for the sample[a]	Range of estimates (millions of 1985 dollars)	Judgmental best estimate (millions of 1985 dollars)
Consumer market studies			
1. Dardis (1980)	87.7	0.36–0.55	0.46
2. Blomquist (1979)	3.0	0.38–1.4	0.60
3. Ghosh, Lees, and Seal (1975)	not reported		0.55
4. Ippolito and Ippolito (1984)	varied	0.23–1.24	0.52
Early low-range wage-risk estimates			
5. Thaler and Rosen (1975)[b]	11.0	0.02–0.84	0.64
6. Arnould and Nichols (1983)[b]	11.0	0.62	0.62
7. Dillingham (1979)	1.7	0.39–1.2	0.43
Early high-range wage-risk estimates (all based on BLS industry accident rates)			
8. R. Smith (1976)	1.0 and 1.5	3.6–3.9	3.7
9. V. K. Smith (1983)[c]	3.0	1.9–5.8	3.9
10. Viscusi (1978)	1.2	4.1–5.2	4.3
11. Olson (1981)	1.0	7.9	7.9
12. R. Smith (1974)	1.0–1.5	8.4–15.8	8.4
13. Viscusi (1981)			
a. without risk interaction terms	1.04	5.3–6.9	6.9
b. with risk interaction terms	1.04	4.6–13.2	10
New wage risk studies			
14. Dillingham (1985)	1.4–8.3	1.3–5.6	2.2
15. Marin and Psacharopoulos (1985)			
a. manual workers	(d)	2.4–2.7	2.5
b. nonmanual workers	(d)	9.0	9.0
16. Gegax et al. (1985)			
a. all union workers	8.2	1.9	
b. union blue-collar workers only	10.1	1.6	1.6
New contingent valuation studies			
17. Jones-Lee et al. (1985)	0.8–1.0	2.3–4.3	3.1
18. Gegax et al. (1985)	4.2–10	2.2–3.2	2.8

Source: Ann Fisher, Lauraine Chestnut, and Dan Violette, "The Value of Reducing Risk" (September 16, 1986), mimeo. See their bibliography for the full citations of the papers cited.
a. Approximate annual deaths per 10,000 people.
b. Based on actuarial risk data.
c. Assuming 0.4 percent of all injuries are fatal, as reported by Viscusi (1978) for the BLS injury statistics and that the risk premium for fatal injuries is 33–100 percent of the premium for all risks.
d. Their age-adjusted normalized risk variable is not directly comparable to the risk levels used in other studies. However, the average risk of death for the entire sample was 2 in 10,000.

Even if we confine ourselves to the labor market studies, the variation is large even if we look only at the "judgmental best estimates," rather than the full range of results. In fact, the range could be expanded further to include studies that found no evidence of risk premiums, that is, an apparent willingness to pay of zero. Institutional factors appear to have a great influence on the presence of premiums. Thus many studies find premiums only among blue-collar workers and often only among those who have union representation. I will return to the question of the validity of these findings, but first a simple comparison of table 2.3 with table 2.1 should be highlighted.

The highest figures in table 2.3 overlap the range of estimates for the average cost per death for almost all the health standards in table 2.1. Thus it is possible to argue that WTP estimates can justify many of OSHA's health standards, at least if the only choice is between the standard and doing nothing.

However, that rosy conclusion depends on two key assumptions: that the highest WTP figures are appropriate and that less costly preventive measures were not available, that is, that the choice was between the proposed standard and doing nothing. Regarding the first issue, the study that has the soundest methodology produced a WTP estimate of $2.5 million.[6] If we use this figure, then only the ethylene oxide standard could join asbestos in a claim of net benefits, and this would be true only if the lower range of the cost estimates were used. If we also double the average cost-effectiveness figures in table 2.1 as a rough attempt to estimate the *marginal* cost of preventing the last death, then the ethylene oxide standard would present a case of overregulation except under extremely optimistic cost assumptions. Using what appear to be the most reasonable assumptions about costs and workers' willingness to pay, we see that all but the asbestos standard appear to constitute cases of overregulation. How could anyone disagree?

Sources of Disagreement
The first possible reason for disagreeing could be a belief that the facts are wrong—either the costs are overstated or the health effects belittled or both. These issues are taken up in chapter 3. A related position is agnosticism—a belief that the data are so uncertain that we simply do not know what the costs per death prevented have been.

Second, as we have seen, if you assume the low end of the cost range and the high end of the effects range, it is possible to argue that most of the standards conferred net benefits. Although this combination seems unlikely, no one has attempted the difficult task of estimating the probability distribution of the cost and effect estimates; thus it is impossible to say *how* unlikely.

Third, one can be skeptical of the validity of the figures from the WTP literature. Critics have questioned whether workers really have enough information to make reasoned judgments about the trade-offs. The fact that premiums have been found in many studies does not mean that they are the same premiums that would emerge from a study of fully informed workers. Indeed, because the findings are so disparate, you can pick any figure up to $10 million. And, although most studies have found that risk premiums are paid, this may be largely the result of "publication bias," that is, studies with negative findings have less chance of getting published.

This line of reasoning can lead to the conclusion that labor market studies of willingness to pay provide no credible guidance about how much workers really value risk reduction and thus should simply be ignored. However, at the least, we can conclude that the evidence provides no support for figures above $10 million. Although it is appropriate to point out the error of putting too much faith in quantitative methods, it is equally appropriate to point out the error of disregarding quantitative evidence altogether.

A fourth reason for rejecting the conclusion of overregulation is the presence of externalities. Thus, even if workers do not value the prevention of disease more than a certain amount, their diseases impose costs on other people in society. Thus the social value of prevention is greater than the value to the individuals directly at risk. In discussing this issue, I distinguish externalities resulting from altruism—people care about other people— from externalities resulting from unwillingly borne costs. Altruism is discussed later and may be quite important. Imposed costs can be important in some circumstances but are unlikely to loom large for any of the new OSHA health standards except cotton dust and to a lesser degree asbestos. The overwhelming risk posed by the other hazards are diseases that are usually fatal and involve relatively short periods of disability—lung cancer, liver cancer, leukemia. Even if the average medical expense per illness totaled tens of thousands of dollars, there would be little effect on valuations that are already in the millions.

Yet the most important reasons why people have rejected the conclusion that we have overregulated go beyond disputes about which numbers are correct. Instead, their disagreements address the fundamental issue of the appropriateness of placing a money value on preventing deaths. Condemnation for those who propose to "trade off lives for dollars" is a frequent refrain. Yet it is difficult to object to the general argument that we should try to find out whether the good aspects (benefits) of a policy outweigh the bad (costs). Such a weighing requires comparing the benefits of lifesaving with its costs.

Because I do not think that the refusal to acknowledge that trade-off is honest, I address the more germane question of the appropriateness of using WTP estimates as a measure of the benefits of standards. The issues raised in this dispute often overlap and can be categorized in different ways. Here I examine them in the following order: efficiency versus equity and fairness, the role of altruism, and reliance on the market for guidance about valuation versus reliance on the political process.

Efficiency versus Equity and Fairness

At the most obvious level, the use of willingness to pay raises questions of equity because richer people are willing to pay more to reduce risks than poorer people, just as they are willing to pay more for any other normal good. To some degree the equity problem can be solved, at the expense of efficiency, by ignoring the different income levels of people facing different risks and starting off with a uniform WTP figure. In fact, no public official would advocate, for example, that differences in the average income of their patrons should justify a lower value on preventing bus crashes than airplane crashes.

The practice of ignoring income-based differences in the demand for safety raises the problem of deciding *whose* demand should become the basis for a uniform standard. If it is the demand of the poor, then the wealthy may feel underprotected. If it is the demand of the wealthy, then the poor may be overprotected. Is that bad? It is if the poor end up paying for it, that is, if they have to pay $10 for a risk-reduction measure for which they would have been willing to pay only $5. In that case they would have been made worse off.

Identifying who actually pays the costs of new health standards is difficult. In most cases current workers probably do not bear most of the costs. If we assume that industry will pass on a substantial share of the costs, the costs are likely to be widely shared. But most of the health benefits will be concentrated—the workers most affected by OSHA's new standards are blue-collar workers, not CPAs. Because the costs and benefits are not borne and received by the same people, there is, in the absence of a

Table 2.4   Average Weekly Earnings in Industries Affected by New OSHA Health
Standards Are Relatively High

Hazard and standard industrial classification (SIC) code	1985 Average weekly earnings of production worker (dollars)
Asbestos	
329 misc. nonmetallic mineral products	410
Vinyl chloride	
282 plastics materials	495
Coke ovens	
331 blast furnaces	548
Benzene	
291 petroleum refining	657
421 trucking	412 (nonsupervisory)
301 tires and inner tube	560
306 fabricated rubber	344
307 misc. plastic	324
Arsenic	
333 primary nonferrous	573
Lead	
333 primary nonferrous	573
334 secondary nonferrous	NA
336 nonferrous foundries	
332 iron and steel foundries	430
369 misc. electrical equipment	422
Cotton weaving mills	
221	278
Acrylonitrile	
282 plastic materials	495
286 gum and wood chemicals	605
DBCP	
287 agricultural chemicals	471
Ethylene oxide	
384 medical supplies	331
806 hospitals	309 (nonsupervisory)
Total private nonagricultural sector (production or nonsupervisory)	299
Total manufacturing (production workers)	386

Source: Bureau of Labor Statistics, *Supplement to Employment and Earnings* (Washington,
D.C.: Government Printing Office, June 1986).

requirement for unanimous consent, no unambiguous basis for stating whether a policy change improves societal welfare.[7] Benefit-cost analysis attempts to fill that role. If a policy has benefits in excess of its costs, then any losers from the policy could, in theory, be fully compensated by the winners, so that in the end there would be winners but no losers. That result would indeed represent an unambiguous improvement. However, there is no guarantee that losers will be fully compensated and, in practice, they rarely are compensated. The fallback position is to argue that society will be better off if we use a cost-benefit rule. Although some people will be losers in any particular case, the use of the rule will increase society's wealth. In the long run everyone is likely to benefit from the bigger pie.

This argument has considerable merit but shortcomings as well. Regarding our topic, the appropriate caveat is not that "in the long run, we are all dead," but rather that in the short run only some of us will be dead. Those who die because society rejects inefficient lifesaving programs will not be around to benefit from the bigger pie. Does this fact require condemnation of any policy that stops short of a maximum effort to prevent deaths? No. It is inevitable that public policy will create losers who are beyond the reach of compensation. But this fact should spur thinking about who the losers are and how we feel about their plight.[8]

The existence of income redistribution programs suggests that many citizens may be willing to supplement the willingness to pay of low-paid workers. But table 2.4 shows that, except for the cotton dust standard, the workers affected by OSHA's new health standards have earned higher wages than the average for all production or nonsupervisory workers in the private nonagricultural sector. They are also more likely to be in unions than most blue-collar workers are. And, although it is true that low-wage workers appear to face greater *safety* risks than high-wage workers, the evidence we have does not suggest that the same relationship holds for *toxic* risks. Table 2.5 shows that the percentage of workers who say that they face great or sizable risks from toxic hazards changes little with wage levels; if anything, the more highly paid workers say they face greater hazards. Thus there does not appear to be a strong case, at least on income distribution grounds, for subsidizing the willingness to pay of workers to reduce toxic hazards.

The Role of Altruism

Few hazards pose equal risks to all people. Either they pose a risk only to a subset of the population (as most occupational risks do) or they pose

Table 2.5   Among Blue-Collar Workers, Low Earners Are Less Likely to Face Toxic Hazards; High Earners, More Likely

Wage per hour (dollars)	No toxic problem	Toxic problem	Percentage with toxic problem
Less than 2.50	47	4	8
2.50–3.49	45	26	21
3.50–4.49	68	20	23
4.50–5.49	65	23	26
5.50–6.49	47	13	22
6.50–7.49	45	17	27
7.50–8.49	40	12	23
8.50–9.49	23	5	18
9.50–10.49	8	7	47
10.50 +	12	8	40
Total	450	135	23

Source: 1977 Quality of Employment Survey (Institute for Social Research, University of Michigan).

different degrees of hazard (as many air pollutants do) depending on geography and health status. Thus there is usually an "us" who are faced with the decision of whether to help "them." Equity concerns may motivate a positive response, as may the belief that people have a right to be protected. More generally, concern for the welfare of others can supply an additional reason for being willing to pay for risk reductions.

The individuals at risk are likely to take some account of the concerns of those who are closest to them, their families. When family members draw on the same resource pool (as spouses do), their joint valuation on reducing the risk to one of them may be no higher than the willingness to pay of either one of them individually and could be lower. The chief exception is that children cannot add to the willingness to pay because they have no way of drawing on their future income stream. Thus a strong case can be made for some societal supplement to the risk reduction efforts undertaken on behalf of parents of young children.

While acknowledging that market estimates do not reflect the altruistic concerns of nonfamily members, economists writing about willingness to pay typically express the view that "unless such concerns are especially strong . . . they will not substantially affect the value of life obtained using workers' own preferences." [9] Direct evidence bearing on this issue is slim. Even if the public places a relatively high priority on preventing workplace cancer deaths, the actual amount they are willing to pay may not be large. After all, the total amount of charitable contributions to health programs and hospitals in 1980 totaled only $6 billion, about $75 a household, and much of that went to programs helping children. [10] In contrast, if one believes that risk premiums equal $2 million per fatality, then workers collectively receive over $10 billion for the more than 5000 workplace fatalities they experience and perhaps an equal amount for nonfatal injuries.[11] It is not enough to invoke the benevolence of third parties as if that ended the discussion. The *magnitude* of that benevolence has to be considered.

People's willingness to pay for risk reduction may be quite dependent on certain characteristics of the risk context. This issue is quite important because it bears directly on whether the large differentials that we find in the cost per death prevented for different programs are justified.

It is unclear whether individuals place an equal value on reducing the different risks that they personally face. Experiments by psychologists have shown that the same individual may be both risk taking and risk averse in making choices (mainly about money bets), depending both on the size of the gains and losses and on how the choices are posed. But studies of actual behavior are too few, cover too restricted a set of hazards, and raise too many serious problems of comparability to provide much insight.[12] The mere fact that a person accepts a higher level of risk in one context (for example, mountain climbing) than in another (for example, commercial aviation) does not mean that he or she values a marginal reduction in risk differently in the two cases.[13] Mountain climbing may have such great benefits that it justifies accepting great risks.

There is some evidence that, when they consider how much society ought to spend to prevent different types of deaths, individuals do consider to what degree potential victims are responsible for their plight. It does seem plausible that there is greater variation in the valuations of "third parties" than in the valuations of the people directly at risk. However, several studies indicate that even for "third parties" the differences in how much should be spent are rarely more than two- or threefold. One reason for this limited range is that individuals often disagree about which programs deserve priority. Thus, even though individuals may rate preventing their highest-valued death ten times as much as the lowest-valued one, differences in ranking reduce the range in the aggregated assessments.

Evidence from one study is presented in table 2.6.[14] Groups of respondents were shown a list of eight programs for reducing risks and told to assume that they would each cost the same and each prevent ten deaths. The programs included one on occupational safety (to enforce standards to prevent fatal falls in the construction industry) and one dealing with occupational health (enforcement of workplace toxic substance standards to prevent fatal cancers). Respondents were told that limited resources

Table 2.6   Median Ratio of the Value Placed on Preventing Ten Deaths from Workplace Cancers to the Value Placed on Preventing Ten Deaths in Other Programs

Sample	1st Quartile	Median	4th Quartile
SDSU Sample $N = 50$[a]			
Bike lanes	0.50	0.85	1.50
Crib slats	0.40	0.89	1.90
Roadside obstacles	0.82	1.38	2.87
Paramedic services	0.54	0.87	1.20
Pollution	0.92	1.13	1.54
Median barriers	0.56	0.88	1.71
Construction falls	0.70	1.20	2.55
ICL Sample $N = 18$[b]			
Bike lanes	0.63	0.86	1.75
Crib slats	0.55	0.88	1.33
Roadside obstacles	0.71	1.10	2.75
Paramedic services	0.69	0.89	1.58
Pollution	0.64	1.00	1.50
Median barriers	0.45	0.63	1.07
Construction falls	0.60	1.00	2.00
UCSD Sample $N = 35$[c]			
Bike lanes	0.40	0.60	1.20
Crib slats	0.20	0.46	0.94
Roadside obstacles	0.40	1.00	2.00
Paramedic services	0.50	0.86	1.25
Pollution	0.91	1.10	1.50
Median barriers	0.20	0.67	1.00
Construction falls	0.38	0.86	1.17

a. San Diego State University.
b. Institute for Continued Learning.
c. University of California, San Diego.

prevented all the programs from being implemented and were asked to rank them on the basis of whether we should value the deaths prevented by one program more than the deaths prevented by another. Then the respondents were asked to take the program that they ranked lowest and say how *much* more we should value the other programs in relation to it. Respondents were given information about the average age of the victims and the latency period, if any, for the deaths.

Consider the finding that in the first sample (SDSU), the median judgment was that the prevention of the cancer deaths merited spending 20 percent more than the prevention of the construction deaths (half the respondents thought it merited spending less than that amount; half, more). In the second sample (ICL) the median rating judged the two programs equally valuable; and in the third sample (UCSD) construction falls came out ahead. Thus, although there are differences in how people value the prevention of deaths in different programs, there is no strong evidence here that people value the prevention of workplace cancer deaths substantially more than other deaths. Two other studies that have posed questions in similar ways also found that aggregate differences in the valuation placed on the prevention of different deaths rarely exceeded twofold.[15]

It is important to remember that the question being answered with this method is different from the one posed by WTP studies. Those studies try to determine how much the individuals at risk are willing to pay for a given reduction in risk; that figure can then be used to calculate a willingness to pay to prevent a death. In contrast, the approach here asks individuals how much they think that society should be willing to pay to prevent one kind of death versus another. The answers in this survey depend, at least in part, on ethical, personally disinterested judgments. Although an individual's willingness to pay depends on such factors as risk aversion, wealth, and initial level of risk,[16] the "ethical" rating expresses judgments about the value of the lives saved and the culpability of the victims for their fates.

One way to view the findings in table 2.6 is that they show the variation in third-party valuation in reducing particular risks.[17] In order to calculate overall societal willingness to pay, however, we need several other pieces of information. First, we need to know the absolute magnitude of this third-party caring. We do not have any reasonable estimate. Second, we need to know the absolute magnitude of individuals' willingness to pay. We do have many estimates, mainly from the labor market, of this figure. Third, we need to know how much variation there is in individuals' willingness to pay to reduce risks in different contexts. We do not, however, have credible evidence about whether individuals value a reduction in their own risks more in some settings than in others.

I did suggest, however, that an individual's willingness to pay was less likely to be sensitive to the risk context than third-parties' valuations were. If we accept this assumption, then we can draw an important conclusion: The justifiable variations in spending to prevent deaths should not exceed the ratios found in studies such as the one presented in table 2.6. Of course, no great credence should be placed in those specific numbers. What is important is the repeated finding that the differences that third-parties believe are justified do not exceed two- or threefold. Thus an agency's claim that differences of tenfold or twentyfold are justified lacks credibility.[18]

Efficiency versus Rights and Politics versus the Market

As a technique, benefit-cost analysis is least problematic when all the resources involved—both the inputs and the outputs—are traded on markets. Is the expenditure on labor and pipe that is required to build an irrigation system justified by the increased crop that can be harvested? When a good is traded in markets, its price is determined by supply and demand. The price reflects the value that the marginal consumers place on the good. The fact that they buy must mean they value it at least as much as the price. Those who value it less than the price will not purchase it. Thus the analyst can use market prices to measure the value of the goods and services that go into a project and that come out of it.[19]

But public policymakers are frequently interested in project results that are not traded in markets, at least not explicitly. Clean air, quiet, reductions in anxiety, improved health, the sense of living in a just and humane society, liberty—this list covers a few of the nontraded goods. In some cases the analyst can find methods for placing a value on these concerns. For example, several studies have tried to estimate the value of reducing noise at airports by comparing property values in neighborhoods that are similar in almost all respects expect for the noise from airplanes.[20] But as the nature of the concern becomes more subjective and, especially, as it touches on more fundamental values, the ability of such analyses to guide the public policy debate becomes more subject to challenge.[21]

In theory, the WTP method can measure whatever it is that people value about reducing the risks they face. This value may reflect the loss that their family and friends would feel. It may reflect individuals' sense of the justness or unjustness of the risk situation they find themselves in. Yet, in the eyes of critics, the use of the WTP method is itself part of the problem.

The use of willingness to pay "explicitly assumes that what we wish to achieve as a society is the maximum satisfaction of preferences or interests of the sort that individuals might express in the market." [22] This rejection of market guidance is tied to the view that the issues involved are moral:

How can cost-benefit analysis claim to be either neutral or comprehensive if it cannot deal with a wide range of moral, cultural, aesthetic, and political concerns? There may be some issues which raise few important cultural or moral issues; for example, the commodities markets may be left to determine the prices of hog bellies or potash. This does not show, however, that markets or market analysis can give us adequate policy for public safety and health. On the contrary, where moral, political, and cultural values—not simply economic ones—are at stake, we need to make moral, political, and aesthetic judgments. Cost-benefit analysis does not replace these "subjective" judgments with "objective" or "neutral" ones. Rather it distorts or ignores the non-economic values it cannot handle. [23]

This sweeping criticism confounds the practice of performing benefit-cost analysis with a practice of relying on market-based estimates of willingness to pay as a measure of the benefits. Because, as I have argued, it is hard to oppose the general practice of weighing the good versus the bad in making decisions, the validity of the critique really depends on the role of markets in guiding decisions.

Perhaps the first question to ask about any market is whether participants are well enough informed to make intelligent choices. The question of how much information is enough can probably not be answered satisfactorily. Instead, we look at the outcomes of choices to see whether people seem to be behaving reasonably in light of the preferences we think they have. Or we look to see whether risk premiums are being paid, an outcome consistent with a functioning market. Some of the information problems posed specifically by toxic hazards are discussed later. [24]

A specific criticism of economists is that they believe that decisions arrived at collectively are necessarily less valid than decisions reached through individualistic processes and that what people say should be done is a less valid guide for public policy than how they behave. One reason for doubting this credo is that a "self-control" problem may be involved and people may support measures that constrain their choices. [25] Thus smokers who say they want to quit but don't may support programs or policies that make it difficult for them to smoke. Similarly, some workers may realize that they would take extra risks in order to earn more money but feel that they really shouldn't do it. In these cases the inferences drawn from market behavior may not fully capture the complexity of preferences. Nevertheless, although keeping such complexities in mind is desirable, it would be rash to justify ignoring behavior altogether on the grounds that preferences may be more complex.

Another potential shortcoming of the market pertains to its difficulty in reflecting altruistic preferences. However, one might raise the question of why, if altruism is really substantial, more producers do not advertise on the basis of ethical attributes. For example, why didn't some textile companies take the lead in reducing cotton dust exposures and advertise the fact to gain market share among altruistic consumers? One problem is that a fairness issue may be involved, especially with regard to free riding on public goods. I may be willing to pay a little more for my shirts so that textile workers do not get brown lung disease but may feel that it is unfair for me to pay when not everyone else does. I may support a rule requiring safer conditions and higher costs even if I would not have chosen to pay extra for a safely made shirt at the store. Here again, however, posing the hypotheticals does not address the crucial issue of the magnitude of altruism, which other data suggest may not be terribly large.

But to some the lack of altruism is precisely the type of problem that public policy should address. Economists are criticized for taking preferences as "given" and for ignoring that politics is in large part composed of battles over what our preferences ought to be. The belief that the presidency should be a "bully pulpit" nicely expresses the view that political leadership should be creative and uplifting. In a debate that harks back to Edmund Burke, economists often reply that overriding preferences is undemocratic and usually undesirable.

Yet the lines are not so clearly drawn. Proponents of highly protective regulation often in the same breath point out that surveys show that the public seems to approve of strict regulation of health and safety even after they are reminded that they, as consumers, bear much of the cost. Sometimes, proponents also claim that, because Congress appears to have endorsed strict protection, it is antidemocratic for anyone to argue for less. In this case it is the economists who argue that the importance of existing preferences should be minimized and who look to the "bully pulpit" of the Office of Management and Budget (OMB) to argue for "what's right" and to explain the need for efficient use of scare resources. Thus each side can tar the other with the charge of elitism. The real issue, however, is to figure out how to reconcile the somewhat different messages that the market and the political process are conveying.

A "rights" approach is sometimes the most appropriate guide to public policy. The choices about when to create such rights are not made primarily on cost-benefit grounds. But, although the balancing of costs and benefits that lies at the heart of utilitarianism is not a sufficient guide to social action, it is almost always a necessary one. Discussion of rights does not obviate the need for trade-offs. Instead, it leads to discussion of which rights take precedence. Often a more sensible approach would look at whether the gains from stricter standards outweigh the costs.[26]

Some situations clearly do call for restricting the sway of the market.[27] For example, we do not allow buying and selling votes, much less human beings. In the latter case the reason is chiefy moral. In the former the primary reason is that the practice would undermine the legitimacy of democratic institutions, with potentially grave consequences. Where there is a consensus that we should prohibit markets for these types of reasons, it would be improper for public policymakers to look to the market for guidance about the value of the proscribed activity. Where a consensus is absent—often when markets have been regulated but not prohibited—the issue of looking to them for guidance becomes more controversial. But what relevance do these examples have to occupational safety and health?

The OSH Act declares that it is Congress's intent "to assure so far as possible every working man and woman in the Nation safe and healthful working conditions."[28] Despite the use of the word "possible," many observers have interpreted the act to confer a "right" to such conditions. They then object to cost-benefit analysis because it ignores "rights" in its search for the optimal balance between costs and benefits.

The evidence indicates that a market for workplace risk, although undoubtedly imperfect, does exist. Attempts to suppress trade-offs for risk can never be more than partially successful because there is no way that all occupations can be made equally safe; thus, so long as workers are free to choose their jobs, some compensating differentials will be required to attract workers to the riskier ones. Are such transactions immoral? Are they different from trade-offs that workers might make between wages on the one hand and pleasant working conditions, job security, or good benefits on the other? The basis for distinguishing hazard pay from these others is a belief that health is a special type of good. Just as we should not deprive people of life-preserving medical care just because they cannot pay, so we should not deprive them of life-preserving environmental conditions because they cannot pay.

This analogy to Medicaid (the federal program providing medical care for the poor) breaks down because, as we have seen, the redistributional argument for OSHA is not very strong. But the analogy could be shifted to Medicare, which is provided to the elderly without regard to income. Yet the problems with Medicare would also have analogues in the occupational health field. What level of medical care (environmental conditions) do people have a right to? Is everyone going to be forced to consume the same level of medical services (safety measures)? How do we provide incentives to pay attention to costs so that medical services (hazard abatement) are not taken to the point where their marginal benefits are almost zero?

The inadequacy of the rights approach to deal with this class of problems can be clearly seen if we pose the issue of the right of a vulnerable group, such as asthmatics, to be protected against air pollution. As one writer points out:

In the real world, one person's right is another's duty, and it often clarifies the discussion to focus more precisely on who owes this duty and what it is going to cost him or her. . . . Suppose taking X quantity of pollution from the air of a city will keep one asthmatic from being forced to leave town and cost 1,000 workers their jobs? Suppose it will keep 1,000 asthmatics from being forced out and cost one job? These are not equivalent choices, economically or morally, and the effort to decide them according to some abstract idea of moral importance only obscures the true nature of the moral problems involved.[29]

It is hard to believe that the existence of a market for risk threatens the legitimacy of our economic institutions or that trade-offs for marginal increments for risk are viewed by most people as immoral. In contrast, if workers were continually accepting certain death to feed their families, a moral crisis would assuredly arise, along with demands that such unsafe jobs be prohibited. Of course, this prohibition would not address the desperation that had led individuals to take those jobs, but it would help to restore faith in the justice of the economic system.

Finally, some assert that policymakers' use of explicit figures for the value of life should be discouraged because it will lead to an erosion in respect for life. Talking about trade-offs between lives and dollars certainly does raise troubling ethical issues. How much of our own money, for example, should we spend to keep our elderly relatives alive? At least in the realm of public policy, however, the correctness of this prediction of eroding respect is by no means self-evident. For example, through the early 1980s the Federal Highway Administration (FHWA) and most of its state counterparts employed a figure of around $200,000 for the benefit of preventing a highway fatality, although they denied that this represented any attempt to estimate the "value" of life. A good share of the credit for the FHWA's recent adoption of higher values goes to economists, who pointed out the findings of more recent human capital studies as well as the WTP literature. In this case explicit analytic focus on the value of death prevention led to higher values being used. Which, if either, is more likely to erode respect for life—a low, unstated, and implicit value or a higher explicit value?

And, of course, *any* policy decision places a value on life, implicitly if not explicitly. A decision to spend $10 million to prevent ten deaths implies a value of at least $1 million per death prevented. Analysts assume that explicitness will lead to decisions that are more consistent with society's preferences because the basis for the choice will have to be articulated and defended. How are the fifty state highway departments supposed to make intelligent decisions about the worthwhileness of thousands of safety investment decisions each year without some sense of how much should be spent to prevent a fatality? "More consistent" does not necessarily mean less protective; for example, if OSHA had looked at the costs and effects of the 1972 asbestos standard, it might have realized that a lower PEL would have been justified.

The ultimate argument for ignoring market studies is that treating life as "priceless" or putting a high value on it is an important symbol of our society's commitment to humane values. It expresses the kind of values that we want our society to embody. The problem with such symbolism is that, if we do end up spending $10 million or $20 million to prevent a cancer death, we are not going to be able to prevent many of them. It is only because we prevent so few deaths that we can afford to pat ourselves on the back for spending so much on those few.

However, to a certain degree, the "symbolic" argument can be defended within a WTP framework. The reason is that the marginal valuation placed on preventing deaths will decline as the number of deaths prevented increases. One reason is simply that societal wealth will have been depleted; after preventing 50,000 deaths at an average cost of $10 million (a total cost of $500 billion), the willingness to pay for the prevention of the remaining deaths will be lower because wealth is lower. A second reason is that the success of early prevention efforts will have lowered the level of risk; with higher probabilities of survival, people may tend to place a lower value on further increments of risk reduction.[30]

Thus, in concept, although preventing 100,000 deaths at this average cost might be unacceptable, preventing a few might still be justifiable. The validity of this level as a spending guideline for present marginal decisions is not necessarily vitiated because it appears excessive when applied to 100,000 people.

However, a theoretical possibility should not be confused with the most likely case. Realistic opportunities do currently exist for preventing thousands of premature deaths if we are willing to spend the money.

Examples include air bags for cars, improved emergency services, and making hypertension diagnosis and treatment programs more freely available. However, if we try to spend on programs costing $10 million per death prevented, we will quite quickly run into resource constraints long before we reach the point where the marginal value placed on preventing additional deaths has dropped very much.

It is not only appropriate but necessary to weigh the costs and benefits of risk reduction programs, and this requires placing a value on the reductions in risk. The potential willingness to pay of those at risk is an important piece of information for policymakers to consider. Because they are the major beneficiaries, the workers' assessments of the gains should be extremely pertinent to the choice made by those to whom the decision-making authority has been delegated. Consider a situation in which all members of society face the same risks from a hazard. To find out how much to spend to reduce the risks, what could be more sensible than to find out how much individuals would be willing to sacrifice toward that end?[31]

However, it is highly improbable, even on purely theoretical grounds, that the number generated by studies of risk behavior should automatically be inserted in a calculation that produces an estimate of net benefits to society. Instead, we should also consider equity, external caring, and any special circumstances of the particular risk context that is being addressed. Few benefit-cost analysts would object to this second step; however, viewing the proper process as having two steps raises new problems. One risk is that the hard numbers drive out the soft, and the second step of the analysis becomes vestigial. The second risk is that, because the second step has few guidelines and no clear bounds, policymakers become essentially free to disregard evidence about the preferences of those at risk. Not surprisingly, even those economists who acknowledge the relevance of the second step often imply that it should carry relatively little weight.

The Relevance of WTP Estimates to OSHA Health Standards

Although many shortcomings and inconsistencies in the studies of labor market risk premiums have been noted, the weight of the evidence is that such premiums are paid in some settings.[32] Studies that use the rate of on-the-job fatalities as the measure of risk tell us how much a group of blue-collar workers values reducing the risk of accidental death. Because the studies have produced estimates that differ substantially, the policy implications for reducing accidental workplace deaths must be hedged. At the low end they cluster around several hundred thousand dollars (in 1985 dollars); at the high end they go above $5 million. However, I am interested here in whether the same range of values applies to preventing a death resulting from long-term toxic exposures.

One of the sharpest distinctions between studies finding small premiums and studies finding large ones is that the former studies typically use the total fatality rate among members of an occupation as the measure of risk, whereas the studies finding large premiums use the on-the-job fatality rate. On-the-job deaths are overwhelmingly accidents. In contrast, the occupational death rate reflects the overall mortality experience of an occupation, including the fatal diseases that may afflict workers before or after retirement.

There are three possible reasons why the occupation measure leads to lower estimates of risk premiums. The first is that occupational measures create some downward bias because of self-selection. For example, above-ground miners turn out to have higher overall mortality rates than underground miners, largely because the underground miners who contract lung disease transfer to jobs topside. The high mortality rate of bartenders is also in part a product of self-selection. Thus the measured risk in these studies for these two occupations will exceed the true job-related risk. The result is that workers will appear to be relatively poorly compensated for the risks attributed to their jobs.[33]

A second possible explanation for the small size of the premiums in studies using a measure of total occupational mortality is that the disease risks are not well perceived and thus not well compensated. Evidence of cases where workers were uninformed is abundant.[34] The third possible explanation is that a reduction in the risk of death from a disease with a long latency period is not valued as highly as a reduction in the risk of a death occurring this year. These last two explanations have quite different policy implications. If the former is true, then employers face weak incentives to control hazards; and policies are needed both to provide information to workers and to regulate exposures. If the latter is true, the need for these policies can be viewed as less pressing; any standards that are set should be relatively lax to reflect the low value placed on reducing the risks. If both are true—that is, workers place a low value on reducing risks from diseases with long latency periods *and* they are ignorant of these risks— then there will still be a need for government action, either providing information or setting standards, but the stringency of the standards should still be guided by the worker's low valuations.[35]

No studies have been published that specifically try to estimate the magnitude of risk premiums associated with exposures to workplace carcinogens, although one team of researchers reported that they had run a test that found no statistically significant premiums.[36] Viscusi investigated whether workers who said they faced health hazards received wage premiums and found that the risk coefficient, although positive, was not statistically significant. That study's relevance may be limited for my purposes by its use of an aggregated measure of health hazard; only two of the dozen component hazards concerned toxic chemicals; the rest involved dampness, temperature, dirtiness, noise, and other physical conditions. In another study, Viscusi carried out a simulation in which chemical workers were asked what their responses would be if new hazards were introduced into their workplace. He found that workers said they would demand substantial premiums to deal with the more serious hazards.[37]

Table 2.7 shows an analysis of wage premiums that looked only at whether workers said they were exposed to "sizable" or "great" hazards from chemicals or fumes and dust. For those who did, a variable labeled "TOXPROB" was set equal to 1.[38] Although the statistical significance of the TOXPROB coefficient varies with the sample, the findings indicate that, if we look only at blue-collar occupations, workers who believe they are exposed to serious toxic hazards do appear to get higher pay. To test whether the TOXPROB coefficient was picking up the effects of other hazards not included in this regression, nine other hazard variables were included in another regression (not shown); the coefficient and significance of TOXPROB increased.[39] The regressions also indicated that, unlike safety hazards, risk premiums for toxic hazards are not provided only at unionized plants (column 2).[40] Nor are they provided only at larger plants (column 4); in fact, the interaction term between risk and plant size indicates that toxic premiums are smaller there.

Of course, we do not know how well workers understand the risks they face. In the case of safety Viscusi has shown that worker's perceptions of hazards are highly correlated with the injury rate in the industry in which they work.[41] But for health hazards we lack a good objective measure of relative health risks among industries with which to compare workers' perceptions. It is noteworthy that the size and significance of the estimate of wage premiums for toxic hazards is similar to the estimate for all hazards from the same survey. Thus, on average, workers get about the same premiums when they perceive "great" or "sizable" toxic hazards as when they perceive "great" or "sizable" hazards from any source.[42] But we do not know whether the perception of a "great" toxic hazard involves the same probability of dying as the perception of a "great" safety hazard.

Table 2.7 Workers Who Believe They Face Serious Toxic Hazards Do Receive Compensation

Variable[a]	Blue-collar, no interaction[b]		Blue-collar, union-toxic interaction[c]		Blue- and white-collar, no interaction[d]		Blue-collar, size and toxic interaction[e]	
	Coefficient	Standard error	Coefficient	Standard error	Coefficient	Standard error	Coefficient	Standard error
TOXPROB	.31[f]	.18	.28	.27	.09	.17	.57[h]	.22
Union	1.41[h]	.18	1.39[h]	.20	1.01[h]	.15	1.39[h]	.18
Union × TOXPROB			.07	.36				
Bigsize × TOXPROB							.90[g]	.40
Experience	.05[h]	.01			.06[h]	.01		
Experience squared	−.0005[g]	.0002			−.0008[h]	.0002		
Tenure	.02	.04			.10[h]	.03		
Tenure squared	.00	.00			−.002[g]	.001		
Education	.01	.01			.04[h]	.01		
Black	−.73[h]	.25			−.79[h]	.22		
Female	−1.21[h]	.21			−1.34[h]	.19		
Too Fast	−.01	.16			.17	.12		
Repetitive	−.43[g]	.17			−.78[h]	.13		
No control	.01	.16			−.36[h]	.13		
Bad health	−.86[g]	.41			−1.02[h]	.35		
Urban	.62[h]	.17			.79[h]	.14		
Craft	1.57[h]	.30			−.11	.21		
Operative	.90[h]	.29			−.51[h]	.20		

a. Also included were variables for industry, region, and firm size. For definition of variables, see appendix A.
b. N = 585, R² = .52.
c. N = 585, R² = .52.
d. N = 1166, R² = .44.
e. N = 585, R² = .53.
f. Significant at the .10 level.
g. Significant at the .05 level.
h. Significant at the .01 level.

Thus uncertainty about the true size of the hazards prevents us from arriving at an implied value of preventing a death.

In summary, the empirical evidence regarding risk premiums for health hazards fails to help much in figuring out what value policymakers should place on preventing deaths from long-term toxic exposures. However, other considerations can supply some insight.

A central issue is whether workers would demand as much for a given reduction in the risk of a cancer death thirty years from now as for the same reduction in the risk of an accidental death this year. There are at least two reasons why reduction of toxic risks might be valued more. First, cancer, as well as other fatal occupational ailments, such as obstructive pulmonary disease, is often painful and dreaded. Second, workers and especially the public may feel that accidents are partly or largely due to the carelessness of the workers, whereas deaths resulting from toxic substances involve no fault on the worker's part. Yet we saw that, although survey respondents do feel that such a distinction should affect valuations, the differences tended to be small.

There are many reasons why workers might place a greater value on preventing the more immediate death. Not only are the years of life lost because of most toxic exposures fairly far in the future (most cancers have a latency period of fifteen to forty-five years), but the number of years lost is, of course, on average less than the number of years lost as a result of accidents. The average age of the workplace accident fatality is about 41. The average age of the workplace cancer victim is likely to be 55, 65, or even higher, depending on the type of cancer, the level of toxic exposure, and the demographics of the industry work force. Age 20 through 50 is the period when most people have their greatest family responsibilities. Death would deprive children of a parent and parents of a chance to see their children grow. During those years people tend to be in good health and otherwise in their prime.[43]

The delayed effects of toxic exposures raise the question of whether to discount them and, if so, at what rate. Analysts have reached no consensus on this issue; however, it seems proper that discounting practice should be guided by the preferences of the affected people. As an analogy, if we were trying to decide how to measure the reduction in the quality of life caused by a certain disability, we would want to base it on individuals' preferences about the relative value of being in that disabled state versus perfect health. Similarly, with discounting we should consider preferences about future versus present outcomes. This position contrasts both with those who argue that costs and benefits should always be discounted at the same rate and those who argue that discounting is a "psychological frailty" that should be repudiated.[44]

It seems plausible that most people would place a lower value on preventing risks that materialize in the future. In nonhealth areas evidence indicates that many people, especially blue-collar workers, have high discount rates. This can be seen in the high rates at which people will borrow money.[45] More pertinent, it can be seen in the refusal to give up behaviors that are hazardous in the long run but pleasurable or difficult to give up, such as smoking. Smoking has declined less among blue-collar men than among other men. The prospect that differences in attitudes toward the future could create a growing gap between the health status of blue- and white-collar workers is upsetting. But with discount rates, as with WTP valuations, policymakers are not bound to accept income- or class-based distinctions if they find the results invidious. If they choose, they can use the same discount rate for all groups. They could, of course, accept the argument that discounting is a "psychological frailty" and abandon it altogether. However, it is not necessary to do so in order to avoid possible inegalitarian results. Moreover, although the evidence is not at all solid, it seems likely that failing to discount would not do as good a job at capturing the typical person's preferences as would discounting at a low rate.

If we chose to discount the prevention of a death at a 5 percent discount rate, then a cancer death occurring twenty-five years in the future would count as only 0.295 death. Thus the cost per death prevented would go up more than threefold. If we use a 10 percent discount rate, this future death would count as only 0.092 death, and the cost per death prevented would increase more than tenfold.[46]

Another perspective comes from comparing the valuations needed to justify OSHA's cancer standards with the costs of various medical programs. Table 2.8 shows that the cost per life year added (discounted at 5 percent) for these medical programs was under $100,000 for all but one program and well under $50,000 for most. In contrast, a $5 million valuation on the prevention of a cancer death at age 55, which would follow a twenty-five year latency period and cut off seventeen remaining years of life, implies that the value of each year of life added (again discounted at 5 percent) is over $1.5 million. Yet even this $5 million valuation would not be enough to justify several of OSHA's standards.

The OSHA costs of $2 million to $20 million per death prevented translate to costs per discounted life year roughly 25 to 250 times higher than the $20,000 price tag carried by the medium-priced medical program. Even without discounting the disparities are great. It seems hard to recon-

Table 2.8   Cost-Effectiveness of Medical Programs: Some Representative Studies

Medical condition	Program evaluated	Cost per year of life added (dollars)
Hypercholesterolemia	Changing diets	6,700–24,000
Hypertension	Screening and treatment	17,000–36,000
Coronary disease	Coronary care units	7,200
	Mobile coronary care units	10,300
End-stage renal disease	Facility dialysis	53,000
	Home dialysis	34,000
	Transplantation (with facility dialysis of failures)	29,000–43,000
Tuberculosis	Screening children	60,000–216,000
Phenylketonuria	Screening neonates and dietary treatment	12,000
	Follow-up screening of initially negative screens	72,000
Breast cancer	Screening with physical exam by trained laypeople	9,600
	Screening with mammogram (marginal effect)	79,000
Measles	Immunization	5,000

Source: Donald M. Berwick, Shan Cretin, and Emmet Keeler, *Cholesterol, Children, and Heart Disease: An Analysis of Alternatives* (New York: Oxford University Press, 1980), pp. 272–273. See this book (which presents these figures in 1975 dollars discounted at 5 percent) for specific references to the various studies. This table converts those figures to 1985 dollars using the medical care component of the Consumer Price Index.

cile the much higher spending for OSHA's cancer prevention with the widespread belief that people are more willing to spend money on treatment than on prevention.[47]

An Assessment

At the beginning of this chapter I argued that a cost-effectiveness framework did not provide an adequate basis for assessing OSHA's program of standard setting—or those of other risk-regulating agencies. Are the costs per death prevented by OSHA's toxic standards greater than those of most other health measures? Yes, but the agency can reply that its spending is not too high; rather, spending by others is too low. Is it true that with our current level of spending we could prevent more deaths if we reallocated spending away from high-cost programs and toward low-cost ones? It is true, but the agency can reply that, in the absence of an actual government budget for all health spending, there is no reason to think that a less costly OSHA standard would lead to, for example, more highway safety construction. Finally, we saw that the thrust of the cost-effectivess critique could be parried by the argument that the prevention of occupational disease deaths *deserves* higher spending levels than the prevention of most other deaths. Thus the OSHA standard can be shown to be undesirable only if it costs "too much" in some absolute sense. We need to move from cost-effectiveness to benefit-cost analysis.

These defenses of OSHA raise important issues. In this chapter I have tried to address them in a serious fashion. I have argued that the best estimate of workers' willingness to pay for risk reduction indicates a value of around $2.5 million per death, essentially for the prevention of fatal accidents. If we inject this figure into some other programs, such as highway safety construction, then we will indeed conclude that they are spending too little; however, that valuation would still not justify the most likely costs for most of OSHA's carcinogen standards. Moreover, I have argued that the value workers place on preventing distant occupational cancer deaths is probably less than the value placed on preventing accident deaths, although the evidence on this point is meager and unclear.

A public decision about what level of protection to seek should consider more than the best estimate of workers' willingness to pay. Consideration of third parties' concern for reducing risks will justify greater protection. How much greater remains difficult to pin down. A few small-scale studies do indicate, however, that, although preventing occupational deaths and job cancer deaths may merit greater spending than for most deaths, the differentials, if any, do not appear to be large. Thus, although a defense of small cost differentials might be hard to rebut, a defense of OSHA's higher-cost standards on the basis that the prevention of occupational disease deaths is valued more highly than most other deaths appears suspect.

Spending $10 million or probably even $5 million to prevent an occupational disease death is excessive. That is the conclusion that this analysis leads to, although it depends on too many subjective and uncertain assumptions to be certain.

One purpose of this book is to provide a framework in which the case for cost-effectiveness can be made more effectively. The strategy for providing this framework is not to point out the myriad opportunities for preventing deaths at a lower cost in other programs. Politically, those opportunities are of limited relevance. But if it is true that strict regulation retards the pace of OSHA standard setting, then the high implicit valuations on some workers' lives causes a low implicit value on other workers' lives. One cost of overregulation becomes the deaths that are not prevented because of the ensuing underregulation. As a normative position, a believer in strict protection can still argue that it would be desirable to have both more standards and undiminished stringency. However, if the argument here is correct, for any given distribution of political power, greater stringency probably does not lead to more overall protection.

Thus, if the estimates of costs are not seriously overstated and the estimates of effects are not seriously understated, the charge of overregulation is probably sustained. But how good are the estimates?

Before turning to those issues, one important observation is in order. If we use the criterion of $2.5 million per death prevented, the *overall* OSHA program of setting new health standards might be judged a *success*. In other words, if the choice had been between having no new standards and having all of them, we are better off with the latter. If we look at the standards in table 2.1, for which we have estimates of both costs and deaths prevented, and add them up, we find total annual costs of between $738 and $957 million a year and total deaths prevented of between 427 and 497. The average cost per death prevented comes to between $1.49 and $2.24 million a year. The reason why the average cost per death prevented in the aggregated standards is far lower than the average of the individual standards is that asbestos accounts for about 80 percent of the deaths prevented and imposes quite low costs. Again, many caveats beset this conclusion. In particular, the asbestos case raises the important question of whether and to what extent exposures would have been reduced, and deaths prevented, even in the absence of the standard. Both industry's fears of liability and labor market pressures have been adduced as possible contributors to reduced exposures.[48] Suppose that these factors would have led to some reductions but not to ones as sharp as those resulting from OSHA's standard. In that case the costs per death prevented *attributable to the OSHA standard* would be much higher than the estimate in table 2.1 because of the assumptions that the marginal cost curve rises as exposures are reduced and that OSHA could claim credit only for the expensive reductions.

The argument that by some measures we are better off with the set of new OSHA health standards than we would have been without them deserves a hearing. But the recurring pattern of overregulation has more bearing on current policy choices.

Are We Overregulating? What Are the Costs and Health Effects?

In this chapter I provide a guide to the economic and scientific uncertainties that beset efforts to estimate the cost per death prevented of OSHA's health standards. In all policy debates, and especially in those concerned with toxic substances, uncertainties about the costs and effects of policy options are pervasive. In these debates facts are weapons. But claims of ignorance can also be weapons; many have claimed that the uncertainties should lead us to err on the side of caution. Any method we adopt for addressing them has implicit policy judgments built in. Those methods that are likely to overestimate effects or understate costs will lead to lower estimates of the costs per death prevented and make regulation seem more attractive, and vice versa. Ideally, we would like to have best estimates and confidence intervals around those estimates. At a minimum we need to be aware of the direction of the likely bias that our methods foster.

What Are the Costs?

How reliable are the cost estimates on which the assessments in table 2.1 of the costs per cancer death prevented are based? Isn't it true that the cost estimates are usually based on information supplied by industry and usually turn out to be overestimates? The answer is yes, although the figures in table 2.1 have already been adjusted to try to take account of that bias. In this section I examine the difficulties with cost estimates and explain how those cost figures were calculated.

The Appropriate Concepts of Cost
What costs should be included in the figure that is used to generate the estimate of costs per death prevented? A cost is a forgone benefit. The appropriate measure of cost captures the benefits that society gives up by adopting a standard. Usually, we focus on the resources (labor and capital) that are expended as a result of this decision and that could have been used in some alternative project. But the types of cost imposed by OSHA standards are really more complex. They involve public and private costs of adopting a standard; public costs of enforcing a standard; costs of the resources used in compliance measures; foregone productivity, including unemployment; losses in consumer surplus; and the costs of foregone

liberty, added discomfort, and other factors not included elsewhere. Let us look at each category separately.

1. First, there are the costs of adopting the standard. These include governmental costs for standard setting, all the work of gathering information on costs and health effects, and writing and justifying the standard. OSHA's budget for health standard setting has averaged about $5 million a year. With only about one new standard issued a year, that comes to an average of $5 million per standard. However, a large share of these costs go for administrative overhead, for other activities unrelated to the promulgation of particular toxic hazards (such as the development of generic standards for carcinogens and the labeling of hazardous materials), and for standards that are never promulgated. I would estimate that the cost to the government of each additional standard averages between $1 million and $2 million. In addition, private parties also incur costs in providing information that the government requests, as well as in presenting their own arguments, first to the agencies and ultimately to the courts. These costs depend in part on the number of parties affected by the standard, but they probably average $1 million to $2 million as well.

2. Although in most cases a new standard simply means that OSHA is enforcing a stricter PEL than it formerly did, the lower PEL makes violations more likely and therefore increases the number of employer appeals and the number of cases in which OSHA must monitor an employer's program for abating the violation. Also, when a new standard is adopted, OSHA often tries to increase its inspections at plants where workers are exposed to the substance. If the enforcement budget is fixed, the cost of all these extra measures is the foregone benefit from not inspecting the workplaces that will be neglected. Usually, we are not talking about more than a hundred inspections a year.[1]

3. Most studies focus on the cost to the employer of complying with the new standard. Of course, the financial impact on an employer will depend on all kinds of tax and accounting considerations. These are irrelevant to an analysis of the costs to *society*. If $100,000 has to be spent on labor and capital to install new controls, then those resources are not available to society for other purposes.

4. Productivity losses are a subcategory of compliance costs. For example, exposure to chemical fumes might be reduced by installing controls or by reducing the volume or slowing the pace of the process that produces them. The last procedures do not necessarily require new spending, but they may increase the unit cost of the output.[2]

5. Losses resulting from unemployment are an indirect type of produc-

tivity loss, although in this case they are borne by workers, not the employer. With unchanged demand the higher costs of production can lead some firms to cut back or close down. Workers who lose their jobs will often suffer some spell of unemployment, which imposes costs on them and on the economy.

6. When the higher costs are passed on in higher prices, consumers will buy less of the goods. To the extent that they had valued the goods above what they had been required to pay for them, they suffer a loss in "consumer's surplus."

7. Finally, there are a variety of costs that have not been accounted for elsewhere. These include the loss of liberty that some employers or workers experience from the constraints imposed on their behavior by the standard. Those workers who would have liked to take greater risks in exchange for greater compensation can no longer do so legally. (Other workers, of course, are protected against pressures to take risks that they really did not want to take.) Workers who are now required to wear personal protective equipment, such as respirators, may experience new discomforts as the price of protection.[3]

These seven categories suggest that the cost side of the equation is not necessarily less complicated than the benefit side. But several of these categories appear to involve costs that are small enough to ignore safely. Ignoring small items is a defensible strategy when the big ones are subject to a considerable margin of error, as they are here. Categories 1, 2, 5, and 6 can probably be disposed of in this way. I also do not try to monetize category 7, although it should be considered in the total analysis.[4]

Why Estimating the Costs Is Difficult

Not surprisingly, almost all the efforts to estimate the costs of health standards have focused on categories 3 and 4. Yet, even if we stick to these two categories, we encounter formidable obstacles. The firm itself is often uncertain about the costs of controls. And even if firms have good information, OSHA faces the problem of obtaining it. Finally, even after the standard has been implemented, retrospective attempts to assess the costs encounter new difficulties.

The View from the Firm
To a degree, firms can reduce their uncertainty about the costs of reducing toxic exposures by mounting more elaborate studies. Firms undertake new investments all the time, and, because good estimates of costs are impor-

tant, they have learned how to improve them. In contrast to those voluntary investments, however, compliance with OSHA standards is rarely viewed as meriting elaborate study. Firms often would prefer a less strict measure than OSHA proposes, but they are eventually likely to adopt whatever standard OSHA requires. Because the ultimate decision is not fully in their hands, the value of extra information is reduced. But even if the firm wants to know the costs, it must overcome several obstacles.

The firm may have a rough idea of what it will cost to add conventional exhaust ventilation to existing operations, so-called retrofitting. It will have a less clear sense of the costs of alternative approaches; yet, over time the firm will have an incentive to find cheaper methods and is likely to discover some that are less costly. For example, because retrofitting is expensive, the firm may decide that it is worthwhile to accelerate the purchase of new capital equipment. The new equipment may both reduce hazards and increase productivity. But if it does, analysts face a problem of "joint costs"—there is no nonarbitrary way to apportion the costs between OSHA compliance and expanded output.

In a number of cases OSHA has required firms to take innovative steps, including the development of new technology, to meet its standard. In those cases, where the firms are often skeptical that the PEL can be attained, their cost estimates are obviously of little relevance. More generally, firms may not be able to predict accurately the effectiveness of particular measures in reducing exposures, which undermines the validity of their cost estimates.

The View from OSHA
For every one of its changes in a toxic substance PEL, OSHA has hired a consulting firm to estimate the costs of compliance. The quality of those studies has varied widely, although they have tended to improve over time. The first task of the consultants is to find out where workers are exposed to the substance and to estimate how many are exposed at different levels. The costs of control depend largely on how many workplaces will have to install controls, how many operations will be affected, and the extent to which exposures must be reduced. None of this information is readily available, except for the identification of the major industries that are affected.

The accuracy of the data that are collected depends on the variety of industries affected by the standard, the willingness of firms to cooperate, and the extensiveness of the consultant's study. The standard on coke oven emissions required changes only in coking facilities at steel plants. In contrast, the lead standard addressed over forty different industries. Even within an industry different plants may use different processes and raise different compliance problems. Even when they use the same process, different plants have often undertaken different degrees of prior efforts to control exposures. All these sources of variability present a major sampling problem for consultants, who usually lack any basis for stratifying their sample to account for these differences and in any event usually also lack the time and money to visit more than a small number of plants. Often the consultants' estimates for an industry are based on extrapolations from a single "model plant." And estimates for whole industries are drawn from analogies to other similar industries. Critics of these estimates constantly question the representativeness of these "models" and the validity of the analogies.

Most of the information about costs collected by the consultants comes from estimates provided by the companies. Firms frequently refuse to cooperate with consultants, often because they simply do not want to bother making estimates. When they do cooperate, or when they submit their own independent cost estimates directly to OSHA, the validity of their estimates is tainted by their incentive to overestimate. Reports that compliance costs would be large and, especially, that the attainment of a proposed PEL cannot be achieved or would bankrupt the firm are more likely to make OSHA hesitate about issuing a strict standard. OSHA needs to have information to convince a court that its standards are feasible in both the technological and the financial sense. Firms that argue that standards are not feasible and those that withhold information make OSHA's task more difficult. Thus the incentive to undermine OSHA's position combines with the plant engineer's own tendency to estimate costs conservatively (which, in this case, means not to count on uncertain prospects that may reduce the costs of compliance).

In some cases OSHA has gotten especially useful information from firms that have taken more extensive steps to reduce exposures than other firms in their industries. (These cases are discussed in chapter 7.) These firms may less strongly oppose or even support an OSHA standard because it will impose relatively greater costs on their competitors.

Retrospective Studies: What Did Compliance Really Cost?
A few attempts have been made to examine compliance costs retrospectively. Ideally, retrospective studies would provide a truer estimate of the cost impact of OSHA standards. In addition, the studies could help us to assess the direction and size of the errors in OSHA's original estimates. In practice, retrospective studies avoid some (but not all) of the problems of

prospective estimates but also encounter new ones. The primary new problem is trying to decide what portion of any new control expenditures is actually attributable to the OSHA standard. We saw in the case of asbestos that worries about lawsuits and pressures from workers for higher risk premiums could also induce firms to reduce exposures. When new information about a hazard is generated, it is plausible that *some* new control efforts would often have been launched even in the absence of an OSHA standard. In those cases both the costs and the benefits attributable to the OSHA standard are less than what one would otherwise have estimated. And because of the assumption of a rising marginal cost curve, the cost per death prevented is higher.

For five standards—asbestos, vinyl chloride, coke oven emissions, cotton dust, and lead—we have some retrospective insights on compliance costs. These are discussed in more detail in appendix B. For both asbestos and cotton dust the costs appear to have been roughly half of what OSHA's contractors had predicted. A comparison for vinyl chloride is thwarted because the consultants had agreed with the industry that compliance with the OSHA standard was not feasible at any cost. That conclusion was quickly revealed to be incorrect. For coke oven emissions, comparisons are difficult because it is clear that engineering controls have not always been implemented as quickly or with as much success as OSHA had predicted. For example, from 1979 to 1982 OSHA sampled exposures for almost 1900 coke oven workers and found that 49 percent were still exposed to airborne levels above the permissible exposure level and thus were required to wear respirators or rotate out of the area.

In this case firms had to bear not only the costs of engineering controls but also the cost of an extensive respirator program. On the other hand, delays in implementing engineering controls saved money. The net costs imposed by the respirator programs are uncertain, depending on how extensive they were before the standard.

The ultimate costs of the lead standard also remain uncertain, depending on the feasibility problems that will be encountered in the primary and secondary smelting industries. Estimates of the costs of the arsenic standard have been confounded by the infeasibility of engineering controls in some settings and by the agreement of labor and management to work together to design new solutions that will be acceptable to OSHA. Here again, there are offsetting factors: The overoptimism about technology tends to lead to underestimates of costs, but the search for more flexible, local solutions promises to reduce them.

Conclusions on the Costs of Standards

My review of the retrospective studies shows that the cost estimates of OSHA and its consultants have often proven to be overestimates. The asbestos, cotton dust, and vinyl chloride standards clearly fall in this category. In these cases OSHA's contractors exaggerated the difficulty of finding technological solutions. However, in other cases (for example, lead smelting and coke ovens), OSHA appears to have been overoptimistic.

We lack retrospective studies for the acrylonitrile, ethylene oxide, and benzene standards. The benzene standard was overturned by the Supreme Court and never implemented, although OSHA will promulgate a new standard in the late 1980s. In these three cases it seems likely that the costs were also overestimated. All three involve the petrochemical industry (as the vinyl chloride standard did) and do not pose the type of feasibility problems faced in old smelting operations. The costs may have been as little as half of the figures cited by OSHA. In table 2.1 I presented a range bounded by these two figures.

A similar range is presented for the costs of the arsenic standard. Point estimates should be considered only as the best guess within a range that could easily be plus or minus 50 percent.

Estimating Health Effects

Before any conclusions about overregulation can be drawn, we have to look at the health effects side of the equation as well. Although estimating costs is no less difficult than estimating effects, the former can be more narrowly bounded. People may differ in their cost estimates by a factor of 2 or sometimes even 5 or 10; they will almost ever differ by a factor of 100 or 1000 or more. In contrast, disparities of that magnitude are not rare in the debates over the number of deaths attributable to some toxic exposures. Fortunately, however, such disparate estimates are usually not found in the handful of standards for which OSHA has set new standards. In this section I illustrate those uncertainties and explain why they exist.[5] Then I look at OSHA's way of handling them and the criticism it has aroused. Finally, I review the implications for estimates of the impact of OSHA's standards and the overall judgment about overregulation.

Table 3.1   Types of Evidence Used to Justify OSHA Changes in PELs

Substance	Primary type	Chief supporting type
Asbestos	epidemiology	–
Vinyl chloride	epidemiology	bioassay
Coke oven emissions	epidemiology	–
Benzene	epidemiology	–
Arsenic	epidemiology	–
DBCP	bioassay and epidemiology	–
Cotton dust	epidemiology	–
Lead[a]	–	–
Acrylonitrile	bioassay	epidemiology
Ethylene oxide	bioassay	epidemiology

a. The chief issue in the lead standard was the prevention of so-called subclinical effects, including reduced nerve conduction and decreased ability to synthesize heme. Laboratory studies using human subjects and blood studies were the primary types of evidence.

Sources of Evidence and Their Limitations

What information is available to determine whether current exposures are hazardous and how much disease could be prevented by enforcing a lower PEL? In some cases there are acute effects and the hazard is obvious. For hazards without such symptoms, more sensitive methods are required.

Aside from clinical observations there are four primary methods to help identify carcinogens. Two of them—structural activity relationships and short-term tests—have had at most a trivial impact on the new standards that OSHA has issued to date.[6] As table 3.1 shows, epidemiological and clinical evidence have usually played the major role, supported by bioassays, in OSHA's arguments that existing exposures are hazardous. As we will see, epidemiological evidence has also predominated in efforts to quantify the health effects.

Despite the crucial role they have played, epidemiological studies are subject to serious limitations, both for identifying hazards and for estimating the magnitude of the risks they pose. First, there is typically a lag of fifteen to fifty years between the time of first exposure and the onset of disease. This lag hampers efforts to find out what level of exposures workers experienced. Monitoring of exposure levels was less common in earlier years, especially, of course, when there was little or no awareness that a particular substance was hazardous. Second, epidemiologists need to control for other possible causes of the diseases that the chemical is suspected of causing. Workers may have also been exposed to other hazardous chemicals, not just the one under investigation in a particular study. Lifestyle and other environmental factors also must be considered. Smok-

Table 3.2   Sources of Uncertainty in the COWPS Attempt to Estimate the Number of Occupational Cancer Deaths Prevented by OSHA's Acrylonitrile Standard

Factors leading to overestimates of deaths prevented	Factors with uncertain impact	Factors leading to underestimates of deaths prevented
1. COWPS assumed a linear dose-response curve with no threshold.	1. Exposure levels from 1950 to 1955 may have been higher or lower than 20 ppm.	1. Not all exposed workers were traced.
2. Many facilities are already at or near 2-ppm exposure levels.	2. The average latency period may be longer or shorter than twenty years.	
	3. People in the sample may have smoked more or less than other Du Pont workers.	
	4. Because of sampling error, the number of excess deaths could be larger or smaller than 4.	

ing is often a suspected cause, but data on smoking habits frequently are unavailable. More important, researchers do not know all the risk factors that they should be controlling for. Third, the sample of workers in any particular study is frequently not large. As a result of these shortcomings, epidemiological studies are essentially useless for identifying small increases in risk; realistically, only excess risks greater than 30 percent will ever be identified.[7] In many cases, even considerably larger effects could not be conclusively established. For example, a prominent asbestos researcher, Philip E. Enterline, has shown that a study to detect a lung cancer excess among workers exposed to the current PEL of 2 fibers for twenty-five years would probably require following a sample of tens of thousands of workers for another twenty-five years. Assembling this large a sample is a highly unlikely prospect.[8] Partly because of the inability of epidemiology to detect small excess risks, OSHA adopted the position in its Cancer Policy that nonpositive epidemiological studies should be given no weight when they conflict with positive bioassay results.

To illustrate the problems described, table 3.2 shows the uncertainties plaguing the attempt by the Council on Wage and Price Stability (COWPS) to use an epidemiological study to estimate the number of cancer deaths that would be prevented by OSHA's reduction in the PEL for acrylonitrile from 20 ppm to 2 ppm. In this case COWPS relied on the preliminary results of a study conducted by Du Pont, which followed 470 males who worked at one of its plants from 1950 to 1955. For workers exposed between 1950 and 1952, there had been eight cancer deaths through 1975 as opposed to four deaths expected, a difference that was just statistically significant at the .05 level.

COWPS estimated that acrylonitrile exposures for the workers had averaged 20 ppm, a figure taken not from Du Pont (which offered no estimate) but from Monsanto, which based the figure on its assessment of industry practices at the time. COWPS assumed a twenty-year latency period for the disease, which meant that only exposures before 1955 could have contributed to the diseases that had appeared by 1975. Based on this assumption, COWPS estimated the excess risk of cancer per year of exposure to acrylonitrile.[9] Then it applied this risk to the estimate that 3400 workers were exposed to acrylonitrile levels between the current PEL of 20 ppm and the proposed PEL of 2 ppm. For the sake of both convenience and "conservatism," it assumed that all these workers were actually exposed at 20 ppm. Then COWPS assumed that the dose-response curve was linear and had no threshold and calculated that a 2-ppm PEL would prevent 90 percent of the eight cancer deaths that would occur at exposures to 20 ppm, or seven deaths a year.

Although COWPS often chose to make what it considered conservative assumptions in estimating the risks, the uncertainties listed in table 3.2 preclude any definitive judgment about the direction of the bias in its final estimate. The acrylonitrile story has an interesting sequel, for as additional years of experience were analyzed by Du Pont, the rate of excess cancer deaths diminished. Although there was still a small excess, it was not statistically significant.[10] Those newer findings do not exonerate acrylonitrile, especially in light of positive findings in bioassays, but they do reinforce a sense of skepticism about the precision that quantitative risk analyses can attain. But despite their shortcomings for demonstrating that a risk exists, epidemiological studies potentially remain quite useful for providing rough estimates of the maximum possible effect of exposures.

Bioassays

Although epidemiological studies and the clinical observations that often precede them provided the basis for the majority of the new health standards OSHA has issued, it seems probable that bioassays will play a larger role in the future.[11] For the OSHA standards promulgated through 1986, however, quantitative risk assessments have been based on bioassays in only one case, ethylene oxide.

Bioassays usually pose the problem of extrapolating from high-dose to low-dose exposures in its sharpest form. The brouhaha about saccharin gave front page treatment to the rats who drank the equivalent of eight-hundred diet sodas a day. The use of high doses is a concomitant of the small number of animals used in the tests, usually fifty of each sex in two species at each of two dose levels, plus the controls. The fundamental assumption underlying the bioassay is that high-dose testing assesses the toxic properties of the chemical. If it is a central nervous system depressant at the doses tested, it is probably one at lower levels as well. If it is a carcinogen at high doses, it is probably one at lower doses as well.[12]

During the 1970s, many researchers and regulatory agencies chose to assume that carcinogens had a dose-response curve that was linear and had no threshold. In other words, the dose-response curve should be drawn as a straight line from the data points to the origin. The implication was that there was no level of exposure that was entirely risk free except zero. These assumptions were consistent with what was known about relatively well-understood carcinogens such as radiation, cigarette smoking, and asbestos. And, as we have seen, the large number of nonpositive studies at low doses cannot exclude the possibility that there is some small effect. Because we lack good data at low dose levels, it would be helpful to have a powerful theory, but no method for predicting low-level risks has any clear claim to superiority. This is unfortunate because, although the proposed models do not differ much in their predictions at higher dose levels, they vary dramatically (by factors of 10 to 1,000,000) in their predictions of health effects at low levels.[13]

The other crucial policy judgment that emerged during the 1970s was the decision to treat chemicals for which there was strong evidence of carcinogenesis in animals as if they were human carcinogens. The data show only that almost all the known human carcinogens have also been shown to be carcinogenic in bioassays. The more pertinent issue—whether all animal carcinogens are human carcinogens—is again one that cannot be resolved. Many committees of scientists have gone on record asserting that, if there is strong evidence that a chemical causes cancer in animals, it should be considered to be a human carcinogen. Again, as discussed later, this is a policy decision, not a scientific judgment.

Extrapolation from animals to humans raises at least as many problems as extrapolation from high to low doses does. Some animal strains are much more sensitive to particular toxic agents than others. Which, if any, present the best analogy to humans? Often the method of administration—for example, feeding versus inhalation—is not the same for animals as for exposed humans. Should this invalidate the comparison? Should the extrapolation of the dose be based on the relative weight of humans and mice, the surface areas of their bodies, or some other factor? This issue alone can introduce scaling differences up to fortyfold in extrapolating effects to humans.[14] More broadly, there are questions about whether the test animals metabolize the toxic agent in a fashion similar to humans. Bioassay results also depend crucially on accurate pathological work to identify the tumors in experimental and control animals. Yet a number of celebrated cases show that agreement among pathologists cannot be counted on.[15] All these problems have led some experts to conclude that

today few experienced experimental oncologists would make any attempt to extrapolate mathematically the degree of human risk from animals.... Exact estimates as to the number of cases of a cancer that might be expected to occur in man based on a single experiment are silly and simply ignore biological realities. The fact that no better methods exist does not make these statements any better or more valuable.[16]

Nevertheless, reliance on bioassays has grown because there are both strong political and analytical pressures to quantify risks and because there is often indeed no alternative basis for doing it. (See the hypothetical dialogue in appendix C for more discussion of whether poor data are better than no data.)

Health Effects of OSHA's New Standards

Having provided some background on the limits of the available types of data, in this section I proceed to show how the estimates of the health effects reported in table 2.1 were calculated. As noted, except for ethylene oxide, we are relying on human data. Because OSHA itself provided no estimates of health effects for the standards it promulgated during the 1970s (except for coke oven emissions and, in the 1980s, for reconsiderations of the benzene and arsenic standards), most of the figures are based on other sources.

Asbestos
The estimate of 396 deaths prevented a year by the 1972 asbestos standard is based on a 1974 study by economist Russell Settle.[17] Settle relied on epidemiological studies by Selikoff that indicated that there were 4 excess asbestos-related deaths annually per 1000 workers in the manufacturing and insulation industries. He multiplied this number by the current employment in those industries to get the figure of 396 deaths. As an estimate

of the impact of reducing the PEL from 12 fibers to 2 fibers, this number is likely to overestimate the impact in those two industries for three reasons.

First, most of the exposures causing the excess deaths found in the studies occurred twenty to forty years earlier, when exposures were well above the levels prevailing in 1972. Settle cites Selikoff to the effect that exposures in 1972 averaged 5 or 6 fibers in these industries. Exposures thirty years earlier could easily have been several times that level. Using a linear dose-response hypothesis, the overestimate of the effect would also be several-fold.

Second, the estimate assumes that exposures would have remained at the 1972 level in the absence of a new standard. In the case of asbestos, with the great growth in product liability and consumer concern, this assumption seems implausible. When a firm would have taken some steps to reduce exposures on its own, OSHA can claim credit only for the relatively expensive reductions that the firm would not have undertaken. However, this criticism may not be fully valid in the asbestos case: At least some of the reduction in exposure occurred because some firms completely stopped making asbestos products rather than because of additional dust control measures. In these cases there is no basis for attributing the more expensive reductions to OSHA.

A third and less important factor is that the 2-fiber PEL did not eliminate asbestos-related disease, although Settle's calculations assumed that it did. This error probably does not lead to more than a 10 percent overestimate.

On the other hand, Settle noted that other construction workers might also benefit from the measures to reduce exposures to the insulation workers employed on the same construction site. If so, the health effects would grow without any additional cost. The figures here were much more speculative; Settle used estimates ranging from 0 to almost 2000 deaths prevented among these workers.

In addition, other researchers have suggested that the effects of low-level exposure are somewhat greater than Settle assumed. For example, Julian Peto has speculated that 10 percent of workers exposed for 50 years to 2 fibers would die of asbestos-induced disease.[18] This is a rate of 2 per 1000 per year (that is, 10 percent of 1000 equals 100 deaths; over 50 years, that comes to 2 per 1000 per year), which is half of the rate Settle used to predict the effects of exposure levels 2.5 to 3 times as large (that is, to 5 or 6 fibers). Even if Peto is correct, Settle's estimates are still probably too high. The big uncertainty is the impact of the standard on other construction workers not directly affected.

Vinyl Chloride

Only one attempt to estimate the health effects of the OSHA vinyl chloride standard has been made.[19] The estimate is built on three key assumptions: First, that the twenty-one angiosarcoma deaths in the United States linked to vinyl chloride exposures through 1976 constituted all of the deaths caused by exposures during the preceding forty years; second, that the number of deaths during the forty years after 1976 would be the same in the absence of a new standard; and third, that the OSHA standard will prevent future diseases. This set of assumptions leads to the conclusion that the new standard will, on average, prevent one death every two years, or 0.5 death a year. Obviously this estimate is extremely crude. Vinyl chloride exposures were dropping over this period, so the assumption that the number of cases would remain constant seems unreasonable. On the other hand, more recent studies suggest that vinyl chloride can cause brain and other tumors as well as liver angiosarcoma.[20]

The EPA's Carcinogenic Assessment Group (CAG) has used animal inhalation studies to estimate the carcinogenic potency of vinyl chloride. Use of their estimate indicates that the lifetime cancer risk from occupational exposures is of the order of 1.2×10^{-3} for each part per million. Multiplying this risk times the estimate of the average exposure level of vinyl chloride workers at the time the standard was adopted gives a lifetime total of about one hundred cancer deaths, or just over two per year for a forty-five-year work life.[21] A few of these deaths may occur with the exposures allowed by the OSHA standard, so the best estimate from this source is about two deaths prevented a year. Thus a range from 0.5 to 2 deaths a year seems plausible.

Coke Oven Emissions

In the preamble to the coke oven emissions standard, OSHA claimed that the new PEL would prevent 240 cancer deaths a year. The Council on Wage and Price Stability (COWPS) estimated that the range was from 8 to 36 deaths. The figure in table 2.1 uses the high end of that range, relying on a risk assessment conducted by Charles Land of the National Cancer Institute.[22] Land used both a linear and a quadratic model; the linear model estimated higher risks and was used by COWPS. If we assume that the standard reduced exposures from 0.40 mg/m³ to the new PEL of 0.15, the excess risk would have dropped by 0.023 or 0.035, depending on the assumption about the latency period. For 20,000 workers this becomes 460 to 700 cancers, or 10 to 16 a year, assuming a 45-year work life.

Redmond has noted that Land's estimates may overstate the excess risk resulting from coke oven emissions because steelworkers in the Pittsburgh area (where the epidemiological studies were conducted) have higher lung cancer rates than the general American population.[23] Thus some of the risk attributed to coke ovens appears to be due to some other factor affecting steelworkers. Finally, as noted, many coke facilities have not achieved compliance with the PEL of 0.15 mg/m^3, at least not through engineering controls. However, if compliance has been achieved through the use of respirators, then the estimate here remains plausible.

Benzene

One of the most famous risk estimates was performed for benzene by Harvard physicist Richard Wilson, who argued that the reduction in the PEL from 10 ppm to 1 ppm would prevent only one death every few years, leading to a cost per death prevented of $200 million or even $300 million.[24]

Recently, OSHA scientists have reviewed the epidemiological literature and estimated that 45 years of exposure to 10 ppm of benzene will cause 44 to 152 added cases of leukemia. At 1 ppm the linear model reduces those figures by 90 percent. Assuming that 30,000 workers were exposed to an average of 3 ppm of benzene, they calculated that a reduction to 1 ppm would prevent 300 to 960 deaths, or 7 to 21 per year.[25] Critics of that estimate have focused on whether the exposures of the workers who became ill were really as low as the authors assumed. If the exposures were understated, the risks at lower exposures will be overestimated.[26] Table 2.1 uses the range of 7 to 21 deaths prevented annually, although the number could be lower.

Arsenic

There have been several epidemiological studies on which to base a risk assessment of arsenic exposure. The EPA's Carcinogenic Assessment Group concluded that each microgram (μg) of lifetime environmental exposure increased the risk of lung cancer by 8.1 percent. A conversion to forty-five years of occupational exposure (that is, forty hours for forty-six weeks a year) reduces lifetime exposure by $\frac{7}{8}$ to 1 percent. Thus the OSHA consultant's finding that 1700 workers were exposed at an average of 300 μg would generate an excess risk of 300 percent. Because the lifetime risk of lung cancer is 0.047, the excess would be 0.141 (0.047 times 300 percent). A reduction from 300 μg to the new PEL of 10 μg would reduce the excess risk by 0.136. For the 1700 workers this amounts to 231 cancers, or 5 a year over 45 years.

The 1 percent estimate is at the low end of the linear risk estimates prepared by OSHA to show the Ninth Circuit Court of Appeals that the arsenic standard met the Supreme Court's test of addressing a "significant risk."[27] The high end of that range came to 3 to 4 percent per microgram of exposure, although these are risks for lung cancer, not lung cancer deaths, which are somewhat lower. If applied to deaths, these figures would increase the annual number of deaths prevented to 15 to 20. (Estimates using a quadratic model generate risks that are roughly tenfold lower.)

Speakers for the industry have noted that these estimates are all based on extrapolation from doses that are mostly at or above the 500-μg range, far above the 10-μg PEL adopted by OSHA. Because arsenic is an essential trace mineral for humans, they argue that there must be a threshold effect.

Table 2.1 uses a range of 5 to 20 deaths per year prevented by the standard.

Acrylonitrile
As discussed in the text, more recent evidence indicates that the risk from acrylonitrile exposure is not as great as the study that was the basis of the 1978 risk estimate had indicated. In addition, several of the assumptions used in that analysis will certainly tend to lead to overestimates. The assumption that all workers exposed between 2 and 20 ppm were exposed to 20 ppm is the clearest example. Although the evidence suggests that even the initial estimate of risk was high, we cannot be certain that it was. Table 2.1 uses the estimate of deaths prevented from the COWPS analysis, although it is probably too high.

Ethylene Oxide
The ethylene oxide standard is the only one in table 2.1 for which bioassay data rather than epidemiology provided the sole basis for the risk estimate. The model used was the one developed by the EPA's Carcinogenic Assessment Group. At the existing PEL of 50 ppm, OSHA estimated a maximum likelihood risk of 63 to 109 cancer cases per 1000 workers exposed for 45 years.[28] (The upper 95 percent confidence interval was 101 to 152 per 1000.) OSHA assumed that 80,000 workers were exposed to an average level of 10 ppm. In fact, however, surveys by its consultant indicated that a range of 2 to 4 ppm described the range of exposures much more accurately.[29] Using the OSHA risk estimate with this lower exposure estimate predicts between 2 and 9 cancer cases per 1000 workers. For 80,000 workers, the totals would be 160 to 720 lifetime cases, or between 4 and 16 a year. The use of the EPA model is especially likely to make this an overestimate.

"Conservative" Assumptions and the Burden of Proof
In the range of estimates presented I have not extended the range of health effects to zero, despite industry claims that they may be nonexistent. The chief reason for this decision was to subject the overregulation hypothesis to a more difficult test. But the use of larger, more "conservative" risk estimates is a practice that has drawn harsh criticism from industry.

One specific criticism is that regulators' no-threshold model of cancer causation ignores our growing understanding that there are many different mechanisms of carcinogenesis. The no-threshold model depends on the assumption that a single molecule of a chemical can cause a cell to mutate, setting the stage for the process of tumor formation. But only some mechanisms fit this "genotoxic" model; other carcinogens rely on different ("epigenetic") mechanisms. Another complexity that regulators ignore is that the carcinogenic response depends not on the dose that is administered to animals but on the dose that actually finds its way to the organs. The relationship between the two doses depends on the complex process of metabolism that falls under the topic of pharmacokinetics. Interpretation of bioassays requires an analysis of this issue.

Many scientists agree that many of these new distinctions and emphases are probably valid. OSHA's unwillingness to consider them has led to the charge that it is "freezing science" in its efforts to uphold protective regulatory policy.[30] Indeed, if an agency such as OSHA is truly to be guided by the "best available evidence," as its statute requires, then some of these complexities will eventually have to be acknowledged. However, substantial uncertainty still usually exists about whether, for example, any particular chemical is an initiator of DNA changes or a promoter of existing tumors, or both. In the face of that uncertainty, should OSHA simply try to decide which is most likely? Or should it also be guided by its mandate that workers be protected to the extent feasible. Again the issue comes down to the proper standard of proof to use. If OSHA should use whatever assumptions appear "more likely than not" based on the scientific evidence, then industry critics may be correct. However, if OSHA should be more protective, perhaps it should continue to use the no-threshold assumption unless the evidence against it becomes overwhelming. Thus the validity of the "freezing science" criticism really depends on this policy judgment.[31]

Others have criticized the use of conservative assumptions on the grounds of obfuscation. As Lester Lave argues: "Unfortunately current practice is to employ assumptions of various degrees of conservation at each stage to arrive at an overall estimate that is so muddled it cannot be interpreted beyond showing that it is conservative." [32] Instead, he suggests that analyses present "best estimates" along with indications of the range of uncertainty and the probability of higher and lower figures.

This suggestion has considerable merit. The use of conservative assumptions to estimate health effects has an equivalent impact to raising the value placed on preventing those effects. If a best estimate is ten deaths prevented and conservative assumptions lead to an estimate of a hundred deaths prevented, the cost per death prevented declines tenfold. We would have to use a value of lifesaving tenfold higher to justify the smaller impact. But, as Lave points out, we rarely know how much of a bias our conservatism builds in. It is not surprising that defenders of strict regulation uphold the use of conservative assumptions or that critics condemn it.

Lave also points out that the use of conservative assumptions, by overstating the risk most in those cases where we know the least, will systematically allocate relatively more resources into reducing poorly understood risks. [33] We may spend less for a program that is fairly certain to prevent a hundred deaths than for one where our best estimate is forty deaths but where the uncertainty is greater. The appropriateness of this policy depends on how individuals feel about this uncertainty.

There is abundant evidence that individuals often are risk averse in their individual behavior; the existence of the insurance industry depends on that fact. For an individual or a family the loss of a breadwinner or a house or the occurrence of a major illness can be catastrophic. Thus they are willing to pay more than their expected loss (the probability of a loss times the size of the loss) in order to avoid anxiety and enjoy the "peace of mind" that insurance can bring.

There is also evidence that the presence of uncertainty does make some people less tolerant of the risks posed by hazards. The magnitude of the aversion to uncertain risks is not clear, however. For example, researchers found that, when they introduced uncertainty into a problem of choosing which risks to address, most respondents still chose the option that minimized the expected number of deaths, although the number who chose to address the more uncertain risk increased. [34]

One can question the appropriateness of risk aversion as a policy for society in this area. Society does not face the same risk of financial disaster and, although some potential hazards (for example, nuclear war, carbon dioxide buildup, depletion of the ozone layer) are so large that risk aversion will be warranted, the hazards where OSHA may have overregulated do not appear to threaten more than a maximum of several dozen deaths per year. It seems difficult to argue that uncertainty of this magnitude justifies a large degree of risk aversion.

Of course, to the group that is exposed to the hazard the risks may appear catastrophic; and other members of society may choose to take that perception into account in their decisions about how much to contribute to reducing the risk.

Implications for a Judgment about Overregulation

Are the estimates of costs and cancer deaths prevented in table 2.1 accurate? This chapter should have fostered respect for the uncertainties that beset attempts to make these calculations. However, it also presents substantial evidence that the figures in that table are likely to be roughly right. And where they are wrong, they are more likely to lead to understatements of the cost per death prevented than to overstatements.

Unless retrospective studies were available, I have assumed that the compliance costs estimated by OSHA's contractor were overestimated by as much as a factor of 2. This overestimate has been projected to other standards where it seemed appropriate. The estimates used here assume that no changes would have occurred in the absence of a new standard; to the extent that this is incorrect, it will usually lead to an underestimate of the cost per death prevented that is *attributable to OSHA*. For standards where compliance with the PEL by means of engineering controls have proven infeasible on a wide scale, the impact on costs is uncertain.

In calculating the range of health effects, I have incorporated some "conservative" assumptions. I have worked on the assumption of a linear dose-response curve with no threshold, which may overstate the risk and certainly will not understate it. I use recent risk estimates that include higher figures than those used in earlier studies.

If anything, the figures on costs and effects in table 2.1 probably will tend to understate the cost per death prevented. Thus, while acknowledging again that the case is not a certain one, the claim that we usually have overregulated seems the most plausible one.

These criticisms of particular OSHA health standards should not necessarily be taken as an argument against regulation. Indeed, as I argue in the next chapter, we probably need to set standards more frequently, but they need to be more cost-effective.

Are We Underregulating?

The conclusion that OSHA has usually set standards too strictly is not inconsistent with the argument that there are many hazards for which *some degree* of *further* regulation would be desirable. Yet no consensus on this latter issue exists. Indeed it has rarely been explicitly considered. Those who are skeptical that underregulation exists can point to the high cost of the standards OSHA has adopted as evidence that stricter standards are unlikely to be good deals for society, especially if they believe that the hazards that OSHA addressed were the best candidates for regulation. I argue that this last belief is not well founded and, more important, that the finding of overregulation from standards requiring 95 percent reductions in exposures does not mean that more moderate reductions would not have been justified.

A cost-benefit perspective on hazards, including toxic substances, suggests that the risks society should tolerate will tend to decline over time. First, we are likely to discover better methods for reducing hazards; this will cut the costs of achieving additional reductions in exposures. Second, the demand for reducing risks will increase as incomes grow, increasing the marginal benefits from reduced exposures. The result is that the marginal benefits will exceed the marginal costs over a broader range of exposure reductions. In addition, given the limited knowledge on which most exposure limits were based and the likelihood that most pre-OSHA standards were set moderately, we are more likely to uncover new evidence of harm than new evidence of safety.[1] Therefore new information will tend to increase the value we place on achieving lower exposures. However, these reasons do not tell us the appropriate number of exposure limits that should be reduced in this decade or the next or how far they should fall. Thus the general argument that exposure limits should be reduced over time does not tell us whether the reductions that OSHA has made constitute an adequate response.[2]

The Ideal Evidence Is Not Available

In order to demonstrate that OSHA's program for protecting workers from toxic substances suffers from underregulation, one needs to demonstrate that there are hazards "out there" for which further regulatory measures would be worthwhile. The paucity of information about what is "out there" makes this a daunting task. Ideally, we would need information about the nature of the dose-response relationships, the number of workers exposed at all concentration levels believed to be potentially hazardous, and estimates of the marginal costs of reducing exposures by various amounts.

As we saw in chapter 2, roughly accurate data on worker exposures and much less certain data on compliance costs can be collected at considerable expense, usually several hundred thousand dollars per hazard. Information on dose-response curves requires either bioassays or epidemiological studies. The preconditions for a useful epidemiological study of a hazard are often not met; a bioassay takes several years to complete, its costs approach $500,000, and its relevance to humans can be hotly contested. Needless to say, it is rare for either type of study to give clear-cut quantitative answers.

In order to save money, OSHA has commissioned studies of costs and exposures only when it has already made a tentative decision to set a new standard.[3] The upshot is that neither we nor OSHA has a precise basis for ascertaining how well it has selected from the universe of hazards or how many good candidates remain. Nevertheless, I marshall evidence suggesting that underregulation is indeed a problem.

The Size of the Disease Problem

Images of how big a problem is may have important political ramifications. The late 1970s witnessed a lively and politically charged debate about the contribution of occupational exposures to cancer prevalence in the United States.[4] The threat of a workplace cancer epidmic supported stronger efforts to regulate hazard-producing industries. In contrast, the belief that the vast bulk of cancer is related to individual lifestyles (smoking, diet, exercise, sexual practices) focuses attention away from the workplace.

Yet it is a staple of policy analysis that estimates of the total size of a "problem" rarely have much value for policymaking. The chief reason is that policy decisions involve choices about what to do in particular cases; the relevant information is the incremental costs and benefits of different options, not the total costs attributable to the "problem."

Nevertheless, a belief that the occupational disease problem is large would be extremely pertinent to an assessment of the claim that underregulation exists. When combined with the evidence in table 2.1 that most of OSHA's new health standards have prevented only a small number of deaths, the two facts would constitute strong evidence of the inadequacy of the current regulatory approach. After all, if such strict rules usually have had such a small impact on such a big problem, something is very wrong.

Unfortunately for this argument, the key study that claimed to demonstrate that the number of occupational disease deaths was large was fatally flawed. No one really knows how big the occupational disease problem is.[5] (Appendix D provides both the story of the debate on the magnitude of the cancer problem and a review of the fallacies in that study.)

One obvious alternative to the use of a measure of diseases is a measure of *exposure* to toxic substances. If exposures are getting worse, implying that the future disease burden may be increasing, then the case against the current regulatory system is strengthened. The prospect that hazardous exposures have grown rapidly has been raised by environmentalists who note that US production of synthetic organic chemicals grew from 4 billion pounds in 1940 to 22 billion in 1950 and to 228 billion in 1979.[6]

Despite increased production of hazardous chemicals, the available evidence suggests that, at least for those hazards that are recognized, the average exposure level to any particular chemical has *decreased* substantially over time. Some evidence on declining exposures comes from epidemiological studies; in the few cases where there is credible data on past exposure levels, the levels were generally well above current exposure levels. Some additional evidence on long-term trends in the chemical industry appears in the company-reported data shown in table 4.1.[7] Underscoring the absence of a necessary link between chemical production and worker hazard is the case of sulfuric acid. Although by far the leading single chemical in production volume—84 billion pounds a year, about 5 percent of all chemicals—the ninety-six OSHA inspections that sampled for sulfuric acid between 1979 and 1981 turned up only nine workers exposed above the OSHA PEL.[8]

The conclusion that the exposure of the average worker to a particular known hazard has tended to decline over time does not necessarily mean that occupational disease risks have declined. First, the total number of exposed workers may have increased. In fact, the total number of workers exposed to chemicals has increased but not at anywhere near the pace at which chemical production has risen; from 1950 to 1979 the chemical industry work force less than doubled. Second, each worker may be exposed to a greater number of hazards, some of which may be unrecognized. We know little about the roughly 53,000 chemicals in use or the 1700 that are added each year.[9] The National Research Council report on toxicity testing concluded that

Table 4.1   Exposures to Many Toxic Substances in the Chemical Industry Are Decreasing

Substance	Exposure (ppm)	Time-weighted average (ppm)
Styrene		
Monomer production		
1942	24 (area samples)	
1945	1.4 (area samples)	
1972	0.1–6.0;	1.0
1973	0.2–5.4	1.0
1980	0.01–3.3	0.4
Polymer production		
1955	<200 (area samples)	
1963	97 (area samples)	
1973	<0.1–19 (10 time-weighted averages)	
1975–1976	0.1–1.2 (42 time-weighted averages)	
1980	0.03–0.2 (19 time-weighted averages)	
Benzene (used as a manufacturing solvent)		
Manufacturing area		
1952–1953		17–36
1965		5–17
1973		3.8–4.0
1978		0.03–1.3
Lab technician		
1961		16
1974		4.0
Fabrication area		
1952–1953		35
1965		11–32
Vinyl chloride monomer: Copolymer production operations		
Unit I, Dry end		
1950–1959		5–10
1960–1963		5
1979		0.7
Unit I, wet end		
1950–1959		10–385
1960–1963		10–80
1979		0.8
Unit II		
1950–1959		5–825
1960–1963		5–240
1975		10
1979		1.0

Table 4.1 (continued)

Substance	Exposure (ppm)	Time-weighted average (ppm)
Acrylonitrile: Plastic production		
1955	13 (area samples)	
1959	4 (area samples)	
1965	17 (area samples)	
1973		0.2–19 (6 samples)
1973	3 (area samples)	2.3–2.5 (2 samples)
1975–1976		0.1–4.5 (37 samples)
1980		0.02–0.9 (19 samples)

Source: Fred Hoerger, "Indicators of Exposure Trends," in *Quantification of Occupational Cancer*, Richard Peto and Marvin Schneiderman, eds. (Cold Spring Harbor, Mass.: Cold Spring Laboratory, 1981), pp. 444–446.

of tens of thousands of commercially important chemicals, only a few have been subjected to extensive toxicity testing and most have scarcely been tested at all. Many other constituents of the human environment, including natural chemicals and various contaminants, are also potential candidates for testing. Although it can be convincingly argued that many chemicals do not need to be tested, because of their low potential for human exposure or for toxic activity, it is clear that thousands or even tens of thousands of chemicals are legitimate candidates for toxicity testing related to a variety of health effects.[10]

A study of the "premanufacturing notifications" required for all newly produced chemicals (under the provisions of the Toxic Substances Control Act) also found that the amount of testing data reported on those forms was usually far less than what was needed to make a reasonable assessment of toxicity.[11]

The response from the chemical industry is that the great majority of these chemicals involve trivial human exposures. Indeed, most new chemicals do start at small production volumes. Fewer than a hundred chemicals account for 80 percent of the total weight of chemical production. From a review of the data on the top fifty chemicals, several authors from Dow Chemical concluded that "the data base on these chemicals is significant, and the priority data gaps, as perceived by either industry or government, are being filled."[12]

Despite this response, it seems reasonable to conclude, in view of the increase in the total number of chemicals and the uncertainty about their toxicity, that we do not know whether the *combined* threat from all toxic exposures is declining.

Because these discussions of total disease deaths and aggregate trends in exposure encounter such severe data problems, it will prove useful to disaggregate the analysis to get closer to understanding whether under-regulation exists.

Toxic Substances in the Workplace: The Nature of the Problem

One approach to understanding the nature of the occupational toxic substances problem is the following taxonomy of the diseases caused by toxic substances.

1. Diseases resulting from exposures that exceed the OSHA permissible exposure limits (PELs).

2. Diseases resulting from exposures below the existing OSHA PEL.

3. Diseases resulting from exposures for substances for which OSHA has no PEL but for which the American Conference of Governmental Industrial Hygienists (ACGIH) or other groups have proposed exposure limits.

4. Diseases resulting from exposures from existing substances for which neither OSHA nor anyone else has proposed exposure limits. In most cases, the diseases caused by these hazards have not yet been recognized.

In rough terms, category 1 presents problems of OSHA enforcement; categories 2 and 3 present problems of standard setting; and category 4 raises problems of identifying hazards through testing and surveillance. Yet it will become clear that these different problems are related, at least in terms of a strategy of how best to approach toxic substance problems. The strictness of standards affects both the likelihood of noncompliance and the social desirability of noncompliance. And uncertainty about whether substances are really harmful has to be factored into decisions about whether and how strictly to set standards. The suspicion that a group of chemicals presents a risk may justify modest precautions, but not draconian exposure limits.[13]

Diseases from Exposures above the PELs

The hazards in category 1 are of two sorts: (i) those that can cause disease only with exposures above the PEL, that is, where there is a threshold that is higher than the PEL; and (ii) those that can cause disease at exposures below the PEL as well, for example, carcinogens, under the assumption that there is no threshold for carcinogenesis. For this second group, category 1 includes only that portion of the total number of diseases that would be eliminated by reducing exposures down to the PEL.

Even though exposures to many better known hazards have been decreasing, exposures that exceed the PEL for those substances still appear to pose a significant public health problem. A crude measure of the relative number of workers overexposed to different hazards can be constructed from the number of workers found exposed above the PEL in OSHA inspections. Table 4.2 presents this information for the hazards with the most frequent overexposures.[14] It is worth noting that many of the diseases that these exposures can cause are quite serious ones, including cancer and obstructive lung disease.

Because all of the category 1 diseases would be eliminated if all workplaces complied with all of the PELs, we could treat them as presenting a problem of enforcement, not of standard setting. Before dismissing them in this way, however, consider the relationship between noncompliance and the level of the PEL that is apparent from table 4.3. Setting a lower PEL will tend to create a higher rate of noncompliance. A likely explanation for this finding is that the marginal costs across substances increase sharply as exposures are lowered, and the perceived benefits to employers (both from less disease to workers and lower penalties from OSHA) increase less rapidly.[15] The finding in table 4.3 does not, of course, mean that lower PELs are not desirable. It does indicate that the health benefits from lower PELs are likely to be less than a model of full compliance would predict. It also means that the agency will incur a relatively heavy administrative cost in enforcing lower PELs, because of the likely flow of employer appeals from citations (which grew to a rate of over 25 percent of all health citations in the late 1970s) and the need to document violations and monitor their abatement. The finding also helps to explain why so many of the most toxic hazards tend to have relatively high violation rates: They also tend, for protective reasons, to have low PELs. The important implication for the overregulation/underregulation argument is that less strict PELs would not sacrifice worker protection as much as one would predict from a simple comparison of the PELs.

Diseases from Exposures below the PELs: The Comparison of OSHA PELs with ACGIH TLVs

The best way to discuss diseases caused by exposures below the OSHA PELs or by hazards for which OSHA has no PEL is to compare OSHA's exposure limits with those of the American Conference of Governmental Industrial Hygienists (ACGIH). In 1943 the director of industrial medicine at Eastman Kodak commented on the recent attempts to develop "maximum allowable concentrations" (MACs) for toxic substances:

It must be emphasized that the MAC values are not absolute, immutable. A few are based upon a considerable amount of careful clinical evidence, but many are very

Table 4.2   Most of the Hazards to Which Workers Are Most Commonly Found Overexposed Can Cause Serious Diseases

Hazard	Number of workers found overexposed	Health effect
Lead arsenate	2,829	lead or arsenic poisoning; possible carcinogen
Lead, inorganic	2,635	lead poisoning
Silica	1,963	silicosis
Nuisance dust (organic)	1,340	irritation of nasal passages
Carbon monoxide	1,333	dizziness; asphyxiation
Coke oven emissions	865	lung and kidney cancer
Arsenic	788	lung cancer
Coal tar pitch volatiles	708	lung cancer
Toluene	524	nervous system depression
Copper fume	505	respiratory tract irritation; fever
Iron oxide fume	492	benign pneumoconiosis
Mercury, inorganic	372	chronic neurologic effects
Cotton dust	369	byssinosis
Asbestos	288	lung and gastrointestinal cancers; mesothelioma asbestosis
Copper dust	254	respiratory tract irritation; some ulceration
Carbon disulfide	229	nervous system damage; may worsen heart disease
Vinyl chloride	207	liver and other cancers
Chromic acid	196	some compounds cause lung cancer, perforated nasal septa; kidney damage
Silver	175	irritation of mucous membranes, eyes
Methyl ethyl ketone	148	irritation of mucous membranes, eyes, skin
Hard wood dust	132	respiratory irritation; skin sensitization
Styrene monomer	125	irritation of mucous membranes, eyes; nervous system depression
Welding fumes	124	respiratory irritation; metal fume fever
Cristobalite	116	silicosis
Dust (total)	101	irritation of nasal passages
Total	16,818	

Sources: OSHA Management Information System, April 1979–July 1981: Nick H. Proctor and James P. Hughes, *Chemical Hazards of the Workplace* (Philadelphia: Lippincott, 1978).

Table 4.3   The Lower the PEL, the Higher the Percentage of Samples That Exceed It

Substance	OSHA PEL (time-weighted average) (mg/m^3)	Samples above PEL/all samples[a]	Percentage of samples above PEL
Acetone	2400	0/217	0
Ethyl alcohol	1900	0/65	0
Ethyl acetate	1400	1/175	0.6
Cyclohexane	1050	0/81	0
2-ethoxy ethanol	740	0/50	0
N-butyl acetate	710	0/102	0
2-ethoxy ethyl acetate	540	0/128	0
Naphtha	400	4/69	6
Butyl alcohol	300	0/120	0
2-butoxy ethanol	240	0/124	0
Carbon disulfide	60	22/54	41
Carbon monoxide	55	6/332	2
Ammonia	35	0/82	0
Benzene	32	5/310	1
Acrylonitrile	4	6/124	5
Carbon black	4	7/50	14
Chromium, insoluble	1.0	12/582	2
Copper dust	1.0	76/549	14
Antimony	0.50	6/294	2
Chromium, soluble	0.50	2/528	0.2
Cotton dust	0.20	55/105	48
Coal tar pitch volatiles	0.20	147/517	28
Cadmium dust	0.20	25/484	5
Coke oven emissions	0.15	205/422	48
Copper fumes	0.10	142/1104	13
Cobalt	0.10	6/124	5
Chromic acid	0.10	55/306	18
Cadmium fumes	0.10	18/324	5
Arsenic	0.01	206/845	24
Beryllium	0.002	8/94	9

a. Samples are from OSHA Management Information System, April 1979–July 1981. The hazards in this table are the first thirty where more than fifty samples had been taken and where the levels can be expressed in milligrams (for example, excluding asbestos).

tentative in character, and are meant as nothing more than the best estimate as to a safe level. The values are being, and should be, constantly revised as new evidence is presented to indicate that lower values must be set to safeguard the health and safety of individuals exposed, or that higher levels are safely permissible. There is always a danger that the values will be so "frozen" by time and usage that the newer, more accurate data will be ignored. This is especially so when the values are incorporated in codes by the various governmental agencies, and these codes have the force of law and the consequent fixation which characterizes such facilities. These dangers place a responsibility upon the individuals in charge of guiding the governmental control regulations, but thus far, in the main, the activity has been well considered and reasonable.[16]

Four decades later, the dangers appear greater. The most important piece of evidence for the underregulation hypothesis comes from the growing disparity between the OSHA PELs and the threshold limit values (TLVs) established by the private ACGIH. Under the terms of the OSH Act, Congress told OSHA to use the 1968 ACGIH list, with roughly four hundred chemicals, as its initial set of toxic substances standards. Since that time OSHA has reduced the exposure limits for ten substances (although it established "work practice" standards without PELs for thirteen other chemicals). Meanwhile, the ACGIH has reduced the exposure limits for approximately one hundred substances and has added exposure limits for about two hundred more.

If these ACGIH changes are reasonable and address significant hazards, then the case for underregulation is strong. In the absence of actual analyses of the costs and benefits of these changes, we need to examine two issues: whether the ACGIH process and its criteria for standard setting give us confidence that the changes are likely to be reasonable ones and whether the changes address hazards with serious toxicity and nontrivial human exposures.

The reasonableness of the TLV changes depends on three factors: the criteria used to establish them, the quality of the data on which they are based, and the deliberativeness of the process itself. Before looking at each of these, however, a brief review of the history of the ACGIH and its TLVs is in order.

In 1938 the professional staffs of public occupational health units, many newly formed, joined together with others in the universities to form the private ACGIH. By 1981 it had more than 2300 members worldwide, all in government or educational institutions. In 1946 the ACGIH Committee on Threshold Limit Values issued its first list of recommended exposure limits.[17] Several states incorporated the ACGIH limits as official regulations soon after they were issued and others followed. In 1949 the list was incorporated in the model code of regulations of the International Labor Organization. In 1960 the list was adopted by the United Kingdom Ministry of Labor as maximum permissible concentrations. In the same year the US Department of Labor adopted the TLVs as rules applicable to all federal contractors under the Walsh-Healey Federal Contracts Act.[18] Because the enforcement of regulations under Walsh-Healey was notoriously weak, the immediate impact of this action was small. But in 1970 the OSH Act called for the secretary of labor to adopt within two years "any national consensus standard, and any established federal standard, unless he determines that the promulgation of such a standard would not result in improved safety or health for specifically designated employees."[19] Given the available data, such a determination would have been difficult to make; in any event, no one tried. The United States became one of the roughly twenty countries that by 1980 had "either adopted the TLVs as legal standards or as guides to legislative action."[20]

Criteria for ACGIH Exposure Limits
As the statement made in 1943 suggests, the quality of the evidence underlying the TLVs is highly variable. The resulting uncertainty surely makes some of the TLVs much more protective than others. But what were the criteria used by the TLV Committee of the ACGIH? How protective were they trying to be?

The TLV Committee has not made it easy to ascertain the criteria it uses in establishing TLVs. It has made no explicit statements about the appropriate trade-offs between health and economic costs. (Its lack of explicitness is consistent with the insight that getting agreement on particular cases is usually easier than getting agreement on principles.[21] People may agree to support a particular decision for many different reasons and despite conflicting principles.) The preface to the list of TLVs for chemical contaminants states that

threshold limit values refer to airborne concentrations of substances and represent conditions under which it is believed that nearly all workers may be repeatedly exposed day after day without adverse effect. Because of wide variation in individual susceptibility, however, a small percentage of workers may experience discomfort from some substances at concentrations at or below the threshold limit; a smaller percentage may be affected more seriously by aggravation of a pre-existing condition or by development of an occupational illness.[22]

This sounds somewhat more tolerant of illness than section 6(b)(5) of the OSH Act, which requires OSHA to set the standard that "most adequately assures, to the extent feasible, on the basis of the best available evidence, that no employee will suffer material impairment of health or functional capacity even if such employee has regular exposure to the hazard ... for the period of his working life." However, the term "feasible," which I discuss in detail later, is ambiguous and has no explicit analogue in the ACGIH statement. To get more insight, we really need to look behind the formal statements.

A long-time chair of the TLV committee explained that the TLVs are based on the premise that, "although all chemical substances are toxic at some concentration experienced for a period of time, a concentration exists for all substances for which no injurious effect will result no matter how often the exposure is repeated."[23] This reflects the traditional assumption in toxicology that "no-effect" thresholds do exist. The usual procedure is to find the highest exposure level at which no adverse effects are detected (for example, in bioassays or in industrial experience) and then apply a "safety factor" to establish a safe level. Obviously the magnitude of the safety factor is crucial in determining just how "safe" that TLV is. According to a 1971 paper by a leading figure in the ACGIH, the magnitude varies among hazards, primarily on the basis of the following four factors: (1) the seriousness of the toxic response; (2) the nature of the toxic response (for example, for such irritants as ammonia or such narcotics as trichloroethylene, a safety factor of only 1.5 to 2 is considered adequate); (3) a larger safety factor being used when the supporting data are less adequate; and (4) the fact that "for some substances with a cumulative effect, the safety margin is rather small, but has been retained through long industrial use and medical experience. Example: lead, mercury vapor, arsenic."[24]

The examples cited in this 1971 article provide an illustration of how today's margin of safety may evaporate tomorrow. Within a few years of its publication, arsenic became a well-documented human carcinogen, the evidence supporting a reduction in lead exposures grew, and animal studies suggested that trichloroethylene might be a human carcinogen. For four of the five hazards listed here, the ACGIH reduced the TLVs between 1968 and 1981.

For a small group of relatively rare substances with high carcinogenic potency, the ACGIH had recommended that "no exposure ... shall be permitted."[25] But many of the substances now known or suspected to be carcinogens did not have TLVs established on that basis in the 1968 list, which became the basis of OSHA's PELs. In the years since 1968, it has become common for the TLV Committee to consider carcinogenic effects. However, unlike OSHA, it has worked from the assumption that the threshold concept was appropriate for carcinogens. In dealing with evidence of cancer from bioassays, the committee classified substances in terms of the estimated potency of the carcinogenic effects, which were then to be taken into account in setting the TLVs. For bioassays conducted at high doses, the committee refused to accept the results as evidence of carcinogenicity.[26]

Thus, if we compare the ACGIH's treatment of potential carcinogens with OSHA's, we find that the ACGIH is (1) less likely to acknowledge that certain substances should be classified as carcinogens at all; (2) more willing to believe that, even if a substance is a carcinogen, exposures to it may not be harmful at low doses; and (3) more willing to distinguish among carcinogens on the basis of evidence of potency in recommending exposure limits. Taken together, these practices comprise a much less stringent approach to setting individual standards.

A team combining scientific and economic experts recently examined the documentation underlying the TLV changes and concluded that

unlike OSHA, they are not compelled by law to ignore economic costs in their standard setting. Indeed, reading between the lines of the documentation one sees a rejection of the idea that chemicals can be controlled to the point that they have no observable effects on comfort or health. Their philosophy . . . is more a balancing of risks with the practicality of reduction.[27]

Insights into the Cost-Effectiveness of ACGIH Changes   Table 4.4 compares the PELs that OSHA has adopted in its new standards with the TLVs that the ACGIH has adopted for the same hazards. In one case, asbestos, the ACGIH adopted a much stricter standard. In three cases the exposure limits were the same; in the remaining four cases the OSHA figures were stricter. Thus, although the ACGIH has adopted several hundred more exposure limits than OSHA has, it has frequently been unwilling to adopt limits that are as strict and costly as OSHA's.

In the two cases where the ACGIH adopted the same exposure limit and where we have estimates of the cost per death prevented, the estimated cost ranged from $2.6 million to $5.2 million for acrylonitrile and from $1.1 million to $9 million for ethylene oxide. This is the low end of the OSHA range of costs. I suspect that it represents the high end of the range for the ACGIH changes since 1968. The main reason is that the exposure reductions for these two hazards, 90 percent and 98 percent, respectively, represent unusually large percentage reductions for ACGIH. Of its roughly one hundred changes, the median reduction was 50 percent. In only about a dozen cases was the reduction 90 percent or greater.

The extent of the reduction in exposures in large part determines whether

Table 4.4 Measures of the Stringency of Standards

Substance	Date of promulgation	New OSHA PEL	Ratio of ACGIH exposure limit to OSHA PEL[a]	Total annual cost (millions of dollars)	Cost per cancer prevented (millions of dollars)
Asbestos	June 1972	2 fibers in 4 years	1 : 10 (1980)	173	0.4
Vinyl chloride	October 1974	1 ppm	5 : 1 (1977)	40	40
Coke oven emissions	October 1976	0.15 mg	no ACGIH limit	200–400	6–50
Benzene	February 1978	1 ppm	10 : 1 (1974)	94–188	4.5–32
DBCP	March 1978	1 ppb	no ACGIH limit	6	?
Arsenic	May 1978	0.01 mg	20 : 1 (1978)	95–190	4.8–38
Cotton dust	June 1978	0.2 to 0.75 mg depending on process	1 : 1 (2 mg) (1973)	95	NA
Acrylonitrile	October 1978	2 ppm	1 : 1 (1979)	18–37	2.6–5.2
Lead	November 1978	0.05 mg	3 : 1 (1971)	460–690	NA
Ethylene oxide	June 1984	1 ppm	1 : 1 (1982)	18–36	1.1–9

a. The figure in parentheses is the year in which the most recent ACGIH change occurred. Until 1980 the ACGIH asbestos limit was the same as the OSHA PEL. In that year it adopted different limits for different types of asbestos. The lowest was 0.2 fiber.

the costs of a new standard will be reasonable. As I indicated earlier, even if the costs of the 95 percent reductions typically mandated by OSHA's earlier health standards were excessive, some reduction in exposures probably could have been justified on cost-benefit grounds. A rough rule of thumb used by industrial hygienists is that successive, equal percentage reductions in exposures through the use of engineering controls cost equal amounts. For example, the cost to reduce an exposure by 90 percent is roughly equal to the additional cost required to reduce it from 90 to 99 percent, which is equal to the cost required to go from 99 to 99.9 percent.[28] If we combine this role of thumb with the assumption that health benefits increase linearly with exposures, then the marginal cost per health effect will increase tenfold with each of these decrements in exposure. The implication of such a steeply rising marginal cost curve is that reductions of 50 percent are far less costly than reductions in the 90 to 100 percent range.

The proposition that the marginal costs of successive reductions in both exposures and deaths will increase as exposures get closer to zero is supported by the cost studies that have been made in the course of OSHA standard setting.[29] Table 4.5 shows estimates of the incremental costs per death prevented for different exposure limits for arsenic and acrylonitrile and the incremental cost per case of byssinosis prevented for different exposure limits for cotton dust. (In those cases where the costs do not increase sharply, the reason is that the lower exposures were judged not to be achievable through engineering controls; instead, the extra reductions would be achieved through the use of respirators, a much cheaper method but one that OSHA allows only when the infeasibility of engineering controls has been demonstrated at a particular plant.)

Unfortunately for the purpose of estimating what less strict exposure reductions would cost, OSHA's economic studies have usually focused on exposure limits that are quite strict. Among the more moderate is the 0.1 mg/m³ exposure level for arsenic, shown in table 4.5. (Note that this level was ten times higher than the one OSHA promulgated in 1978.) It represents an 80 percent reduction from the 0.5-mg level that OSHA adopted from ACGIH. The ACGIH has reduced its TLV to 0.2 mg, which, judging from table 4.5, probably entails forgoing the prevention of fatal cancers at a cost of less than a million dollars. Although there are some ACGIH TLVs whose adoption would require large costs per death prevented, the great majority probably would not.

The Reasonableness of ACGIH Procedures Since the 1950s the size of the ACGIH TLV Committee has grown and its procedures have become somewhat more formalized. These changes reflect the growing number of

Table 4.5 Marginal Costs of Disease Prevention Increase Sharply as Exposure Limits Are Reduced

Substance	Marginal cost per death prevented at given exposure limit (millions of dollars)							
	0.5 mg/m³	0.2 mg/m³	0.1 mg/m³	0.05 mg/m³	0.004 mg/m³	2.0 ppm	1.0 ppm	0.2 ppm
Arsenic[a]			1.25	11.50	68.1			
Acrylonitrile[b]								
Acrylonitrile production						3.66	23.92	(e)
Acrylic fiber manufacturing						2.43	11.54	4.64
Nitrile elastomer latex manufacturing						8.12	98.46	860.23
ABS/SAN manufacturing						1.51	11.69	94.41
Polyols						(d)	91.74	232.72
Cotton dust[c]								
Yarn preparation	0.056	0.593	6.268					
Mill slashing and weaving	0.022	1.338	1.867					

a. Viscusi, *Risk by Choice* (Cambridge, Mass.: Harvard University Press, 1983), p. 124.
b. Broder and Morrall, "The Economic Basis for OSHA's and EPA's Generic Carcinogen Regulations," in *What Role for Government?* Richard Zeckhauser and Derek Leebaert, eds. (Durham, N.C.: Duke University Press, 1983). p. 251.
c. Viscusi, *Risk by Choice*, p. 125. The cotton dust figures refer to the cost per disease (not death) prevented.
d. Already attained.
e. Not technically feasible.

toxic substances posing concerns and the increased importance that the TLVs played in regulatory affairs. Since the 1970s the ACGIH section on air contaminants has had fifteen to twenty members, representing diverse disciplines, including toxicology, medicine, chemistry, industrial hygiene, and engineering. In 1981 eleven of its eighteen members were employed by the federal government, with the rest from state governments or universities. In 1964 it began to issue Notices of Intent with respect to all hazards for which changes in the TLVs were being developed. This step was taken to encourage responses by industry. After approval of a list at the ACGIH annual meeting, all changes go on a Tentative List for at least two years or until the committee believes that new information is not forthcoming in the near term.[30]

Documentation is required before the committee can propose an addition or revision. An internal review in 1964 showed that 90 of the approximately 350 TLVs listed in that year had been based primarily on data supplied by industry. In almost every one of the ninety cases, the contributors had come from the chemical industry. By the late 1960s it had become customary for the committee chair to meet with interested industrial representatives before the meeting of the plenary committee in order to receive comments and suggestions.[31] Although the basis of many early standards included educated guesses based on impressions about industry experience, the great majority of changes since the 1970s have been occasioned by new animal or human studies.[32] Nevertheless, the effort at documentation of the TLVs and the committee's review of the evidence is much less substantial than the review that OSHA's proposals are subjected to. To what degree the difference affects the accuracy of the review and not just the number of feet of documents that are reviewed is unclear.

Are the Differences between TLVs and PELs Important?

Suppose that we granted that the changes in exposure limits that the ACGIH has implemented since its 1968 list—the one that OSHA adopted—were reasonable. We would still want to know whether the differences between the OSHA and the ACGIH limits had important health consequences. Ideally, we would like to know how many diseases would be prevented if OSHA adopted all of the ACGIH limits.

The first point to acknowledge is that a number of the ACGIH changes apply to simple asphyxiants or to hazards for which OSHA could use its more general nuisance dust standard. In addition, for hazards for which OSHA does not have a PEL, it can sometimes compel abatement by invoking the OSH Act's "general duty" clause, although this is a more unwieldy enforcement tool.[33]

Many other ACGIH limits address chemicals with limited worker exposures; sometimes these are new chemicals, for which the number of workers exposed usually starts small. One piece of evidence for the rareness of worker exposures to many of these chemicals comes from a review of OSHA inspection sampling for ninety chemicals for which the ACGIH had reduced exposure limits for hazards with OSHA PELs. Because the median ACGIH reduction from the level adopted by OSHA is 50 percent, I looked at samples where workers were exposed to levels between 50 and 100 percent of the OSHA PEL during a twenty-seven-month period between 1979 and 1981. Sixty of the ninety chemicals did not have a single sample recorded in that range. Although there is evidence that the results of more than half (and perhaps 80 percent) of all OSHA samples were not recorded during this period, it seems fair to conclude that for many of the hazards adoption of the ACGIH limits would make little difference.[34]

Yet some of the ACGIH reductions do involve chemicals with high production volumes. A review of the list of the fifty highest volume chemicals found thirty whose names matched those on the OSHA list; and of those thirty the ACGIH had reduced the exposure limit in nine cases where OSHA had made no change.[35] (In one other case, vinyl chloride, OSHA had reduced the exposure limit further than the ACGIH did.) The median reduction among these nine had been 50 percent, although one chemical had seen a 90 percent reduction.

Again, the inclusion of several major chemicals among those for which the ACGIH has lowered exposures does not, by itself, demonstrate that any illnesses would be prevented by OSHA's enforcement of those lower limits. Perhaps industry is already complying with them. Thus, for example, scientists from Dow Chemical have stated that "most companies in the chemical industry, at least the large- and medium-sized ones, have occupational health programs staffed by professional industrial hygienists who establish control programs often targeted at or below the ACGIH recommendations."[36]

In only a few cases do we have estimates of the actual number of workers exposed between the ACGIH and OSHA exposure limits. The fifteen chemicals in table 4.6 are those with the largest number of workers found exposed in this interval, according to the OSHA inspection records. For only four of them do we have independent estimates of the actual number exposed; these estimates were made by consultants who were studying possible compliance costs for new OSHA standards. The ratio of exposed

Table 4.6 For Some Hazards a Large Number of Workers Appear to be Exposed to Levels between the OSHA and the ACGIH Limits

Hazard[a]	ACGIH limit as a percentage of OSHA PEL	Samples found within 0.5–0.99 of OSHA PEL, April 1979–July 1981[b]	Estimated number of workers exposed above ACGIH limit but below OSHA limit[c]
Chromium[d]	5–50	52	60,000
Cadmium (fumes)	50	20	
Cadmium (dust)	25	18	
Formaldehyde	50	9	130,000
Nickel	10	17	
Trichloroethylene	50	20	20,000
Ammonia	50	10	
Hexone MIK	50	19	
Iron oxide fume	50	191	
Mercury (inorganic)	50	49	
Mercury (akyl)	10	8	
Perchloroethylene	50	9	
Styrene	50	77	
Sulfur dioxide	40	9	10,000
Toluene	50	55	

a. These hazards were the ones, among those for which the ACGIH time-weighted average exposure limit had been lowered from the OSHA PEL, that had the largest number of samples reported in the OSHA Management Information System for this period.

b. OSHA Management Information System. On average, each sample reflects the exposures of about four workers.

c. The four hazards included in this column were the only ones for which independent estimates of the number of workers exposed at these levels were available. The sources were various contractor studies performed for OSHA.

d. Comparisons for chromium are difficult. OSHA has three different PELs for different types of chromium. The ACGIH has six, and they do not neatly overlap with OSHA's. The 60,000 figure applies to exposures to hexavalent chromium. The fifty-two OSHA samples reflect all types of chromium.

workers to samples in three of these four cases is of the order of 1000 to 1.[37] If we extrapolate by this ratio for the rest of the chemicals on this list, we get an estimate of over 500,000 workers who would be protected by adoption and enforcement of the ACGIH limits. Given the data missing from the OSHA Management Information System (MIS) and the fact that this estimate represents only fifteen hazards, I feel that an estimate of a million workers would be conservative.

It is true that in some cases the lower limit may provide merely an extra margin of safety, but six of the hazards in this table are known or suspect carcinogens. Chromium is an important case. A contractor for OSHA estimated in 1980 that over 60,000 workers were exposed to carcinogenic forms of chromium at levels below the OSHA PEL but above the ACGIH limit. If we take the midpoint of the exposure ranges in that study and apply the EPA Carcinogenic Assessment Group's estimate of the cancer risk from chromium inhalation (adjusting from lifetime exposure to a work life of 40 years of 8-hour days), I calculate that about 18,000 cancers will result if current exposures continued for the next 40 years, or 450 cancers a year.[38] As we saw in chapter 2, this technique of risk estimation is likely to overestimate the risk by some unknown amount, but it suggests that failures to keep pace with the ACGIH limits may have serious consequences.

Potency and PELs: OSHA versus the ACGIH

Another interesting perspective on the relative performance of OSHA and the ACGIH can be gained from figures 4.1 and 4.2. They show the relation between carcinogenic potency (that is, the increase in the number of cancers for a given increase in the exposure dose) and the OSHA PEL or the ACGIH limit for all the hazards for which OSHA has a PEL and for which the EPA has made such potency estimates.[39]

PELs should be set to reflect both potency and the degree of evidence that a chemical is really harmful. For example, suppose that 10,000 workers are exposed to equal exposure levels of two chemicals. The potency estimate for one chemical suggests that a hundred workers will die from continued exposure; the second chemical is less potent, and only ten workers would die from continued exposure. However, the evidence that the second chemical is really harmful is quite strong, whereas the evidence for the first chemical is quite weak. If we estimate the probability that the first chemical is truly a threat at .1 and the probability for the second chemical at .9, then the expected number of deaths from the two chemicals would be 10 and 9. Reducing the PEL by 50 percent would lead to roughly

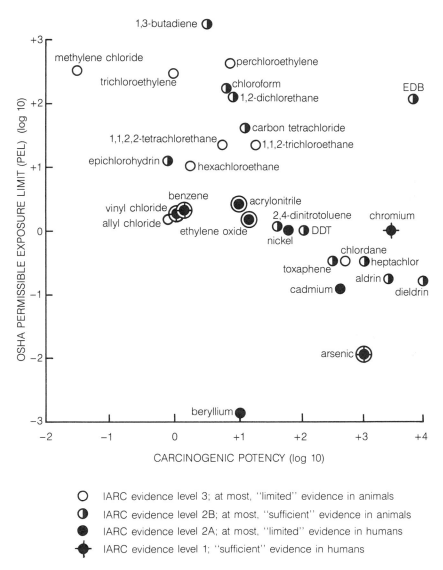

Figure 4.1 Relation of carcinogenic potency, the strength of evidence, and OSHA PELs. A large circle around a data point indicates that an OSHA PEL has been set since 1971.

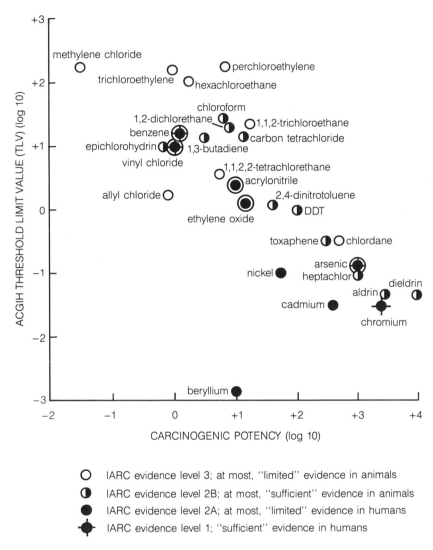

Figure 4.2 Relationship between carcinogenic potency and ACGIH TLVs. A large circle around a data point indicates that an OSHA PEL has been set since 1971.

Table 4.7   Effects of Potency and Strength of Evidence of the OSHA PEL[a]

Variable	Coefficient	t	Significance
Potency	$-.55$	3.459	.0028
Human	-1.13	1.591	.1248
Limited	-1.49	2.266	.0327
Animal	$+.31$	.573	.5718
Constant	$+1.85$	4.275	.0003

Source: See text.
a. This regression excludes beryllium and ethylene dibromide. Beryllium was excluded because it is the only hazard for which both of the following are true: The PEL was not set with cancer in mind, and the PEL would clearly not be reduced even if it were taken into account. EDB is not included here because there is no ACGIH TLV.
   Several chemicals have different PELs for different compounds. For this analysis, chromium was given a PEL of 1 mg/m^3 and cadmium 0.15 mg/m^3. The PEL assigned to benzene is 3.2 mg/m^3, the PEL in the standard overturned by the Supreme Court.
$N = 27$, $R^2 = .52589$, $F = 6.655$

equivalent gains in the expected number of deaths prevented. In contrast, if we had more confidence in the evidence for the more potent chemical and the probabilities were reversed, the expected deaths would be 90 and 1. In this case (given equivalent marginal cost curves for reducing exposures), we should set a much lower PEL for the more potent chemical.

Figures 4.1 and 4.2 also provide a measure of the degree of evidence. The International Agency for Research on Cancer (IARC) has separately classified human and animal evidence; for each, it has rated the evidence as "sufficient," "limited," or "inadequate." The figures recombine these into the four categories shown.

A multiple regression estimates the relative effects of potency and degree of evidence on the OSHA PEL. It takes the form $\log_{10} \text{PEL} = b_0 \log_{10} \text{potency} + b_1 \text{ sufficient} + b_2 \text{ limited} + b_3 \text{ animal}$.[40] "Sufficient" is a dummy variable that takes the value 1 for chemicals with sufficient evidence of carcinogenicity in humans. "Limited" is a dummy variable that takes the value 1 for chemicals with at most limited evidence in humans. "Animal" takes the value 1 for chemicals with at most sufficient evidence in animals. The coefficients for all these dummy variables represent the impact on the PEL of having these degrees of evidence compared to having only limited evidence in animals.

The results in table 4.7 show that a 10-fold increase in potency is associated with a 5.5-fold decrease in the PEL (a coefficient of -0.55). At first, it might seem preferable that this coefficient equal 1 so that the total risk would be held constant; that is, if the potency were ten times as great, then the exposure limit would be one-tenth as large. However, because the marginal costs of controlling exposures increase as PELs are decreased, a coefficient of less than 1 is probably desirable, although the optimal size remains uncertain.

Table 4.7 shows that, when human evidence exists, the PELs are lower. Indeed, the average effect is to lower the PEL by ten to fifteen times. The *degree* of human evidence, whether it is sufficient or limited, appears not to matter. This finding is somewhat disturbing in light of our belief that the degree of evidence should play a role in determining the strictness of standards.

Even more disturbing is that the coefficient for animal evidence shows that having sufficient evidence in animals does not lead to a lower PEL than having only limited evidence in animals. The only evidentiary distinction that appears to matter is between having human evidence of any type and not having it.

The great emphasis on human evidence and the belittling of animal evidence have important implications for underregulation because the list of undisputed human carcinogens continues to be dwarfed by the list of substances for which the evidence of a cancer threat to humans is more equivocal. The IARC periodically convenes panels of experts to assess evidence on carcinogenicity. In a 1979 report IARC panels reviewed 422 chemicals for which there was human or animal evidence on carcinogenicity. The human evidence was judged sufficient for only eighteen hazards and limited for only eighteen more. For 24 other chemicals with human evidence and for the 362 with only animal evidence, the prospects for regulatory action appear limited.[41]

OSHA's insensitivity to strong animal evidence would be even more disturbing than it is if it were not for the positive correlation between potency and degree of evidence. Chemicals that are more potent (that is, more likely to cause cancers for a given dose) are also therefore more likely to show up as positive in carcinogenicity tests. Thus stronger animal evidence will often have some indirect effect on the PEL through its impact on potency, but the effect does not appear to be large.[42]

The variables in table 4.7 explain almost 53 percent of the total variance in OSHA PELs. This figure is reasonably high when we consider that all of the PELs were adopted from the 1968 ACGIH list, except for the five that have been the subject of new OSHA standards—vinyl chloride, benzene, acrylonitrile, ethylene oxide, and arsenic. Considerably less evidence about carcinogenicity was available in 1968 than is available now. OSHA's slow pace of standard setting has not allowed it to avail itself of much of this new information. When OSHA has taken action, it has not addressed the hazards that stood out as having high PELs given their potency. Instead it addressed three of the four hazards with sufficient evidence in humans and two of the five with limited evidence. OSHA's actions have given an increased importance to human evidence and a reduced importance to potency.

This trend is especially evident when we compare the OSHA PELs in figure 4.1 with the current ACGIH limits shown in figure 4.2. This figure indicates that potency has a more important explanatory role for ACGIH than it does for OSHA. A regression analysis of the ACGIH limits confirms that the coefficient for potency is larger and the coefficient for sufficient evidence in humans is smaller.[43] The net effect is that the same variables explain over 71 percent of the variation in the ACGIH limits compared to the 53 percent in OSHA's PELs. Because these are the variables that *should* determine the level of PELs, there is a prima facie case on these grounds that the ACGIH choices are preferable. This conclusion strengthens the case about the relative attractiveness of the ACGIH approach of setting more new standards but setting them less strictly.

Although indicating that OSHA has set quite low PELs for some of the handful of hazards where human evidence is present, figure 4.1 also provides a basis for a first cut identification of cases of underregulation. The key suspects are the hazards with PELs much higher than would be predicted on the basis of potency and evidence. Ethylene dibromide (EDB), for which a new standard is being developed, clearly appears to deserve some reduction in its PEL. So does perchloroethylene. It and acrylonitrile are almost equally potent, and it is unlikely that the difference in evidence between them justifies the 150-fold difference in their PELs.

Of course, given its inability to produce a large number of standards, OSHA should also consider the number of workers exposed to each hazard so that the PEL reduction it chooses will make a meaningful contribution to public health. On this criterion, relatively exotic chemicals, such as 1,1,2,2-tetrachloroethane, would get lower priority. Yet if the roadblocks to faster rule making were removed, it seems likely that even fairly rare chemicals should be addressed.[44]

OSHA's priorities would be more analytically defensible if it could claim to have focused on hazards that, although not the most potent, posed exposures to so many workers that the total health threat was large. The evidence in table 4.8 indicates that this claim would be farfetched. The table includes only carcinogens because the assumption that they have no safe level allows us to try to calculate the diseases that will result from expo-

Table 4.8 Estimates of Future Cancer Caused by Current Workplace Exposures

Toxic substance	Basis for estimate	Lifetime cancers	Annual cancers (lifetime/45)
Promulgated or proposed OSHA standards			
Arsenic	Assumes 1700 workers exposed to 290 μg; 5600 at 50 μg. Risk based on OSHA analysis of epidemiological studies, using linear model.	270–1215	6–27
Asbestos (manufacturing only)	Assumes average exposure of 1 fiber/cc to 14,000 workers and that 3–10 percent of workers exposed at that level for 45 years will die of asbestos-induced diseases.	420–1400	9–32
Benzene	Assumes 34,000 workers exposed to an average of 3 ppm. Risk based on OSHA analysis of epidemiological studies, using 1-hit linear model.	510–1632	11–36
Coke oven emissions	Assumes average exposure of 100 μg for 15,000 workers. Risk based on epidemiological studies and linear model.	210	5
Ethylene oxide	Assumes 76,000 workers exposed to an average of 2–3 ppm. Risk based on multistage model from bioassays.	182–274	4–6
Formaldehyde	Based on distribution of full-time exposures and multistage model using bioassay data		
	a. maximum likelihood	143	3
	b. upper 95th percentile confidence interval	1055	23
Hazards without new OSHA proposals			
Chromium	Uses midpoints of distribution of exposures to hexavalent chromium; assumes all hexavalent compounds are carcinogenic with equal potency. Risk based on EPA CAG analysis of epidemiological studies.	18,000	450
Perchloroethylene	Uses midpoint of exposure distributions and EPA CAG risk estimate from bioassays using multistage model.	24,600	547
Trichloroethylene	Uses midpoint of exposure distributions and EPA CAG risk estimate from bioassays using multistage model.	110,000	2,444

Source: See appendix E.

sures. (Although some of the total exposures are at levels above the PEL, they almost certainly comprise a small proportion of the total exposures.)[45] The list is also limited to the handful of hazards for which we have exposure estimates.[46] These estimates of the number of cancers caused by current exposures to these hazards are all subject to considerable uncertainty. They consider only workplace air exposures, ignoring the use of respirators.[47] Correction for respirator use would reduce the number of expected cancers. An offsetting bias may be that diseases are understated to the extent that the risk estimates focus on only one type of well-documented cancer, ignoring other types whose incidence may also be elevated.

The most striking features of table 4.8 are that (1) the number of diseases caused by the hazards that OSHA chose to address tend to be quite small (keep in mind, however, that for asbestos several million people are exposed to small amounts in construction and the secondary automotive market; and that (2) the expected number of diseases caused by exposures to hazards that OSHA has not addressed are much larger. Of these, chromium is a well-established carcinogen; however, the exact chromium compounds that are carcinogenic and the potency and number of workers exposed to each remain uncertain. The figures in table 4.8 are based on the assumption that all exposures to hexavalent chromium are equally hazardous. The evidence on the carcinogenicity of the two solvents—trichloroethylene and perchloroethylene—is much less compelling. Moreover, if they are carcinogens, they both may work through epigenetic rather than genotoxic mechanisms, in which case the EPA CAG estimates of risk are likely to be much too high.[48] The point, however, is that, even if there is only a 5 percent chance that the CAG estimates are correct, these two chemicals are causing more deaths than most of the other chemicals in table 4.8, and some moderate reductions would appear to be worthwhile. (The large disease burden attributed to them is chiefly a result of the far higher exposure levels that prevail under current standards. The current PEL for arsenic is 0.01 mg/m^3; for acrylonitrile, vinyl chloride, and formaldehyde, between 2 and 4 mg/m^3, and for benzene 32 mg/m^3. In contrast, for trichloroethylene it is 535 mg/m^3 and for perchloroethylene, 680 mg/m^3.)

Table 4.8 makes it clear that OSHA's priorities do not reflect a weighting of potency by the number of workers exposed but rather appear to reflect chiefly the great importance attached to human evidence. The reasons for this approach are discussed in later chapters. Its inconsistency with a more rapid pace of standard setting is clear.

Overregulation, Underregulation, and the Future of OSHA Policy

In this chapter and the last I have tried to convince you that most of OSHA's handful of new health standards are overly strict and that at the same time opportunities to prevent additional death and disease at a reasonable cost have been forgone. Suppose that I have succeeded. Does the prescription to set standards more extensively but less strictly necessarily follow from these findings of overregulation and underregulation?

The answer is no. The validity of that prescription depends on a number of additional assumptions. For example, assume (1) that there is some hazard out there that is doing as much damage as 12 fibers of asbestos, (2) that it has not been addressed under the current policy, and (3) that it would be one of the hazards whose exposure limit would be sliced in half under the proposed policy. My policy prescription looks very good under those assumptions. More generally, the policy of more extensive, less strict standards looks attractive if we are ignorant of the costs and benefits of reduced exposure limits.

But assume instead that we had adopted the policy of less strictness but greater extensiveness in 1970 and that, as a result, we had tripled the number of hazards whose exposure limits we had reduced (all by 50 percent). But an additional result was that we reduced the PEL for asbestos by only 50 percent—from 12 fibers to 6, instead of to the 2-fiber level that became effective in 1976. As we saw in chapter 2, the 2-fiber level probably prevented a large number of deaths at a fairly low cost. It is quite possible that the adoption of this larger number of across-the-board 50 percent reductions would have saved fewer lives and cost more to boot than the policy that OSHA actually carried out.

Thus my policy prescription may not be attractive if the world is characterized by a few hazards for which large reductions in exposure will bring major benefits and many hazards for which even moderate reductions would bring little benefit. In that case public health proponents could justifiably argue that OSHA's slow pace of standard setting is not really a serious problem; although it may take a few years, the serious hazards will be addressed. And it is more important to mount major campaigns against the serious hazards than to wage guerrilla warfare against a host of small hazards.

Of course, this perspective does assume, first, that we are able to recognize which hazards are serious and which are not and, second, that, once the serious hazards are recognized, regulatory agencies will in fact address them. Table 4.8 presented evidence that undermines this second assumption, and chapter 6 supplies more. Regarding the first assumption, we simply do not know what the distribution of hazards looks like. Therefore I cannot say whether this prescription would be valid or not.

However, this agnosticism need not be paralyzing. There is no reason why my prescription would have to be for *uniformly* moderate reductions. In cases where we have reasonably good information, we should carry out a benefit-cost analysis to see what level of reductions would be justified. If that analysis indicated that a stringent standard is justified, it could be adopted. Then for hazards about which we have less information, we could pursue a precautionary but moderate strategy along the lines of the ACGIH changes.

Conclusions

Underregulation occurs when exposure limits are set at a higher level than would be socially desirable. Included in this definition are the cases for which a limit would be desirable but does not exist. The calculation of what is desirable should consider all the social benefits and costs, including the administrative resources used in the standard-setting process itself.

Determining whether some level of reduced exposures to toxic substances would be desirable is difficult. The available data fail to provide the basis for assessing the marginal costs and benefits of exposure reductions. To seek insights, we are forced to turn to more indirect evidence. The economic argument that rational citizens will want exposure limits to decline over time indicates the direction that most changes should take but does not indicate the appropriate magnitude of the changes.

The argument that we are currently underregulating relies heavily on the growing disparity between OSHA's exposure limits and the recommendations of the ACGIH. I have shown that the number of hazards for which the ACGIH, but not OSHA, has made protective changes is quite large. The data, although far from fully satisfactory, suggest that moderate reductions in exposure limits—of the order of those typically adopted by the ACGIH—will often prevent deaths at a cost that seems reasonable, no more than $1 million or $2 million each. Finally, although many of the ACGIH changes pertain to hazards that currently do not involve a large number of exposed workers, a sizable number do, and these present a significant public health problem.

The ACGIH changes often reflect new evidence of possible harm. In only a few cases has it been possible to establish solid evidence that a hazard is a human carcinogen; but for a much larger number of hazards we have lesser degrees of evidence. In most of the cases with "sufficient" human evidence, OSHA has taken strict action. But OSHA appears to wait until the evidence becomes strong before taking any action, regardless of the potential danger of exposure. It has taken few steps to address the much larger number of chemicals with lesser evidence of carcinogenicity. If we could trust OSHA to act reasonably in setting standards for these chemicals, then we would likely be better off taking those actions. In a rational scheme of public health measures, the *possibility* of serious harm can warrant protective action. We should not wait for the toxicological equivalent of the smoking gun. Even if there is only a 20 percent chance that current exposures to a chemical will cause a thousand deaths, if society wants to maximize the number of deaths prevented, we should treat this threat as equivalent to one that will kill two hundred (unknown) people with certainty. But what public health advocates often ignore is that the degree of protectiveness should be calibrated to the probability of harm and the costs of prevention as well as to the magnitude of the potential harm. We should not spend vast resources to reduce every risk, no matter how remote.

Even if there are many potentially desirable new standards, people who are deeply concerned about costs will fear that the measures to cure underregulation would end up making matters worse, overshooting the mark and leading to overregulation and to larger net costs than we incur from underregulation. Public health advocates may question whether a trade-off of greater extensiveness for reduced strictness would prevent more disease. Their answer will partly depend on assumptions about what the world looks like in terms of the severity distribution of hazards (should we worry more about a few big ones or many smaller ones?) and regulators' abilities to identify and act on them. But it also will depend on the particular design of reform proposals.

Before proceeding to design those reforms, we should understand the reasons why overregulation and underregulation have emerged. That diagnosis should lead to a sounder plan for reform.

II

THE POLITICS OF RULE MAKING

Explaining the Slow Pace of Standard Setting

Although most commentaries on OSHA health regulation have focused on the strictness of individual standards, a regulatory program should be judged by broader measures of its impact on the social problem it was designed to address. We should ask not only whether individual standards are set properly but also whether the regulators are choosing appropriate hazards to address and whether the regulatory program deals with a sufficiently large chunk of the regulatory problem. If Congressmen had predicted in 1970 that passage of the OSH Act would create a regulatory system that enforced fewer standards and often less strict standards than private groups were issuing, they would not have been taken seriously. Congress did not anticipate the problem of underregulation and foregone protection that stricter federal standards and enforcement have helped to create.

But although "regulatory delay" is often used as a pejorative term, faster rule making does not necessarily mean better rule making.[1] Allowing adequate time for affected parties to provide information and for regulators to digest it is obviously desirable. There is a cost to setting a standard improperly, especially in a system that makes reconsiderations of a standard difficult and time consuming. Finally, the most important caveat to the underregulation argument is that delay in the promulgation of bad standards is no vice.

The objective of this chapter is to explain the slow pace and limited scope of the standard-setting effort. It provides the chief evidence for assessing the claim that the strictness with which standards are set is a significant cause of the failure to address a large number of hazards. In chapter 6 I go on to examine the defects in OSHA's priority-setting mechanisms and show how these defects are magnified when overregulation and underregulation are present. In chapter 7 I look at the determinants of how strictly standards are set. All three of these chapters raise the question of how reforms might be made, but chapters 8, 9, and 10 take up that issue directly.

Background on OSHA Standard Setting

Before looking at the reasons for the slow pace of standard setting, we need to provide a brief background on aspects of OSHA's history and procedures that we will be discussing later in more detail.[2] As we saw, the OSH

Act required OSHA to adopt all existing federal standards, which included all of the roughly 400 ACGIH TLVs (from that organization's 1968 list) that had been incorporated under the Walsh-Healey Act.

The act gave the head of OSHA (the Assistant Secretary of Labor for Occupational Safety and Health) great latitude in choosing which hazards to address, requiring only that he give "due regard" to the recommendations of the National Institute of Occupational Safety and Health (also established by the act and located in the Department of Health, Education, and Welfare). It required that proposed rules be published in the *Federal Register* and allowed thirty days for comments. Interested parties could also request a hearing on the standard, and OSHA was obligated to respond. Within sixty days after the hearing, OSHA had to promulgate a final standard.

The act provided the following guidance to OSHA about the substance of new standards dealing with toxic materials and harmful physical agents: It will

set the standard which most adequately assures, to the extent feasible, on the basis of the best available evidence, that no employee will suffer material impairment of health or functional capacity even if such employee has regular exposure for the period of his working life. Development of standards under this subsection shall be based upon research, demonstrations, experiments, and other such information as may be appropriate. In addition to the attainment of the highest degree of safety and health protection for the employee, other considerations shall be the latest available scientific data in the field, the feasibility of the standards, and experience gained under this and other health and safety laws.[3]

These standards had to include not merely a permissible exposure limit but also requirements for warning labels and, where appropriate, personal protective equipment, medical exams, and workplace monitoring.

Under certain conditions (described later), the act also allowed OSHA to issue emergency temporary standards (ETSs) without having to go through the procedures just discussed. The emergency standard had to expire within six months, but OSHA was required to initiate preparation of a regular standard when it issued the ETS.

Any person who was adversely affected by either an emergency standard or a regular standard could appeal it in a court of appeals. The filing of such an appeal would not automatically stay the application of the standard, although the court could order such a stay. In its review of challenges to standards, the act stated that OSHA's determination "shall be conclusive if supported by substantial evidence in the record considered as a whole."[4]

The OSH Act can be characterized as granting broad discretion on the substance of regulations but setting forth rigid procedural guidelines. In fact, it turned out that some of the procedures established in the act were ignored, but new ones were mandated by the courts and by the White House. Even more important, the courts, although circumspect in OSHA's first seven years, later intervened to confine its substantive discretion.

The key cases were the Supreme Court decisions on the benzene and cotton dust standards.[5] In 1980 the Court overturned the benzene standard on the grounds that OSHA had failed to demonstrate that exposures at the existing PEL posed a "significant risk." In the next year, after Reagan took office, the Supreme Court upheld the cotton dust standard against the claim that standards be required to pass a benefit-cost test. Indeed, said the Court, not only was a benefit-cost test not required, it was not even allowed in light of the act's commitment to worker protection.

President Nixon appointed OSHA's first two directors: George Guenther, a businessman who served until January 1973, and John Stender, a local union official who served through July 1975. Morton Corn, an industrial hygienist from the University of Pittsburgh, served only from December 1975 to January 1977. President Carter appointed Eula Bingham, a toxicologist from the University of Cincinnati. Bingham served during Carter's full term, giving way to construction executive Thorne Auchter when the Reagan administration took over in 1981. Auchter left in March 1984 and was replaced by Robert Rowland, an attorney.

The new health standards issued from OSHA's inception through mid-1986 are listed in appendix G. OSHA has established new PELS for only ten hazards. Most of its other standards have proposed more generic requirements for such things as hazard labeling and ensuring worker access to exposure and medical records.

Explanations for the Slow Pace

Several simple explanations for the slow pace of standard setting can be suggested. One is that there simply are not hazards "out there" that merit regulation. Regardless of the factual correctness of this assessment, it is quite inadequate as an explanation, at least on one level. After all, OSHA officials did not subscribe to this assessment. They were aware that, despite OSHA's protective mandate, the ACGIH was lowering exposure limits far more frequently than they were. They would have been happy to set many more standards, at least before the Reagan administration. At a deeper level, however, I argue that qualms about the merits of OSHA standards do help to explain the infrequency with which they are issued.

Table 5.1   Length of Rule-Making Proceedings

Rule	NPRM to final rule (months)	Year of final rule	Emergency temporary standard	National Institute of Occupational Safety and Health criteria document to NPRM (months)
Asbestos	5	1972	yes	0
Vinyl chloride	5	1974	yes	2
Coke ovens	15	1976	no	29
Benzene	9	1978	yes (voided)	34
DBCP	4	1978	yes	2
Arsenic	40	1978	no	2
Cotton dust	19	1978	no	27
Acrylonitrile	9	1978	yes	4
Lead	37	1978	no	33
Ethylene oxide	14	1984	no	No criteria document

A second explanation points to the various procedural requirements imposed on OSHA by the statute, the White House, and the courts. Public hearings, studies of technological and economic feasibility, quantitative risk analyses—all of these do lengthen the duration of rule making. In some cases inaction and delays reflect the scarcity of OSHA's resources. In others, delays could not be reduced by adding more resources. A ninety-day comment period after a public hearing can no more be shortened by adding staff than a chamber music piece for a string quartet can be shortened by using an octet. For whatever reasons, some rule making has indeed taken a long time. From the official Notice of Proposed Rule Making (NPRM) to the promulgation of the final rule took forty months for OSHA's arsenic standard, and thirty-seven months for lead. Yet table 5.1 reveals that such long proceedings were exceptional. The actual time required for analysis will be longer for a standard that (like lead) cuts across many industries, but the table indicates that the analysis can usually be done in six months. The length of the proceedings is not simply a function of the analytic requirements.

This conclusion is obvious when we look at the drawn-out reconsiderations of such hazards as noise, asbestos, benzene, cotton dust, and lead. A new exposure limit for noise was the subject of one of the first NIOSH (National Institute of Occupational Safety and Health) recommendations to OSHA in 1972. Rejecting pressure from the EPA and from his own staff, OSHA director John Stender issued a proposal in 1974 calling for an exposure limit of 90 db (decibels) rather than 85 db. The economic impact study had estimated compliance costs of $13 billion for the 90-db standard and $31 billion for the 85-db standard.[6] When Morton Corn succeeded Stender, plans to proceed with an 85-db standard were revived despite a speech by President Ford specifically criticizing the high cost of that measure. Corn later explained that: "For me, the key question on whether to set 85 or 90 was, 'Does the record support 85 for the purposes of preventing hearing impairment.'"[7] He felt it did. Yet Corn also explained that the secretary of labor and White House officials were "reluctant" and "didn't want me to move before the election," but "nobody ever said I couldn't come out with the regulation I thought was best. They only said the justification better be good." Corn went along with the delay but was replaced by the Democrats after Carter's victory. Under his successor, Eula Bingham, noise never received a high priority. A much less costly hearing conservation standard was finally issued four days before Reagan took office in 1981—just in time for it to be stayed by the new administration. A revised and further weakened version was issued in 1983, vacated by a Fourth Circuit Court of Appeals panel in November 1984 but upheld in 1985 by a decision of the full Circuit.[8] Throughout the period, the chief cause of the delay was that the costs appeared so large that opposition remained strong.

On benzene OSHA was sent back to the drawing boards after the Supreme Court repudiated what most justices saw as the standard's high costs and lack of significant benefits. During the next year the cotton dust, lead, and hazard communication standards, along with hearing conservation, were all targeted by Reagan's OMB for reconsideration because of the perception that they were costly and unjustified. Political conflict rather than analytic requirements is the major cause of delay.

A major sign of that conflict is the frequency with which standards are appealed to the courts. All but two of OSHA's final health standards have been appealed. It is instructive to consider those two exceptions.

Both bioassay and epidemiological evidence led OSHA to consider setting a new, lower acrylonitrile standard in late 1977. OSHA's proposal called for reducing the PEL from 20 ppm to 2 ppm. Several major firms testified that lower levels could be achieved. Dow Chemical stated: "We believe that levels of 0.2 ppm and 1 ppm are technologically attainable, but would require significant costs and years of effort." Officials of Monsanto estimated that achievement of the 1-ppm PEL "would take 2 or 3 years beyond the period for completion of their 2 ppm engineering program." OSHA's own feasibility consultant stated in its report that "1 ppm would be technologically feasible except for periodic maintenance operations and tank farm and loading areas."[9] With previous standards OSHA had adopted PELs despite the insistence of affected firms and its own contractors that they were infeasible; in this case it *failed* to adopt a PEL that both acknowledged was feasible. Compared to previous OSHA standards, acrylonitrile looked quite reasonable.

In the case of the pesticide DBCP, the PEL was extremely strict; but the total estimated costs of compliance were by far the smallest of any OSHA standard (only $3.65 million a year), the health effects were dramatic (both sterility and cancer), and the market outlook was poor (because of EPA restrictions on its use). Thus the net costs to the firms because of the OSHA standard were quite small. The only two US producers, both large chemical firms, decided to close down their plants.

In addition, industry did not appeal all of the ETSs that OSHA issued, letting those for asbestos, vinyl chloride, and DBCP go unchallenged. To see the significance of these failures to litigate, we need to understand clearly that the issuance of an ETS speeds up the promulgation of a permanent standard.

Table 5.1 shows that standards that began with ETSs took much less time to promulgate. This is hardly surprising, in large part because the act requires that a permanent standard be issued within six months after an ETS. OSHA could be sued for failing to comply and generally stayed within a few months of the deadlines. The ETS provision was inserted in the statute precisely to address hazards where speedy action seemed essential. However, the act also stipulated that OSHA must first determine that "employees are exposed to grave danger from exposure to substances or agents determined to be toxic or physically harmful or from new hazards" and that the ETS is "necessary" to protect them from the danger. As the table shows, OSHA relied on ETSs heavily in its earlier years. They fell from favor in part because the courts—especially the Fifth Circuit—often vacated them.

The role of the ETS in determining the pace of standard setting is further clarified by the rationale employed to justify an ETS for a second, more stringent asbestos standard in 1983. Somewhat plaintively, OSHA explained that the history of rule making showed that, unless an ETS were issued, new action on the asbestos threat could take years.

The explanation of OSHA's capability to produce a standard within 6 months of an ETS lies in the urgency generated by OSHA's finding of a grave danger, the existence of a specific statutory deadline to complete a rulemaking within 6 months and the need to prevent a gap in protection between the expiration of the ETS and the imposition of the permanent standard for a substance already determined to pose a grave danger.[10]

What OSHA was saying was that it could not put the development of a standard on a "fast track" and keep it there without the spur of an ETS.

Of nine ETSs[11] six were challenged in court and only one of those (acrylonitrile) survived intact. The ETSs for asbestos in 1971, vinyl chloride, and DBCP were never challenged. In all three of these cases OSHA was responding to fresh and unmistakable evidence of serious illness in humans. In the acrylonitrile case positive findings in a bioassay sponsored by the industry had triggered OSHA's ETS. The challenge to the ETS was brought not by the industry association but by a small firm acting on its own. This distinction was one that was not lost on the judges, according to Labor Department attorneys.[12] Moreover, by the time the judges heard the suit, Du Pont had already produced an epidemiological study that indicated that acrylonitrile had caused an increase in the lung cancer rate among its workers.

The requirements of the ETS—that the danger be "grave" and that the action be "necessary"—are rough tests of how strong the health arguments for a new standard are. When industry does not challenge an ETS, it is acknowledging that lower exposures are needed. When the courts uphold an ETS against a challenge, they are reaching the same conclusion.

In striking down ETSs, the courts have emphasized how reluctant they are to allow OSHA to bypass the procedural safeguards (public notice and hearings) that the normal process supplies. But when the causal role of exposures in causing serious disease is acknowledged by all parties, when there are actual sick workers to point to, and when the workers were unlikely to have been aware of the dangers, the courts (and OSHA) are more predisposed to take the ETS route. Thus it would be a mistake to construe OSHA's turn away from the ETS as merely a reflection of legal tactics. It reflected the perception that the persuasiveness of the arguments for several of the new standards was not as strong.

The strength of the health evidence on asbestos, DBCP, acrylonitrile, and vinyl chloride certainly helps to explain industry's decision not to appeal the ETSs. The presence of strong evidence reduced the probability that industry would win, reducing the expected payoff from appeals. However, in all of those cases except DBCP, another factor was that the PELs in the ETSs were moderate: 5 fibers for asbestos versus the final PEL of 2 fibers; 25 ppm for vinyl chloride versus the final PEL of 1 ppm; and 2 ppm for acrylonitrile, which was equal to the final (and uncontested) PEL. In contrast, the one carcinogen ETS for which industry appealed the PEL was the benzene ETS of 1 ppm, which industry claimed would cost several hundred million dollars per death prevented.

Unions also recognized the importance of the ETS and the trade-off between stricter standards and speedier rule making. In the case of vinyl chloride, their desire for a PEL even lower than 1 ppm was tempered by the fear that

an effort to force OSHA to lower the exposure limit further might have delayed the issuance of a standard. If the delay extended beyond October 5, the ETS would expire. Once that happened, with no firm date to aim at, OSHA might delay substantially longer before completing the rulemaking, and the eventual standard might be the same or even weaker than one the unions would obtain by supporting the agency. If the unions were able to convince OSHA to issue a more stringent standard, the nearly inevitable judicial review at the behest of the industries would be even harder to win.[13]

The Role of Resources

Speeding up the pace for one standard does take resources away from others. The paucity of resources is another explanation for the slow pace of standard setting. To develop a permanent standard for vinyl chloride within six months required dropping everything else, according to Grover Wrenn, chief of health standards at the time.[14]

The health-standard-setting operation at OSHA is small. In 1974 there were twelve professionals in the office; at the peak in 1979 there were over forty.[15] By the early 1980s, the number slipped as low as twenty-seven, and twenty of them were primarily occupied with carrying out reassessments of rules that had been issued by the previous administration.[16] The agency could not have produced as many standards as it did under Bingham if its resources had still been at the 1974 level.

The staff grew steadily throughout the 1970s, especially after 1975. Of course, for such a tiny program, even a large percentage increase would cause barely a blip in an agency that employed 3000 people at its height. One explanation for the growth was that first Secretary of Labor Dunlop and then Secretary of Labor Marshall convinced the OMB to upgrade the health standards effort. But what kept the health standards staff from growing to 100 or 200 professionals, a size that might enable several times as many standards to be produced? Rapid growth in a program, even when small in absolute terms, must always surmount the norm of incrementalism. In the absence of an obvious crisis, it is hard to see how much more could have been achieved.

Another constraint was that bigger budgets for rule making were not the chief priority of organized labor. Although labor lobbyists supported increases, they put their greatest efforts into increasing the size of the enforcement program. A larger inspectorate addresses several labor concerns: that OSHA won't respond quickly to worker requests for inspections and that it will not have enough resources to inspect nonunion plants, possibly putting unionized plants at a competitive disadvantage. It is on these types of enforcement issues that national union leaders get requests for help from their local union officials. In contrast, on standards, unions are concerned with OSHA's capability only to the extent that it interferes with its responses to *particular* hazards that they want action on.[17]

An additional factor is awareness on the part of the OMB staff and the appropriations committees in Congress that the economic impact of adding fifty staff to health standards is far greater than the impact of adding fifty inspectors. Those committees have been the lightning rod for much of the criticism of OSHA. Because no other Labor Department agency comes close to OSHA in the number of hostile appropriations riders, committee members are well aware of the agency's unpopularity.

Quality Matters as well as Quantity

Neither its salaries nor its working conditions made OSHA an especially attractive place to quality people. Even compared with colleagues at the EPA and the FDA, OSHA scientists were less buffered from political winds and enjoyed less support from the outside scientific community. As a result, turnover tended to be high and the quality—despite some excellent people—relatively low. As one observer noted:

Constantly struggling against the deficiencies of its available technical staff, OSHA had to rely heavily on NIOSH, consultants, contractors, and often lawyers from the Labor Department's solicitor's office. . . . Often by the time a project was ready to move to the next step in the regulatory process, everyone who had known much about it had left. New people were constantly being trained in both the substance of issues and the procedures that had to be followed. Efficiency and the level of competence of agency work suffered.[18]

For example, Leonard Vance, director of health standards under Auchter, observed in 1983 that one problem in designing a new benzene standard was that none of the people who had helped to write the 1978 standard were still with the agency.[19] Former Assistant Secretary Morton Corn observed that the agency had had no organization and no staff to carry out routine functions; each new standard required an organizing effort from the top.[20] Such efforts clearly were limited by the time that top officials had available. Yet it is hard to accept the notion that a bottleneck at the top is inevitable.

After all, many top agency officials have to make decisions about a far broader and more numerous group of issues than the chief of OSHA does; yet such decisions do get made. Still, it is true that the time required for review depends to a great extent on having staff who are viewed as both capable and like-minded. The frequency with which OSHA leaders claim that certain issues are in limbo because there is no one to take charge of them suggests that more high-level staff could increase the level of agency activity.

The task of writing good standards demands great skill. Peter Hutt, former general counsel for the FDA, claims that "no one who hasn't been involved in trying to get a regulation out in the *Federal Register* can imagine how difficult it is." [21] A 100-page document in the *Federal Register* is the length of a 320-page book. It must marshal scientific, engineering, economic, and legal expertise into an argument that will convince a reviewing court to turn a deaf ear to the challenges of talented industry and union lawyers. Few scientists and engineers have been trained to craft what are essentially policy arguments. Lawyers are trained to do it, but they must rely heavily on the other disciplines. OSHA did not have its own legal staff but relied on the Labor Department's Office of the Associate Solicitor for Occupational Safety and Health.

Because of low salaries and poor working conditions, the talented people who do enter government are probably more likely to have a special affinity for the goals of the public programs; that is, they are more likely to be zealots. Indeed, one factor that made the promulgation of six standards in one year possible under Bingham was her ability to recruit, largely on ideological grounds, a talented handful of people. Several young lawyers were temporarily bootlegged into the agency under various pretexts, and at least one new scientist who could write policy documents played an important role in the lead and cotton dust standards. In addition, outside consultants who had close ties to OSHA's leaders played an unusually important role in developing several key policy components. [22]

To the extent that quality staff matters, highly ideological (probably prolabor) leaders are more likely to be able to attract them. Thus, in the short run, to the extent that staff quality, as well as quantity, affects the pace of standard setting, strict regulation is probably *not* the enemy of more extensive regulation. But, in the long run, the agency's reputation for politicization will tend to undercut the efforts of more moderate leaders to attract the quality of scientist and size of budget that might help to change its reputation and improve the pace.

Courts and Pace

Judicial review has been credited or blamed—depending on the commentator—with increasing the degree of analytic scrutiny that each standard must bear and, consequently, with increasing the amount of time and resources required to produce it. As we have seen, when courts overturned several of OSHA's ETSs, they did delay standard setting and force OSHA to do additional work. The Third Circuit expressed dismay when it found that the entire justification for the 1973 ETS for "14 Carcinogens" took less than a hundred words. It vacated the standard with respect to several chemicals. The chief Labor Department attorney for OSHA reports that it was largely in response to this and another 1973 court decision that OSHA began to prepare far more extensive preambles to its proposed rules.[23]

Reviewing courts (circuit courts of appeals and the Supreme Court) have several different tasks. First, they must assess whether the statute or the agency's actions under it are constitutional. Constitutional issues have not played a major role in the review of OSHA's health standards.[24] Second, they must assess whether the agency's action is consistent with the basic statute or with other pertinent statutes (for example, the Administrative Procedure Act). On so-called factual determinations, this assessment requires judging whether the agency is supported by "substantial evidence in the record as a whole."[25] Thus the agency must have "substantial evidence" that the terms of the statute have been adhered to—for example, that standards are "feasible" and "reasonably necessary" and that they address "significant risks." Although the central provisions of all of OSHA's final standards except benzene have been upheld, many of the secondary provisions have been overturned for failing to meet these tests.[26] For example, the D.C. Circuit's decision on the lead standard stayed its applicability to thirty-seven industries because OSHA had not demonstrated the standard's feasibility there. The message was that OSHA cannot address only the major industries and assume that the courts will let it do what it wants in the minor ones. More extensive and expensive feasibility studies will thus be required.

Yet I have argued that analytical requirements per se were not the chief cause of the slow pace of standard setting. The chief role of the courts in fostering delay is more subtle and pervasive than specifying the hoops that must be jumped through.

My argument is that judicial opinions about standards are influenced by assessments of their reasonableness. Reasonableness, in turn, is largely in the eye of the beholder and thus depends on the public policy preferences of the judges. To the extent that OSHA adopts standards that can be criticized as unreasonably strict (or lenient), it increases the likelihood that the almost inevitable appeal will lead to a reversal. The prospect of reversal has a chilling effect on the development of standards.

Of course, when both the law and the facts are clear, the policy preferences of judges—their views of what is "reasonable"—count for little. But vague statutes and factual uncertainties combine to ensure that these conditions of clarity are often not met. One indicator that they are not is the frequency of split decisions in the opinions of reviewing courts. Although most lawyers and some political scientists balk at viewing judges as purely or perhaps even primarily driven by their policy preferences, my argument requires only that these preferences enter into a significant number of decisions. The consensus among students of judicial politics appears to be that "it is beyond serious question today that the judges of the Supreme Court have their own conceptions of public policy and that their attitudes and values effect the thrust of their decision-making." [27] The importance of "forum shopping" for appeals courts suggests that policy preferences play a significant role there as well.

The Benzene Decision and the Fear of Overregulation
Despite the reversals detailed, OSHA's final standards generally passed judicial muster. (The courts' upholding of OSHA's protectiveness is examined in chapter 7.) The striking exception was the benzene standard.

In mid-October 1978 the Fifth Circuit Court of Appeals delivered the cause of protectiveness at OSHA its first major judicial setback. The Fifth Circuit had already become OSHA's nemesis, overturning several of its ETSs, including the one on benzene. Departing from all other decisions, the court turned the spotlight on a hitherto ignored section of the act, which defined an "occupational safety and health standard" as a standard that "requires conditions, or the adoption or use of one or more practices, means, methods, operations, or processes, *reasonably necessary or appropriate to provide safe or healthful employment or places of employment*" (emphasis added).[28] The court claimed:

Unless OSHA can provide substantial evidence that the benefits to be achieved by reducing the permissible exposure limit from 10 ppm to 1 ppm bear a reasonable relationship to the costs imposed by the reduction, it cannot show that the standard is reasonably necessary to provide safe or healthful workplaces.... This does not mean that OSHA must wait until deaths occur as a result of exposure levels below 10 ppm before it may validly promulgate a standard reducing the permissible exposure limit. Nevertheless, OSHA must have some factual basis for an estimate of expected benefits before it can determine that a one-half billion dollar standard is reasonably necessary.[29]

Thus the court was both imposing a benefit-cost test for OSHA standards and requiring some sort of quantification of benefits as a necessary step to carry out that test.

Alone among regulatory agencies, OSHA had steadfastly denied the possibility of meaningful quantification of cancer risks. In the preamble to the benzene standard, as in others, it claimed that it was "impossible to derive any conclusions regarding dose-response relationships."[30] This unwillingness reflected agency concerns that quantification was the first step to benefit-cost analysis. Precisely as the Fifth Circuit Court had complained, if you do not quantify the benefits, you cannot weigh them against the costs. OSHA stated that in its judgment the benefits would be "appreciable" but that the size of the benefits was not relevant to the selection of the PEL.

OSHA's contention about the meaninglessness of quantitive risk analysis (QRA) was undercut by the fact that other federal agencies did employ it. The EPA's Carcinogenic Assessment Group had performed a risk assessment for benzene, and the oil industry had introduced an assessment by Harvard physicist Richard Wilson that claimed that the standard would cost $200 million for each fatal cancer prevented. OSHA's reluctance to follow the EPA and the FDA reflected the relative lack of support for analysis at OSHA. Labor union pressures combined with staff preferences for protection to override any interest in the use of more analytical approaches. With its much broader mandate, staff at the EPA were aware that not every hazard could be reduced to the lowest feasible level.

The Fifth Circuit's decision stunned OSHA's leaders, who viewed it as a total challenge to their regulatory philosophy and to their view of OSHA's role. Bingham was especially upset because she had a particular interest in benzene. She was not inclined to accept the advice of the solicitor's office, which was to ignore the decision rather than to appeal it.[31]

Despite her decision to appeal, the Fifth Circuit's decision generated a new hesitancy about setting health standards. If OSHA performed QRAs, they might be used as a weapon by those who opposed strict standards. Moreover, OSHA would be acknowledging that the health effects could be quantified. Yet standards without QRAs might be rejected by the courts.[32]

Except for the lead standard, issued just a few weeks after the Fifth Circuit's decision, OSHA issued no more standards on specific toxic substances during the remaining twenty-seven months of Bingham's tenure.

Although other factors besides that decision contributed to the halt, these factors alone would not have generated such a striking hiatus. In this context, the frustration of OSHA's desire for strict standards led to no standards.[33]

In July 1980 a badly split Supreme Court upheld the Fifth Circuit's decision, although not its reasoning. A four-judge plurality argued that OSHA had failed to assume its burden of proof and show that a reduction in the benzene PEL was needed. More precisely, the plurality found in the language of section 3(8) a new concept of "significant risk," which, in the court's words, required OSHA "to make a threshold finding that a place of employment is unsafe—in the sense that significant risks are present and can be eliminated or lessened by a change in practices."[34] OSHA had failed to show that benzene exposures of 10 ppm constituted a "significant risk." Because OSHA had failed to make this threshold finding, the Court avoided the question of whether it must weigh costs and benefits.

The four-member minority (Marshall, Brennan, White, and Blackmun) protested that

the plurality ignores the plain meaning of the Occupational Safety and Health Act of 1970 in order to bring the authority of the Secretary of Labor in line with the plurality's own views of proper regulatory policy. The unfortunate consequence is that the Federal Government's efforts to protect American workers from cancer and other crippling diseases may be substantially impaired.... According to the plurality, a standard is not "reasonably necessary or appropriate" unless the Secretary is able to show that it is "at least more likely than not" that the risk he seeks to regulate is a "significant" one. Nothing in the statute's language or legislative history, however, indicates that the "reasonably necessary and appropriate" language should be given this meaning.[35]

In a separate opinion, Justice Rehnquist provided the fifth vote for overturning the standard. His rationale was that the statute was so vague that it constituted an invalid delegation by Congress. Although the "nondelegation doctrine" had not been successfully used to overturn legislation since the Supreme Court's acceptance of an activist government in the late 1930s, Rehnquist's complaint does point to a fundamental problem of modern government and of regulation in particular:

If we are ever to reshoulder the burden of ensuring that Congress itself make the critical policy decisions, this is surely the case in which to do it. It is difficult to imagine a more obvious example of Congress simply avoiding a choice which was both fundamental for purposes of the statute and yet politically so divisive that the necessary decision or compromise was difficult, if not impossible, to hammer out in the legislative forge.[36]

As its first word on the topic of risk assessment, the Supreme Court's benzene decision has spawned numerous legal commentaries. Many of them criticize the decision for its vague guidelines and its apparent inconsistencies.[37] On the one hand, the plurality said that the burden was on the agency to present substantial evidence that it was "more likely than not" that long-term exposures to 10 ppm of benzene posed a "significant risk." The plurality went on to chide OSHA for relying on assumptions and theories rather than on evidence of harm at 10 ppm. Yet the plurality also acknowledged that "so long as they are supported by a body of reputable scientific thought, the Agency is free to use conservative assumptions in interpreting the data with respect to carcinogens, risking error on the side of over-protection rather than under-protection."[38]

In its complaints the plurality is demanding that OSHA meet a burden of proof that is totally unrealistic given the type of evidence that is available for benzene and for almost every other carcinogen. If any evidence of harm exists, it is almost invariably at levels above current exposure levels. Because evidence at that level does not exist, "assumptions" and "theories" must be used. In any event, the logic of the "significant risk" argument extends beyond the current PEL of 10 ppm. If OSHA must show that a "significant risk" exists at 10 ppm, why not at 9 ppm and 8 ppm and at every level above the proposed new level?

On the other hand, if we look at the other statements by the plurality that sanction the use of conservative assumptions, then we must wonder what they are complaining about. The no-threshold theory that OSHA relied on certainly had scientific support; so did the view that quantitative risk assessments were highly uncertain.

The best way to make sense of the inconsistencies and interpret the plurality's decision is that it expressed their mistrust of OSHA, their belief that it had overregulated in the case of benzene, and their fear of the overregulation it could cause in the future. If more justices had believed that OSHA was doing a reasonable job of balancing costs and benefits, they would not have invented the "significant risk" doctrine and would not have overturned the benzene standard. Thus, if industry witnesses had testified that their risk assessments showed that the standard would cost $200,000 per cancer death prevented instead of the $200 million that they actually claimed, it is hard to believe that the justices would have been so upset by OSHA's refusal to conduct its own assessment. That refusal was perceived by the judges as a symbol of its resistance to a more balanced approach.

The passage that best expresses their fear of overregulation states:

In the absence of a clear mandate in the Act, it is unreasonable to assume that Congress intended to give the Secretary the unprecedented power over American industry that would result from the Government's view of Sections 3(8) and 6(b)(5), coupled with OSHA's cancer policy. Expert testimony that a substance is probably a human carcinogen ... would justify the conclusion that the substance poses some risk of serious harm no matter how minute the exposure and no matter how many experts testified that they regarded the risk as insignificant. That conclusion would in turn justify pervasive regulation limited only by the constraint of feasibility. In light of the fact that there are literally thousands of substances used in the workplace that have been identified as carcinogens or suspected carcinogens, the Government's theory would give OSHA power to impose enormous costs that might produce little, if any, discernible benefit.[39]

At that point, the opinion adds in a footnote that "OSHA's proposed cancer policy indicates that this possibility is not merely hypothetical." In his concurring opinion, Chief Justice Burger concluded: "When the administrative record reveals only scant or minimal risk of material health impairment, responsible administration calls for avoidance of extravagant, comprehensive regulation." Justice Powell's concurring opinion went beyond the plurality to argue that "an occupational health standard is neither 'reasonably necessary' nor 'feasible,' as required by statute, if it calls for expenditures wholly disproportionate to the expected health and safety benefits."

Thus the basis for the benzene decision was concern about overregulation, and a chief effect has been to create an obstacle to efforts to overcome underregulation. The plurality's requirement (borrowed from tort law) that OSHA show that it is "more likely than not" that a risk is "significant" will make it more difficult to regulate hazards where the evidence is only suggestive. The Fifth Circuit has used this language to attack the use of upper 95 percent confidence intervals for risk assessments, even though this may be the sort of "conservative assumption" sanctioned in the benzene decision. After all, if the probability is only 1 in 20 that the risk is that high, then it is obviously *less* likely than not, not more.[40]

The future impact of the "more likely than not" language is hard to assess. So far, courts other than the Fifth Circuit have shown considerable tolerance for agencies' attempts to demonstrate significant risks.[41] At OSHA the benzene decision did have the virtue of forcing the agency to think about the quantitative impact of its standards. In particular, in cases where human evidence for calculating risks has been inadequate, OSHA has had to take the quantitative implications of bioassay data more seriously.[42]

As the benzene decision indicates, it is not always easy to distinguish whether criticisms of procedures mask differences on substance. Some judges feel strongly enough about procedures to hang a reversal on them. Others, who dislike the substance of the agency's decision, will feel more comfortable with overturning it if there are good procedural grounds on which to act. It would be foolish of OSHA to give critics an easy opening; therefore it will try to close the procedural loopholes. That response reduces the likelihood of purely procedural criticisms; however, it still allows judges who are persuaded that OSHA has made the wrong decision to claim that it has failed to amass "substantial evidence" in support of it.

One of OSHA's directors of health standards stated: "Uncertainty about the health effects is usually the chief cause of concern about whether the standard will hold up in court and that makes it a leading source of delay." We saw in chapter 4 that hazards were more likely to be addressed if there was evidence of human illness. This is true despite the widely shared assumption among regulators that chemicals that had been shown to cause cancer in animals should be considered *for policy purposes* to be carcinogenic in humans. Courts have even upheld the reasonableness of this presumption in several cases. Yet it is striking that OSHA has yet to set a new PEL for any chemical for which human evidence was not present. The same is true for the EPA in its choice of the eight substances addressed as hazardous air pollutants under section 112 of the Clean Air Act, which has even more precautionary language than the OSH Act. The absence of human evidence does reduce the confidence with which agency staff approach the task of convincing judges to accept arguments to limit exposures.

OSHA leaders hesitate about issuing standards for the same reason that graduate students postpone taking their comprehensive exams: They aren't sure that they will pass. What are the costs to the agency of having a rule overturned? First, it will deflate the morale of the staff, who will view the decision as a rebuke to either their mission or their competence. Second, resources will be wasted, although some of the work may be recycled if a new rule-making effort is launched. Third, protection for workers is delayed. Fourth, a reversal will undermine the agency's autonomy by weakening its ability to fend off political attacks. If the rebuke is to the agency's competence, its ability to maintain autonomy by claiming expertise is jeopardized. If the court holds that the agency has strayed from congressional objectives, then its ability to maintain autonomy by claiming to uphold a special mandate is endangered.

Postponing a proposal or final action may make it easier to produce a standard with fewer chinks; in some cases it may allow new evidence to be considered. But postponement also entails costs. It delays worker protection and may eat away at staff morale. It can expose the agency to political attack for nonfeasance, for failure to carry out its protective mission. And, as I discuss later, it also can subject it to legal attack for rule making "unreasonably delayed" in violation of the Administrative Procedure Act. In the absence of clear legal guidance about the degree of evidence that is necessary and sufficient to sustain a standard, agency officials must weigh the trade-offs.

One reason that Assistant Secretary Bingham was able to generate a relatively large number of standards was that she was willing to run higher risks of losing than her predecessors. When she took office, her first question to Health Standards Director Grover Wrenn was how long it would take to get an ETS for benzene. Wrenn replied that it would take a month, but he suggested that the normal NPRM process be used instead of an ETS because there was no new evidence. The solicitor's office gave her the same response. She responded that she would get new evidence and she persuaded organized labor to prod the head of NIOSH to write her a formal letter reporting the preliminary results of a study his agency was sponsoring.[43] Despite the opposition of the solicitor's office, she issued an ETS (which was overturned in the courts).

It is possible that Bingham's apparent willingness to take risks reflected her overconfidence that the courts would sustain her. As we saw, once the agency actually lost in the benzene decision, a new caution crept back into rule making.

Other Influences on the Pace of Standard Setting

Suppose that the Supreme Court suddenly reversed itself on the benzene and cotton dust decisions, deleting the requirement that OSHA demonstrate "significant risk" and granting the agency latitude to balance costs and benefits. The agency would be able to proceed more expeditiously, yet several forces would continue to constrain rule making. One is the norm of due process, which is widely shared in American political culture. As Grover Wrenn commented: "When you affect industry or workers in major ways, it's awfully hard to avoid giving them time to respond and make their cases."[44] Congress, as well as the courts, plays an important role in enforcing this norm. Although large firms and major trade associations employ staff who have developed relations with their counterparts at OSHA, Congress plays an important role in facilitating contacts for firms whose involvement in the regulatory process is more sporadic.

In addition, the executive branch has played an increasingly important role in imposing analytical requirements on regulatory agencies. Under President Nixon, a Quality of Life review program was set up in 1971 within the OMB to examine rules from the newly established EPA, whose activities were already beginning to unsettle business. The exact locus of authority for final decisions remained somewhat murky, at least until 1973 when Nixon acceded to EPA chief William Ruckelshaus's threat to quit unless his authority was acknowledged.[45] Under President Ford, an executive order required all executive branch agencies to issue "inflationary impact statements" for their major rules. Although ostensibly addressed to the rule's impact on the overall price level, the first step in these analyses was to estimate the costs of compliance. The newly formed Council on Wage and Price Stability (COWPS) undertook to review these statements and began a practice of issuing formal comments to be placed in the rule-making record.

President Carter substituted a new executive order, which required agencies not only to estimate costs but also to analyze alternative regulatory options and to either choose the most cost-effective option or to explain why they did not. In addition, Carter established the Regulatory Analysis Review Group (RARG). It included key White House officials as well as cabinet members and was intended to provide more clout to the review of selected agency rules. Again the issue of how disagreements between an agency and the reviewers would be resolved remained fuzzy. Charles Schultze, chairman of the Council of Economic Advisers and head of RARG, urged the president to overturn OSHA's cotton dust standard, but the secretary of labor ultimately convinced the president to accept it.

A minor debate rages between those who think that the review process before 1981 led to no change in the content of regulations and those who think it led to a small change. But few dispute that the requirements led agencies to upgrade the quality of their analytic staffs in order to parry the thrusts of the reviewers. In addition, the review process added a small amount to the time required to issue standards. The increase was small because the White House requirement usually overlapped those of the statutes and the courts.

The review process initiated by President Reagan's Executive Order 12291 not only gave the OMB more power to affect the content of rules but also allowed it to hold up rules for significant periods both before the NPRM and before issuance of the final rule. James C. Miller, III, the chief of OMB's regulatory program, predicted in early 1981 that "OSHA will issue some new regulations in the next four years, but mainly it will be working on digesting what it has already bitten off rather than biting off more."[46] There is no doubt that many major standards were held up by the OMB. (See my later discussion in chapter 6 on priority setting in the Reagan administration.) The OSHA hazard communications proposal submitted by Assistant Secretary Auchter was held there for six months. The proposal to regulate ethylene oxide was held there for over a year. In a review of the experience across agencies, the General Accounting Office (GAO) found that thirty of the rules frozen by the OMB in January 1981 were still on ice in April 1982. In 1981 the OMB returned forty-five new rules to agencies for major revisions, and the GAO report observed that "revisions of the regulation and/or analysis by the agency in response to OMB comments may be quite time-consuming" and noted that many agency personnel reported that internal reviews have "become more time-consuming because of the anticipated OMB review."[47]

Attempts to Overcome the Slow Pace

OSHA officials have been well aware of the torpid pace of health standard setting. In a report he issued as he left office in early 1977, Assistant Secretary Morton Corn observed:

With the resources currently planned for the Health Standards directorate of OSHA, I estimate that a productivity rate of 15 to 20 health standards promulgated per year is a noble ambition in 1978 or 1979. Obviously, there are thousands of chemicals in the work environment and this rate of productivity will not adequately address the problem.... The above considerations lead to the conclusion that continued development of standards for individual chemical agents is a self-limiting developmental process. The Agency must seek another way of addressing chemical hazards in the work environment.[48]

Corn's estimate proved to be far too optimistic, but the mistake reinforces the argument for seeking alternative approaches.

The standard on "14 Carcinogens" was the first attempt to catch up.[49] It started with an AFL-CIO visit to the secretary of labor requesting more action on carcinogens. OSHA had not adopted PELs for a group of carcinogens that had been listed in the appendix to the ACGIH list of exposure limits. ACGIH had not assigned exposure limits to these chemicals. OSHA asked NIOSH for information about them. Following a petition from Ralph Nader's Health Research Group and from the Oil, Chemical, and Atomic Workers Union in January 1973 and a lawsuit in April, OSHA issued an ETS for fourteen chemicals in May. The list included six rarely used substances linked to human cancers and eight slightly more common ones for which only animal evidence existed. As we saw, the Fifth Circuit of Appeals overturned the ETS because of an inadequate statement of the reasons for issuing it. The final standard issued in January 1974, which relied on requirements for workplace practices rather than on setting PELs, was overturned on procedural grounds with respect to two of the fourteen chemicals but upheld for the rest. Reflecting on this feat of aggregated rule making, Health Standards Director Grover Wrenn later observed that there was no way that this procedure would have been accepted by the judicial standards of the late 1970s.[50]

The first comprehensive effort to address the slow pace of rule making was the Standards Completion Project (SCP), a staff initiative announced in early 1974. The SCP would not have altered PELs, but it would have added requirements for air monitoring, medical exams, and labeling to each of the PELs that existed. However, OSHA did propose to establish an "action level" equal to half of the PEL for each chemical. Whenever exposures exceeded that action level, the various requirements for monitoring, medical testing, and the like would be invoked. Their exact nature would depend on the severity of the exposure and the particular chemical.

OSHA justified the project as an attempt to make employers more aware of the hazards in the workplace and to ensure that they conveyed that information to workers. In addition, as Grover Wrenn explained: "Our resources are limited, and setting an exposure limit is a very time-consuming process."[51]

OSHA planned to promulgate groups of new standards every two months, completing the 400 hazards in about two years. In fact, it proposed standards for one group of six chemicals in May 1975 and another group of eleven in October 1975. None of those standards was ever promulgated, and no other standards of that type were proposed. Although not formally terminated, the Standards Completion Project was placed on the back burner, and by late 1976 it had evaporated.

The disappearance of the SCP can be attributed partly to the realization that the task was herculean. The size of the task was, in turn, largely a function of the need to amass evidence to ward off legal challenges. It became clear that they would be forthcoming. Exposure monitoring and medical exams can be costly. Industry protested that the action levels that triggered these requirements should not be uniformly set at half the PEL. For less toxic substances they argued that the action level and the PEL should be the same.[52]

The second major reason for the atrophy of the SCP was the absence of any major constituency outside of the agency for whom the SCP was a high priority. Finally, staff also realized that there were probably more efficient methods for achieving the objectives of requiring more monitoring and medical exams.

By 1976, the agency was, in Corn's words, "searching . . . for so-called generic standards. For example, standards would be issued for labeling of compounds, for medical surveillance of employees, and for monitoring the work environment." He cited a labeling proposal that was "on the verge of appearing in the *Federal Register*" and an "imminent proposal" for identification, classification, and regulation of carcinogens.[53] Even these generic rules proved difficult to produce. The "imminent" carcinogen proposal appeared twenty months later. The final carcinogen rule appeared over two years after that. And although an Advance NPRM for chemical labeling appeared that month, it took four more years for OSHA to issue the NPRM itself. No final rule was issued during the Carter administration. Such optimism, however, has not been confined to Corn or to generic proposals.

A recommendation for a chemical labeling rule had appeared in a 1974 NIOSH criteria document and was seconded the following year by the OSHA Advisory Committee on Hazardous Materials Labeling. A major push came from the House Committee on Government Operations, which held hearings on the idea in 1976 and 1977 and recommended that OSHA take action. Four years passed between the Advance NPRM in January 1977 and the proposal in January 1981.

Several factors help to explain the four-year delay between the issuance of the Advance NPRM and the issuance of the NPRM in January 1981. First, OSHA did not accord this standard as high a priority as it gives to standards on specific hazards; with its limited resources, low priority meant little action. Second, industry insisted on protection for trade secrets and warned against what it viewed as unduly alarmist warning labels. OSHA had to take these views into account and to respond to the issues they raised. Third, even in the absence of clear opposition, figuring out how to mesh a new labeling system with existing public (for example, Department of Transportation) and private labeling systems is difficult and time-consuming. The NPRM was issued just in time to be withdrawn by the Reagan administration, which issued its own final rule in January 1983.

A second generic rule also focused on improving the flow of information to workers, this time by ensuring them access to the results of medical exams and workplace air monitoring. Observing that "the denial of direct, unrestricted employee access to exposure and medical information is commonplace, if not the universal practice of industry," OSHA issued a proposal in 1978 and a final rule in 1980 to rectify that practice.[54] This standard was upheld in court, although in 1982 the Reagan administration proposed to modify it.

The most controversial generic rule has undoubtedly been the carcinogen rule. Work on it began in early 1976, with most of the responsibility shouldered by Anson Keller, an attorney who had been Associate General Counsel for Pesticides at the EPA and who had been brought to OSHA by Labor Secretary John Dunlop to work on health standards.

At the EPA's pesticide program Keller had been involved in the first major efforts to distill a set of "cancer principles" to guide regulators. Most of the early standards at OSHA also addressed carcinogenic hazards and raised a recurring set of questions: Was there a no-effect threshold? Should the development of nonmalignant tumors in a bioassay be treated the same as malignant tumors? Should different species, organs, or routes of administration of the toxic material be treated as less valid than others in interpreting evidence of carcinogenicity? Seeing the same issues continually refought fueled Keller's belief that the EPA approach could be fruitfully applied and extended at OSHA. Assistant Secretary Corn supported him and, later, Health Standards Director Grover Wrenn worked closely with him on the elaboration of the policy.

The Cancer Policy proposal appeared in the *Federal Register* in October 1977. It became probably the most massive rule-making procedure that has taken place in the health and safety field. Scores of cancer authorities wrote treatises on the issues it raised, piling up a printed record of a quarter of a million pages. The proposal also spawned a new organization: The American Industrial Health Council (AIHC) was formed by the chemical industry to build a broader critique of OSHA's regulatory strategy. OSHA issued the final regulation in January 1980 with an explanation that occupied just under 300 pages in the *Federal Register*. Compared to the proposal, the final regulation made some concessions to industry complaints about the rigidity of the rule, but few of these represented changes in the heart of the policy.[55]

The original purpose of the Cancer Policy was to speed up the rule-making process. Because disagreement about health effects was believed to be a central cause of delay, the policy called for creating presumptions about the interpretation of health data. OSHA explicitly acknowledged that the presumptions would all err on the side of identifying noncarcinogens as carcinogens, rather than by letting carcinogens slip through. Although other federal regulatory agencies had drafted or were drafting their own cancer principles, OSHA's effort stood out for the boldness with which it announced and implemented this protective stance. Most of the document elaborated OSHA's justification for its presumptions. The following two examples give the flavor of these presumptions:

1. Epidemiological studies that failed to show harmful effects would be ignored unless

(i) the epidemiologic study involved at least 20 years' exposure of a group of subjects to the substance and at least 30 years' observation of the subjects after initial exposure; (ii) documented reasons are provided for predicting the site(s) at which the substance would induce cancer if it were carcinogenic in humans; and (iii) the group of exposed subjects was large enough for an increase in cancer incidence of 50% above that in unexposed controls to have been detected at any of the predicted sites.[56]

In contrast, studies that did show harmful effects could be considered without meeting these criteria. Extremely few epidemiological studies can meet these criteria.

2. The argument that the doses administered to test animals were so high that inferences about carcinogenicity were unjustified would be considered only if

(i) documented evidence is presented to show that the substance in question is metabolized by the experimental animal species exposed at the dose levels used in the bioassay(s) to metabolic products which include one or more that are not produced in the same species at lower doses; (ii) documented evidence is presented to show that the metabolite(s) produced only at high doses in the experimental animal are the ultimate carcinogen(s) and that the metabolites produced at low doses are not also carcinogenic; and (iii) documented evidence is presented to show that the metabolite(s) produced only at high doses in the experimental animals are not produced in humans exposed to low doses.[57]

It is probably fair to say that no one has this type of information.

The policy itself called for setting up two categories of potential carcinogens. Category I would include all those chemicals that caused tumors or reduced the latency period (at sites other than the site of administration) in humans, in a single mammalian species with concordant evidence, or in a single mammalian species without concordant evidence but where the secretary judged the evidence sufficient. Concordant evidence included independent results in the same or another species, positive evidence in a short-term test, or tumors at the site of injection. Category II potential carcinogens would include those chemicals that meet the Category I criteria, except that the evidence is only "suggestive," or those chemicals for which there is evidence in only a single mammalian species without concordance.[58] These criteria appear to give wide leeway to put hazards in

Category I. Basically, all that is needed is one well-conducted bioassay that finds positive results. OSHA can judge that conflicting bioassay results as well as epidemiological evidence are outweighed by the positive finding. If OSHA wanted to have "concordant" evidence, they could turn to the battery of short-term tests.

The act of labeling a substance as a carcinogen or a noncarcinogen became extremely significant in the Cancer Policy because it did not recognize the relevance of either levels of carcinogenic potency (that is, how harmful exposure to it is) or the benefits of the substance. Despite the use of two categories, the policy choice was basically dichotomous; either a substance was a probable carcinogen or it wasn't. For Category I carcinogens OSHA would establish a PEL at the "lowest feasible level." If a suitable substitute existed, the carcinogen would be banned. Category II carcinogens would be regulated as "appropriate and consistent with the statutory requirements" on a case-by-case basis. However, OSHA's earlier history of regulation implies that Category II carcinogens would also be regulated to the "lowest feasible level."

We can contrast this dichotomous policy framework with one in which the labeling of a substance as "carcinogenic," by itself, has no specific regulatory implications; the regulatory action would depend instead on weighing the harm and benefits of reducing exposures.

The implementation of the Cancer Policy would have begun with the preparation of a "candidate list" from which a "priority list" of ten substances would be chosen for Category I and ten substances for Category II. The policy was crammed with "action-forcing" provisions with deadlines for action. Perhaps most important, to facilitate OSHA's meeting the test required for an ETS, the policy stipulated that exposure to any Category I carcinogen "constitutes a 'grave danger' within the meaning of section 6(c) of the Act." [59] Despite these provisions, the policy still gave OSHA great leeway on the basic question of whether to propose to issue a standard at all.

The central question for my purposes is whether implementation of the Cancer Policy would indeed increase the number of hazards for which new standards are set. Although some of the key provisions of the policy were stayed by the Reagan administration, its implementation remains an option for OSHA.

In the preamble to the 1980 policy, the agency discussed why it would speed the pace of standard setting. For its previous rules on carcinogens, OSHA calculated how much time had elapsed between the first notice about the hazard in the *Federal Register* and the completion of judicial review of the resulting standard.[60] Although for four of the seven standards court reviews were still pending, the average duration had already reached thirty-eight months. What OSHA failed to say, however, was that just over half of that period occurred *after* the promulgation of the standard; the average time until promulgation was nineteen months, with judicial review accounting for the rest. Thus nineteen months is the upper bound of any reduction as a result of speeding up the promulgation of standards. Would the deadlines stated in the policy be of much help?

Although OSHA claimed that "the periodic announcement of regulatory priorities and advance notice of identification and classification criteria will enable all participants in the regulatory process . . . to act with greater efficiency and certainty in framing the truly critical issues," the chief mechanism reducing the length of proceedings would be the limitation on the issues that could be raised.[61]

Yet, although the Cancer Policy might convince firms of the futility of, for example, trying to convince OSHA to consider nonpositive bioassay results or to reject positive test results involving high doses, its effects on the length of the proceeding would be constrained by two factors: First, many other important issues would remain to be dealt with, and, second, even if OSHA presumes that certain issues are closed, the courts may not.

What are the main issues that the Cancer Policy would leave open for consideration? The first is whether the evidence indicates that a particular substance should be classified as either a Category I or Category II potential carcinogen. This includes a review of whether the relevant scientific studies are reliable. A second issue concerns whether any employer challenges to the OSHA presumptions meet the criteria OSHA established for considering them and whether any petitions to consider "substantial new issues" should be granted. A third issue is the determination of the "lowest feasible level" of exposure. A fourth issue is whether suitable substitutes for Category I hazards exist, triggering the requirement that no exposures be allowed. A fifth issue is whether the provisions of the model standards are appropriate in the particular case. In addition, the Supreme Court's benzene decision led to a 1980 amendment to the Cancer Policy, requiring that a determination that the substance posed a "significant risk" precede any regulatory action. Finally, it is important to note that the agency still had to address any issues required by executive orders, including, of course, the analysis of regulatory alternatives.

The reaction of the courts to the Cancer Policy provides the second possible source of constraint on faster standard setting. For the most part, courts have been willing to defer to regulatory agencies' interpretation of the data on health effects. In a major 1978 case involving the EPA, the D.C. Circuit Court of Appeals approved the agency's regulation of slightly chlorinated PCBs on the basis of what was known about more highly chlorinated PCBs. The court observed that "the number of toxic substances subject to regulation seems very large. Regulation of many substances could well be extremely difficult if EPA were precluded from drawing inferences from available data on well-known, related substances."[62] Yet there is a broad leap from this comparison of PCB compounds, cited by OSHA in defense of the Cancer Policy, to its own sweeping policy. In the Supreme Court's decision overturning OSHA's benzene standard, Justice Stevens voiced the judicial distaste for agency policies that rely only on general assumptions even though evidence on the hazard in question is available. Foreclosing issues in this way runs counter to a fundamental theme of modern administrative law, which stresses the value of open and full discussion of all the evidence and all the reasons for agency actions. A particular legal concern about the Cancer Policy is whether its presumptions and the resulting decisions to ignore evidence would run afoul of the act's requirement that standards be set "on the basis of the best available evidence."

If OSHA or its lawyers shared my assessment of these prospects, they would be well advised to foreclose issues sparingly and to give employers the benefit of the doubt as to whether the particular case raised issues that deserved special attention. In any event, firms will still have an incentive to try to raise as many issues as possible so that they will be in the record and thus can be used as the basis of a legal challenge to the standard. And so long as the expected costs of complying with standards seem onerous, firms will still have an incentive to do everything in their power to delay them. This includes adding issues to the record or trying to explore a given set of issues in more depth. In addition, it includes challenging the standards. As we saw, these challenges are the direct cause of at least half of the time taken to complete a rule and the indirect cause of much more (because of the burden they place on the agency to nail down its case).

I have presented reasons why we should be skeptical about the effect that implementation of the Cancer Policy would have on the pace of rule making and the number of hazards addressed. Further evidence is presented later, when I review the EPA's experience with section 112 of the Clean Air Act, which is another quintessential action-forcing program that has failed to force action.

I do think that the Cancer Policy's establishment of presumptions would have *some* effect, but I would be very surprised if it reduced the time or resources required for setting a standard by more than 10 or 20 percent. Much of what the Cancer Policy aspired to could have been achieved with less fuss by adroit use of a word processor to repeat the language from earlier standards. This analysis of the Cancer Policy contrasts sharply with the usual assumption that its implementation would cause a dramatic upsurge in rule making, an assumption that aroused either enthusiastic approval or condemnation, depending on the assessment of how appropriately OSHA set standards.[63] An example of this assumption was the Regulatory Analysis Review Group's conclusion that "a reasonable starting reference point for an estimate of the policy's cost impact" was a scenario that envisioned 1,970 substances regulated under the Cancer Policy and an estimated cost of $20 billion annually.[64]

Looking back in 1983, the chief authors of the Cancer Policy, Anson Keller and Grover Wrenn, felt much less confidence than they did when the proposal appeared in 1977 that it would significantly speed up the process.[65] Even by the time the final standard was issued in 1980, a different motivation had become prominent: to bind future leaders to the policies for regulating carcinogens that OSHA had developed. The success of that goal remains uncertain. One long-standing requirement of the courts is that agencies adhere to their own procedures; however, it is unclear how strictly courts would apply this test to the many provisions in the policy. In addition, of course, the Cancer Policy is a standard that future leaders can alter, although they may face some serious political and legal obstacles. In early 1981 the Reagan administration stayed the provisions that called for setting up candidate lists and priority lists. OSHA chief Thorne Auchter's plan to rescind the policy altogether came untracked in 1983 when he decided, in the words of one of his advisers, that "Congress would have my head if I did that." Thus the Cancer Policy is still being reconsidered. It may help to bind future leaders. It certainly constituted a major exercise in intellectual definition for OSHA's leaders. But it would not have more than a modest impact on the number of standards issued.

Finally, it is important to understand that the most common criticism levied at the Cancer Policy—that it is inflexible and tends to "freeze science"—is neither entirely fair nor, by itself, the heart of the problem. It is true that the Cancer Policy, even in its 1980 version, explicitly rejects what seems like the most reasonable approach, namely, to sift and weigh *all* the relevant evidence. However, it is entirely reasonable for a regulatory agency to adopt presumptions that weight some pieces of evidence more heavily than others. OSHA should be free to decide that it cares more about reducing false negatives than about reducing false positives. The problem arises when this policy is joined with one that also regulates strictly.[66] The result is a Delaney clause–type program, in which a sensitive trigger (a loosely interpreted finding of carcinogencity) automatically trips an inflexible and strict regulatory mechanism (a ban or adoption of the lowest feasible level).

The Cancer Policy attempted to solve the underregulation problem by tinkering with administrative procedures. Yet OSHA's regulation of carcinogens has drawn fire because it is viewed by powerful and articulate sectors of the population as costly and inefficient. Given that perception, it was naive to believe that an effort to speed up the pace of *that manner* of regulation would not generate opposition in the White House, Congress, and the courts. Under those conditions, speedy rule making—always at risk of becoming an oxymoron—is not possible.

Industry Initiatives to Facilitate Standard Setting

In early 1983 industry joined the campaign to speed up the pace of rule making. The Synthetic Organic Chemical Manufacturers Association (SOCMA) proposed to OSHA that it forgo attempts to develop elaborate standards that deal with monitoring, warning signs, protective equipment, and medical exams. Instead, it should simply modify the PEL for substances it already regulated or propose new ones. Although OSHA would still face the need to conduct the usual set of analyses on the new PEL, SOCMA predicted that

by focusing primarily on the PEL requirement, OSHA could conduct the rulemaking more efficiently. This will also mean that employees could receive the benefits of reduced permissible exposures more expeditiously than would otherwise be possible, and employers could retain the flexibility they need to protect employees in the most cost-effective manner.[67]

This approach would "reduce the time for issuance of the modified standard, lessen the chances of judicial review, and facilitate compliance, thus providing protection for employees sooner and improving OSHA's effectiveness." SOCMA emphasized that this proposal would "permit employers to use the full arsenal of health protection devices and practices without mandating any one of them."[68]

The device that SOCMA had most clearly in mind was respirators. Many industry groups have continually criticized OSHA for its insistence that compliance with the PELs be achieved by engineering controls, not by the use of personal protective devices such as respirators. In its compliance manual OSHA stipulates that engineering controls must be used by each firm unless they are not "feasible." Thus the issue of feasibility arises in two contexts. In its handful of new health standards, OSHA has to show that the PEL it has chosen is "feasible." In addition, in enforcing both those standards and the 400 other PELs it adopted in 1971, OSHA must show that compliance through engineering controls is feasible in each particular case.

Companies that are cited for failure to comply with the PEL by engineering controls have often appealed to the Occupational Safety and Health Review Commission, an independent agency established by the OSH Act, and, ultimately, to the courts. The commission and the courts have swung to and fro on whether this feasibility test for enforcing standards requires OSHA to weigh the costs and benefits. SOCMA urged OSHA to declare that it did or else to drop the engineering requirement altogether.

The SOCMA proposal again shows the trade-off between stringency and extensiveness. Industry would go along more easily with lower PELs if OSHA would allow the use of less costly methods to comply with them. OSHA leaders received the SOCMA proposal with mild interest. Some believed that the sections of the OSH Act that dealt with new standards, which mandate provisions for monitoring and medical exams "as appropriate," would not permit the stripped-down approach to standard setting that SOCMA advocated. (Further discussion of the reasons underlying OSHA's commitment to engineering controls appears in chapter 7.)

Overregulation and Underregulation outside the Workplace

As we saw in chapter 1, the pattern of strict but infrequent standards characterizes other programs in addition to OSHA. Does the explanation for that pattern in those programs also indicate that strictness is a major reason for the lack of extensiveness?

The program whose mission most resembles OSHA's health program is the regulation of hazardous air pollutants by the EPA. The same types of hazards that OSHA is supposed to control in the workplace, the EPA is supposed to control in the air outside. The 1970 Clean Air Act (CAA), in addition to mandating the establishment of ambient air standards for five major pollutants (including sulfur dioxide, carbon monoxide, and hydrocarbons), also provided (in section 112) for the regulation of pollutants for which no ambient air standard is applicable and which "causes or contributes to . . . an increase in mortality or an increase in serious irreversible, or incapacitating reversible illness."

From 1970 through 1984 only five hazards were regulated under section

112 (asbestos, vinyl chloride, beryllium, mercury, and some uses of benzene). In every case the rules were issued under either court order or the threat of court order. An understanding of the reasons for this meager and begrudged output must begin with a review of rule-making procedures.[69]

The first step in the regulatory process is the listing of a pollutant as hazardous. Within 180 days, the EPA must propose emission standards for polluting sources. It must hold hearings within another 30 days and issue a final rule within 180 days of the proposal unless it finds "on the basis of the information presented at the hearings, that such pollutant clearly is not a hazardous air pollutant." Finally, the administrator must set the emissions standards "at the level which in his judgment provides an ample margin of safety to protect the public health from such hazardous air pollutant."

Thus we have the perfect picture of strict, agency-forcing regulation. Once a hazard is "listed," it is close to legally impossible for the EPA to avoid regulating because it is impossible to prove a negative—that it is *not* a hazardous air pollutant. The timetables would seem to speed the regulation inexorably down the chute into the *Federal Register*. The requirement to protect the public health "with an ample margin of safety," combined with the absence of any mention of concern with costs, makes the protective goal perfectly clear.

By now the results are also clear. Because the act of listing a pollutant as hazardous creates a nondiscretionary duty to regulate, the EPA has been wary about taking that step. Its health assessment documents have taken one to two years to prepare, not counting the three to six months for review by the EPA Science Advisory Board. Graham explains:

In light of the important consequences of the listing decision, the lack of direction from Congress, and the likely opposition from the affected industries, the EPA has attempted to protect itself from judicial reversal by including progressively more sophisticated and comprehensive analyses in its health assessment documentation.[70]

The timetables have generally been ignored because they are impossible to meet. The chief result of their presence has been to facilitate lawsuits by environmental groups.

Most important, because of the presumption that there is no risk-free level of exposure to carcinogens, the protection of public health with "an ample margin of safety" would mean a requirement of zero emissions, which would often require banning a chemical altogether. Despite its mandate to ignore costs, the EPA has not been willing to ignore them or to adopt such drastic measures. Thus, faced by a decision to regulate vinyl chloride in 1974 and "hesitant either to flout the literal meaning of section

112 or to set a standard effectively closing the [vinyl chloride, polyvinyl chloride] and related industries, EPA delayed setting any standard for [vinyl chloride] emissions until October 1976."[71] That standard did consider economic factors and was subject to an Environmental Defense Fund lawsuit.

Both Graham and environmental attorney David Doniger agree that the strict mandate of section 112 has impeded the pace of regulation.[72] A veteran EPA employee, Walter Barber, chief of the Office of Air Quality Planning and Standards, concurred in testimony before Congress in 1981:

While low-cost controls with the potential to reduce emissions and exposure by fifty to ninety percent may be available, it is not clear that they would meet the statutory test of "ample margin of safety" under section 112. On the other hand, uncertainty in the health and exposure data make[s] more stringent and more costly controls less justifiable. The ability to balance the magnitude and uncertainty of health risk with the cost and impact of control techniques is a prerequisite to any accelerated decisionmaking under the statute.[73]

Although environmentalists have been reluctant to acknowledge that less strict regulation is a prerequisite for accelerated rule making and that the latter may be a by-product of the former, they have been willing to consider explicit trade-offs. David Doniger reports that at 1978 hearings on whether to adopt a zero-emissions goal as general policy, an Environmental Defense Fund attorney indicated that his group would concede that some balancing should be allowed, in exchange for a substantial increase in the number of substances that the EPA would regulate.[74]

Environmentalists' chief goal for the program has been to have Congress commit the EPA or the agency commit itself to issuing more regulations. In the 1977 Clean Air Act Amendments, they succeeded in having Congress mandate the administrator to decide within one year whether radionuclides, arsenic, cadmium, and polycyclic organics were "hazardous" under the meaning of section 112. Strictly speaking, they definitely do fit the criterion. However, the Carter administration found a way to avoid even listing cadmium and the organics and issued final regulations for none of the four. During the Reagan administration regulations were proposed under court order for radionuclides and arsenic. Later, the radionuclide proposal was withdrawn by the agency on the grounds that the risks posed by exposures were not "significant," a reading into section 112 of the Supreme Court's decision on the OSHA benzene standard.[75]

The failure to employ section 112 is not the fault of any one administration; Carter's team as well as Reagan's eschewed it. Nor is it the fault of foot-dragging bureaucrats. Risk-regulation statutes are designed to encourage strict, sometimes unreasonable rules. But when you tell people to do something totally unreasonable, they are likely to try to find ways to avoid doing it. Or, if they do not, other political institutions will throw up barriers. The congressional strategy of ordering the EPA to list a large number of hazards as a first step toward producing a large number of rules seems doomed to failure. Forcing more proposals into the front end of the current regulatory machinery will not necessarily ensure that more will emerge as finished products.

Conclusions

The main theme of this chapter is that one important reason that so few standards have been set is that agencies try to set them strictly. Greater strictness increases the total cost of regulation and increases the cost per death prevented. The higher cost of regulation increases the incentive of firms to try to defeat or delay it. In addition, the perception that the cost is unreasonably high makes some policymakers more concerned about the economic implications and more sympathetic to industry objections. Agency officials are well aware of industry opposition and sometimes have made efforts to allay it. But except in the first years of the Reagan presidency, they have responded primarily to the pressures of labor and environmental interest groups, to their congressional supporters, to activist judges, and to the media and a public that are concerned about risks to health—as well as to their own policy views. Thus rule making on these hazards tends to be characterized by major conflict. The conflict is in large part rooted in American history and tradition that have, in turn, fostered adversarial institutions.[76] Yet a *proximate* determinant of the degree of conflict is the strictness of the standards.

Conflict between labor and industry goals provides the underlying basis for the slow pace of standard setting. In collective bargaining the two parties have an incentive to compromise their differences in the interests of reaching an agreement. Delays in reaching agreement are costly to both. But delay in setting standards is often a boon to industry, although in some cases the uncertainties attendant on those delays lead firms to seek an early resolution.

The consequences of conflict for the pace of regulation depend on particular features of the regulatory program and the hazards that it was devised to address. Because OSHA runs a standard-setting program, unless it takes action, firms have great legal freedom to determine the level of hazards in the workplace. In developing a standard, OSHA bears the burden of proof of showing that new controls are warranted. That burden includes convincing courts that the exposures constitute a "significant risk," that the proposed controls are "feasible," and that the agency has amassed "substantial evidence" for all the measures that it will require. It also includes convincing White House reviewers that the standard is reasonable, or else exerting enough pressure on the reviewers to make the political costs of holding back a standard too great to justify. Even if the costs and effects of exposure reductions were certain, people would disagree about whether they were worthwhile. But, in fact, they are often quintessentially uncertain. Faced by uncertainty and unclear guidelines from Congress or the courts about the degree of evidence that is sufficient, agencies often lack confidence that they can meet the burden of proof that will be demanded. (For a more systematic review of the mechanisms though which strictness retards the pace, see appendix F.)

Implications for Reform

How could the pace of standard setting be increased? First, if more staff and better quality staff could be hired, OSHA could work on more standards at any one time. Even if the time required for each standard did not change, more standards could be produced. Second, if OSHA had to carry out fewer procedural requirements (for example, regulatory analyses, quantitative risk analyses, public hearings), then the time required for each standard could be reduced somewhat.

But these two changes do not get to the heart of the problem. The fundamental factor slowing the pace of regulation is the agency's recognition that it does not have the arguments to convince the powerful outsiders who determine whether the individual rules are implemented and whether the agency and its leaders are attacked or praised. In general, the stricter the standards, the more difficult it is to make convincing arguments that they are worthwhile.

Because OSHA is constrained to regulate strictly, the actual standard of proof that it must meet is burdensome. Although such documents as its Cancer Policy espouse a low standard of proof—allowing PELs to be lowered essentially on the basis of a single bioassay—in practice OSHA has not established new PELs on that basis.

The fundamental reform that would clear the way for a faster pace of standard setting is a lower standard of proof, construed broadly to include the reviews of all the influential outsiders, not just the courts. But a lower standard of proof is not desirable if the result would be a larger number of unreasonably strict standards. This was the fear expressed by the plurality in the Supreme Court's benzene decision. More resources for standard setting and a reduction in procedural requirements could legitimately be opposed for the same reason.

Support for curing underregulation depends on creating a sense of trust that the broader scope of regulation will be exercised reasonably. In chapters 7 and 9 I return to measures that might create that assurance: the regulatory budget, which could strengthen agency incentives to issues more cost-effective rules; regulatory negotiation, which could provide some incentives for labor and management to seek such rules themselves; and a specific legislative package that would address over- and underregulation more directly.

But the argument I am making requires an understanding of more than the factors retarding the pace of regulation. The harm of underregulation can be mitigated if agencies do a good job of deciding which hazards to address. Does OSHA? If not, how can its choice process be improved? And, finally, if strictness is indeed a significant cause of the slow pace, what factors contribute to strictness and which might be the promising targets of reform efforts?

Explaining What Is Regulated: The Issue of Priority Setting

Although the ACGIH has changed the exposure limits for several hundred toxic substances since 1968, we have seen that OSHA has changed only ten. Why has OSHA chosen to regulate those particular hazards? Does it matter? It definitely matters because a key measure of the quality of any regulatory program is how well it selects the good candidates and avoids the poor ones. In the extreme the worst candidates are those that pose minute threats reducible only at great cost, and the best pose major threats reducible at low cost.

In this chapter I argue that both the small number of hazards addressed by OSHA, that is, its underregulation, and its tendency to overregulate in setting PELs make the quality of its choices especially important. I describe the factors that have shaped OSHA's regulatory agenda and argue that there is little reason to believe that this set of choices has maximized either public health or efficiency. Finally, I suggest some steps that would help to produce a more satisfactory set of priorities.

The Special Importance of Priority Setting in the Presence of Overregulation and Underregulation

The general point that priority setting has important consequences becomes much stronger in a regulatory system that is characterized by underregulation and overregulation. First, the inability to address more than a small number of hazards each year lends added importance to the choice of priorities. If failure to set a particular standard this year meant only that it would be set next year, the choice would be less consequential than if it meant that the standard would not be set for five, ten, or twenty years, if ever.

And if OSHA does a poor job of picking candidates for regulation, the argument for forcing it to regulate more extensively is strengthened. We cannot assume that the few hazards it does address pose the greatest threat. In chapter 4 I pointed out that we lack the data to judge conclusively how good OSHA's priority setting has been. However, I suggested that OSHA had ignored several large hazards while addressing several quite small ones. I also argued that OSHA's insistence on human evidence as a prerequisite for a new PEL was probably unlikely to lead it to focus on the most cost-effective opportunities for preventing disease. The discussion of priority-

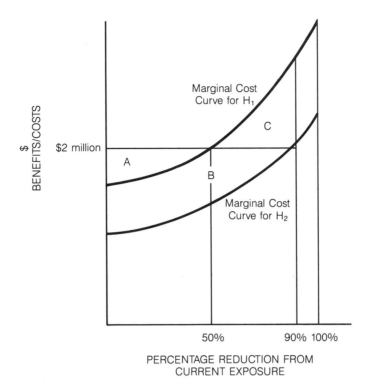

Figure 6.1   A representation of why overregulation tends to increase the variance in net benefits among standards.

setting politics in this chapter makes the analytic deficiencies in that process even clearer.

Just as the sheer inability to address many hazards (underregulation) highlights the importance of priority setting, so does the strictness with which standards are set. Regulating hazards in a uniformly strict manner creates greater variability in the net benefits among standards than does a practice of trying to maximize their net benefits—again heightening the importance of the choice of hazards. Figure 6.1 illustrates how this works. The curves show how the costs of preventing additional deaths change as exposures are reduced to two hazards, H_1 and H_2 The rising slopes of the curves mean that, as exposures are reduced, the cost per death prevented is increasing and at an increasing rate. This assumption is consistent with what is known about compliance costs. The lower position of the curve for H_2 means that, for any given percentage reduction in exposures, the cost per death prevented will be lower for that hazard. (For example, H_2 might be a more toxic chemical, so that a given reduction in exposures to it might prevent more deaths.) Suppose, for the sake of this argument, that the agency is trying to maximize net benefits and places a value of $2 million on preventing a death. Then for each hazard it should reduce the PEL to the point at which the cost of the last death prevented equals that amount. For the hazards shown in figure 6.1, this policy would justify a 50 percent reduction in the PEL for H_1 and a 90 percent reduction in the PEL for H_2. The outcome would be positive net benefits from the regulation of H_2 equal to the whole area above the H_2 curve and below the $2 million line (area A plus area B). For H_1 there would be positive net benefits equal to the small area above the H_1 curve and below the $2 million line (area A).

Because the net benefits from regulating H_2 are greater, it clearly should get priority if the agency can set only one standard in the near future. To choose H_1 instead would mean forgoing the difference between the area A and the much larger net benefits from regulating H_2. Now suppose instead that the agency has a policy of reducing all exposures by some large and uniform amount, for example, by 90 percent. The PEL chosen for H_2 (and the resulting net benefits) would be unchanged, but the stricter PEL for H_1 would turn the net benefits from positive to negative (area A minus area C). As a result, the *difference* in net benefits from regulating H_1 and H_2 grows larger. Thus the costs from making the wrong choice in setting priorities are greater under this type of strict policy, which reflects the actual OSHA practice.[1]

Priority-Setting Methods and Politics

Agencies differ in the methods they use to set priorities.[2] One dimension along which they differ is whether the agency itself or outside groups determines them. A second is whether the criteria used are essentially political or analytical. OSHA retains the formal authority to decide its priorities, but it has been responsive to the political rewards and penalties that different choices would bring. Congress gave OSHA little guidance in setting priorities for standards, stating only that "the Secretary shall give due regard to the urgency of the need for mandatory safety and health standards."[3] The act allows "any interested person" to request that a standard be issued, but, as we saw in chapter 5, it requires OSHA to "give due regard to the recommendations of NIOSH."[4] After relying on NIOSH for guidance in its earliest years, OSHA found that it was being led to address hazards that raised political risks for the agency without providing compensating benefits. The agency discovered that more political rewards could be earned by responding to union priorities and to the newly discovered health hazards that tended to get extensive media coverage.

After 1980 three other forces took on new prominence. First, the Reagan White House, through the OMB, selected the initial regulatory (or, in this case, deregulatory) proposals for the new agency directors at OSHA and elsewhere. Second, the courts, spurred by what many judges took to be the Reagan administration's bad faith, took on a greatly expanded role in mandating agencies to issue rules. Third and specific to OSHA, beginning in 1985 the EPA began referring candidates for regulation to OSHA under the terms of section 9 of the Toxic Substances Control Act.

NIOSH responded to its statutory responsibilities to make recommendations for new standards by setting up a priority-setting mechanism of its own. NIOSH took into account the number of workers exposed as well as the severity of the hazards, but it lacked data on which to base estimates of the number of diseases that might be prevented by new standards. The 1972 NIOSH recommendations ("criteria documents," in the language of the OSH Act) for new standards dealt with asbestos, beryllium, carbon monoxide, heat stress, noise, and ultraviolet radiation. Each of the last four involved exposures to millions of workers; none of them ever developed into a final rule. As we saw, OSHA did devote major energies to developing a noise standard but finally backed off because of the political opposition that its large and widely spread costs would have generated. Both heat stress and ultraviolet radiation (that is, sunlight) are hazards that predominantly occur in agriculture. OSHA approached agricultural standards with some trepidation, although not enough, as it turned out, to keep the agency from getting into political trouble.

Relying on NIOSH to set priorities also became impossible because their production of recommended changes soon far outstripped OSHA's standard-setting output. NIOSH published twenty criteria documents by 1974 and over a hundred by 1980. OSHA would have had to develop a way to set priorities *among* the NIOSH priorities.[5]

To understand why OSHA leaders would be concerned with the reaction of outside groups and their congressional supporters, we need to review OSHA's political position in the early 1970s. Throughout its first years, OSHA was plagued by constant legislative attacks, spearheaded by small business and farm groups, which focused on the enforcement by "police state" tactics of what seemed to them often picayune requirements. Although large firms and their trade associations ply their influence in the agencies and the White House, small business groups and especially farmers see Congress as their access point to the bureacracy. Although critical amendments to the OSH Act never got anywhere in the labor-dominated authorizing committees, critics managed to place restrictions on OSHA enforcement in agriculture in the annual appropriations bills. Although none of them dealt with rule making, the concern within the agency was that critics would seize on its mistakes to gain enough support to amend the act on the floor, where many bills had been introduced to require standards to meet a cost-benefit test.

The cross-pressures that OSHA has been subjected to are especially evident in the agricultural area. Although farm groups have regularly opposed new standards, OSHA felt strong pressure in favor of an ETS on pesticides from the House Education and Labor Committee in 1972. A lawsuit by the United Farmworkers also pressed OSHA to issue an ETS. Although OSHA had previously planned to issue a permanent standard at a more leisurely pace, the agency issued an ETS in the following May, only to see it voided by the Fifth Circuit Court of Appeals.

Later, in 1975, the chair of the Senate Labor Committee urged OSHA to issue a "field sanitation" standard, providing toilets and drinkable water to migrant workers in the fields. Even more potent pressure came from another lawsuit (described later), which led to a court order to issue a proposed standard. OSHA issued the proposal while appealing the court's decision. A few weeks later that proposal was the subject of angry criticism during the debate on the Department of Labor appropriations bill. One Congressman called OSHA the mandator of the "privy on the plains." The criticism led to the enactment of an appropriations rider, renewed every year since then, exempting small farms from OSHA jurisdiction. OSHA decided not to proceed with the field sanitation standard.[6]

Another example of how political pressures influence priorities came in the cotton dust standard. A critical but often overlooked factor in determining the cost and complexity of a standard is its scope. Thus, should an asbestos standard deal only with manufacturing or with construction as well? Should the benzene standard cover gas stations as well as oil refineries? In the cotton dust case an important issue was whether to include cotton ginning operations in the standard and thus to make them comply with the same PELs. Although technical issues influenced the final choice, a major reason for OSHA's decision to deal with cotton ginning separately (and somewhat more leniently) was that the chair of the House Appropriations Committee came from a Texas district with one of the strongest concentrations of ginners.[7]

Many accounts of relations between Congress and agencies emphasize the subordination of the agencies. But Congress is not a monolith. Not every committee can employ all the tools that are at Congress's collective disposal. Moreover, not all agency activities are equally susceptible to congressional influence. In the case of OSHA the powers of the labor-dominated authorizing committees were restricted by the hostility to OSHA that pervaded both chambers. As one authoritative observer commented:

Because of the potentially strong opposition to OSHA in Congress and the uncertainty as to what would occur if the Act were opened for amendment on the floor of Congress, OSHA, with rare exception, has opposed all amendments of the Act, even those that otherwise would have been deemed desirable. This position has been supported by the labor unions; the House and Senate Labor Committees, concurring in this point of view, have consistently refused to report out bills to amend OSHA. As a result, the Act has never been amended.[8]

Thus one thing the labor committees cannot threaten to do if OSHA fails to be protective enough is to amend the act. Organized labor and its supporters are also limited in budgetary strategies: Because they want the agency to have more money, it would be self-defeating to threaten to reduce its budget in order to influence agency policy. And even if labor had the votes to pass an appropriations rider requiring OSHA to promulgate a new standard, it would be stymied because a rider is out of order if its effect is to amend existing law by imposing *additional* duties not previously required of the executive department.[9]

Despite these limitations, congressional committees have played a role in prodding OSHA to be responsive to organized labor's priorities. Although Congress is reluctant to get involved directly in such issues as whether a PEL should be 1 ppm or 2 ppm, it is quite comfortable telling an agency to "do something." The absence of substantial congressional attention to OSHA's standard setting before 1981 did not reflect an inability to intervene but rather a lack of any strong push by organized labor to solicit congressional help in this area. Labor leaders felt that OSHA was responsive. In contrast, after Reagan took office, a spate of hearings was held in the House of Representative to castigate OSHA and the EPA for their inaction on specific hazards.[10]

OSHA's alternatives to relying on NIOSH for its priorities were either to choose them on its own or to rely on the statutory procedure of petitions from outside parties. Staff interest in choosing priorities has been high enough to fund several teams of consultants to devise mechanisms for OSHA to use, but their reports have gathered dust. The political incentive to respond to petitions from powerful clients has been too strong to resist.

Thus most of OSHA's choices about which hazards to address reflect the sustained interests of particular unions: asbestos (a broad coalition of unions), coke oven emissions (Steelworkers Union), arsenic (Steelworkers Union), benzene (Oil, Chemical, and Atomic Workers Union), cotton dust (Textile Workers Union, backed by the AFL-CIO), and lead (Steelworkers Union).

In other cases the development of standards was triggered by new evidence of human illness. In two cases (vinyl chloride and acrylonitrile) the evidence was first presented to OSHA by the firms involved. In the third case (DBCP), the local union developed most of the evidence. In all three cases, however, labor unions quickly submitted petitions for new OSHA standards. The identification of a new cause of worker illness tends to draw media attention, which puts political pressure on OSHA to take some kind of action. At the regulatory agencies this has been tagged the "carcinogen of the week" phenomenon. However, unless a strong client "adopts" that hazard, it is likely to be bumped in priority by the well-publicized hazards that follow it.

Constrained to act strictly once it has decided to set a standard, OSHA's chief tool for avoiding political dangers has been the authority to select the hazards it addresses and to define their scope. With cotton dust, noise, ultraviolet radiation, and heat stress, the agency backed away from strict regulation because of fears of Congress. However, the 1980s saw new developments that threatened to take that tool out of OSHA's hands.

Priority Setting in the Reagan Era

In its first two years, the Reagan administration confounded the traditional political science picture of regulation as an activity to which presidents paid as little attention as they could. Instead the new administration presented regulatory reform as one of the three key elements, along with tax reform and budget cuts, of its domestic program.

Probably the major change was that the *White House*, through the OMB, was to determine regulatory priorities and the agency leaders were picked for their political loyalty and for their lack of ties to groups that traditionally supported the agencies' programs. The new head of the auto safety agency captured this policy best when he explained that his unfamiliarity with that topic had been no barrier because White House officials had decided that they wanted "somebody who had not been previously involved in this precise subject matter."[11] His agency was told to rescind its rule requiring passive restraints. At OSHA the new assistant secretary (Thorne Auchter) was told to reassess its recently promulgated rules for cotton dust, lead, hearing conservation, and hazard labeling. The bulk of OSHA's shrunken health staff was put to work on task forces on those four issues.

The increasing assertion of OMB authority to set priorities (as well as to slow down rule making and influence the content of the rules) generated a reaction at several levels. I have already mentioned the increase in congressional hearings about OSHA and the EPA; the drumbeat of criticism about the EPA led in 1983 to Reagan's dismissal of agency head Ann Burford. The fallout from that dismissal included a new willingness of leaders at other agencies to buck the White House when criticisms from other sources got too hot. One source of that criticism came from the courts. To understand how the rules changed in these years, we need some understanding of the previous practice.

Judicial Pressures to Issue Rules

When OSHA does not adequately respond to demands for new standards, the affected groups may try to get the courts to command OSHA to issue them. In fact, however, unions did not find it necessary to resort to this tactic often during the 1970s. As we have seen, a farm worker lawsuit did prod OSHA to issue a pesticide standard. And in 1978 the Textile Workers Union filed a last minute suit when President Carter appeared to have agreed to back his economic advisers' plans to delay and weaken the cotton dust standard OSHA was about to issue. However, the major lawsuit of this type in the 1970s arose when the National Congress of Hispanic American Citizens sued in December 1973 to compel OSHA to issue several standards, including one on field sanitation, on which some preliminary work had begun. The district court judge ruled that OSHA's failures to observe the timetables in the act were illegal and ordered it to issue final rules.

In 1977 the D.C. Circuit Court of Appeals reversed the district court, citing the "traditional agency discretion to alter priorities and defer action due to legitimate statutory considerations."[12] So long as the discretion was being exercised honestly and sincerely, the courts had no right to intervene; failure to observe the statutory timetables was, by itself, not an abuse of discretion.

On remand, however, the district court judge complained that OSHA lacked any published criteria for selecting hazards and therefore that its refusal to issue a field sanitation standard was unreasonable. Again, she ordered it to act as soon as possible. Again the D.C. Circuit overturned her, ruling that OSHA's argument that other hazards deserved higher priority was reasonable and in good faith. However, the court did state that

> where the Secretary deems a problem significant enough to warrant initiation of the standard setting process, the Act requires that he have a plan to shepherd through the development of the standard—that he take pains, regardless of the press of other priorities, to ensure that the standard is not inadvertantly lost in the process." [13]

Assistant Secretary Bingham filed a timetable in 1980, estimating that a standard would be issued in forty-four months. For a third time the district court judge charged bad faith. OSHA entered into a settlement agreement with proponents of the standard in 1982. In 1984 a new proposed standard was issued, but at the end of 1986 no final action had yet been taken.

After thirteen years it is clear that this legal strategy to force OSHA to issue a standard has had only limited success. Some of the lawsuits do appear to have prodded OSHA to move more quickly, although none of the lawsuits begun in the 1970s scored ultimate victories in court. In the field sanitation case, success probably would have crowned the effort if the appeals court had changed its stand. Indeed, this is what happened in the rule making on ethylene oxide (EtO) begun during the Reagan administration. In September 1981 OSHA rejected a petition for an ETS from the Public Citizen Health Research Group; however, OSHA did state that it would initiate a regular rule-making procedure and four months later issued an Advance NPRM. Meanwhile, the Health Research Group went to district court in search of an order for OSHA to issue an emergency standard.

In 1983 the district court agreed that the record before the agency "represented a solid and certain foundation that workers are subjected to grave health dangers from exposure to ethylene oxide and levels within the currently permissible range" and therefore that OSHA's rejection of the emergency standard constituted an "abuse of discretion" and ordered the agency to issue an ETS within twenty days. [14]

The D.C. Circuit slapped down both the district court and OSHA:

> While it is a close question, our review of the record indicates that, in ordering an emergency standard, the most drastic measure in the Agency's standard-setting arsenal, the district court impermissibly substituted its evaluation for that of OSHA. Nonetheless, we fully agree with the district court that "OSHA has embarked upon the least responsive course short of inaction." ... We therefore hold that OSHA must expedite the rulemaking in which it is now engaged. ... OSHA's failure to date to issue even a notice of proposed rulemaking—some eighteen months after announcing its intention to commence rulemaking—is in our judg-

ment, and in light of the risk to current and future lives, agency action unreasonably delayed.[15]

The court directed OSHA to issue a proposal within thirty days and "to proceed expeditiously thereafter toward issuance of a permanent standard for EtO."

The chief legal basis of the court's decision was section 706(1) of the Administrative Procedure Act, which outlines the scope of review of agency actions by the courts and requires that they "compel agency action unlawfully withheld or unreasonably delayed." What constituted "unreasonable delay"? The court acknowledged that it would "hesitate to require the Assistant Secretary to expedite the EtO rulemaking if such a command would seriously disrupt other rulemakings of higher or competing priority. But we do not confront such a case." Apparently, delay in issuing a standard is unreasonable if the agency has given it too low a priority. And the court took upon itself the authority to decide which priorities were appropriate. It evaluated the three rules that OSHA claimed priority for (labeling, asbestos, and ethylene dibromide) and concluded that "none of these proceedings appears to approach in urgency the need for prompt issuance of a new EtO exposure standard and OSHA has provided us with no reasoned explanation for why it has protracted the EtO rulemaking."

Is the court's ruling in this case good public policy? I am skeptical of the judges' competence to assess the relative merits of the arguments for regulatory priority. For example, in the EtO case they implied that, because asbestos is a carcinogen and ethylene dibromide is both a carcinogen and a mutagen, ethylene dibromide deserves to be placed on a faster track—as if one should simply add up the number of effects rather than look at the chemical's potency and the number of workers exposed. Yet, although the competence of the courts is questionable, at least until recently no one else has been in a position to review agency priorities.[16] Thus, if the courts had not reviewed them, agency discretion would have been unchecked, or, more accurately, agencies would be less insulated from signals or pressures from interest groups, Congress, or the White House.

What is striking, however, about a comparison of the D.C. Circuit's decisions in the field sanitation cases and the EtO case is the dramatic plunge in its willingness to defer to the agency on priority setting. One differentiating factor in the minds of the judges could be that EtO involves life-threatening hazards. But, as in the change from the benzene to the cotton dust decision in the Supreme Court, I think that the most likely explanation is the court's reaction to the change in administrations. As the court had explained, the key issue in assessing reasonableness was the perception of the agency's honesty and good faith. The court was far less willing to accept that OSHA under Reagan was sincerely trying to implement the statute in the manner that Congress (as interpreted by the courts) had intended. Even if a factually identical case had arisen during Bingham's term, the different context—the judges' belief that Bingham *was* committed to issuing standards—probably would have led the court to uphold the agency.

Challenges to agencies for unreasonable delays in rule making had been rare until the 1970s.[17] In the 1980s they became frequent. The chief legal adviser to the AFL-CIO on OSHA expressed organized labor's strategy for standards under Reagan in three words: "Mandamus, mandamus, mandamus."[18] (A mandamus is a writ issued by a court commanding the performance of an official act or duty.) In a program characterized by such infrequent standard setting, there is some merit in the prodding that the courts can give.

The danger of this strategy and of the court's decision in the EtO case is that, by making it more difficult for an agency to halt rule making once it has begun, it will induce agencies to become more reticent about initiating proceedings until they are certain they want to set a standard. This new source of delay in issuing proposals or advance notices of proposals, reminiscent of the problem with listing pollutants under section 112 of the Clean Air Act, would be unfortunate because the responses to those proposals generate much of the information that the agency uses to make more intelligent decisions about the content of the standards.

Although some offsetting benefits may flow from requiring agencies to be more explicit and rational about their priorities, the prospect that courts will no longer defer to agency decisions makes it more costly for the agency to change its mind and will tend to lock in its past decisions. In this respect, more formally rational policies may lead to less reasonable ones, especially in an area where new information about hazards is constantly being generated. Here as elsewhere, protection against abuses of the regulatory process may often be purchased at the price of costly rigidity.

The EPA, the Toxic Substances Control Act, and OSHA

Section 9 of the Toxic Substances Control Act (TSCA), adopted in 1976, gives the EPA administrator the discretionary authority to refer chemicals to other agencies when he or she concludes that there is a "reasonable basis" to believe that they "present or will present an unreasonable risk" and that action by the other agency could reduce the risk sufficiently so that no EPA action would be needed. Until 1985 the EPA had not used section 9 to refer chemicals to OSHA; but after the OMB blocked its efforts to address hazards with sizable workplace exposures, it referred to OSHA both 1,3-butadiene and methylene dianiline (MDA), both suspect carcinogens.

Under section 9 the EPA asks OSHA for its determination on whether the risk is unreasonable. If OSHA concludes that it is not, neither OSHA nor the EPA can regulate. If OSHA concludes that the risk is unreasonable but fails to state an intention to take action within a period specified by the EPA, then the EPA retains regulatory authority.

In both the 1,3-butadiene and MDA cases, OSHA has assumed authority. It issued an Advance NPRM for 1,3-butadiene and initiated plans to bring affected parties together to "negotiate" a standard for MDA. (See chapter 8 for a discussion of negotiating standards.) Despite these actions, these hazards may not be accorded high priority because of their lack of sponsors within the agency. Yet for OSHA to have turned down authority over them would have been a bureaucratic gaffe, clearly exposing its inability to control its own turf. Thus the EPA appears to have the means to exert some control over OSHA's agenda. That it has not chosen to make referrals in the past suggests, however, that it too prefers not to surrender its authority. Nevertheless, if the OMB constrains the EPA's rule making in this area, referrals may increase.[19] If they do, will the impact on OSHA's priorities be positive? The answer depends on the criteria the EPA uses for its priorities; however, the mere fact that the EPA has had to rely heavily on bioassay data in its administration of TSCA augurs well for redressing OSHA's neglect of hazards without direct evidence of human harm. Still, OSHA's fears of White House and judicial distaste for standards based only on bioassay data are likely to remain a deterrent to action.

Better Priority Setting

OSHA needs better information for setting priorities for standard setting. In essence, that information could identify cases of underregulation. The exact data needed will depend on the criteria that are used for ranking. For example, if a benefit-cost ranking is desired, information about exposure levels, dose-response curves, and incremental control costs will be needed. But the elements in this example are not always, indeed not usually, available. Thus the criteria that can be used depend on what data are available.

Gathering complete information about all possible candidates for regulation is prohibitively expensive. Thus a strong argument has been made for a system of tiered screening. The first tier considers a little information about each of a large number of candidates; the second tier considers more information about a smaller set, and so on until an actual standard is set on the basis of thorough studies.[20] Compared to the present system, which involves essentially no screening, this proposal has the drawback of adding to costs. Some data gathering will be repeated and, of course, information will be gathered on hazards for which no standards will be forthcoming. Offsetting these costs are the anticipated benefits resulting from better choices.

Better information about worker exposures is a crucial ingredient in assessing priority-setting choices. Currently, the largest and most useful exposure database is the one generated by OSHA's own sampling in the course of enforcing standards.[21] Its main shortcoming is that inspections are not conducted randomly, which raises questions about the validity of extrapolations from inspected plants. One solution would be for OSHA to allocate a small number of hygienists to random inspections of plants in industries where chemicals of interest are known to be used. For example, suppose that fifteen hazards seemed to be possible candidates for regulation in the coming years. An average of twenty random inspections for each hazard would create a solid basis for estimating the distribution of exposures.[22] Indeed, it would be superior to the exposure data that OSHA usually has for predicting the health effects of its final standards. The 300 inspections required would constitute fewer than 5 percent of the health inspections OSHA conducts annually.

Dose-response estimates, with which the exposure information must be merged, are often not available. Crude proxies, including estimates of the relative potency or toxicity of different chemicals, will often have to be used. Efforts to develop rules of thumb for estimating the marginal costs of hazard abatement are also still in their infancy.

These problems do not rule out use of a more analytical approach to priority setting; yet the uncertainties that currently exist indicate the need for judgment to be exercised in drawing implications for policy. Indeed, even if the uncertainties disappeared, there are still too many subjective factors that enter into a choice of regulatory priorities to allow a mechanical process to dictate them. Nor would the interest groups involved accept a purely mechanical process.

The development of such information can, however, inform the process and open it up to more intelligent outside criticism. Pressures from the OMB and even from labor groups have led OSHA to consider convening concerned parties to discuss what its priorities should be.[23] The requisite data have not been developed in the past in large part because OSHA viewed them as more likely to be harmful than helpful. Yet once the data are developed, they will be hard to dismiss.

As I argued at the beginning of this chapter, a better choice of priorities will ease some of the problems caused by underregulation—the hazards addressed will be more likely to be ones worth addressing. Therefore, on average, the resulting standards will be more likely to have bigger net benefits, or at least smaller net costs. However, by themselves, better priorities will probably not go very far to ensure that the final standards will prevent illnesses at a lower cost than previous standards have done. If a standard is set strictly enough, even good candidates for regulation will end up imposing net costs. There may be more agreement that something should be done about a hazard but still substantial disagreement about what that "something" should be. In turn, that disagreement will continue to throw up obstacles to a speedier pace of rule making. Thus, although better priority setting is useful in itself and an important ingredient in a move to a more extensive, less strict system, the key reforms must be those that operate directly on the pace of rule making or on its strictness.

Explaining Why Standards Are Strict

In previous chapters we looked at the pace and scope of standard setting and at the way in which decisions are made about which hazards to address. In this chapter I focus on the reasons why standards are set as strictly as they are. If, as I have argued, the strictness of standards is one cause for the failure to set them, then it is important to understand the causes of strictness in order to assess the options for relaxing it.

The topic of strictness has received more scholarly attention than the issues of pace or priority setting. Most studies have focused on explaining the *average* level of strictness of American occupational health standards compared to those of other countries or to other types of hazards in the United States. This explanation is important and will be attended to here. However, I give special attention to explaining the *variation* in strictness *among* OSHA's health standards. The factors explaining variation are not necessarily the same as those that explain the average level of strictness of OSHA standards. For example, invoking Americans' distrust of big corporations and lack of faith in government's ability to control them may help to explain why American standards are tougher than Britain's,[1] but it is unlikely to explain why one OSHA standard is stricter than another. The reason for emphasizing this second issue is that an understanding of the reasons for variation among US standards seems more likely to uncover factors that policymakers here can actually manipulate.

As explained previously, strictness here means unreasonably costly. The factors influencing the degree of strictness include political parties, interest groups, professional values, administrative procedure and the courts, and the broader American political perspective on regulation. I review the role of each of them.

This review addresses how these factors affect the particular policy choices that lead to more costly standards. The most obvious of these choices is the decision to set a low PEL, but others include OSHA's unwillingness to allow differential PELs that would allow industries where compliance is more costly to meet less strict standards; and the requirement that exposure limits be met, where feasible, by engineering controls rather than by use of less costly personal protective equipment. A fourth choice concerns the length of time that a standard allows before compliance is required. This is the one area where OSHA has proven more flexible.

Variations in Strictness: The Role of Political Parties

We have seen that the typical OSHA standard carries a high cost per death prevented, although the 1972 asbestos standard is a striking exception. But asbestos does not exhaust the variation among standards. Although clear conclusions about the relative cost per cancer death are difficult, the data in table 4.4 do show that these estimates correlate highly with another measure of strictness—the ratio of the ACGIH recommended limit to the OSHA PEL. Arsenic, benzene, and vinyl chloride all had estimated costs per cancer prevented of about $20 million; for all three the OSHA PEL is at least five times lower than the ACGIH TLV. The OSHA lead standard is three times lower than the ACGIH TLV and is also the most costly of all the standards. The next four standards on the list appear to have been noticeably less strict. The estimates of cost per cancer prevented range from $1 million to $9 million, and the OSHA PELs are no stricter than the ACGIH recommendations. Finally, asbestos stands at the bottom with a much stricter ACGIH standard and a much lower cost per cancer prevented.

One task in my discussion of strictness is to explain these disparities. One explanation is the party in power. Of the four stricter standards three were promulgated in 1978, while Eula Bingham headed OSHA in the Democratic Carter administration. Of the five less strict standards, three were promulgated during Republican administrations. Of course, it is possible that, rather than party, the important differences are between administrations or even between agency leaders within an administration. Because Carter was the only Democrat and Bingham the only head of OSHA during his four years, any inquiry into the effect of presidential administration or agency leader—rather than party—must be limited.

The party hypothesis may seem obvious; after all, Democrats are known to have stronger pro-environment and, especially, pro-labor voting records than Republicans. However, the party hypothesis actually rests on an assumption that is by no means self-evident, at least not in the literature on regulation. It assumes that presidents affect regulatory outcomes, presumably through their selection of agency officials and through later control. The Reagan presidency certainly does square with this assumption, but, in fact, ideological or programmatic screening of appointees by presidents has been more the exception than the rule. Many scholars also claim that, before Reagan, presidential oversight, whether exercised through the secretary and under-secretary of a department or by White House officials, was conspicuously absent.[2]

For now, it is sufficient to note that none of the three—party, administration, or agency chief—can explain all of the variation found in table 4.4. The same year that Assistant Secretary Bingham issued the arsenic, lead, and benzene standards, she also signed less strict rules for cotton dust and acrylonitrile. And under President Nixon OSHA issued by far its least strict rule (asbestos) as well as one of its most strict (vinyl chloride). Finally, the one standard issued under Reagan (through 1985) was about as strict as Carter's acrylonitrile rule.

Organized Labor: The Prime Mover for Strictness

Organized labor was the prime mover behind the passage of the OSH Act, and unions have played the leading role in prodding OSHA to set standards and to set them strictly. What explains labor's support for strictness? Are there circumstances under which unions might be willing to accept less strictness?

Before turning to these questions, it is important to document the union role in OSHA's adoption of strict standards. The unions appealed several of OSHA's standards on the grounds of insufficient strictness. Perhaps most notably, they appealed the 1972 asbestos standard on the grounds that OSHA had impermissibly considered economic feasibility in setting the PEL. In contrast, unions were least heavily committed in the case of the acrylonitrile standard and this became the least strict of the other standards. With union interest low, Assistant Secretary Bingham let the director of health standards make almost all of the decisions. He agreed to the 2-ppm PEL when industry leaders signaled that they would not appeal it.[3]

Answering the questions requires some understanding of what motivates labor union activity on safety and health issues. The candidates include membership pressures, leaders' desires to improve the health status of their members, and leaders' desires to gain more members or to increase the strength of the union in the industry.

Membership pressures do not appear to have played a large role in activating unions. Despite efforts to develop a "brown lung" movement among retired textile workers that would be a counterpart to the Black Lung Movement that forced the United Mine Workers to demand federal action on mine safety, sustained grass roots pressures appear to have been exceptional. The coke oven workers, who had a long-standing caucus within the Steelworkers Union, were the one other group who did press demands for union action on their problems.

Thus when union leaders decided to demand federal action on a hazard, they were not responding primarily to worker demands. That does not mean that they were free of membership constraints on their actions. The major one was that the standard not visibly eliminate the jobs of current workers. In the one case where a major plant's demise was predicted with near certainty—the Tacoma smelter affected by the arsenic standard—OSHA increased the PEL to try to avoid that result.[4]

Of course, in the long run some or all of the costs of complying with a standard are likely to be passed on to consumers, with an ultimate reduction in the quantity demanded and in employment. But impacts that are felt only in the long run and affect potential workers more than current ones will tend to have lower salience to union leaders, who care more about present than future members.

Yet union leaders are far from indifferent about the size and strength of their organizations. Potentially, these concerns may induce them to seek strict standards. First, if unionized firms have lower compliance costs, they may gain a competitive advantage over nonunionized firms as a result of a strict standard. Second, if a standard does force some firms into bankruptcy, the remaining firms may emerge in a stronger position. If the remaining firms are disproportionately unionized, the standard can increase the union's ability to gain extra benefits for its members. Third, efforts to comply with standards may require increases in employment that more than offset future declines resulting from regulation-induced price hikes.

Is there any evidence about the importance of such "strategic" behavior in unions' actions to get health standards? Only one standard entailed any major increases in employment. The coke oven standard—the only one that specified the exact equipment and procedures that firms had to utilize—was projected to increase coke oven employment by about 5000, a major jump from the 20,000 already employed. In every other case, the economic impact analyses of the standards estimated that small employment gains resulting from compliance activities would be outweighed, usually by small amounts, by the decreases from the decline in the quantity demanded.

Some data can also be brought to bear on the issue of whether unions may have been using standards to reduce the competitive disadvantages faced by unionized firms in industries with significant nonunion sectors. Table 7.1 shows the percentage of production workers covered by collective bargaining agreements in the industries that were the focus of the new OSHA standards. For the three standards in which the steelworkers were dominant—coke ovens, arsenic, and lead—the table shows that unions represented virtually all production workers. Moreover, the steelworkers themselves represented almost all of the workers exposed to coke oven

Table 7.1   Union Representation in Industries Affected by New OSHA Health Standards

Hazard and standard industrial classification (SIC) code	Percent covered by collective bargaining	
	All workers	Production workers
Asbestos		
329 misc. nonmetallic mineral products	56	82
Vinyl chloride		
282 plastics materials	55	84
Coke ovens		
331 blast furnaces	77	98
Benzene		
291 petroleum refining	31	63
421 trucking	61	71
301 tires and inner tube	65	100
306 fabricated rubber	50	65
307 misc. plastic	32	42
Arsenic		
333 primary nonferrous	73	90
Lead		
333 primary nonferrous	73	100
334 secondary nonferrous	73	100
336 nonferrous foundries	56	65
332 iron and steel foundries	75	87
369 misc. electrical equipment	49	56
Cotton		
221	20	22
Acrylonitrile		
282 plastic materials	55	84
286 gum and wood chemicals	66	70
DBCP		
287 agricultural chemicals	40	57
Ethylene oxide		
384 medical supplies	31	46
806 hospitals	9	10

Source: Coverage estimates are from Richard B. Freeman and James Medoff, "New Estimates of Private Sector Unionism in the United States," *Industrial and Labor Relations Review* (January 1979), 32(2): 143–174. The identification of industries affected by the standard was based on various sources.

emissions and arsenic (in copper smelters) and bargained for them on an industry-wide basis. Thus the opportunities here for strategic behavior related to the nonunionized sectors were minimal.

For the petrochemical hazards—vinyl chloride, benzene, and acrylonitrile—unionization was somewhat lower and strategic behavior more plausible. However, the costs of compliance relative to firm size in these industries tended to be so small that significant competitive effects seem unlikely.

The cotton dust standard presents a different story. Ninety-five percent of textile mills using cotton were in the South and only 5 to 10 percent of southern mills were unionized. Although some of the biggest firms (for example, J. P. Stevens and Milliken) were notoriously nonunion, it is probably still true that unionized plants tended to be found at the stronger firms in the industry. Thus a goal of providing a competitive advantage by driving weaker firms out of business cannot be dismissed. Here too, however, it is neither the only explanation for union action nor the most likely.

The dominant explanation for unions' actions on standards is that they are seeking to improve conditions in the workplace. By placing the issue outside of collective bargaining, union leaders believe that the union will not have to give up as much to gain health improvements. In partially unionized industries a federal standard may help to improve conditions without putting unionized workers at a competitive disadvantage. It is less clear whether and to what extent union action is motivated by the leadership's belief that strict standards are supported by the members and make good political sense or by a more paternalistic concern for their welfare. There is evidence for both views.

The frequency with which health and safety topics are discussed in union newspapers suggests that they are a good political issue for union leaders. More than most issues, they help mobilize a sense of class conflict—of "us" against "them." [5] For this purpose it helps to draw the line sharply: Unions want the "lowest feasible limit," and the companies want to sacrifice lives for profit. Of course, it strains credulity to think that union leaders, who have to engage in the constant trade-offs of collective bargaining, are truly shocked by the idea that the costs of health measures must be weighed against other costs. However, the fact that many citizens *are* shocked is precisely what makes the issue a good one to push from collective bargaining to the public policy agenda.

In at least one standard, lead, the PEL was not the prime concern of the unions. One union official even acknowledged that a 0.05-mg PEL was seen only as a bargaining chip. For years organized labor had argued that standards should include a provision guaranteeing that workers who were transferred from a job because of the effects of their exposures would be protected against a loss of wages or seniority. OSHA had omitted the provision from the coke oven standard. It was included in the cotton dust standard but later voided by the Supreme Court, which held that OSHA had justified it on the impermissible grounds of protecting workers' wages rather than on health grounds. In the case of lead OSHA made a careful argument that, unless workers were protected in this manner, they would refuse to participate in the exams necessary to protect them. (This argument was accepted when the standard was challenged.) The provision for "medical removal protection" (MRP), as it came to be called, was the driving force in determining the PEL. According to the calculations of OSHA's consultants, unless the PEL was lowered to 0.05 mg, the number of workers with blood-lead levels in the impermissible range and thus subject to the MRP provision would be so large that the industry's labor force would be decimated, a clearly infeasible result.[6] The lead standard provides a case where union leaders appeared as concerned with workers' incomes as with their health. Yet a good case could be made that the MRP provided the most potent incentive for employers to ensure that workers were not overexposed.

In general, it does seem clear that a paternalistic concern for workers' health often plays a role. Interviews with union leaders and their staffs elicit frequent statements that workers are too shortsighted about their health.[7] In collective bargaining they are viewed as too willing to sacrifice health measures for other near-term benefits.

Union opposition to allowing respirators to be used instead of engineering controls reflects similar concerns. Indeed, there is considerable irony about OSHA's and unions' opposition to allowing respirators to be used as a primary method for complying with new standards. A review of the results of OSHA inspection sampling shows that for several of the new standards a large proportion of the exposed workers are exposed to levels above the PEL and that most of them are wearing respirators. As table 7.2 shows, this conclusion applies to arsenic, lead, and coke ovens, the three standards that OSHA's chief supporter, the Steelworkers' Union, has a major stake in. More than seven years after these standards were issued, there are still no prospects for a major drop in respirator use. When asked to explain why they persisted in their demand for engineering controls in the face of this paradoxical result, steelworker leaders responded that the principle of engineering controls must be upheld in order to let workers know that their current discomfort with respirators is only temporary.[8]

Table 7.2   For Several Hazards Addressed by New Standards, a Large Percentage of Workers Remain Exposed above the PEL and Must Wear Respirators

	Percentage of sampled workers	
Industry	Exposed below PEL	Exposed above PEL
Coke oven emissions[a] (January 1979–December 1982), $N = 1877$	51	49
Lead, primary smelting[b] (1981–1982), $N = 2790$	20	80
Lead, secondary smelting[b] (1981–1982), $N = 1799$	25	75
Lead, battery manufacturing[b] (1981–1982), $N = 8936$	59	41

Source: Robert Goble, Dale Hattis, Mary Ballew, and Deborah Thurston, "Implementation of the Occupational Lead Exposure Standard," paper 83-11 (Cambridge, Mass.: Center for Policy Alternatives, June 15, 1983), mimeo.
a. From the fourteen inspections where coke oven emissions were sampled by OSHA Management Information System.
b. From surveys by Charles River Associates for OSHA in all 6 primary smelting plants, 22 out of 65 secondary smelting plants, and 67 out of 266 battery plants.

This rather messianic view suggests that paternalism does play a role in union policy.

Unions have also opposed the proposal to set different PELs for different industries—stricter ones for those where compliance is inexpensive and looser ones where it is costly. Here the objection is that workers should not be exposed to greater risks merely because they work where compliance is costly. This view reflects an ideological commitment that protection should not be sacrificed for efficiency. In practice, a differential standard is likely to offer a lower overall level of protection than a uniform standard set at the "lowest feasible level." This view also reflects a fear that standards might be set more laxly for nonunion sectors, creating a possible competitive disadvantage for unions. Corporate leaders are at least as concerned about competitive disadvantages as their union counterparts, and jockeying between rival industries (for example, the primary and secondary smelting industries in the case of the lead standard) can be intense.[9]

Implications for Policy Change

In summary, union leaders want strict standards primarily because they want to protect workers, subject to the constraints that visible job losses and serious competitive disadvantages are not created. Does this conclusion suggest any insights into the potential for their acceptance of less strict standards? Because health is their main concern, union leaders could support less strict standards if they were part of a package that appeared to guarantee greater protection. In other words, if they were convinced that "overregulation causes underregulation" and that there was a change that promised more protection, union leaders might buy it. The union staff who are most involved in health and safety issues are aware that overregulation can be counterproductive (as we saw in chapter 5 in the discussion of the vinyl chloride standard). They would have to convince top officials to instruct union lobbyists to seek legislative change. However, union leaders are unlikely to take the initiative in seeking amendments. Only if there are strong pressures from industry to amend the OSH Act will these trade-offs become politically relevant.

The industrial unions that have provided the strongest support for OSHA's health standards have been hit hard by the challenges to American competitiveness. The Steelworkers Union lost half of its members between 1980 and 1986, and few believe that the loss can be regained. This ebbing strength raises the possibility that changes could be effected even in the face of union opposition.

Industry

Do strict standards really serve the interests of some regulated firms? Do they secretly support the adoption of tough regulations in order to gain a competitive advantage? If so, has their support actually been an important reason why OSHA has chosen strict standards? During the 1960s economic analyses of industry price and entry regulation pointed out the large inefficiencies resulting from these programs. Partly as a result, "public interest" explanations for regulatory programs gave way to explanations based on their redistributional consequences.[10] More recently, safety and environmental regulations have begun to be subjected to similar scrutiny. Instead of a story about environmental or safety proponents prevailing over industry opponents, the revisionists claim that some, if not all, firms within the industry have something to gain from regulation and that industry support is necessary to explain the adoption of the regulations. The impetus for this revision has again come from findings that regulation does have differential impacts on firms and regions.[11]

In the case of OSHA the major example of firms' strategic use of the regulatory process that has been proffered concerns cotton dust. Two economists argue that "we do not expect that regulation could exist without the coalition of interests between the environmentalists and producer groups."[12] Their analysis tries to show that larger firms, especially those with heavy use of cotton, experienced increases in the value of their common stocks after NIOSH began work on the development of a recommended standard. In late 1974 NIOSH recommended a PEL of 0.2 mg/m^3. In late 1976 OSHA proposed the same PEL. The final standard, issued in June 1978, allowed higher exposures for some parts of the textile industry.

A more sophisticated analysis has arrived at contrary conclusions about whether big textile firms benefited from the cotton dust standard.[13] But the issue here is—assuming that some firms believed they would benefit— what evidence is there that they influenced OSHA's decision?

There is good reason to believe that Burlington Industries, the largest firm in the industry, had taken many more steps to comply than most other firms and that, in general, there was a negative correlation between firm size and exposure levels.[14] Thus the incremental costs to reach lower exposure limits likely were less for those firms. However, the position advanced by the American Textile Manufacturers' Institute (ATMI), which included Burlington, in 1973 and 1974 was that any new regulation should rely primarily on medical monitoring.[15] The argument was that, because byssinosis is detectable in its early stages and is reversible at that time, monitoring would be an effective preventer of disease. Moreover, because the etiology is unknown, the dose-response curve in dispute, and engineering controls costly and infeasible, the ATMI argued that the case against a lower PEL was strong. Thus its support for a cotton dust standard based on medical monitoring of workers was a far cry from OSHA's proposal to achieve a PEL of 0.2 mg/m^3 with engineering controls—a change that was estimated (incorrectly) in 1976 to cost upward of $8 billion.

Dr. Harold Imbus, medical director of Burlington and the key figure in its interaction with OSHA, states that "in 1974 nobody in the textile industry that I'm aware of wanted or thought they could comply with a 0.2 mg standard."[16] However, Imbus did support OSHA's 1978 standard in most respects. He believed that a PEL below 0.5 mg would be desirable, although he still thought 0.2 mg was too low.[17] Burlington did not join the ATMI in its suit against the standard.

When the final standard was being written in 1978, Imbus and Burlington were viewed by some within OSHA as having broken with the rest of the industry. In its preamble to the standard, OSHA frequently cited controls adopted by Burlington as evidence that reductions were feasible. Indeed, it is in this respect that Burlington's position was critical. Like other regulatory agencies, OSHA always knows less about economic and political feasibility than the industry. Gaining confidence that controls really are feasible facilitates the development of a standard and makes it easier to argue for a lower PEL.

Although not every standard-setting procedure saw a firm play Burlington's role, several did. On coke oven emissions, National Steel, which appeared to be the low-cost complier, again provided data that facilitated OSHA's task. On formaldehyde, where OSHA has avoided taking action, Dow and Monsanto drew the fire of the Formadehyde Institute for denying its claim that a 1-ppm PEL would be infeasible.

Did these actions mean that these firms really wanted lower standards? In some cases, such as formaldehyde, the answer is probably yes. After all, if their provision of information helped OSHA make the case for such reductions, wouldn't they have "stonewalled" if they had really been opposed? But that conclusion will not always be correct, for it fails to consider the dynamics of the standard-setting process. OSHA asks firms for information. Firms often ask OSHA to become more sensitive to particular industry problems. But if firms are not cooperative and forth-coming with information, OSHA's incentive to be sensitive is reduced. Firms may ultimately gain from a higher probability of beating OSHA in court, but they have to weigh this against the foregone opportunities to win accommodations at an earlier stage.

Thus, aside from the threat of a lawsuit, the major way in which firms influence standard setting is through the information they provide or fail to provide to the agency. Although their motivation may be to gain a competi-tive advantage over rivals, other motives are no less plausible. Chemical firms may want to lower exposures to chemicals that they produce so that the firms they supply will not make their employees sick. Then, if workers do get sick and sue the producer, the potential number of lawsuits will be reduced. Or a firm that wants to protect its employees may want a standard to avoid putting itself at a competitive *dis*advantage. It is fair to conclude, however, that the great bulk of firms in the affected industries have not been supporters of the standards that OSHA has set. Although industry divisions increase the flow of information that makes it easier for OSHA to justify stricter standards, the conventional argument that firms oppose strict standards remains generally correct.[18]

The Statute and the Courts

Policymakers at OSHA are free to decide how strict standards should be, but only so long as they stay within the range prescribed by the OSH Act. But because the statute is hardly transparent on this issue, the courts have had the final role. During the Bingham years, a good generalization is that policymakers set the lowest PEL that they thought the courts would accept.

Under Reagan it is probably fair to say that they set the highest they thought the courts would accept. The fact that standards under Reagan do not appear to be radically less strict than those issued under Bingham is testimony to the role the courts have played in confining discretion.

The central provision of the OSH Act dealing with health standards says:

The Secretary ... shall set the standard which most adequately assures, to the extent feasible, on the basis of the best available evidence, that no employee will suffer material impairment of health or functional capacity even if such employee has regular exposure to the hazard dealt with by such standard for the period of his working life.... In addition to the attainment of the highest degree of safety and health protection for the employee, other considerations shall be the latest available scientific data in the field, the feasibility of the standards, and experience gained under this and other health and safety laws.[19]

Union officials were breathless at the level of protectiveness they believed the act guaranteed.[20] They viewed the 1972 asbestos standard, which called for a reduction from 12 fibers to 5 fibers and then to 2 fibers in 1976, as failing to meet the act's specifications. They challenged OSHA's use of feasibility considerations, which had led it to delay adopting the 2-fiber PEL. Industry also challenged the standard, noting that the evidence collected by OSHA did not support the view that a 2-fiber standard was necessary to prevent disease.[21]

In April 1974 the D.C. Circuit Court of Appeals issued its decision on the challenge to OSHA's asbestos standard. The decision went beyond resolving the propriety of considering feasibility and "provided a framework for all subsequent discussions of the scope of court review of OSHA standards."[22]

The court wrestled with the meaning of the requirement that OSHA show "substantial evidence" for its choices in a context where "some of the questions involved in the promulgation of these standards are on the frontiers of scientific knowledge, and consequently as to them insufficient data is presently available to make a fully informed factual determination."[23] Compared to the review of such factual determinations, "judicial review of inherently legislative decisions of this sort is obviously an undertaking of different dimensions." What were the dimensions?

What we are entitled to ... is a careful identification by the Secretary ... of the reasons why he chooses to follow one course rather than another. Where that choice purports to be based on the existence of certain determinable facts, the Secretary must, in form as well as substance, find those facts from evidence in the record. By the same token, when the Secretary is obliged to make policy judgments where no factual certainties exist or where facts alone do not provide the answer, he should so state and go on to identify the considerations he found persuasive.[24]

As for the secretary's choice of "a relatively low limit" for the asbestos PEL: "Inasmuch as the protection of the health of employees is the overriding concern of OSHA, this choice is doubtless sound, but it rests in the final analysis on an essentially legislative policy judgment, rather than a factual determination, concerning the relative risks of underprotection as compared to overprotection." [25]

The court's review was certainly deferential to the agency. However, the deference was not to the agency's expertise but rather to its legislative role. Furthermore, the court made it clear that the legitimacy of that role, and thus OSHA's freedom from closer scrutiny, depended on continued service to worker protection as its overriding goal. The agency's own incentives to make that its priority were thus reinforced by the court.

The chief substantive issue in the case was the Industrial Union Department's (IUD) challenge to OSHA's use of arguments about economic impact to justify delaying the effective date of the 2-fiber PEL. The decision rebuffed that challenge, holding that the economic impact of standards should be considered. But what did such consideration entail? The court's guidance was neither clear nor consistent. At one point, it opined that "it would comport with common usage to say that a standard that is prohibitively expensive is not 'feasible'." But what does "prohibitively expensive" mean? Later we are told that "Congress does not appear to have intended to protect employees by putting their employers out of business—either by requiring protective devices unavailable under existing technology or by making financial viability generally impossible." [26]

But the concept of economic feasibility does not

necessarily guarantee the continued existence of individual employers. It would appear to be consistent with the purposes of the Act to envisage the economic demise of an employer who has lagged behind the rest of the industry in protecting the health and safety of employees and is consequently financially unable to comply with new standards as quickly as other employers. As the effect becomes more widespread within an industry, the problem of economic feasibility becomes more pressing. [27]

The court gave examples. If only a few leading firms could comply, OSHA might properly delay the compliance date in order to avoid increasing industry concentration. Competition with imports or even domestic substitutes might also be legitimately considered.

These examples have nothing to do with the weighing of benefits and costs, at least as economists construe them, but a great deal to do with protecting the equities of existing firms. From an economic perspective, if an industry's production generates too high a level of some social "bad," then society may be better off without the industry. The court's reasoning recalls the justifications given for older forms of price and entry regulation, that they slow the pace of change, protecting the equities of existing firms against market uncertainties and the threats posed by new technologies. In contrast, social regulation often has the explicit goal of speeding the pace of change, best exemplified by the notion of "technology-forcing" discussed in the next section. To some degree, the two notions can coexist, because both agencies and courts show more concern for the economic well-being of firms when they enforce standards than they do when they set them.[28]

Technology Forcing

In his brief defending OSHA's vinyl chloride standard from the challenge of the Society for the Plastics Industry, a Labor Department attorney argued that the language of "feasibility" did not prevent OSHA from requiring exposure limits that could be met only if new technology were developed. OSHA had acknowledged that compliance in many job classifications would require such developments:

Since there is no actual evidence that any of the [vinyl chloride] or [polyvinyl chloride] manufacturers have already attained a 1 ppm level or in fact instituted all available engineering and work practice controls, any estimate as to the lowest feasible level attainable must necessarily involve subjective judgment. Likewise, the projections of industry, labor, and others concerning feasibility are essentially conjectural. . . .

   We agree that [polyvinyl chloride] and [vinyl chloride] establishments will not be able to attain a 1 ppm level for all job classifications in the near future. We do believe, however, that they will, in time, be able to attain levels of 1 ppm [time-weighted average] for most job classifications most of the time. It is apparent that reaching such levels may require some new technology and work practices. . . . In any event the [vinyl chloride] and [polyvinyl chloride] industries have already made great strides in reducing exposure levels.[29]

The Second Circuit Court of Appeals agreed with OSHA and the Labor Department attorneys and chided the plastics industry for its lack of self-confidence:

We cannot agree with petitioners that the standard is so clearly impossible of attainment. It appears that they simply need more faith in their own technological capabilities, since the record reveals that, despite similar predictions of impossibility regarding the emergency 50 ppm standard, vast improvements were made in a matter of weeks. . . . In the area of safety, we wish to emphasize, the Secretary is not restricted to the status quo. He may raise standards which require improvements in existing technologies or which require the development of new technology, and he is not limited to issuing standards based solely on devices already fully developed.[30]

In a decision on a safety standard, the Third Circuit agreed that standards were not infeasible "when the necessary technology looms on the horizon." [31] In all of the ensuing challenges to health standards, the reviewing courts have subscribed to the same views. Although they have ruled that OSHA had failed to demonstrate the feasibility of a standard in a particular industry, the result has only been that the requirement to comply through engineering controls is stayed in those industries until OSHA conducts the requisite studies. The courts have generally acted as if they believed that feasibility was a foregone conclusion. The mounting of a serious study was treated as a necessary condition for establishing feasibility, but it was also a sufficient condition.

In fact, although OSHA has had some noteworthy successes in technology forcing—vinyl chloride and cotton dust being paradigms—it has also had some failures. OSHA's predictions about the prospects for reducing lead exposures in smelters were clearly overoptimistic. More generally, widespread respirator use in industries with heavy exposures to lead, arsenic, and coke oven emissions testifies to the incorrectness of the belief that engineering solutions were really "looming on the horizon," at least if we assume that five to ten years is sufficient for such "loomers" to arrive. In the future, as the failures become better known, judges might not be willing to show as much deference to OSHA's judgment.

Cotton Dust and Cost-Benefit Analysis

In its benzene decision the Supreme Court had dodged the cost-benefit issue by ruling that OSHA had not even met the threshold issue of showing that benzene exposures posed a "significant risk." But the benefit-cost question quickly faced the Court again when it agreed to review OSHA's 1978 cotton dust standard.

In 1979 Judge Bazelon had announced the D.C. Circuit Court's decision to uphold OSHA's cotton dust standard (except for its application in the cottonseed oil industry, which was remanded for further feasibility studies). [32] In concluding that "in the OSH Act . . . Congress itself struck the balance between costs and benefits in the mandate to the agency," the decision appeared to preclude OSHA from using benefit-cost analysis. Thus, although OSHA could not set a standard unless it determined that a "significant risk" existed, once that threshold was met, it was still obligated by section 6(b)(5) to set a "safe" limit, or if any exposures were dangerous, to set the lowest feasible limit. The industry association appealed.

By the time the case was heard in 1981, the Reagan administration had taken office and issued Executive Order 12291, which states that, to the extent permitted by law, regulatory actions should not be undertaken unless the "potential benefits to society for the regulations outweigh the potential costs." [33] Fearing that the Supreme Court might uphold the standard, the administration tried unsuccessfully to convince the Court to dismiss the case. In the absence of a Supreme Court decision, OSHA could treat the 1979 decision as "only the view of the D.C. Circuit" and thus not necessarily the final word. It could then apply the executive order to OSHA regulations unless a circuit court specifically ordered it not to, rather than risk a Supreme Court decision that would bar its use.

The Supreme Court voted 5 to 3 to affirm the circuit court's decision, holding that

Congress itself defined the basic relationship between costs and benefits, by placing the "benefit" of worker health above all other considerations save those making attainment of this "benefit" unachievable. Any standard based on a balancing of costs and benefits by the Secretary that strikes a different balance than that struck by Congress would be inconsistent with the command set forth in Section 6(b)(5). Thus cost-benefit analysis is not required by the statute because feasibility analysis is. [34]

The majority, which was composed of the benzene case minority plus Justice Stevens, relied heavily on the dictionary definition of feasibility ("capable of being done") and its view of the legislative history. Rehnquist, joined by Chief Justice Burger in dissent, again argued that section 6(b)(5) should be voided for vagueness. Stewart dissented on the narrower grounds that OSHA's feasibility arguments in this case were not supported by substantial evidence. Powell, who had called for a cost-benefit test in his benzene case concurrence, did not participate in this decision, but clearly would have voted on the minority's side. Thus again the Court was as divided as it could be.

The majority decision in the cotton dust case depended on adding Justice Stevens to the dissenters in the benzene case. We do not know why Stevens, critical of the agency's failure to assess whether the risks it was addressing were "significant," joined those who opposed balancing costs and benefits. My interpretation of the benzene decision was that the plurality (including Stevens) was essentially upbraiding the agency for acting unreasonably, both in failing to use a tool such as risk assessment and in asserting that costs were no object. Now that the Reagan administration was in command, these fears of overregulation had eased. It seems plausible that some of the justices believed that his unprecedentedly aggressive program for regulatory "relief" for industry would tip the scales too far in the other direction.

Whatever the reason, the cotton dust decision does constrain efforts to regulate less strictly and exempts OSHA's health standards from the cost-benefit requirements of Executive Order 12229. Judicial mistrust of Reagan's deregulation effort also helped to derail the OMB's plan to relax the cotton dust and lead standards. After its lengthy deliberations, OSHA made only minor changes to relax the strictness of the standards. Along with staff pressures, industry divisions, and the cotton dust decision, another important constraint on attempts to relax the standards was the legal rebuff the administration had suffered in its attempt to rescind the Department of Transportation's passive restraint rule.

In June 1982 the D.C. Circuit Court of Appeals said that the recision of that regulation was a "paradigm of arbitrary and capricious action." A year later, in the *State Farm* decision, the Supreme Court upheld the principle that the procedures for setting and rescinding rules were symmetric.[35] In contrast, the administration had claimed that decisions to rescind a regulation should be treated in the same manner as decisions not to regulate at all, which had been treated by the courts (at least in theory) as largely within the discretion of the agency. These new rulings clarified that, in order to deregulate, agencies would have to establish that the rules they had earlier shown to be "reasonable" or "feasible" in fact were not. That burden of proof was onerous and Labor Department attorneys believed that it would cripple attempts to relax the lead and cotton dust standards substantially.[36]

The concept that decisions to rescind a rule must be based on a body of evidence of equal weight to that used to establish the rule seems like a reasonable and balanced approach. However, such a balance is illusory for OSHA health standards. As we have seen, the courts reviewing those standards acknowledged that many of the key choices were based on policy preferences implicit in the statute. The choices did not, indeed could not, simply emerge from a weighing of the evidence. And, except for the Fifth Circuit, reviewing courts have agreed that OSHA should exercise its policy discretion on behalf of the "overriding objective" of worker safety. So long as uncertainty is to be resolved on the side of safety, the process of deregulation and regulation cannot be symmetric. Deregulation usually entails reducing safety and thus will be subject to stricter review. The implication of the *State Farm* decision for OSHA would appear to be that, however difficult it is to establish a rule, disestablishing it is more difficult.

Implications for Reform

The constraints imposed by the cotton dust decision could be relaxed by amending the OSH Act to allow a balancing of benefits and costs. This change is examined in more detail in the next chapter. However, the close votes in both the benzene and cotton dust decisions indicate that these are hardly settled areas of the law. Another possibility is for the Supreme Court to alter its interpretations.

The majority in the cotton dust decision relied heavily on its construal of congressional intent. The judicial concept of "legislative intent" is difficult to square with the political scientist's insight that the objectives of legislation are often "multiple, conflicting, and vague." [37] Although a legislative history is sometimes littered with cues left by legislators for sympathetic judges to pick up, the OSHA case reflects another pattern—intentional obfuscation. Judges, who have to decide specific disputes by discerning what statutes mean, usually have a professional and intellectual stake in not acknowledging obfuscation. In any event they have limited themselves to reviewing the formal documents preceding the legislation—the committee reports, floor debates, and hearings—which are hardly a sufficient basis for understanding why legislators did what they did.

In an interview several years after the passage of the OSH Act, the chief counsel for the Senate committee that wrote the bill explained that "in the Act the issue was not directly dealt with. That was intentional. We were afraid that if we said 'economic feasibility,' nothing but costs would be considered." On the House side, subcommittee counsel Daniel Krivit agreed that "the Act left it open and Congress did not face up to the issue of costs; although most of us believed costs would be a factor taken into account. We did have a few purists who thought that they should not be." [38] These comments do not speak directly to the issue of cost-benefit analysis, but they do indicate that legislative intent on the issue is somewhat chimerical.

The Supreme Court majority in the cotton dust decision argued that "Congress thought that the *financial costs* of health and safety problems in the workplace were as large or larger than the *financial costs* of eliminating these problems." The legislative history is indeed replete with statements that the costs of protecting workers would be justified. However, it is a long intellectual jump from this prediction about the overall program to a conclusion that Congress thought that any standard, no matter how strict, would be justified.

Moreover, the "feasibility analysis" endorsed by the majority still raises several problems of interpretation. First, what is "capable of being done" depends on the time frame. The acceptance of technology forcing acknowledges that standards have been adopted even though compliance was not currently feasible. Although such forcing was to be allowed only when adequate new technologies were "looming on the horizon," neither agencies nor courts have shown themselves terribly prescient in identifying these candidates. Second, what is "feasible" also depends on the scale of resources devoted to a task. The Supreme Court appears to have accepted the earlier views of the D.C. Circuit in *IUD v. Hodgson*, that "financial feasibility" should also be taken into account and that the criterion was whether most of the firms in an industry would be bankrupted. Although this view is consistent with the objective of protecting workers' jobs, it does imply that more protection will be afforded to workers in such industries as chemicals and oil than in industries with a higher proportion of production in marginal firms.

The tone of the debate and the language are clearly protective. A conclusion that the OSH Act *requires* cost-benefit analysis would be difficult to defend. The Supreme Court's conclusion that it *forbids* cost-benefit analysis is less implausible, but hardly compelling. A more reasonable conclusion, in both legal and policy terms, would be that the statute does neither, merely telling the regulators to be protective without giving clearer guidance about analytical procedures or substantive outcomes.[39] This was the factual conclusion of both Rehnquist and Burger. They then went on to draw the legal conclusion that such broad delegation was illegal. However, another reaction to this view of the facts is to grant the agency discretion to carry out balancing. Its leaders could then be required by the White House to adhere to requirements for some sort of cost-benefit analysis. (The cotton dust decision currently prohibits OSHA from complying with any such directives.)

The most recent trend in Supreme Court decisions would support a broad grant of discretion to agencies. After striking down deregulation efforts in such cases as the cotton dust one and *State Farm*, the Court's 1984 *Chevron* decision evinced a new willingness to defer to agencies unless Congress had addressed the precise issue and clearly indicated what interpretations were impermissible.[40] At least one judge of the D.C. Circuit has publicly acknowledged that *Chevron* has led her to rule differently on many challenges to agency rule making.[41] Another Supreme Court review of the act's provisions on feasibility could lead to a more flexible interpretation.

Given the high valuations implicit in most OSHA standards, greater use of benefit-cost analysis is likely to lead to less costly standards. However, although the advocates of cost-benefit analysis have been those critical of the strictness of standards, cost-benefit analysis is not inherently antagonistic to protectiveness. For example, Congress, the agency, the OMB, or even the courts could state that $20 million is an acceptable value for society to place on preventing a workplace disease death. Such statements might give new life to the debates about the allocation of resources among different lifesaving programs. In practice, all of these institutions are more likely to prefer to keep their valuations implicit and avoid the political heat that explicit valuations would generate.

Professional Consensus and the Science Base

Like their brethren at the EPA and the FDA, OSHA policymakers are required to take scientific evidence seriously. Although the evidence is always inadequate and often conflicting, the science base cannot simply be contravened. Thus the scientific consensus sets limits on what OSHA can do, and disagreements among scientists allow greater use of policy discretion. Understanding the nature of scientific views helps to explain the apparent anomaly of OSHA's 1972 asbestos standard, which was far laxer than any other PEL set by OSHA. One scholar has called it the one instance in which OSHA "reached a conclusion in a final standard that seems to have been outside the zone of reasonableness established by available knowledge."[42] How did OSHA reach that conclusion?

As recent lawsuits have revealed, at least some of the firms producing asbestos were aware by the 1930s that it could cause asbestosis, a progressive scarring of lung tissue that could be fatal. Although firms suppressed evidence of danger, parts of the medical community were aware of the disease. From 1963 to 1966 new research appeared that linked asbestos to lung cancer and to mesothelioma, a cancer of the lining of the lung. In 1969 Dr. Irving Selikoff, a leading asbestos researcher, recommended a 2-fiber/cc standard, a level that had recently been adopted by the British. At that time the AGGIH TLV was 12 fibers. In 1970 the AGGIH adopted a 5-fiber proposal; but because by statute OSHA had incorporated the *1968* list of TLVs, its standard remained at 12 fibers.

In December 1971, six months after OSHA began operating, the AFL-CIO's Industrial Union Department petitioned OSHA for an ETS for asbestos.

Assistant Secretary George Guenther acceded to the petition, issuing an ETS with a PEL of 5 fibers. Guenther had been a Pennsylvania businessman who was appointed to head the Bureau of Labor Standards before

Table 7.3   Estimates of Instances of Excess Disease among 100 Workers at the End of 40 years of Exposure to Asbestos

Average exposure[a]	Asbestosis		Bronchogenic cancer		Mesothelioma	
	Panel[b]	Selikoff	Panel[b]	Selikoff	Panel[b]	Selikoff
2	0 (20–0)	55	0 (1–0)	12	0 (0.1–0)	4
5	1 (55–0)	85	0.3 (5–0)	20	0 (0.2–0)	7
12	9 (70–6)		1.5 (10–0.05)		0.1 (1–0)	
30	19 (75–9)	95	3.4 (15–1)	20	0.1 (2–0)	5

Source: Arthur D. Little, Inc., *Impact of Proposed OSHA Standard for Asbestos: First Report to the U.S. Department of Labor* (Cambridge, Mass., April 1972), table 2, p. 18; Paul Brodeur, *Expendable Americans* (New York: Viking, 1974), p. 146. Brodeur did not provide Selikoff's estimates for the 12-fiber standard.
a. Number of fibers (> 5 ml) per cc (8-hr time-weighted average).
b. The first figure in the panel estimates is the median; the figures in parentheses show the range of the estimates.

coming to OSHA. He asked NIOSH to produce a criteria document on asbestos. In this and future criteria documents, NIOSH reported what was known about health effects and recommended a PEL that was designed to be the most protective level that could technically be achieved.

On January 12, OSHA endorsed the 5-fiber limit in its NPRM. At the end of the month NIOSH called for a PEL of 2 fibers but suggested that the 5-fiber standard be retained for two years to grant employers time to comply. Thus it appeared that OSHA might be on a collision course with the health-based recommendations of NIOSH. OSHA commissioned a consulting firm (Arthur D. Little) to assess the costs and health effects of a 2-fiber and a 5-fiber PEL. Their study polled ten medical experts on asbestos about its health effects. They were asked what percentage of workers would experience asbestos-related disease at the different exposure levels. The unions observed that almost all of these experts had been financially supported by the asbestos industry and pointed instead to the views of Selikoff, who had refused to participate in the poll. Table 7.3 juxtaposes the views of the panel of experts and those of Selikoff, which were reported later. Based on the panel estimates the study concluded that "reduction of the exposure of workers to asbestos dust from present levels to 5 fibers/cc will significantly reduce asbestos related diseases and achieve more than 99% of the benefits attainable from the control of dust levels." Although the table suggests that "99%" is an exaggeration, the consultant also estimated that compliance with a 2-fiber PEL would cost twice as much as with a 5-fiber PEL, and it is easy to see how it concluded that "a 5-fiber standard appears to be cost-effective at this time."[43]

Despite the Arthur D. Little study, when Guenther issued the final standard in June 1972, it leaned more toward the NIOSH recommendation than to OSHA's original proposal. The one difference was that OSHA allowed four years before the 2-fiber PEL took effect, whereas NIOSH had wanted only a two-year delay.

Labor and management both lashed out at the decision. Although OSHA was aware of the views of Selikoff, it chose to view them as an outlier, as indeed they were in the context of the Arthur D. Little panel. In the light of current knowledge, 2 fibers appears to be too loose a standard, but we need to consider how OSHA leaders perceived the issue. In the preamble to the standard, they explained that

no one has disputed that exposure to asbestos of high enough intensity and long enough duration is causally related to asbestosis and cancers. The dispute is as to the determination of a specific level below which exposure is safe.... Most medical opinion is divided between a two-fiber standard and a five-fiber standard.[44]

Citing the statutory requirement for the "protection of every employee, even of one who may have regular exposure to asbestos during a working life which may reach, or even exceed, 40 years," OSHA asserted that "the conflict in the medical evidence is resolved in favor of the health of employees."

Critical to this dismissal of Selikoff was OSHA's subscription to the belief that a "safe" level of exposure to asbestos existed. This belief in a "threshold" for carcinogenesis was inconsistent with the views of many scientists. However, in early 1972 the consensus that later emerged on this issue—at least among scientists in the regulatory establishment—had not yet crystallized.[45] For example, as late as 1973, the EPA relied on a 1971 National Academy of Sciences study that endorsed the threshold concept for asbestos, although other panels of scientists had suggested that for regulatory purposes carcinogens should be presumed to have no "safe" level.[46]

Although some branches of the EPA were regulating on the no-threshold assumption, OSHA's standards were being written by engineers who had relatively little familiarity with the new scientific interpretations and who certainly lacked the confidence to assert scientific leadership. If they had possessed these qualities, they might have tried to work with Selikoff and others to push for even stricter standards. At that point we would have seen whether Guenther's concerns for feasibility and industry interests overrode the protective argument. However, from the perspective of the time the

1972 standard can be judged reasonably protective. It allowed some delay, but it was below the ACGIH limit and reached the level NIOSH and the British had recommended.

It is also important to realize that no one at the time presented any data about the costs per life saved by the standard. Only later (beginning in 1975) would White House economists present these estimates. In 1972 neither Guenther nor anyone else had any idea what the figures were. No one could point out, "You're not being very protective. You're only willing to require industry to spend an average of $200,000 per death prevented."

In 1974 OSHA adopted its second PEL, a 1-ppm limit for vinyl chloride. Certainly in retrospect and even at the time this standard can be judged much stricter than the asbestos PEL.[47]

What explains why OSHA was more protective in the vinyl chloride case? The most important explanation is simply that the policy of regulating carcinogens had shifted in response to a different view of the existence of thresholds. Thus the initiative came not from the White House or OSHA's appointed leadership but from the desire of the growing number of OSHA scientists to affiliate themselves with the views that more established scientific groups at other agencies were developing. Indeed the fact that there were some health specialists within the agency, albeit few, was something new. In the spring of 1973 there were only ten professionals in the entire Office of Standards Development for both safety and health. By the end of 1974 the number had grown to twenty-three, with most of the increase being health professionals.[48] As their numbers grew, so did their self-confidence. Of course, the diffusion of the no-threshold assumption was facilitated by support from organized labor and environmentalists and lack of clear opposition from the White House. These political factors should remind us that, although it is true that OSHA's policy changed in response to a new view of thresholds, it would be only somewhat less accurate to claim that the view of thresholds changed in response to a change in policy.[49]

Engineering Controls versus Respirators

Another case in which professional beliefs have played an important role in shaping OSHA's policy is in the area of respirator use. The cost of meeting a PEL depends greatly on the methods that can be used to achieve it. OSHA has come under heavy fire from economists for requiring that compliance be accomplished by engineering controls rather than by allowing the use of personal protective equipment. No one questions that protective equipment is less costly, although defenders of engineering controls argue that a high quality respirator program may not be that much less costly than engineering cotrols. One recent example is a study of reducing the asbestos PEL from 2 fibers/cc to 0.5 fiber. In 1982 dollars the costs using engineering controls were estimated at $134 million a year; using respirators, at $54 million a year.[50]

OSHA's position has been that

respirators are capable of providing good protection only if they are properly selected for the types and concentrations of airborne contaminants present, properly fitted and refitted to the employee, worn by the employee, and replaced when they have ceased to provide protection. While it is theoretically possible for all of these conditions to be met, it is more often the case that they are not.[51]

Although the evidence on this point is anecdotal, it is likely that few respirator programs are conducted optimally. The important question, however, is how large the degradation in protection really is and how it compares to engineering controls, which are also subject to degradation because of inadequate maintenance. For example, if optimal respirator use would provide a fiftyfold reduction in exposures, but the actual program provides only a five- or tenfold reduction, this still may compare favorably with the protection from a fivefold reduction as a result of engineering controls.[52]

Although OSHA's preference for engineering controls may be reasonable, at least in a more flexible form, what demands explanation is the rigidity of its position and the refusal to even inquire into the effects of altering it. Not until the Reagan administration did OSHA, at the OMB's prodding, announce that it was considering a change in that policy and request public input on the effectiveness and costs of the different approaches.

What explains the strength of OSHA's preference for engineering controls? Kelman has emphasized the professional ideology of industrial hygienists. Invariably, the textbooks in professional schools emphasize the problems with personal protection and label it as an inferior solution. They "impart a feeling that relying on personal protection is seen as a confession of failure, a betrayal of the can-do approach of the engineer, a renunciation of pluck and determination for laziness and defeat."[53] In addition, the emphasis on engineering controls traditionally involves more demand for the hygienists' services and higher status. Nevertheless, hygienists who work for industry do appear less rigid in their endorsement of engineering controls. OSHA's proposal to elevate personal protection led to a ringing condemnation from the AGGIH, which is dominated by governmental and university-based hygienists. The American Industrial Hygiene Association (AIHA), which more closely represents those in industry, opposed it more mildly and emphasized the importance of professional judgment:

> The AIHA would like to go on record as stating that the elimination of workplace hazards is superior to the use of engineering controls. Where elimination is not feasible, engineering and other control strategies should be the primary methods for reducing or eliminating exposures in the workplace. However, personal protective equipment may be necessary pending more long-term solutions. We recognize that there are times where personal protective equipment is ultimately the only feasible control. The decision to recommend engineering controls, personal protective equipment or other control strategies depends on the nature of the hazard in question and should be based upon the professional judgment of an industrial hygienist.[54]

Thus, although professionals in industry are less rigid than their counterparts elsewhere, all hygienists share an ideology that judges personal protection as second best. This does have important consequences, for it means that industry and other opponents of the engineering controls requirement have difficulty getting experts to back their position.

Before Reagan, union opposition was a sufficient reason for OSHA to eschew reliance on respirators. Since then, lack of professional support for respirators has become the most influential factor.

Increased reliance on personal protective equipment was a major priority in the OMB's guidance to the new OSHA leader. It figured prominently in the reconsiderations of both the lead and cotton standards, which the OMB directed Assistant Secretary Auchter to undertake. Yet, in fact, in neither case did OSHA issue rules that changed the primacy of engineering controls. Part of the reason was that several of the firms that had already invested in engineering controls were not anxious to see less conscientious rivals be relieved of the requirement to follow suit. Another factor was professional opposition. In fact, when the OMB pressed OSHA to relax its requirement for engineering controls in the cotton dust standard—in a session where Presidential Science Adviser George Keyworth served as the arbitrator—its case collapsed when a prominent researcher with industry links wrote complaining that the OMB had misinterpreted his work as supporting the effectiveness of respirators.[55]

In proposals in 1983 and 1984—for ethylene dibromide and asbestos—OSHA did state its intent to allow more use of respirators; however, in the only standard actually promulgated (ethylene oxide in 1984), the engineering requirement remained virtually intact. Thus, despite strong pressure from the OMB and the absence of any court-imposed constraints, the personal protection alternative made little headway.

Implications for Policy Reform

Changes in the science base can force officials to transform the way they regulate. As we saw in chapter 3, a better understanding of carcinogenesis may enable us to distinguish much more clearly the conditions under which exposures are harmful. It has been stated that the existence of thresholds for exposures to carcinogens is a trans-scientific question that can never be answered with confidence.[56] Yet it does seem evident that answers to a host of related questions will be forthcoming and can either reinforce or undermine the assumptions on which the no-threshold view is based. If the no-threshold view is undermined, the greater difficulty in finding scientific supporters will make it harder to justify strict regulation. Courts, White House reviewers, and the agencies themselves will find that the "best available evidence" points the other way.

Of course, it is not apparent that scientific opinion is tending toward that view. And, as I argued previously, a tipping point—a preponderance of the evidence—would probably have to be reached before many would give up the assumptions that undergird protective policy. Thus, although changes in scientific understanding will certainly shape future policies, they are not predictable and can hardly be relied on to justify relaxing the strictness with which standards are set.

Broader Causes of Strictness

Thus far we have focused on OSHA health standards and variations among them. Not all US government programs dealing with safety and health are as costly as OSHA health standards. Even OSHA's safety standards are probably not as costly, although we lack the data needed for a conclusive answer. Comparison of OSHA health standards with safety and health regulations from the EPA, the NHTSA, and the Consumer Product Safety Commission found that the EPA and OSHA had by far the most costly standards, whereas the traffic safety measures that required direct budgetary outlays (for example, to straighten highways) had the lowest cost.[57] Many of the traffic measures had costs in 1976 dollars of less than $200,000.

Most explanations for these differences fall into two broad categories. The first includes those explanations that derive from the preferences of citizens or elites regarding how to value different deaths. For example, the ability of victims to avoid the risk and the ex ante or ex post identification of the victims have been posited as possible explanations. In chapter 2 we saw that some people do appear to value the prevention of different types of death differently, although the magnitude of the variations were typically only a fewfold. The second category of explanations includes those that derive from differences in the political power held by various groups.[58] It should be evident that the distinction between these categories can be overdrawn. The ability of a group to get its way on a particular issue is affected by the distribution of preferences on that issue. Even more pertinent, citizen preferences are not magically converted into public policy. They must be mediated through political institutions.

A thorough study of that mediation process cannot be conducted here, but I can suggest some insights, beginning with a discussion of studies that have compared regulation in different countries. In one of the earlier studies, comparing occupational safety and health regulation in the United States and Sweden, Kelman concluded that the values of agency officials, not pressures from outside groups, were the most important determinants of decisions in the period from 1970 to 1976. These decisions

tended to favor more over less protective alternatives because these officials tend to hold what may be called pro-protection values, arising out of the ideology of the safety and health professions and out of the mission of the organizations they work for. No plausible case can be made that these decisions arose out of technical expertise, and the political system outside the agencies will be shown to have great difficulty influencing agency behavior, which explains the astonishing finding that the important differences between the relative strength of labor and business in the United States and Sweden, and the differences between a Republic Administration in one country and a Social Democratic administration in the other, had little impact on the content of regulations.[59]

Experience under the Carter and, especially, the Reagan administrations certainly is not consistent with Kelman's conclusion about the impact of the political system.[60]

And, although professional values and expertise have helped to shape the strictness of OSHA's policies, they have not been as potent as Kelman suggests. If professional values had been overwhelmingly important, it would be difficult to explain why OSHA frequently adopted PELs that were much lower than those adopted by the ACGIH, the organization that represents chiefly the governmental and academic industrial hygienists who are the most protective in their profession. If professional values alone were so important, then we should expect to find that the OSHA and the ACGIH choices were the same.

Table 7.4 International Comparison of Exposure Limits for Hazards with New OSHA Standards

Substance	United States	Britain	France	Germany
Acrylonitrile	1978: reduced PEL from 20 ppm to 2 ppm	1979: reduced limit to 5 ppm	1978: reduced limit to 1 ppm in new factories; 3 ppm in old	1979: reduced limit to 6 ppm
Asbestos	1972: reduced PEL from 12 fibers to 5. 1976: 2 fibers	1969: 2 fibers 1979: more stringent limits set	No exposure limits given	1979: 0.05 and 0.1 respirable fiber
Benzene	1978: reduced PEL from 10 ppm to 1 ppm [reversed by Supreme Court]	1978: 10 ppm	keeps 25 ppm limit	1979: 8 ppm
Vinyl chloride	1974: reduced PEL from 500 ppm to 1 ppm	1972: 200 ppm 1975: 25 ppm 1975: 10 ppm 1978: 5 ppm 1981: 2 ppm	1975: 5 ppm 1980: 1 ppm in new–factories; 3 ppm in old	1979: 5 ppm in existing plants; 2 ppm in new 1980: 3 ppm

Source: Ronald Brickman, Sheila Jasanoff, and Ronald Ilgen, *Controlling Chemicals* (Ithaca, N.Y.: Cornell University Press, 1985), table A1.

All of the studies of comparative risk regulation agree that, although the American system is characterized by far more conflict, the substantive outcomes appear to be similar across nations. The main quantitative evidence presented in support of this conclusion comes from Brickman et al., whose study of the regulation of fourteen chemicals in the United States, Britain, France, and Germany observes that "no country appears notably more or less aggressive than another when regulatory records are compared over a period of years."[61]

Yet the evidence, at least for occupational exposures, actually seems to indicate that OSHA has been stricter in individual standards than these others. Table 7.4 shows the figures that Brickman et al. cite for the four hazards for which OSHA has promulgated new PELs. (Although other countries did reduce exposure limits for some of the other ten chemicals in this sample, they never set a limit below the OSHA PEL.) For asbestos, not surprisingly, other nations have adopted limits that are more protective than OSHA's 1972 standard. However, for the others, OSHA's standard is clearly the most protective for benzene and vinyl chloride and is approached only by France in acrylonitrile. Although the differences in limits may appear small, the fact of rising marginal cost curves may make the cost differences between these rules significant. Of course, the overturning of the 1-ppm benzene standard by the Supreme Court left the United States with a standard no stricter than Britain's or Germany's. However, the point here is that the agency in the United States had tried to act more strictly, not necessarily that the final outcome is greater protection.

Sweden appears to have matched the US changes more closely. Here, however, it is worth noting that the policy actions in the two countries cannot be viewed as totally independent. This dependence goes beyond the fact that scientific findings are shared by all countries. Kelman provides several examples of Swedish officials adopting strict standards in order to avoid the embarrassment of being less strict than the United States. On vinyl chloride Kelman reports that the Swedish agency had been "considering a 5 ppm exposure limit, even though, given the OSHA decision, any decision higher than 1 ppm would have been embarrassing for the government. It is unclear how the decision would have gone had OSHA made a different decision, but the OSHA move made 1 ppm a virtual certainty." [62] On asbestos, OSHA's 1975 proposal (which, ironically, it did not follow through on until 1986) to reduce the exposure limit from 2.0 to 0.5 fiber/cc spurred a front page article, "Sweden Lagging Behind U.S.," and an immediate lowering of the limit to 1.0 fiber. [63]

Vogel argues that the costs imposed by particular regulations in the United States have not been substantially greater than in Britain. Because comparative data on costs are lacking, we cannot assess this claim directly. What we can do is compare the practices and policies employed in the two countries. Here all of the studies testify to the following differences in Britain: Rules are developed through a bargaining process between labor and management, and each has a veto on the final choice; standards are often set above the lowest feasible level; technology forcing is eschewed; and the rules can be applied flexibly to different employers, rather than requiring all industries to meet them. [64] With these differences in policy, it is difficult to believe that the differences in costs are not substantial.

Vogel's explanation for the tougher American regulations, is, I believe, more on the mark:

The contemporary American public's suspicion of technology is directly linked to both its hostility to business and its mistrust of government: it is not so much science and technology per se that the American public finds threatening as the extent to which they appear to be controlled by private companies—companies that are regarded as both inherently irresponsible and too powerful to be effectively regulated by government. Threats to the public's health and safety have not been seen, as they are in Britain, as an inevitable component of production and consumption in a highly industrialized and affluent society; rather they have become identified with the profit motive of America's largest firms. [65]

Thus government agencies are not to be trusted to work out reasonable requirements by sitting down privately with industry.

A complement to this explanation is the more open and entrepreneurial politics practiced in the United States, especially since the 1960s. Compared to members of Parliament, members of Congress have both greater ability to raise issues and greater incentive to do so. Their greater ability comes from the lack of party discipline in voting, their independent sources of campaign funds, and their frequent positions as chairs of subcommittees. The incentive comes from the apparent political attractiveness of most risk-regulation policies and the media's interest in covering stories about corporate misconduct and bureaucratic foot-dragging. One effect of the shift of regulatory authority from the states to Washington is that regulatory issues receive more media attention.

Greater media attention lends greater importance to popular values. When health choices are made without much media attention and when (as in Britain) politicians have little opportunity or incentive to criticize the result, public attitudes impose relatively little constraint. For example, there is less likelihood that regulators will be forced to consider popular aversion to "trading off lives for dollars." The American evidence suggests that criticizing lax health and safety policies decisions has been a politically rewarding activity for politicians. For example, a tabulation of all the dozens of hearings reported in the Congressional Quarterly's *Environment and Health* showed that all but four featured criticisms that agencies had been too lax. Of these four, one concerned saccharin, one the auto interlock that prevented cars from starting unless seat belts were fastened, and two involved agriculture. Thus, unless the costs of protective regulation are visibly borne by the public or by electorally significant groups such as agriculture or small business, entrepreneurship on behalf of strict standards will be rewarding.[66]

Conclusions

Many factors have combined to produce occupational health standards that have a high cost per death prevented. The statute clearly puts a high priority on worker protection, and the courts have identified it as the overriding objective of the act. Organized labor, which helped to place protective language in the act, has continued to speak out for the "lowest feasible" PELs and against reliance on personal protective equipment, policies that lead to high costs. Under President Carter, the unions got their pick as OSHA's head; even under Republican presidents, organized labor has been able to rely on congressional supporters, media criticism, and the threat of legal action to give weight to its demands. Although the affected firms have not been the chief advocates of any OSHA standards, the existence of compliance cost differentials among them has facilitated OSHA's acquisition of the "substantial evidence" that it needs to support strict standards. The state of scientific knowledge about many hazards is so uncertain that even moderate risk aversion among policymakers can support quite protective standards. Such risk aversion is probably encouraged by the mistrust of corporate practices and government capabilities that currently exists.[67] In addition, there are characteristics of workplace disease that strike a protective chord in many citizens. Stories about callous corporations make good news; attacking them is good politics.

What are the chief opportunities for getting agencies to issue less strict standards? The most direct are either for Congress to amend the statute or for the Supreme Court to reverse its cotton dust decision and allow explicit balancing of costs and benefits. The latter probably has a higher near-term probability, but both should be pursued. Allowing balancing is desirable in itself and should have some effect on reducing obstacles to rule making and thus speeding the pace. However, as I argue in the next chapter, a more satisfactory solution to overregulation and underregulation will require additional legislative changes. They should be pursued in a package, some making it easier to issue less strict rules and some facilitating a faster pace.

Congressional action does depend on either greater labor acceptance of the idea of trading off strictness for extensiveness or a weakened labor movement that is incapable of resisting. If labor is too weak, however, we may get a cure to overregulation but not to underregulation. The ideal would be for labor leaders to embrace the change. I argued that their main concern in this area is workers' health; thus convincing them that health can be improved should be effective. In chapter 10 I return to how this policy change might be carried out.

Shifts in scientific views on such questions as the existence of thresholds for carcinogenesis may occur over time, but they cannot be easily controlled by policymakers. What about the broad features of American political culture and its institutions that foster conflict? Obviously, they too are not easy to change. However, the task is to design both specific compromises and new methods for regulatory decision making that will foster more sensible outcomes despite the existence of those features. I turn now to that task.

III

DIRECTIONS FOR REFORM

8

Generic Reform of Regulatory Procedures

In the preceding chapters I have argued that standard setting for toxic substances at OSHA is plagued by both overregulation and underregulation. I have tried to explain why both have occurred, emphasizing that overregulation is an important cause of underregulation. More generally, any standard-setting program in the United States that produces strict standards is likely to encounter a similar dilemma. Regulators should set standards more frequently but less strictly. But how is this to be accomplished?

In chapter 10 I present a three-step proposal for addressing this problem directly through legislative action to amend the OSH Act: (1) allowing benefit-cost balancing; (2) establishing a two-track system in which standards with low total costs would not have to meet the evidentiary standards of major proposals; and (3) adopting all the changes in exposure limits recommended by the ACGIH in the years since 1968. But a first question is whether other strategies can deal with this problem in an adequate enough fashion to make this proposal superfluous. To answer that question, we need to step back and examine the major proposals that have been made for regulatory reform. These fall into two broad categories. The first includes proposals for generic reforms in the *procedures* for making regulations. Prominent examples include the regulatory budget, regulatory negotiation, and extensions of regulatory review. The second category includes substantive strategies that rely on what have been loosely called "alternatives to regulation." Two of the most prominent are "information strategies," which try to strengthen market forces by supplying information about risks, and "toxic tort strategies," which try to use the liability system to provide stronger signals to firms to prevent disease. Both of these policy tools have been proposed as alternatives to reliance on the "command and control" approach exemplified by standard setting.

In this chapter I look at the regulatory budget, regulatory negotiation, and extensions of regulatory reform. In chapter 9 I turn to information strategies and the use of the tort system. Although this discussion should illuminate the general merits and feasibility of these options, my main purpose is to assess whether they can correct OSHA's twin dilemma.

Table 8.1   Categories of Regulatory Reform Procedures

Affected branch	Type of procedure	
	Analytical	Political
White House	Regulatory review	Regulatory budget
Congress	Sunset provisions	Regulatory budget
Courts	Strict review	Deference to regulatory negotiation

Generic Strategies for Reform of Regulatory Procedures

The literature on regulatory reform frequently suggests that the policy problem should be defined in terms of economic inefficiency and political unresponsiveness. The meaning of "economic inefficiency" is reasonably clear, but "political unresponsiveness" is hardly unambiguous. One connotation is a call for participation in rule making, but this is a democratic, populist theme that is quite distinct and often opposed to economists' calls for efficiency.[1] In the minds of many economist critics, inefficiency and unresponsiveness are linked because the current political institutions do not provide the means or incentives to curb inefficient behavior by the agencies. As Robert Litan and William Nordhaus write:

Decisions of fundamental political importance are left to unelected agency officials or not decided at all. From an economic perspective, the absence of a workable oversight process has led to inefficiency, since agencies have been given little or no incentive to balance regulatory costs and objectives against each other and thus to require private dollars to be spent first on those programs producing the greatest benefits.[2]

Arguments that regulatory agencies are totally unresponsive—"out of control"—are surely overstated.[3] They generally appear quite responsive to the spirit of the statutes that created them and to the court decisions interpreting the statutes. They have been sufficiently responsive to the congressional committees that authorized them so that, except in the case of the Federal Trade Commission, no efforts have been made by the committees to reverse their courses. We have no evidence that strict safety and environmental regulation runs counter to public opinion; if anything, the public seems supportive.

Indeed, it is precisely because they recognize these types of responsiveness that the more politically sophisticated critics of regulatory inefficiency are skeptical of regulatory reform proposals that call for more and better analysis. We can distinguish proposals that rely primarily on analytical improvements from those that rely on altering decision-making procedures to change incentives, that is, on "political" methods. In table 8.1 the analytical proposals include White House review of rules, sunset laws, and requirements for heavy evidentiary tests by reviewing courts. The political methods include the regulatory budget and regulatory negotiations.[4]

During the 1970s all three branches of government gave more attention to regulatory issues as the growth of regulatory problems increased the costs and salience of regulation for the economy and the public.[5] Congress increased oversight of its new creations, although falling far short of what some observers deemed desirable. The courts adopted more of a "hard look" at agency rules, demanding the accumulation of more and more supporting evidence. The White House initiated a regulatory review program that required agencies to conduct more thorough analyses of regulatory impacts and options.

The achievements of White House review during this period are usually portrayed as meager. Christopher DeMuth's often cited analysis provided several reasons for this outcome.[6] First, for legal and political reasons, the review process stopped short of requiring agency rules to meet a benefit-cost test. Second, and most important, presidents had no incentive to stand behind the reviewers and insist that agencies toe the line. President Carter made it clear that the analysts in the Regulatory Analysis Review Group were to act as kibitzers, not as superregulators. Third, in any event the process could only touch a portion of regulatory activities and the reviewers could not match agency expertise with available resources. Fourth, "the process by its very nature cannot affect the rate at which regulations are generated, and thus their aggregate economic impact." Fifth, the review process was based on the "unpromising idea" that regulatory decisions would be improved by centralizing decision making. As an alternative, although with some ambivalence, DeMuth proposed the regulatory budget as a promising option for a decentralized approach to controlling costs.

Before examining the regulatory budget, a brief review of the critique of regulatory review—especially in light of the experience of the Reagan years—is in order.[7] The view that presidents currently have little to gain by being in the middle of disputes about agency rules seems correct. They will make enemies of the losers and draw attacks for "political interference" in agency rule making. The Reagan presidency shows, however, that a president can play a much more directing role in regulation than had previously been seen. Careful choice of agency chiefs who would take directions, at least initially, from the White House and the far greater effort to provide central guidance sharply (if briefly) reversed the direction of regulations at the EPA, OSHA, and the NHTSA. The role of Executive Order 12291 is somewhat less clear. It required agencies, to the extent allowed by law, to choose options that maximized net benefits. It also required them to submit regulatory analyses in private to the OMB before proposing a rule and again, later, before issuing a final rule. Agency actions had to wait until OMB criticisms had been satisfactorily answered. Some rules were held up by the OMB for many months, and there is no doubt that the procedure delayed the issuance of rules. However, losses in the courts and political damage caused by congressional attacks on the EPA's subservience to industry caused the White House to back off and encouraged regulators to become more independent. The experience demonstrates again that presidential support is essential if reviewers are to win most disputes with agencies.

DeMuth's point that the review process cannot affect the rate at which regulations are generated is hard to accept. The added delays of OMB review under Reagan testify to that. More generally, rule making proceeds slowly precisely because of the combined impact of political controversy and procedural requirements. The willingness of courts to scrutinize agency rules and the ability of all parties to trigger that scrutiny gives the agency a strong incentive to make its case as complete and airtight as possible.[8]

Regulatory review under Reagan has proven to have greater potential for constraining agency actions than critics writing before he took office had been willing to acknowledge. Yet the search remains for a procedure that is not so dependent on the anti-regulatory views of the White House and that would build in incentives for cost-effectiveness, rather than relying on outmanned outside review.

The Regulatory Budget

The concept of a regulatory budget has won the admiration of many prominent analysts of regulation.[9] They note that the size of nonregulatory programs is constrained by congressional appropriations and, ultimately, by the size of government tax revenues. In contrast, the costs of most regulatory programs are borne directly by the firms and individuals who have to comply with them. No budget limits the size of these regulatory costs and neither the president nor Congress review them in the aggregate.

In its basic outline the regulatory budget would be established by Congress and the president for each agency, perhaps by starting with a total budget and allocating it among them.[10] Despite some glaring problems, the allure of the concept is easy to understand. By mandating the establishment of a budget constraint, the regulatory budget would clarify the opportunity costs of adopting a regulation and encourage cost-effectiveness. The knowledge that agencies would be competing against each other would lead them to propose their "best" regulations in order to win OMB and congressional approval. The simultaneous consideration of all new regulations also allows their joint impact on particular industries and the economy as a whole to be taken into account. The placement of the budget decisions in the hands of Congress and the president also forces them to assume responsibility for the overall magnitude and priorities of regulation. The establishment of a new regulatory committee to review the regulatory budget and the requirement for approval by the full Congress and by the president will weaken the powers of the authorizing committees, which are often viewed as too supportive of the single-mission agencies. Much has been made of the fact that the regulatory budget establishes new institutional mechanisms that are action forcing. The president could not avoid becoming involved, as he could in the regulatory review process. And once a budget cap was established, legislators would be able to defend votes against particular programs by arguing that other, more valuable programs would have had to be sacrificed.

There are numerous analytical difficulties with the regulatory budget. First, it is not clear what the basis for establishing the size of the budget would be. Unlike the expenditure budget, there are no analogues to revenues and deficits that constrain the regulatory budget's size. Analytically, the obvious option would be to include in the budget all regulations that meet a benefit-cost test. This would maximize the net benefits from regulation. However, if this is the criterion, then the regulatory budget is really a mechanism for enforcing the use of cost-benefit analysis in the regulatory review process, the implications of which I discuss later.

If one believes that the chief problem with regulation is that there is too much of it, then the size of the regulatory budget becomes easier to resolve: Start shrinking it. The actual size does not matter as much as the fact of having a smaller budget, which will induce more cost-effective behavior. Indeed, without a reduction in regulatory "budget authority," the incentives for cost-effectiveness will be greatly if not fully attenuated. Of course, the potential flaw in this resolution is that the benefits from greater cost-effectiveness may be outweighed by the elimination of worthwhile projects that will not fit in the budget.

Second, as every commentator has emphasized, estimating the full social costs of regulations can be devilishly difficult, especially when the programs restrict output or behaviors rather than merely requiring outlays for compliance. A typical example is that the EPA, rather than requiring firms to install pollution devices, could enhance air quality in certain regions by prohibiting new plants from opening. The costs of the latter strategy are much more difficult to calculate. The fear is that a regulatory budget would focus on the more direct costs, creating incentives for agencies to rely on more indirect—but possibly more costly—regulations. That fear, probably more than anything else, has led supporters of the regulatory budget concept to waffle about its practicality. Some have suggested that experiments with the regulatory budget be tried at one or two agencies, preferably ones such as OSHA where the policy instruments rely more heavily on direct costs.[11] Proponents of an experiment have not, however, specified how it would produce insights that would help to address the problem of indirect costs. A regulatory budget limited to OSHA and the NHTSA might still be worthwhile; however, the limitation could shrink potential benefits to the point where the major institutional changes a regulatory budget would require would not be justified.

If the regulatory budget were really set up solely on the basis of budget numbers, without regard to the merits of agency proposals, it could achieve the purpose of decentralizing analysis; neither central analysts nor Congress would have to weigh benefits. However, such an approach requires taking the numbers seriously, either trying to measure all costs with all the pitfalls that raises or limiting the budget to direct costs with its set of possible perverse incentives. With a budget, even if the initial amounts were arbitrary, an iterative process would be set in motion. Congress could review the agency's behavior and decide whether it wanted to move in the direction of more or less. Although inexact, it is little different from the process in the expenditure budget. One problem, however, is that regulatory expenditures are often lumpy, especially as we move from all regulations down to those in specific agencies or programs. Some years might see no regulations; others, several costly ones. If the budget is based simply on feedback based on past agency behavior, the budget might be far larger than the agency actually wants or needs. Its budget (or some arbitrary portion of it) could be carried through to the next year or it could be declared lost; the latter policy would create incentives to use it, not lose it.

One way to overcome the lumpiness problem is to include the costs of past as well as currently proposed regulations. These costs are a better measure of the impact of the agency and could give it an incentive to amend an old rule in order to promulgate a new, better one. However, this step introduces new complications: We must estimate the costs of every rule the agency has ever promulgated, or at least those estimated to still be imposing costs. Presumably, each year the enforcement of old rules is imposing costs, although how much employer spending would have occurred in the absence of regulation is a persistent and thorny question.

The same question is raised by conventional efforts to estimate benefits and costs. However, the problem is less thorny precisely because of the greater symmetry of benefit-cost analysis; that is, to the extent that benefits are understated (overstated) by incorrectly assuming that employers would (not) have reduced emissions on their own, the costs too will be understated (overstated).[12] When costs alone are being measured, these errors will cause more mischief.

The broad alternative—which avoids all the problems of hard-to-estimate costs, perverse incentives, and lumpiness—is to base budgets directly on the merits of proposals, or, actually, as Litan and Nordhaus have suggested, to vote on particular proposals rather than on budgets. This change, however, dramatically changes the nature of the procedure. Instead of a decentralized procedure in which agencies respond to the budgets, analysts and Congress would be deciding on whether the rules are worthwhile.

Like every other commentator on the regulatory budget, Litan and Nordhaus believe that the analytical problems it raises, especially the problem of measuring indirect costs, preclude its adoption, at least at this time. In the hope of preserving many of the benefits of the regulatory budget, Litan and Nordhaus have developed what they believe is a more feasible proposal for a "legislated regulatory calendar" (LRC).[13] As with the regulatory budget, the OMB would review agency proposals and develop a set that the president would submit to Congress. In Congress it would be reviewed by a new regulatory committee; in addition, Litan and Nordhaus concede that regulations for particular agencies may have to be sent to the traditional authorizing committees as well, in order to defuse their opposition to the new procedure. Both committees would send their recommendations to the full body, but there would no longer be any budget ceiling for the agencies or for the total.

Several aspects of the legislated regulatory calendar deserve attention. The first concerns the timing of the process and the ability of the LRC to specify the exact content of the regulation. As one option, Litan and Nordhaus propose that the agency be unable to modify the proposals authorized by Congress.[14] Although they do not emphasize how radical a change this would constitute, it would transform rule making from an administrative process to a legislative one. The task of building a record based on public hearings or other solicitation of information would become secondary. For all agencies this solicitation has been an important contributor to the quality of rule making, although more for some than for others. OSHA, for example, relies especially heavily on the feedback it gets to its initial proposals, whereas the EPA is often virtually "locked in" at the time of proposal.[15] Prior legislative review of regulations would mean review without all of the available information having been considered. There are cases in which early reviews can be useful; for example, the concept of screening candidates for regulation requires early decisions on a large number of hazards using information that is cheap and easily available. However, as one gets closer to the final regulation, it will often be worthwhile to get more information.

If, as a second option, agencies are allowed to modify the proposals in the legislated regulatory calendar, Litan and Nordhaus argue that "the guidelines written by Congress should be sufficiently clear that the issue of whether a particular change is permitted by Congress is not a source of endless litigation."[16] Litan and Nordhaus note that one way to achieve that would be to require Congress to reauthorize *any* change made by the agency. But Litan and Nordhaus expect that agencies would respond to a legislated regulatory calendar by stating proposals in terms that would allow them flexibility in later stages. This leaves open the question of exactly what issues would be resolved by Congress: For example, in the case of an OSHA health standard, would it be the industries covered by the standard, the PEL, monitoring and medical exam requirements, the effective date, the use of personal protective equipment? Because they propose that floor amendments not be allowed, Litan and Nordhaus predict that the content of regulations will be designed in negotiations between the agency and the senior members and staff of the congressional committees.

Litan and Nordhaus suggest that the LRC would "place a congressional imprimatur of lawfulness on the rules authorized through the legislated regulatory calendar," protecting agencies from challenges that they lacked statutory authority. However, they state that it "would not affect the agencies' evidentiary burdens, which are discharged by receiving public comments after proposals are announced."[17] Yet this seems odd indeed, first because the agencies will now be severely constrained in responding to those comments and, second, because the usual effect of legislative involvement is precisely to slash the evidentiary burden. Congress does not need "substantial evidence" for its laws in order to be upheld. Shouldn't greater involvement of elected officials lead to more judicial deference?

An assessment of the LRC idea requires addressing several related questions: Is adoption of the LRC politically feasible? If it were adopted, what form would it take, and would it have the effects Litan and Nordhaus predict? In that form, would the LRC be desirable? Although many of his colleagues supported Senator Lloyd Bentsen's bill (S.51 in 1980) to establish a regulatory budget process, the support led to no serious action and can best be interpreted as position taking on the "overregulation" issue.[18] In fact, several major obstacles stand in the way of congressional approval of either the regulatory budget or the LRC. If Congress had wanted the responsibility of reviewing each new regulation, it could have limited the authority of agencies to issue rules, requiring a return to Congress. Or, as it did in some cases, Congress could write the specific regulations itself. The hazard-specific rules established by legislation (for example, on auto emissions and PCBs) have tended to be simple, blunt rules (a ban on PCBs; 90% reduction in all auto emissions). Or, in a number of cases, Congress created provisions for a legislative veto, to be used if the public response to a rule indicated that its repeal would win political credit.

Why has Congress chosen not to exercise more direct control over the issuance of regulations, opting instead to delegate it to the agencies? If we start with a model of vote-seeking politicians who allocate their always scarce time among credit claiming, position taking, and advertising, then we need to ask whether congressional review of all regulations makes electoral sense. Each regulation is a unique bundle of complex, often highly technical issues. The regulations carry no funds to distribute to constituents or to the districts. Responding to public outcries with either a legislative veto or legislative hearings would be a more efficient use of time. Regulations do, of course, confer benefits on some groups and costs on others. But the fact that Congress usually delegates the decisions suggests that the political costs of responsibility are often viewed as outweighing the political benefits. A legislated regulatory calendar would not allow the luxury of picking and choosing when to intervene.

The example of the fiscal budget reforms of 1974 has been proposed as a possible object lesson that dramatic institutional reforms—such as the LRC—are possible. However, one leading analyst of the budget reforms has observed: "Mere discontent with its own procedures would not, by itself, have been sufficient stimulus to cause Congress to devise a budget process. Congress needed a firm indication that the legislative branch would lose power and esteem if it persisted without a budget process of its own."[19] This explanation is based on the institutional concerns of congressional leaders rather than on the electoral needs of its members, but it also portends poorly for the prospects of the regulatory budget. Although control over the regulatory agencies (especially the agencies outside of the executive branch) has been considered a special purview of Congress, it has not been as central to the congressional mission as is control over spending. The absence of bipartisan attacks on the Reagan administration's aggressive regulatory initiatives illustrates the less central role of regulatory oversight. As Litan and Nordhaus noted, special opposition to regulatory budget or legislated regulatory calendar would be likely from the leaders of the authorizing committees that oversee them. Although the process would give them more opportunities to intervene, it would also subject their influence to the control of the entire Congress. Moreover, the leaders are often ideological supporters of the agency missions. In one fell swoop the legislation enacting the regulatory budget or LRC would wipe out a host of key provisions in current statutes: the authority vested in agency leaders to decide whether to issue rules, the mandates for balancing or not balancing costs and benefits, timetables for proposing rules, and more. Defenders of those programs can be expected to put up a fierce fight.

If a legislated regulatory calendar were enacted, would it tend to curb regulatory expansion and promote efficiency? The answer is not certain, but there are good reasons to believe that it would not. In his analysis of the 1974 Budget Reform Act, Allen Schick has pointed out "that Congress could not subscribe to a biased procedure, that is, to arrangements which explicitly favored spending cuts over increases. To have done so would have curbed the legislative power of Congress by making future outcomes dependent on budget procedures rather than on majority will." [20] Thus bills that foreordain restrictive outcomes (like Bentsen's, which mandated a 5 percent reduction each year in the budget total) would be especially unlikely to pass. In addition, a legislated regulatory calendar would not provide the political justification for opposing protective measures that a regulatory budget could, that is, that you could not support protective measure x because it would have precluded the adoption of protective measure y, which was even better.

Thus a legislated regulatory calendar would not change the context in which Congress would review regulations. Legislators would continue to respond to their current perceptions of the political costs and benefits of expanding or shrinking health, safety, and environmental rules. The chief problem facing those worried about the inefficiency of risk regulation is that most people are not. The costs are not well perceived, and it is not clear who really bears them. Thus their magnitude does not seem overwhelming, and the benefits of appearing to be a society that cares about protecting its citizens can easily appear larger. Congress, which often does a good job of reflecting public preferences, favors protective regulation—except, as we saw in chapter 7, when it hits directly at farm or small business constituencies or when consumers are directly affronted, as with seat-belt interlocks or saccharin. This analysis of the politics of regulation is not supportive of the view that a legislated regulatory calendar would be restrictive. Indeed, it seems at least as likely that Congress would add or toughen rules as that it would limit them.

We also need to question whether the incentives for cost-effectiveness in either a regulatory budget or a legislated regulatory calendar would be as strong as proponents hope. The prediction that these procedures will spur cost-effectiveness is based on the assumption that agencies are trying to maximize their overall protective effects. Thus, if you constrain their total costs, they will try to make better use of their more limited resources. In fact, because of the greater political rewards, OSHA has usually followed the strategy of letting organized labor and the media determine its priorities. The hazards have not been picked on the basis of an analytic approach to maximizing public health gains. This is true despite the fact that political and administrative constraints prevent OSHA (and other standard-setting agencies) from producing many new rules. We could say that these constraints already impose a form of de facto regulatory budget. These agencies' failures, despite these constraints, to pursue a health-maximizing strategy does not inspire confidence that they would behave much differently under the constraints of a true regulatory budget.

In summary, the regulatory budget is intellectually attractive because, by creating a budget constraint and placing the decisions in the hands of Congress and the president, it would force trade-offs and encourage, although not guarantee, more cost-effective behavior on the part of the agencies. Political solutions in this area are attractive because the issues that regulators must address involve major clashes of values and interests. Yet once we move from the regulatory budget to the LRC, Congress becomes involved in the details of rule making, not in setting the priorities and limits—just the opposite of what Litan and Nordhaus correctly view as its proper role. Such detailed and binding congressional involvement is especially troubling so early in the rule-making process, before any public comment has been received. From an analytical perspective, legislative drafting of regulations is troubling. Not only is less information likely to be available at that time, but to the extent that Congress is not pulled by the goal of assuaging public fearfulness, it will often be pushed by the organized business groups whose interests are at stake. The history of direct congressional involvement in air pollution policy—the blunt 90 percent reductions in auto emissions in the 1970 Clean Air Act or the concession to the "clean coal, dirty air" coalition in the 1977 Clean Air Act Amendments—

does not inspire much confidence that a greater role would lead to more efficient rules, unless the institutional framework had been substantially altered.

Regulatory Negotiations

The practice of "negotiating regulations" has its roots in collective bargaining and environmental mediation. When industrial relations scholar and arbitrator John Dunlop was secretary of labor in the Ford administration, he argued that the give and take of collective bargaining provided a better model for rule making than the adversarial process being practiced. The growing practice of environmental mediation brings the parties in disputes together to try to find compromise solutions, usually for cases involving particular sites or projects.

The leading analyst of regulatory negotiations observes that "to the extent that rulemaking has political legitimacy, it derives from the right of affected interests to present facts and arguments to an agency under procedures designed to ensure the rationality of the agency's decisions." [21] However, the issues addressed by the agencies involve policy judgments and values, not simply factual determinations. Although the rule-making procedure "confines and structures agency discretion, it does not provide a forum suitable for the resolution of the political questions or for the exercise of subtle value choices." [22] The adversarial system, which is the basis of current rule making, provides no opportunities for the political agreements that normally lend legitimacy to such disputes.

Critics also charge that the current rule-making process spawns ill-conceived and inefficient rules. One reason for this outcome is that the parties have nothing to gain by expressing their true concerns because they have no way of ensuring that a concession on one issue will gain concessions on another. Parties "raise every issue to nearly equal prominence and place far more issues in contention than may be necessary." [23] The issues raised may not really be the ones bothering the parties, but the particular forum may not allow the true concerns to be raised. "If the parties are unable to define the true issues of concern, the decisionmaker and other parties will have difficulty in addressing the parties' positions and in making informed trade-offs when developing the factual basis of a rule and striking the inherently political choice embodied therein." [24]

This process can be contrasted with the bargaining that goes on in a legislature or in labor-management negotiations. In these contexts, opportunities to trade votes across issues will tend to elicit the true concerns of the parties and incentives to compromise are generated by the costs incurred if no agreement is reached. At least in the absence of major externalities, bargaining outcomes will tend to be more efficient than rule making because, as in any voluntary exchange, each party will make only those trades that increase its well-being. Thus in a bargaining situation it would probably be counterproductive for a union to attempt to require firms to spend large sums on measures that workers placed little value on because those funds have a clear opportunity cost. In a nonbargaining context it becomes much less certain what, if anything, is being given up by the imposition of a costly requirement. It is important to recall, however, that the exchanges that will voluntarily be made may be quite different if the distribution of wealth or power changes. The establishment of regulation or changes in the regulatory rules—that is, what will be required if no agreement is reached—can dramatically alter the power of the parties and the types of voluntary agreements that will be made.

Harter has explored the conditions conducive to the success of regulatory negotiation as well as the major issues about how it should be conducted. The criteria for successful regulatory negotiation include the following:

1. The parties can impose costs on each other and thus have an incentive to bargain.

2. The number of parties is small enough to bargain.

3. The parties have foreclosed the pursuit of other options.

4. No new information is expected to emerge that might alter either side's calculations of its self-interest or its ability to convince third parties.

5. Someone else will make the decision if they do not.

6. Several different issues are involved, allowing trade-offs across issues; preferably, none of them involve such fundamental values that no compromise is possible.

7. The regulatory agency will implement, or at least consider, the argument.[25]

Procedurally, an agency would pick a mediator who would identify the parties who should participate and arrange for representation from them. A *Federal Register* notice would request public comment. One question is whether the agency should participate fully in the group. Another is whether the meeting should be open to the public. Harter argues that open meetings would hinder honest communications and that agency participation would both provide useful guidance about the parameters of an acceptable proposal and circumvent the "not invented here" syndrome. He observes that some sort of consensus would have to be achieved as a prerequisite for formally presenting the proposal to the agency.

The chief procedural issue in the regulatory negotiation proposal concerns judical review. If any party, whether involved in the process or not, can go to court and subject the rule making to the same standards of review that currently are used, then regulatory negotiation has quite limited appeal. Harter proposes that the court would determine whether the plaintiff's interest was represented in the negotiation group. If it was, the petitioner would bear the burden of demonstrating that the group "failed to consider an issue central to the rule and that there is a substantial likelihood that it would have been substantially changed if the issue had been considered." Harter proposes that a party that refuses to participate fully in the negotiations should be prohibited from challenging the regulation before the courts, barring extraordinary circumstances. If a party tries to get involved but is rejected by the mediator or agency, then the agency or mediator could be taken to court to show that its rejection of that party was not arbitrary and capricious. If it fails, then the agency's defense of its standard would be judged by the traditional standard of review. Otherwise, "a rule should be sustained to the extent that it is within the agency's jurisdiction and actually reflects a consensus among the interested parties." [26] This greater judicial deference should flow from the political legitimacy of the process. "The negotiation process guarantees that the concerns of interested parties are addressed, thereby eliminating the need to review the entire factual basis of the agreement. Therefore, judicial review of the factual basis of the negotiated rule need only consider the possibility of arbitrariness and irrationality." [27]

Similarly, Harter argues that a "regulatory impact analysis" would not be required because it "is largely an analytical surrogate designed to aid an agency in replicating the kind of decision the parties would make if they were permitted to make the kind of trade-offs that would be done in the process of a regulatory negotiation." [28]

Before turning to an assessment of the regulatory negotiation, a review of recent experience with it should shed some light on its promise and problems. Congressional hearings on regulatory negotiation in 1980 focused on the experience with environmental controversies. In several cases the procedure appeared to facilitate the emergence of consensus positions. [29] Federal agency use of regulatory negotiations has been scanty. The Federal Aviation Administration convened a group to consider a controversial rule on flight duty status of pilots and adopted the suggestions of the group in a proposed rule. The EPA is proceeding with a group on the criteria for penalties for nonconformance with diesel emissions standards. The most ambitious effort has been at OSHA, which funded a group to examine revising its benzene standard.[30]

Participants included the industrial hygienists from all of the labor unions with significant representation in the affected industries and representatives of the rubber, steel, oil, and chemical industries. Largely because of its own desire to stay independent, OSHA only sent observers. Although OSHA's noninvolvement precluded the group's identification as an "advisory committee" and thus subject to the open meeting requirement of the Federal Advisory Committee Act, the meetings were kept open and the press regularly attended. The labor and management participants had never spoken with each other and were initially quite hostile. Early discussions broke off after a few months, in February 1984, over the issue of the permissible exposure level; most of the industries wanted a PEL in the range of 2–5 ppm, although the steel industry wanted a higher one; labor wanted to reinstate the 1-ppm standard that had been invalidated by the Supreme Court in 1980. However, meetings started again a few months later, and by mid-July agreement had been reached on most issues, including a PEL of 1 ppm. The major concession that industry got in exchange was that, if OSHA found exposures between 1 and 2 ppm, the firm could (if it showed that it had a responsible monitoring program) average that value in with the last several measurements. Only if the average of those was still above 1 ppm would OSHA cite a violation. Thus firms would have greater certainty that fluke variations would not trigger enforcement proceedings. Such a bargain provided an incentive to conduct more extensive monitoring than would actually be required by the proposed standard. Another sign of flexibility not found in previous standards was that the levels of exposure that would trigger various requirements (medical exams, monitoring) were not uniform but varied with the requirement.

Despite agreement by the regulatory negotiation committee members, the proposal was not accepted by several of their principals. Several unions refused to recommend the proposal to OSHA. Participants attributed the disavowal to several causes: First, new research results had appeared that some of the unions interpreted as supporting a PEL below 1 ppm; second, a new OSHA director of whom the unions were profoundly mistrustful had just been appointed; third and related to the second point, the unions were worried that several of the concessions they felt they had made would be used against them in later proceedings.

This concern with precedent distinguishes regulatory negotiation from its antecedents, environmental mediation and collective bargaining. In mediation, where each conflict is site specific, the participants bargain together only once and the problem of precedents usually does not arise. In collective bargaining the concern with precedents is pervasive but arises in what is perceived as a stable, ongoing relationship. If a union gives up something in one year, it expects reciprocity the next time; if it does not get it, management will face trouble the time after that. With the regulatory negotiation, however, it is not evident that there will be a next time. Similar problems must be confronted whenever uncertainty exists and are inescapable in the evolution of new institutions. Whether courts will apply the standard of review that Harter recommends remains to be seen; in the meantime parties will not know whether their participation will be a waste or even a liability. Congress could, if it desired, help the regulatory negotiation process grow by passing legislation prescribing the looser review standard for rules adopted through a regulatory negotiation procedure.

Would Congress want to encourage regulatory negotiation? Because that practice reduces the role of the agency in the formation of the rule (although it retains final authority), Congress might see the regulatory negotiation as a threat to its own influence, which derives partly from helping parties gain access to the bureaucracy. However, my sense is that this role is sufficiently small in standard setting at such agencies as OSHA, the EPA, and the NHTSA so as not to pose a major obstacle.

The agencies themselves are likely to prove ambivalent. Although they will value the opportunity to avail themselves of regulatory negotiation for particularly nettlesome issues, they would dislike the loss of control that mandatory use of it would entail. Although the agency retains the authority to issue or not issue a rule, once a rule is developed by a regulatory negotiation procedure, the agency would face considerable pressure to propose it.

Supporters of strict regulation often worry that regulatory negotiation will compromise the statutory commitment to reducing risks. In addition, the legal staff of an agency may object to regulatory negotiation because its role would be curtailed if the focus becomes what the parties can agree on rather than what the courts will accept.

The point that the regulatory negotiation procedure transforms lawyers from advocates to counsels and tends to diminish their role implies that regulatory negotiation would meet stronger objections in the EPA setting than at OSHA. In the benzene regulatory negotiation the participants from the unions were all technical people. The union lawyers were the ones who were more reluctant to go along. But compared to the lawyers in environmental groups, the union lawyers have relatively little power. Indeed, in many cases, the environmental lawyers *are* the environmental groups.

Attorneys at the Environmental Defense Fund and Natural Resources Defense Council—who play the major role in EPA litigation—cannot be expected to embrace a procedure that emphasizes other skills and constrains their own. In addition, both environmental and labor groups face the problem that regulatory negotiation demands a relatively great commitment of their time. The number of technically trained people affiliated with them is far less than industry commands. If several regulatory negotiations were occurring simultaneously, their resources would be stretched thin.

All these considerations probably justify the conclusion that "direct bargaining between interests will probably never play a major role in the development of regulatory policy and regulatory decisions."[31] Would greater use be desirable? In most circumstances the answer is probably yes. The dangers include the potential for greater strategic use of the regulatory process and the more general problem of exploitation of excluded parties. For example, the regulatory negotiation would probably make it easier for large firms and unions—who are more likely to participate than smaller firms and unorganized workers—to encourage the adoption of policies that would impose relatively greater costs on rival, nonunion firms. It would be up to the agency to take steps to counter these trends, either by guaranteeing representation of the otherwise excluded groups or by amending the regulatory negotiation proposal. Because either of these steps would make it more difficult to reach agreement, the agency might be reluctant to take them unless it feared a lawsuit that would unravel the compromise.

Regulatory Review Again

Although both the regulatory budget and regulatory negotiation are intellectually attractive, especially because they offer political solutions to the dilemmas of rule making, the feasible improvements they offer are uncertain and probably modest. That same assessment probably applies as well to regulatory review programs, but their impact has grown over time. Since 1981 the OMB's authority to hold up rules has certainly slowed the issuance of new standards and in some cases led to more moderate rules.[32]

In January 1985 a new executive order (EO 12498) expanded the OMB's oversight of the regulatory process to require that agencies submit annual "draft regulatory programs" to the OMB for approval. When disagreements arise about what to include, the OMB can ask the president or a cabinet council to resolve them. Except in emergencies or when the agency is responding to new statutory or judicial mandates, the OMB could prevent it from issuing any regulation not included in its regulatory programs.

The executive order displays several parallels to the Litan and Nordhaus proposal, except that it is the OMB, not Congress, that must approve the package of agency plans. Although the new process will be constrained by statutory action-forcing provisions, by court orders, and by political pressures, it will extend centralized control over the agendas of regulatory agencies. Its implementation will spawn new legal conflicts on several fronts. As the review function becomes more powerful, does it run afoul of the president's duty to execute faithfully the laws enacted by Congress? Will proponents of regulation make increasingly successful use of the Administrative Procedure Act's strictures against unreasonable delay?[33]

Regardless of its legal status, is this extension of OMB authority desirable? Just as it is for the fiscal budget, the concept of the president shaping a consistent regulatory program is an attractive one. However, the centralized control that the president exercises over agency spending is one he shares with Congress, whereas his centralized control over regulation would be more unilateral. The increased authority of the OMB makes some enhanced role for Congress both more likely and more desirable, although the exact form it should take remains unclear.

The secrecy of the Reagan review process, which has bothered analysts who believe that public critiques have served a useful educational role, would become more troubling as OMB power increased. For such protective regulatory programs as OSHA and the EPA, secrecy plays a substantive role as well, shielding regulators from media attention and the resulting pressure to issue strict rules.

The new review process can address the problem of overregulation and also push agencies to do a better job of choosing which hazards to address. But even under an administration less hostile to regulation than Reagan's, the procedure of Executive Order 12498, by itself, without an augmentation of agency staff or the cooperation of the courts, is not a tool for fostering more extensive regulation.[34] Indeed, it is likely to slow the process by diverting staff to preparation of the annual "regulatory programs."

An effective tool might be crafted if the OMB coordinated regulatory review with its budgetary review, expanding the budget allocated to rulemaking activities at agencies that set reasonable rules and shrinking it at others. Unfortunately, such budgetary fine-tuning would be difficult to implement because it requires the cooperation of the appropriations committees.

Other suggestions that have been made focus on increasing the size and skills of the White House review staff. Even under Reagan it has never involved more than twenty professionals. None were scientists, although the White House science adviser participated in some cases.[35] A recent recommendation by a National Academy of Sciences panel to establish a centralized body to formulate guidelines for risk assessments makes good sense.[36] Agencies have powerful incentives to produce assessments that bolster the arguments they want to make. Although there is some value in having competing assessment groups, it is outweighed by the value of comparability across hazards and across agencies. But like the other centralization measures discussed in this section, this one addresses overregulation more than underregulation.

9

Reform Strategies That Do Not Rely on Rule Making

The three-step strategy for reforming rule making presented in the next chapter makes sense only if there are no alternative strategies that would do a better job of addressing the overregulation/underregulation dilemma. Despite attractive features, the generic procedural reform proposals reviewed in chapter 8 did not by themselves appear capable of adequately addressing both horns of this problem. Can more direct use of other policy instruments fill the gap? In this chapter I review two of the most prominent candidates: providing information about risks to workers and facilitating lawsuits for occupational disease damages.

Substantive Strategies: Information

It is commonly stated that workers know more about safety risks than they know about health risks. Certainly, they are better able to perceive that a hazard exists and to estimate the seriousness of the physical damage that might result. It is less clear that workers have a good sense of the probability that a given situation (for example, slippery floors) will lead to an accident of a certain severity. For regulatory purposes, however, the important point is that often nobody else does either. Experts know much more about health hazards than workers do but not that much more about safety. This differential in expertise does create a stronger case for a government role in health than in safety.

However, that role may not have to take the form of standard setting. Precisely because experts do have considerable information, one important intervention strategy is to provide that information to workers. Potentially, workers can become better informed about health hazards than they can about safety hazards. They can learn what their exposures are and can sometimes learn what level of disease risk is associated with that exposure. In contrast, no one is going to be able to tell them the probability that they will fall on a slippery floor and seriously strain their backs.[1]

Thus health hazards may lend themselves quite well to interventions that rely on providing information. Ralph Nader and many economists have backed proposals to provide more information to workers about the risks they face. Yet the reasons why they back them differ sharply. The Naderites are profoundly mistrustful of market forces and skeptical of employers' declarations of concern for worker health. They favor more information as a "right" and as a way to give workers the tools to protest and to protect their interests. Most economists emphasize the efficiency and power of market forces. Workers who prefer low-risk jobs will be less likely to take and hold on to high-risk ones, and vice versa. If more hazard information leads to an upward shift in appraisal of risks, workers' demands for higher wages or their higher rate of quitting will gradually but inexorably induce managers to reduce risks.

Could anyone object to providing more information to workers? Obviously, industry has an incentive to oppose the supply of information that would lead workers to demand higher wages. More generally, measures to generate and disseminate information impose social costs and we have to ask if the information will generate sufficient benefits to justify them. For example, in the waning days of the Carter administration, OSHA issued a standard on labeling that included a provision for warnings on every hundred feet of pipe. By one estimate, the initial compliance costs would have been almost $3 billion with annual costs of $1.25 billion.[2] Another example is HR 1309, introduced in 1985, which would require the federal government to inform all workers exposed to a chemical whenever an epidemiological study found that a population exposed to it had a relative risk of more than 1.3 for any disease. Here the opposition centered on the cost of government resources diverted to informing people about findings that would often be false positives and the possible alarm, often unwarranted, that those notified might experience.[3]

The criteria for assessing an information strategy are clearly multiple: To what extent will it improve efficiency by leading to better matches of worker risk preferences? Does it accord with notions about workers' rights to be informed about hazards? Does it strike the proper balance between false-positive and false-negative errors; that is, is it unduly alarmist or overly reassuring? How effective will it be in preventing illnesses? How much will it cost? Will trade secrets be respected?

Yet the most relevant issues in the present study are not whether we should supply more information to workers—I assume that we should—or even what methods should be employed. The rule-making deadlock is a serious dilemma only if adequate alternatives to standard setting are unavailable. Thus the question is whether information strategies can supplement or even supplant rule making to an extent that allows us to be indifferent about the resolution of that deadlock.

Disgruntlement with OSHA's standard setting has led several analysts to consider supplanting them, although the extent to which toxic substance standards would be foresworn remains fuzzy. Philip Harter and George

Eads have proposed that OSHA devote fewer resources to standards and more to information development.

Standards would be reserved for emergency situations, particularly intractable problems, and areas that demand a uniform approach. Because of this limitation, such standards would not require the time and resources currently necessary for the promulgation of a standard; they would not generate the large opposition that has plagued OSHA rulemaking ... standards would not be the primary line of attack against normal occupational health and safety problems.[4]

The exact scope of the limitations remains unclear, although the authors do give examples, citing the vinyl chloride standard as an example of an emergency response, the ethylene oxide standard as an intractable problem, and the hazard communication standard as an area demanding a uniform approach. They also adopt the framework of the overregulation/ underregulation dilemma, noting that, although an emphasis on information would be unlikely to provide as stringent protection as new OSHA standards provide, the scope of its impact would probably be wider.[5] In their view the wider scope would result not only (or perhaps even primarily) from direct market forces but also from the impact of better information on lawsuits, criminal prosecution, and use of OSHA's general duty clause. They acknowledge, however, that these mechanisms may impose large transaction costs.

Viscusi has argued more clearly for substituting information for standards.

After abolishing the current set of health and safety standards, we should base OSHA policies on the following three elements: 1) provision of risk information to workers, 2) greater merit rating of workers' compensation, and 3) penalties on hazardous firms to promote health and safety for selected risks....

The third component of the policy is intended to address the instances in which a market process in conjunction with greater risk information will not generate efficient risk levels. In these exceptional instances, which should pertain almost exclusively to dimly understood health risks, OSHA should consider additional forms of intervention. If workers find it difficult to process risk information pertaining to very low-probability risks, which often has a deferred impact on their well-being, a more direct regulatory strategy should be considered. Justification for such intervention should be required on a case-by-case basis; the existence of a workplace hazard should no longer be taken as a self-evident reason for government regulation.[6]

Viscusi suggests that OSHA consider a commitment to the principle that "no substance-by-substance regulations will be permitted unless it can be shown that an informational alternative is unworkable."[7] "Unworkability" is undefined, but setting the burden of proof in this fashion would appear to place a major barrier to new standards. In contrast, if the burden of proof were reversed and informational strategies had to be shown "workable," they too would find it a difficult test to meet.[8] The following review of the analysis for OSHA's hazard communication standard indicates why this is true.

Costs and Impacts

The estimate that firms would have incurred expenses of over $1 billion a year to comply with the January 1981 OSHA labeling proposal shows that the costs of information are not necessarily cheap. Even the 1983 Reagan proposal was estimated to require an initial $580 million with annual costs of $230 million.[9] For the manufacturing sector, which was all that was covered by the proposal, the initial cost was $41 per worker and the annual cost was $17. What will be achieved as a result?

The impact of hazard communication depends on the changes in worker and employer behavior resulting from better information. Better information could lead to downward revisions in risk estimates, but most expect that the general trend will be upward. Some workers may realize that they are in far riskier jobs than they thought. If they quit and are replaced by less risk-averse workers, society is better off. The first worker might have required $500 to compensate him for the risk, whereas the second might require only $200. Thus the total disutility from risk has declined by $300 because of the better matching of worker preferences with risks.

Employers may learn that a product they thought was safe carries risks. In some cases a good substitute will be available at little or no extra cost. The shift will be made and risk will be reduced.

The increased perception of hazards may lead some workers to ask for better controls or substitution of the hazardous product. Employers will accede if workers are willing to bargain away something the firm values more. The results of voluntary bargaining will be a relatively efficient outcome; both sides will be better off, and the employer has the incentive to reduce the risk in the least costly manner. Even without explicit bargaining, new risk perceptions will reduce the attractiveness of certain jobs. Employers will have to decide if reducing the risks is a less costly option than raising wages.

It is clear that information can facilitate relatively efficient risk-reduction measures. However, we can also "underinform" and "overinform" in the sense of conveying risk messages that are too reassuring or too alarmist. Overinforming may generate large social costs if workers demand high premiums to face trivial risks.

I noted before that the long-term decline in exposures to most health hazards was consistent with the view that firms do respond to market forces. During most of the postwar period, government regulation, workers' compensation, and fears of liability provided only weak incentives to reduce exposures; yet exposures to many hazards appear to have become better controlled. Currently, speakers for major chemical firms claim that they try to adhere to changing ACGIH recommendations despite the absence of legal force behind them.[10] In several recent cases firms have responded to new bioassay evidence of harm by reducing exposures.

Nevertheless, the evidence on the impact of information is mixed. Big chemical firms continue to violate not only ACGIH levels but also OSHA PELs. In addition, there is some evidence that, at least in the short run, recommendations to reduce exposures levels, by themselves, will not always lead employers to lower exposures. Table 9.1 compares changes in the percentage of samples taken by OSHA inspectors that exceeded the PEL for two groups of hazards. For the first group, there were no changes in recommended exposure levels from 1971 to 1979. For the second group, either the ACGIH or NIOSH issued a recommendation for a lower PEL. The hazards included were limited to those for which at least fifty samples were taken in both the period from January 1, 1973, to December 30, 1975, and the period from April 1, 1979, to July 21, 1981. The second group was limited to cases in which new recommendations appeared after 1974 and before 1980.

For this small number of hazards, table 9.1 shows that the proportion of samples above the PEL declined slightly more in the second group. However, because the initial violation level was higher in that group, the percentage reduction was lower. The differences in the changes between the two groups were not statistically significant. Although changes in inspection policy can undermine direct comparisons over time, this test relies on differences between the two groups of hazards and there is no reason to assume that any policy changes would have affected one set of hazards more than another.

Although this test raises some doubts about whether firms respond to information when it takes the form of scientific advice to lower exposures, it does not address the effects of improving the flow of information to workers. There is enough anecdotal evidence of uninformed workers being harmed by hazards they were unaware of to ensure that the OSHA hazard communications proposal could prevent some diseases. However, the estimate of the magnitude of that impact raises difficult problems. The first step is to assess how much occupational disease is occurring. As we saw in chapter 3, this assessment requires quite uncertain assumptions about the

Table 9.1 Do Exposures Decline When *Recommended* Exposure Limits Are Reduced?

Substance (code)	Proportion of samples exceeding PEL in period 1	Proportion of samples exceeding PEL in period 2	Change in proportion	Percent change	Change in recommendation	Period 1		Period 2	
						Number of samples	Number of inspections	Number of samples	Number of inspections
Group 1. No change in recommended exposures									
Acetone (0400)	.1554	.0112	.1442	93	none	1168	145	205	148
Cobalt (0720)	.0142	.0504	−.0362	255	none	141	24	119	47
Ethyl acetate (1040)	.1242	.0000	.1242	100	none	338	49	175	62
Ethyl alcohol (1060)	.1825	.0000	.1825	100	none	219	34	63	48
Hydrogen chloride (1430)	.1806	.1059	.0747	41	none	288	71	104	69
Manganese (1620)	.0705	.0265	.0440	59	none	779	165	657	190
Selenium (2230)	.0000	.0666	−.0666	undet.	none	53	15	60	14
Group average	.1039	.0369	.0670						
Group 2. Change in recommended exposures									
Hydrogen fluoride (1460)	.0370	.0266	.0104	28	From 8 ppm 8-hr TWA to 10 ppm C/10 min[a]	81	16	75	32
Methyl chloroform (1720)	.0548	.0228	.0320	58	From 50 ppm C to 2 ppm C	693	109	143	155
Perchloroethylene (2020)	.2614	.1814	.0810	31	From 100 ppm TWA to 50 ppm	329	77	112	108

Sodium hydroxide (2260)	.1458	.0101	.1357	74	From 2 mg TWA to 2 mg C	144	41	98	58
Styrene (2290)	.2254	.1066	.1188	53	From 100 ppm TWA to 50 ppm TWA	2666	226	356	109
Sulfur dioxide (2290)	.2999	.1874	.1125	38	From 5 ppm 8-hr TWA to 0.5 ppm 10-hr TWA	1087	153	65	23
Group average	.1707	.0890	.0817						

a. TWA = Time-weighted average; C = ceiling.

proportion of cancers and disabling pulmonary conditions that have occupational origins. The second step is to estimate what proportion of those cases would be prevented by the hazard communication proposal. This estimate is even more arbitrary. OSHA suggested a figure of 20 percent for cancer and 10 percent for other diseases; the OMB suggested 5 percent.[11] However, neither it nor anyone else presented any analysis to support those specific figures. Although they are plausible, figures of 1 or 2 or 15 percent seem equally plausible. Viscusi estimated that a 5 percent effectiveness level would be necessary to generate net benefits.

Despite uncertainties about estimating its effects, three reasonable conclusions about an information strategy can be drawn.

1. The fact that proponents estimated the high range of its impact at 10 percent indicates that few people think that its total impact on the occupational disease problem is likely to be dramatic.

2. The more impact it has, the more costly other strategies will become. The reason is that the illnesses prevented by providing information will tend to be the ones that can be prevented relatively cheaply.

3. It will be difficult to tell how well an information strategy is working. Estimates of effectiveness are severely limited by the available data. Effects on diseases with long latency periods will not show up for many years and, even then, will often go undetected. As a proxy, we could measure changes in exposure levels, but current exposure data are not accurate enough to reliably detect the changes associated with a 5 to 10 percent reduction in overall disease rates. We do have measures of acute diseases associated with chemical exposures, but these are widely acknowledged to be underreported, perhaps by a factor of 10 (the estimate used in the OSHA regulatory analysis). The better understanding that the hazard communication standard will impart to workers is likely to lead them to report more acute, chemical-related diseases. This reporting phenomenon will be confounded with any preventive effects of the standard.

Viscusi has suggested that the effects of the standard can be monitored by observing whether the information it provides leads to changes in risk premiums and turnover.[12] However, in the absence of baseline information about worker beliefs about the level of risks, a clear understanding of what new information they receive as a result of the standard, and a model of how workers value reductions in chronic disease risks, it will be difficult to interpret any change or lack of change resulting from this nationwide policy. Were workers' estimates of risks altered by the new information? Did they ever actually get new information as a result of the standard? Was the lack of change in premiums due to the fact that workers heavily discount the risks of disease occuring several decades in the future? The difficulty of gaining feedback about the effects of the policy does count against it.

Proposals to go beyond the information provided through the hazard communications standard have been made by Viscusi and others. Many of these appear desirable, for example, that firms inform all new and prospective workers what the injury and illness rate in the firm is and how it compares to other firms in the same and other industries. However, my point is that an information strategy is not likely to render the rule-making strategy I have proposed ineffective.

The real issue gets down to the relative desirability of standards and information strategies. If the assumption is that OSHA's future rules will resemble its past ones, then the argument for forsaking standards is strengthened. But the argument against more reasonably set exposure limits is much weaker. Indeed it relies primarily on the point that such limits ignore the heterogeneity of worker preferences toward risk.[13]

Government Constraints and Worker Preferences
Government standards do constrain liberty in ways that information strategies do not. They prevent workers and employers from agreeing to some wage-risk combinations that they find attractive. Because willingness to take risky jobs is inversely related to wealth, these restrictions may impinge most on lower income workers. Viscusi argues that "uniform standards do not enlarge worker choices; they deprive workers of the opportunity to select the job most appropriate to their own risk preferences. The actual 'rights' issue involved is whether those in upper income groups have a right to impose their job risk preferences on the poor."[14]

Yet if we turn to an analysis of the role of unions, we find that Viscusi is somewhat inconsistent. Like others, he notes that unions alter the nature of a firm's labor market policymaking. In a purely competitive market it is the marginal workers—those who are potential hires or quits—who influence a firm's choices about what wages and working conditions to offer. Workers who are tied to the firm, perhaps through seniority and pensions, will be ignored in its calculations. But it is precisely these more experienced workers who tend to dominate union policymaking. Because they are older and wealthier than the marginal workers, they will tend to demand higher premiums for risks. Viscusi observes that "if unions advance the interests of these relatively immobile employees, the market outcome will be more efficient."[15]

The fact remains that unions restrict the liberty of the marginal workers

Table 9.2   Workers Facing Toxic Hazards Are Less Likely to Believe That Their Employer Keeps Them Informed of the Dangers

Do you think your employer keeps (would keep) you fully informed about (any) dangerous or unhealthy conditions that you may (might) be exposed to on your job?[a]

Worker's perception of personal hazard	Yes	No	Percent no
Worker says he faces no sizable or great hazard	251	20	7
Worker says he faces sizable or great hazard other than toxic hazard	117	43	27
Worker says he faces sizable or great toxic hazard	76	56	42

a. This table is for the blue-collar subsample. The wording in parentheses was used with the workers who said they faced no sizable or great hazard.

to make risk-wage trade-offs in order to protect the interests of the more senior workers. Yet in the union case Viscusi acknowledges that such restrictions may, on balance, reflect worker preferences better than a competitive market would. Where unions are absent, government standards can potentially play a similar role. Although unionized workers are more likely to face toxic hazards than the 80 percent of the work force that is not unionized, nonunionized workers account for half of all the workers who say that they face a major hazard from toxic substances.[16]

Even where unions are present, it is also possible for government action to reflect the preferences of a majority of members. In their views a government standard may be superior to collective bargaining for several reasons. One important one is that a standard will impose the same requirements on many of their firm's competitors, making it more likely that costs will be shifted forward to consumers rather than backward to their paychecks.

Opponents to heavy reliance on information strategies often either do not believe that workers can understand the information about health risks (or at least not "properly" understand it) or doubt that the market will force firms to pay the premiums that would compensate them. Previously we reviewed the evidence bearing on these issues and the difficulty in drawing unambiguous conclusions. What do workers believe about their firms' efforts to keep them informed? One survey finding clearly suggests that many workers are skeptical and that the skepticism is greater among those exposed to toxic substances. Table 9.2 shows that workers who say they face sizable hazards are more skeptical than workers who believe they face little or no risks and that those who face toxic hazards are the most skeptical of all. These workers would presumably not be happy if they had to rely more on their employer for protection.[17] The hazard communication standard may make them better informed and less skeptical, but these changes remain to be seen.

Substantive Strategies: Disease Prevention Resulting from Workers' Compensation and Tort Liability

According to one former union leader active in occupational health: "History shows that the lawsuit is the only adequate preventive measure against occupational and environmental cancer."[18] In this section I turn to the effect of the current set of workers' compensation and tort liability laws on disease prevention and then look at the impact of proposed reforms. Here again the focus of my interests is whether the likely effectiveness of these systems is so much greater than that of enforcing standards that the stalemate of rule making can be viewed with equanimity.

The purpose of both workers' compensation and tort liability is twofold: to compensate injured people and to foster incentives to prevent future injuries. During the years surrounding World War I, state workers' compensation systems were established to supplant the tort system as a way of supporting injured workers. Workers gave up their right to sue, which had proven not to be worth much before most courts of that period, in exchange for a no-fault system with modest levels of compensation for all injuries arising out of the course of employment.

Several decades later a clear consensus has emerged that workers' compensation programs largely fail to compensate workers afflicted with serious occupational diseases. Indeed, even for injuries, where compensation is more adequate, the effect of the programs on prevention has been difficult to detect. One reason could be that the ex post compensation they provide for injuries simply substitutes, to a large degree, for the ex ante compensation that workers receive in risk premiums. If this is true, it is especially unfortunate that occupational diseases, which are probably less well compensated ex ante, are also less well compensated ex post. Only about 3 percent of all workers' compensation claims are for disease, and one-third of these are for dermatitis. The number of disease deaths receiving compensation is so low that, even under the most restrictive estimate of occupationally caused disease deaths, only a small fraction are getting compensated.

The reasons why occupational diseases are poorly compensated are well known, and many of them impede recovery under the tort system as well as under workers' compensation. Doctors are often poorly trained to diagnose occupational diseases. When the diseases occur after long latency periods, frequently after the workers have retired, the diagnosis is especially likely to be missed even for diseases with a clear occupational connection (for example, silicosis). Some states still have statutes of limitations that require that claims be filed within a limited period after the exposures ended. Long latency periods also increase the probability that the employer or producer will have liquidated or declared bankruptcy, reducing the chances of recovery.

The long latency period also increases the difficulty of establishing the occupational connection in the first place. Epidemiological studies to identify excess rates of disease are hampered by the need to follow workers over long periods and to estimate exposures that they faced decades ago.

The identification problem is most severe when the same disease can be caused by both occupational exposures and nonoccupational factors. Lung cancer is a prime example. Even when the occupational connection is established, it is scientifically impossible to say whether any given individual's lung cancer was caused by the toxic exposures or by nonwork factors. This impossibility jeopardizes workers' claims. The extent of jeopardy will vary, depending on state statutes in the case of workers' compensation and state interpretations of the common law in the case of tort law. In tort law the usual requirement to show that the exposures were "more likely than not" the cause of the disease is obviously undermined by the presence of competing causes and the difficulty of producing clear-cut epidemiological findings.

In some respects workers' compensation limits the incentives for workers to file claims. The programs do not fully compensate workers for their losses. The relatively low level of awards for death or permanent injury (compared to jury awards in tort cases), combined with regulations that limit attorney's fees to a moderate percentage of the award, gives lawyers an incentive to turn down cases unless the probability of winning is high. In most states workers' compensation is the exclusive remedy for a claim against an employer. Thus the tort system cannot be used to increase the employer's expected liability costs.

In 1973 plaintiffs' attorneys opened a new legal front for occupational disease victims by winning a so-called third-party suit against the firms that had supplied asbestos fibers to the employer of a worker who died of asbestosis. In many states these suits were facilitated by the recent introduction of a "strict liability" standard. This standard did not require any showing of fault, as earlier negligence standards did. If the product was "unreasonably dangerous," the supplier could be held liable. Evidence that the suppliers had known about the hazards of asbestos but had not conveyed warnings about those hazards to workers often provided the basis for a finding that asbestos was "unreasonably dangerous." Jury awards exceeded workers' compensation payments several-fold and plaintiffs' attorneys garnered at least one-third of them. In addition, several states allowed punitive damages when corporate misconduct appeared unusually severe. In the first half of 1982, punitive damage awards averaged $600,000.[19] These awards were especially painful to the supplier firms because their liability insurance would not cover them.

The Impact of Liability on Prevention
The ensuing flood of tens of thousands of asbestos suits and the filing for bankruptcy by Manville, the industry's largest firm, are well known. The number of workers exposed to asbestos and the levels of their exposures also declined during this period. Was the liability threat the major cause of the improvement? Consistent with the claim that opened this section, economists Leslie Boden and Carol Jones have argued that "the most powerful occupational disease remedy in the asbestos experience has been product liability suits."[20] Thus an examination of the asbestos experience should provide insight into whether compensation payments (whether from the tort system or workers' compensation) can provide strong incentives for occupational disease prevention. My discussion begins with general arguments and then turns to alternative explanations for the reductions in asbestos exposure.

Long latency periods are a major cause for skepticism about the effectiveness of these measures. Under what conditions would financial incentives be strong enough to induce managers to care about the impacts of their decisions twenty or thirty years in the future, especially when those impacts are highly uncertain? Many studies of corporate decision making emphasize the characteristic high discount rates and correspondingly short time horizons. At a 15 percent discount rate the present value of a million dollar payment in thirty years is only $15,000. This sum does not loom large when compared with the estimated costs of millions of dollars per disease prevented for compliance with OSHA standards.[21]

Others who have noted the incentive for corporate officials to overlook liability costs that may occur far in the future have speculated that firms would "structure incentives and career lines and pension rights to avert that temptation."[22] However, when we look inside the "black box" of corporate decision making, it does not appear that the environment encourages managers to take a longer view. One study of product liability decision making asked firms

whether they had considered tracking individuals responsible for design decisions later found faulty, not for retribution, but to establish the principle that poor decisions taken at one time will be held against an individual even if several years had elapsed and he had moved within the company. Only one firm said that this had seriously been considered and that it had been rejected.[23]

Do these findings imply that firms will take no preventive action because of the liability costs associated with long latency diseases? Not necessarily. First, at least in carcinogenesis, it is believed that some chemicals have a "promoting" effect, not just an initiating effect. Even though the disease will not occur for decades after initial exposures, continued exposures will affect the incidence of disease. Cigarette smoking is an apparent example; risks drop when smokers quit even though the smoker has been puffing for decades. In that case the impact of reducing exposures could show up more quickly in a reduced number of victims and a reduced number of claims. With that expectation suppliers might find preventive actions worthwhile; in the face of uncertainty about the nature of the carcinogenic mechanism, they could choose to follow a risk-averse strategy and assume that "promotion" occurred. However, among known occupational carcinogens this effect has rarely been noted and long latency periods are the rule. Second and less important, although the latency periods of most chronic diseases associated with exposures are lengthy, they do vary considerably. For leukemias associated with benzene, ten years, not thirty, is the average latency, and shorter periods are possible. Again, firms will often not know what latency period is associated with a given hazard.

Even when the liability system can impose near-term costs, the burden is on suppliers, not employers. Because employers remain exempt from these suits in almost all cases, it is hard to see how the tort system could claim major credit for their efforts to reduce exposures. However, liability may lead to reduced workplace exposures through less direct routes. First, suppliers may decide that the expected liability costs of supplying a product for some uses are so great that prices have to be increased or that the particular product use must be discontinued. In either case use of the product and the number of workers exposed to it are likely to decline. Second, suppliers may try to induce or pressure users into using better controls in order to reduce the supplier's expected liability. For example, in 1980 Manville adopted a policy that it "will not sell asbestos or asbestos-containing products where adequate precautions are not likely to be observed." However, implementation of this policy appears to have been difficult in the face of conflicting incentives to boost sales.[24]

Thus there are usually good reasons to believe that expected liability costs should have little impact on occupational disease prevention efforts, although there are circumstances in which the impact could be greater.

Getting back to the asbestos case, there are several rival explanations to the view that liability is primarily responsible for declining exposures. Boden and Jones consider several of them. They observe that the only study of risk premiums for asbestos workers during this period did not uncover any increase after 1971.[25] As for workers' compensation, awards for asbestos cases did not increase in constant dollars and the percentage of workers filing claims did not grow from 1972 to 1976. In contrast, the average tort awards increased by 50 percent, and the percentage of workers getting them more than tripled during that period and grew much more later.[26] Undoubtedly, these changes did accelerate substitution away from asbestos. Costs for product liability insurance rose throughout the industry and suppliers of fibers would try to pass some of them through in higher prices. In addition, manufacturers of asbestos-containing products also faced higher product liability premiums.

These higher prices would, of course, reduce the quantity of asbestos products purchased. Yet, in addition to liability-induced increases in the price of asbestos, it seems likely that in many cases the demand curve itself shifted downward as potential consumers decided that products with asbestos posed an unacceptable health risk. A prime example was the media attention to the presence of asbestos fibers in hair dryers. Home insulation was another use of asbestos that was sensitive to consumer worries. Even firms producing asbestos vinyl floor tile, which presents no health risk, explored alternatives because they felt that consumers were concerned about any form of asbestos.[27]

Non-OSHA regulatory activity also helped to push down demand for asbestos. At the local level the spraying of asbestos was banned in many cities. The EPA was considering bans on various uses of asbestos, and uncertainty about regulatory intentions and the expectation that at least some uses would be banned doubtless contributed to many corporate decisions to search for substitutes.

Finally, OSHA regulations requiring engineering controls also raised the costs of using asbestos.[28] Like many others, Boden and Jones tend to minimize OSHA's impact because they focus on the small size of the penalties for violations. Yet once a firm is cited—and plants employing the great majority of asbestos product manufacturing workers were inspected for asbestos hazards at least once during the 1970s—the incentive to comply is strong because of the potential for penalties for each day out of compliance past the scheduled abatement date. Firms are often successful in getting extensions in their abatement dates, especially when there is no union to push OSHA to enforce its timetable, but most followup inspections of health problems find that the firm has abated the violation.[29]

The most thorough set of case studies of asbestos industry plants indicates that most undertook compliance efforts shortly after the new standard took effect in June 1972, although these steps did not necessarily keep them from being cited.[30] The citations triggered additional measures. In the asbestos textile market most of the firms operating in 1972 had closed by 1978, several of them to avoid complying with OSHA's 1976 PEL of 2 fibers/cc.[31] Paul Brodeur has reported on the impact of an early OSHA inspection at a notoriously hazardous plant that later generated hundreds of asbestos-related lawsuits: "In spite of the mildness of the penalties that accompanied them, the OSHA citations caused considerable consternation to the management of Pittsburgh Corning by setting March 31, 1972 as the date for completing extensive improvements in the ventilation and dust control systems."[32] Within a month following the inspection, the firm decided to close the plant rather than to comply.

To help to distinguish the impact of tort law from the impact of OSHA's regulation, we can disaggregate exposures into two components: the number of workers exposed to asbestos and the average level of exposure of those workers. Reductions in the number exposed are primarily due to substitution away from asbestos products. These substitutions may be due to expected liability costs, concerns about consumer acceptability, and increases in the cost of workplace controls. In contrast, reductions in the average level of exposures within an industry would appear to be chiefly the result of OSHA or worker pressures. Producers of asbestos fibers have a difficult time exerting control over the use of exposure controls in particular plants. Given this reasoning, it is highly significant that the bulk of the overall reduction in risk has come from lower average exposures, rather than from a drop in the number of workers exposed.

Thus the results of OSHA sampling at inspected firms indicate that average exposure levels fell by from 50 to 67 percent in different sectors from the early 1970s to the late 1970s.[33] Because OSHA sampling was not conducted randomly, it cannot provide a definitive answer to the question of how average exposures changed; however, other surveys, reported in table 9.3, are consistent with the conclusion that the number of workers exposed above OSHA's PEL of 2 fibers/cc has declined sharply. In contrast, estimates of the number of workers exposed to asbestos, shown in table 9.4 have declined much less.

Table 9.3   Changes in Workplace Asbestos Exposure Levels

	Estimated exposure levels (fiber/cc)		
Source	1972 NIOSH survey[a]	1976 Weston survey[a]	1983 JRB survey[b]
Asbestos cement pipe	0.2–6.3	0.5–2.0	1.0
Asbestos cement sheet	0.1–16.6	1.0–3.0	1.0
Floor tile	NA	0.5–1.0	0.2–0.5
Asbestos paper	0.4–3.4	0.8–1.9	0.2–0.75
Friction materials	0.1–14.4	1.0–3.3	1.5
Gaskets, seals	0.2–13.6	0.5–2.5	0.2–0.75
Paints, coating, sealants	0.0–16.3	1.0–2.5	0.0–0.75
Textiles	0.1–143.9	1.0–4.0	0.75–1.5

Sources: The NIOSH and Weston surveys are reported in Carol A. Jones, "Models of Regulatory Enforcement," Ph.D. Dissertation, Department of Economics, Harvard University (July 1982). The 1983 JRB survey is reported in Leslie I. Boden and Carol A. Jones, "Occupational Disease Remedies: The Asbestos Experience," paper presented at the National Science Foundation–Carnegie–Mellon University Conference, Regulation at the Crossroads, Airlie House, Virginia, September 12–14, 1985, mimeo, table 11.
a. Range of typical exposures.
b. Estimated current exposures.

Table 9.4   Changes in the Number of Workers Exposed to Asbestos

Sector[a]	Number of workers exposed to asbestos				
	1976[b]	1978[b]	1979[b]	1979[c]	1983[c]
Primary manufacturing	15,905	15,888	20,074	17,700	13,356
Maritime	3,840	4,000	3,637	3,804	3,044
Secondary fabrication	25,610		23,965	26,610	17,204

Sources: RTI estimates reported in their *Asbestos Dust: Technological Feasibility Assessment and Economic Impact Analysis of the Proposed Occupational Standard* (September 1980). JRB estimates reported in Boden and Jones, "Occupational Disease Remedies," Table 11.
a. Estimates have been made for other sectors, but the ones presented are the only ones that appear comparable over time.
b. As estimated by Research Triangle Institute (RTI).
c. As estimated by JRB Associates.

Reforms

Even for the most massive toxic tort case in history, the impact on worker exposures appears to be fairly modest. This conclusion must be tentative in light of the empirical obstacles to identifying the distinct effects of the different changes occurring in those industries. Nevertheless, with this conclusion, it is hard to see how the tort system could supplant the enforcement of standards.

But perhaps there are changes in the tort system or workers' compensation that would provide much greater incentives for disease prevention. Before looking briefly at such reforms, it is useful to review the criteria for assessing policy changes in these laws. Even if changes could enhance those incentives, they may have other consequences that are not so desirable.

The first two criteria are increased effectiveness in preventing disease and an improved level of compensation benefits. For both of these objectives it is possible to go too far, compensating too generously and preventing too much disease. However, at the present time the desired direction of change is fairly clear.

Other criteria include reducing transaction costs, improving horizontal equity to beneficiaries, and improving fairness in distributing the costs. The importance of transactions costs is highlighted by the estimate that only about one-third of all the dollars paid to resolve asbestos suits ends up in the pockets of claimants. The remainder goes to pay for the litigation costs of the two sets of lawyers. The tort system is a costly method for ensuring that workers get compensated.

Horizontal equity refers to "equal treatment of equals." Although the question of equal with respect to what often arises, it is evident that the current systems fall short by any measure. Two claimants with identical factual cases have fared markedly differently at the hands of juries. Many workers do not file cases at all because of ignorance or lack of access to attorneys. A broader problem is that the size of awards depends on characteristics whose germaneness can be questioned. A disease without occupational connections leaves a person to his own devices. A work connection can get him workers' compensation benefits; a product liability suit may bring a jackpot. These differences have been justified by the preventive incentives that are needed when someone is to blame. However, we have seen that, in the case of occupational diseases, the preventive effects are moot. Arguably, when effects on prevention are modest or uncertain, the distinctions are not justified and all people with a given disease should be compensated in a similar manner. That solution does not, however, comport with the strongly held belief that, if a company causes your problem, it ought to pay for it. This view is justified, in part, on the grounds of fairness in the distribution of costs: Why should taxpayers pay for your compensation if Company X is to blame? The combination of a blame-worthy party with "deep pockets" and a blameless victim generates a tendency toward high awards. In addition, juries are more generous in setting such awards than taxpayers and their representatives because they view the case in isolation from its total fiscal impact. Thus the criterion of fairness in apportioning costs often conflicts with the criterion of horizontal equity.[34]

Quite diverse and conflicting concerns have motivated proponents of reform. Table 9.5 briefly characterizes several of the major reform proposals and assesses them in terms of the criteria discussed.[35] The purpose of this review is not to perform a policy analysis of these alternatives but to point out that none of the changes are likely to increase substantially the incentives to prevent long latency diseases. Proposals to improve access to compensation frequently seek to reduce employer resistance by employing measures that would *reduce* prevention incentives. Thus payments are to be funded by industry-wide pools, by disease-specific funds with taxpayer contributions, or by liberalizations of the social security disability system.

One proposal calls for the establishment of a federal administrative agency to hear claims of toxics-induced injury.[36] Once a claimant has met a threshold test showing the plausibility of a causal role for toxics, the burden of proof would shift to the defendant. In this way firms would be given an incentive to develop information in order to protect themselves from claims. Once a chemical has been linked to a particular disease, it would be "certified" and future claimants would not have to remake the causal arguments. Employers would be unlikely to accept such a drastic reform without guarantees that the level of benefits would be kept modest. In any event this reform would not address the disincentives to prevent disease caused by long latency periods.

The proposal to restore the right to sue employers for negligence would also be effective only to the limited extent that employers think that liability might be incurred in the short run.[37] Restoring the right to sue faces little chance in the face of the prevailing view that the tort system has run amok and the widespread support for reining it in.[38]

Conclusion

I have been quite critical of the regulatory reform measures discussed in this chapter. Yet, with the exception of some of the proposals for facilitating use

Table 9.5 Proposals to Change Workers' Compensation and Tort Liability: An Assessment

Proposal	Increase compensation	Increase disease prevention incentives	Reduce transaction costs	Increase horizontal equity	Increase fairness in apportionment of costs	Comment
1. Remove statutes of limitations in workers' compensation. Create presumptions that diseases following certain exposures were occupational.	Yes	Yes, modestly; unless payments are made from an industry-wide trust fund	Yes	Yes, for diseases covered	Yes	May also compensate many workers without occupational disease
2. Allow suits for negligence against employers but let compliance with government standards and the provision of information to workers constitute a defense.	Yes	Yes, modestly	No	No	Yes	
3. Establish special administrative body to review disease claims; place burden of proof on firms (Sobel proposal).	Yes	Yes, modestly	Yes	Yes	Yes	May also compensate many workers without occupational disease
4. Establish hazard-specific compensation systems with funds provided largely from the federal government. Bar third-party suits for these hazards.	Yes	No; might reduce them	Yes	Yes, for people exposed to that hazard. No, otherwise	No?	
5. Restrict product liability suits through raising the burden of proof, placing caps on awards, limiting attorney fees, and encouraging courts to defer to administrative agencies.	No	No; might reduce them	Yes	Yes	No	

of the tort system, these proposals will probably do more good than harm. What they are unlikely to do is adequately address underregulation as well as overregulation. Thus there is indeed a need for the type of proposal presented in chapter 10.

Yet it will become clear that my proposal also faces obstacles to its implementation. The "complete reformer" would therefore do well to keep a diversified portfolio. For the most part, the various types of measures— generic procedural reforms, information and compensation strategies, and changes in the statutes governing agency rule making—are complements, not substitutes. And even where they are substitutes, the overlap is probably not serious.[39]

10

New Strategies for Reforming Rule Making

Staff at OSHA, like their counterparts in other agencies regulating toxic substances, have been well aware of the slow pace of standard setting and the paltry number of hazards that have been addressed. In an attempt to speed up the process, both OSHA and the EPA developed generic policies for regulating carcinogens, although both policies were set aside when the Reagan administration took power. The centerpiece of these policies was a set of presumptions about how to interpret evidence regarding carcinogenicity. By applying them, the agencies hoped to avoid reviewing the same issue de novo in each rule making. These presumptions always erred on the side of caution; that is, they were more likely to lead to identification of a noncarcinogen as a carcinogen than vice versa. Combined with policies of regulating carcinogens strictly, these generic rules raised the prospect of a regulatory system that was both extensive and stringent. As we saw in chapter 5, it was fear of this prospect that led the Supreme Court in 1980 to overturn OSHA's strict benzene standard on the grounds that OSHA had failed to show that it was addressing a hazard that was "more likely than not" to present "a significant risk." The impact of this decision appears to be to raise the standard of proof that OSHA must meet, although, as I have argued, the de facto burden of proof tends to vary with judges' assessments of the reasonableness of specific rules. The following year, the Supreme Court's cotton dust majority held that OSHA must set new exposure levels at the lowest feasible level. Thus the Court has helped to enshrine a system of rule making that is strict and infrequent, just the opposite of what seems desirable. How can we make the transition to a system that is extensive but not so strict?

In the last two chapters I focused on so-called generic approaches to regulatory reform that aim at altering the basic rules of the game under which a host of different regulatory programs have to operate. Reform strategies for particular programs can also flow out of a more generic diagnosis and strategy. The diagnosis of overregulation and underregulation of risk regulation is not limited to OSHA. It can apply whenever agencies try to set standards for a large body of hazards. Thus the strategy for OSHA outlined in the first part of this chapter may have wider applicability. The final section turns to a discussion of the political prospects for reform.

Changing the Statutory Mandate

The cure for strictness that has been proposed most often is to amend the statutes to allow or require cost-benefit analyses of standards. At OSHA this amendment would overturn the Supreme Court's decision on the cotton dust standard, which held that section 6(b)(5) of the OSH Act precluded such balancing. Although the Supreme Court's decision does not rule out all moves toward greater cost-effectiveness, it does make rule making less flexible.

If language allowing cost-benefit analysis had been in the act when Reagan took office, OSHA probably would have proceeded more expeditiously both in revising earlier standards (for example, setting looser exposure limits for cotton dust and lead) and in addressing new hazards. However, most OSHA leaders in prior administrations would probably not have changed their behavior even if the statute had granted them the freedom to weigh costs and benefits. Indeed, even if the statute were amended to *require* cost-benefit analysis, it is still likely that courts would grant substantial latitude to agencies about how to value risk reductions. But that latitude would have its limits; therefore a requirement to weigh costs and benefits would induce greater moderation because of fears of losing in court.

Perhaps more important, even an amendment permitting cost-benefit balancing would strip OSHA of its exemption from Executive Order 12291, which *requires* agencies to adopt the rule with the greatest net benefits unless their statutes prohibit it. Thus, so long as the president wanted to maintain this requirement, statutory permission could have a similar effect to statutory requirement.

Because OSHA is already required to estimate the costs and quantify the health effects of the standards it proposes, these amendments would not add to the time required to issue standards. Indeed, the proposition that more moderate standards are less likely to be challenged suggests that relaxing the mandate should quicken the pace of standard setting, although the impact may be modest.

Whatever its actual consequences, any amendment facilitating cost-benefit analysis would be perceived by organized labor as striking at the ideological heart of the act and would be adamantly opposed. In the absence of much stronger conservative shifts in Congress, especially in the memberships of the relevant authorizing committees, that amendment seems to have little chance unless the unions are offered something important in return.

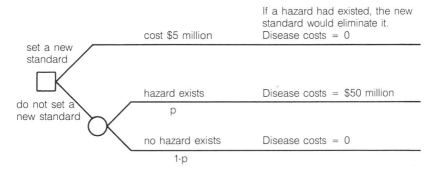

Figure 10.1 Why a standard may be justified even though a hazard probably does not exist. If the probability that the hazard exists (p) is greater than .10, then the expected cost of setting a new standard will be lower than the expected cost of failing to do so.

It is possible, however, that new legislation may not be a prerequisite for reduced strictness. I argued in chapter 7 that the majority's reading of section 6(b)(5) in the cotton dust decision is on shaky ground. The Court in the cotton dust case was closely divided, and a few Reagan appointments may be enough to overturn it and allow cost-benefit balancing without any amendments. This prospect alone may make it worthwhile for the unions to seek something in return for accepting an amendment to section 6(b)(5) before their bargaining chip is taken away.

Changing the Standard of Proof

Along with the new policy permitting regulators to balance costs and benefits should go a revision in the standard of proof that they must meet. Carrying benefit-cost thinking one step further, we see that the most sensible change would be to use the standard of proof that minimizes the expected costs of controlling the hazard *plus* the expected costs of not controlling the hazard.[1] This strategy is illustrated in the decision tree in figure 10.1. Suppose that there is some evidence that a chemical is hazardous. If it turns out to be hazardous, the best estimate of the health damage it would cause is $50 million. The damage could be prevented by a standard that would impose costs of $5 million on firms. The expected cost of regulating—the top branch in figure 10.1—is $5 million. The expected costs of failing to regulate—the lower branch—will be equal to $5 million if the probability that the potential hazard exists is equal to 10 percent ($50 million times 0.10 equals $5 million). If we want to minimize expected costs, the standard should be adopted if the probability of the chemical turning out to be hazardous is 10 percent or more. Thus even a small probability that a chemical is hazardous could legitimately spur action if the potential hazard is serious and the cost of reducing it is low. By the same reasoning, the standard of proof should be high if the cost of control is high and the potential damage less severe. I have argued that the courts are, in fact, sensitive to these issues and tend to review more stringently when they doubt that a regulation is substantively reasonable. Nevertheless, the policy formally announced in the benzene decision was that the standard of proof should be the same in all cases, and this decision will cause some mischief.[2]

One way to incorporate both the balancing of costs and benefits and the flexible standard of proof would be new statutory language stating that, in promulgating new standards, the secretary shall choose the standard that, based on a consideration of the costs it would impose, the probability that the substance is harmful, and the magnitude of the harm that would occur if the substance is harmful, would constitute the most reasonable step to effectuate the act's objective of protecting workers. In addition, Congress should explicitly reject the benzene plurality's requirement that OSHA show that it is "more likely than not" that a "significant risk" exists. It should also signal its desire for greater deference by removing the current requirement that OSHA have "substantial evidence" for its choices, replacing it with the stipulation that courts can overturn choices only if they are "arbitrary and capricious."

Of course, this new language represents a broad delegation from Congress to the agency. Although it provides more guidance than the present statute about which factors to consider, it provides even less guidance about how to carry out the balancing. In particular, it substitutes "balance" for the current prescription to choose the most protective exposure level that is feasible. Thus this amendment offers no substantial concessions to legislators who support strict standards.

If such sweeping legislative change proves difficult, it may be possible to rely on the Supreme Court to follow a reversal of the cotton dust decision with a reversal of the benzene one. This combination would be beneficial. Reversing the cotton dust decision would tend to produce less strict standards, which, I have argued, courts would tend to subject to less harsh scrutiny. Reversing the benzene decision should make it clear that the standard of review had been loosened. Yet, although the benzene decision symbolizes the threat of judicial review facing the agencies, the standard of proof would remain fairly high even without it. Major reforms in the standard of proof therefore will require some type of legislative action. If the broad delegation proposed is not feasible, the next best option might be to create a "fast track" for a subset of new standards for which a lower standard of proof would be especially appropriate.

One proposal along these lines has been offered by attorney Peter Huber. His analysis starts with the observation that Congress usually employs standard setting to deal with "old risks" and screening programs to deal with "new risks." Standard-setting programs (such as OSHA) place the burden of proof on the regulators, giving industry an interest in regulatory delay. Screening programs (such as the FDA's review of new drug applications) place the burden on those whose activities create the risk, giving industry an interest in reducing delay.[3]

A major rationale for the distinction is political. "Old risks" have constituencies and the constituencies have a stake in the status quo. Moreover, law and tradition afford a greater status to those equities than to the forgone profits of a product that never gets to market. In addition, there are circumstances in which requiring stricter regulations for new risks can be an efficient policy. The obvious case occurs when installing hazard abatement equipment at existing plants (that is, retrofitting) costs much more than installing it at the design phase of new plants.

Economists have sharply criticized distinctions that lead to less strict regulation of old risks and old facilities. They point out that the foregone benefits from preventing the introduction of new products are no less real than the costs of higher prices for existing products. In addition, new products and facilities will often be *less* hazardous than older ones; measures that increase the costs of new ones relative to old ones will tend to retard their introduction, which could lead to an *increase* rather than a decrease in risks.[4] Finally, even when stricter regulation of new risks can be justified on the grounds that the marginal costs of abatement are lower for any given level of exposure control, stricter controls are justified only up to the point at which they equalize the marginal costs of controlling the different sources of risk. Lower control costs at new plants do not justify a "blank check" approach to their regulation.

Although these points are valid, the argument against distinguishing new from old risks fails to consider a critical facet of the underregulation problem: New chemicals are usually used in small volumes and standard-setting agencies with limited administrative resources are especially unlikely to address "small" problems, that is, those that affect relatively few workers and are likely to have both small benefits and costs.[5] Because they are able to set so few standards and because administrative costs do not vary much with the size of the hazard, staff prefer to tackle big hazards unless strong interest groups or media pressure deflect them. This preference is certainly reasonable, but it means that the underregulation problem will be greatest for these smaller and newer hazards.

There is another reason for treating "small" hazards differently. When the choice involves costs of $10 million instead of $1 billion, the degree of analysis that can be justified by the quest for a better decision is reduced. In addition, with new or less common hazards the amount of information that is currently available (for example, from bioassays) is likely to be less. Thus generating the information needed to meet a high standard of proof could easily involve costs that are not justified.

Noting that the benzene decision requires OSHA to demonstrate that a "significant risk" exists before it can regulate, Huber argues:

To place such a burden on OSHA is, in effect, to reject screening regulation by that Agency, leaving OSHA without a regulatory tool which might be necessary in some circumstances for effective, reasonably prudent regulation.

The solution is simple. Congress should empower OSHA to divide its regulatory terrain between old and new sources of hazard and between old and new workplaces in much the same way as the Clean Air Act directs the EPA to regulate separately old and new sources of pollutants. . . . When the uncertain nature of the hazard is coupled with the severity of the potential harm, screening is administratively convenient, bypasses the often severe informational problems of regulating new technology, and leads to substantively sound results.[6]

In fact, what is needed is not really screening but a lower standard of proof for standard setting.

One method for implementing this policy would classify all toxic substances for which OSHA does not currently have exposure limits as "new" chemicals, for which standards could be issued with less evidence. Another approach, probably more sensible, could use a cost threshold (perhaps a present value of $25 million, increased with inflation) to distinguish the hazards that could be placed on this "fast track."

Huber does not give specific suggestions for what the lowered standard of proof should be for this category. I think that the language I suggested would be especially appropriate for this class of hazards. Not only would Congress lay the "significant" risk doctrine to rest, but it would also state clearly that evidence of potential harm (for example, potency estimates from bioassays) could be used to predict consequences. A change in the statutory basis of judicial review from the "substantial evidence" test to an "arbitrary and capricious" test would also help. Although some judges might ignore the change, it would constitute a clear signal that more deference should be given to agency decisions for this category of hazards.

Taken together, these changes would give the agency the flexibility it needs to reduce risks in a moderate fashion. The promise of more relaxed scrutiny for more moderate rules would also provide a stronger incentive to behave that way.

The prescriptions suggested are not ideal. On the one hand, neither the criterion of newness nor the criterion of low cost would capture all the hazards that are being underregulated. On the other hand, the use of either would surely produce cases of overregulation. But unless some sort of "fast track" process is established, ongoing efforts to address underregulation will be crippled.

Policies for Closing the Underregulation Gap

Although establishing a regular process for setting new standards more rapidly is important, it might not be able to overcome the gap that has opened since 1968—the year that the ACGIH prepared the list of recommendations that OSHA adopted as standards when it began operations in 1971. What options are available for closing this gap?

One strategy for remedying the lack of extensiveness in OSHA health regulation would be to adopt all the changes that the ACGIH has made since 1968. In theory this could be done administratively. In fact, however, changing the exposure limits for a hundred substances and adopting limits for two-hundred new ones would be impossible given current rule-making requirements. With many industries facing changes in several exposure limits simultaneously, the problems of estimating compliance costs and feasibility would become overwhelming. And for some of the hazards the evidence to establish that a "significant risk" exists at current exposure limits may be nonexistent. Finally, based on past experience, a multiple-hazard rule aggregates the political opposition, ensuring that the rule will be appealed. If any standard emerged, it would be appealed and would face poor prospects in court.

A second strategy is for Congress to mandate the adoption of the ACGIH changes, freeing them from judicial challenge. This option has attractive features. It throws the ball back to Congress, which should resolve the fundamental trade-off between strictness and extensiveness. Congress bears the chief responsibility for the slow pace of standard setting, and it should be asked whether it really intended to cast the 1968 exposure limits in stone.

Yet the general strategy of relying on Congress to mandate *specific* agency actions is in analytic disrepute. It is important to understand why this is so and what the implications are for this strategy at OSHA. Actions such as the congressional ban on PCBs and the mandate to reduce auto emissions by 90 percent have fostered two fears: that mandated standards would be adopted without the benefit of any analysis and that they would, given the incentives facing Congress on most protective issues, be very strict. In a penetrating study of the regulation of hazardous air pollutants by the EPA under section 112 of the Clean Air Act, John Graham presents an example of the first criticism. Environmental groups are trying to get Congress to pass a law "listing" a large number of hazards under section 112. Once a substance is listed as "hazardous" under section 112, the EPA has little choice but to regulate it stringently. Graham comments:

Grafting a priority list of 37 pollutants unto section 112 is inadvisable because the priorities should change as new scientific data are gathered. As an expert administrative agency with scientific staff, the EPA should be in a better position than Congress to evaluate the carcinogenic risk of various pollutants and to establish sensible priorities for rulemaking. Members of Congress lack the time, the attention span, and the expertise to modify priorities in the face of evolving patterns of scientific data.[7]

The objection of inadequate analysis is certainly persuasive in some cases. I argued that the legislated regulatory calendar is flawed because it requires Congress to attempt an independent review of every standard, a role it is ill-prepared to play. And, of course, it would be a mistake for Congress to mandate speedy action on a host of specific hazards so long as an agency is constrained to act strictly.

The proposal to legislate adoption of the ACGIH changes is less subject to these objections. The major reason is that the members of the ACGIH have already conducted a review of the health evidence, although not as extensive a review as OSHA conducts. And although the ACGIH conducts no formal economic analysis, costs are considered and balanced in an informal fashion.[8]

Viscusi has objected to this proposal to adopt the ACGIH recommendations.[9] His first concern is that they are based on an overly casual analytic process. His second is that, even if the analysis is sound, there is no reason to think that the criterion used by the ACGIH will maximize net benefits. I think that Viscusi misinterprets the importance of the fact that professionals from industry and government were able to agree on these recommendations. Rather than taking this agreement as evidence of their reasonableness, he emphasizes the potential for firms to use the process to create problems for their rivals. "To adopt the ACGIH standards as mandatory guidelines would in effect enable Du Pont to set many OSHA regulations."[10]

Although these criticisms have some merit, they do not address what seems to be the central point: Ninety-eight percent of OSHA's current health standards are *already* based on ACGIH recommendations. And they are now *old* recommendations; the most recent were made in 1968 and most were adopted by the ACGIH ten or twenty years before that. Thus the appropriateness of relying on standards developed by private groups is not really the issue, or at least not in the way suggested by Viscusi.

Perhaps a more relevant concern about adoption of the ACGIH changes is that in the future the locus of conflict will be shifted one step backward and will sabotage that organization's deliberative process. Every "one-time" adoption raises qualms about another.

Th other two parts of the strategy advocated here can help to avoid pressure for future one-time adoptions by providing the means for keeping standards up to date. However, implementation of the two-track strategy may rely in part on following the lead of the ACGIH. That organization's future recommendations will surely be one important source of guidance about the need for new exposure limits.

Yet fears for the safety of the ACGIH process may be overstated. As we saw in chapter 4, it has been the source of the exposure limits adopted by many countries over a period of decades. Although the ACGIH process has become slightly more formal during this period, there is no evidence that it has been "sabotaged" as a result of the organization's growing importance for public policy.

Industry is more likely to be concerned about the costs that it will incur as a result of adopting the new ACGIH limits than about the effects on the ACGIH. Despite general reasons to think that most ACGIH recommendations would impose a reasonable cost per disease prevented, the total costs could be substantial. Opposition to shouldering these costs may impede any bargain. As a consequence, measures to reduce the uncertainty and the total costs imposed by the adoption of so many changes should be considered. The cost of achieving a given exposure limit can be reduced in two major ways: allowing compliance with respirators rather than through engineering controls or extending the period before the new limit takes effect or before it must be achieved through engineering controls.

Respirator programs have a poor reputation for effectiveness among the industrial hygiene profession, and unions firmly uphold the principle of engineering controls. Yet we saw in chapter 7 that unions have tacitly acknowledged that long-term respirator use will be required to achieve many of the PELs mandated by the new standards that they won. In order to take advantage of this concession to practicality while avoiding a fight on the principles, Congress could state that the new ACGIH limits would become effective quickly and that compliance by means of engineering controls would ultimately be required but that compliance through other methods would be allowed for five or perhaps even ten years.

The best legislative package of reform would include an allowance or requirement for the balancing of benefits and costs, an explicit provision that the burden of proof be calibrated in some way to the costs of the proposed rule, and, as a catch-up measure, the adoption of the ACGIH changes. It would be a mistake to lower the burden of proof in the regular standard-setting process without also establishing some mechanism to encourage balancing. The arguments I presented suggest that in the long run more balanced standards will meet less opposition and facilitate the standard-setting process. Nevertheless, the highest legislative priority is probably adoption of the ACGIH changes, if only because the regulatory review process appears capable of prodding agencies to give some consideration to costs. In addition, the regulatory burden imposed by overly strict standards is, I have argued, self-limiting.

Prospects for Reform

Some important features of the current political impasse are captured by the two-by-two table in figure 10.2 It shows four policy alternatives. The current policy—strict rules and a slow pace of rule making —is box C. The

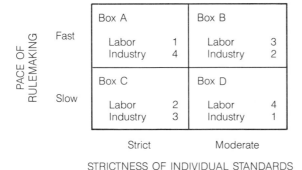

Figure 10.2   Interest group preferences on the strictness and pace of rule making. "1" signifies the most preferred option; "4," the least preferred.

argument of this book is that a shift to box B—less strict rules and a faster pace—would be socially desirable.

Labor and industry preferences regarding each policy are shown in the boxes. Thus organized labor's first preference would be for strict rules and a fast pace of rule making (box A); but this is industry's least favored policy. Not surprisingly, labor's least favored choice is box D, less strict rules with no faster pace. I have labeled this as industry's first choice, although this judgment is more uncertain because of divisions among firms.

The more critical labeling judgments concern policies B and C. It is currently correct to say that organized labor prefers the existing policy (box C) to the less strict, more extensive alternative (box B). Labor is not convinced that workers would be better off under policy B, and support for the current policy is more ideologically satisfying. In contrast, I think that most of American industry would prefer policy B to the current policy. It promises to be more cost-effective and more reasonable. Certainly it would be more attractive to the big chemical companies who claim that they already use the ACGIH exposure limits as their targets. Thus they might incur relatively low compliance costs if OSHA adopted them. They would gain an advantage over domestic competitors who had lagged in hygiene efforts. Perhaps equally important, they would gain leverage for reducing exposures at the firms that purchased their chemicals. Lower exposures there will ultimately result in fewer diseases. Given the recent growth in lawsuits against suppliers and the far higher awards received by successful plaintiffs compared to recipients of workers' compensation, these big chemical firms might be pleased to see the enforcement of lower PELs even if it means a small contraction in demand for their products.

If we accept this distribution of preferences as roughly correct, we can draw two implications:

1. If a policy change requires the agreement of both parties, there will be no change because there is no alternative that both prefer to the status quo.[11] The strong antipathy of at least one of the parties to policies A and D probably guarantees that they are not real options in the next decade or two, unless the existing distribution of power changes markedly.

2. If labor union leaders could be convinced that policy B is preferable to the status quo, then a shift would make both parties better off in their own terms. However, even if both did prefer B to C, they would still face the problem of how to make the transition. Labor would fear that, if it gave up

on strictness, it might end up with policy D, not B. Industry would fear that allowing a faster pace might lead to policy A, not B.

Thus there are two critical steps that are required. The first requires a shift in how elites view the role of standard setting. Labor leaders, politicians, and some business groups must be convinced that a policy of more extensive, less strict rule making would be preferable to the status quo. If it can be shown to be substantially more cost-effective, then it could both protect more workers and cost less than the current system. The second step requires the invention of specific bargains and institutional mechanisms that can reassure each party that the outcome it fears most is unlikely to be realized, allowing them to make the transition to policy B.

The difficulty of taking each step is increased by uncertainty. In the first case, uncertainties about the nature of the hazards that are "out there" make it difficult to rule out the possibilities that the new policy would either fail to regulate a new hazard strictly enough or regulate too many trivial hazards. Advocates of strict protection may fear that the new policy would not provide adequate protection against a serious new hazard. I pointed out in chapter 4 that the less strict, more extensive policy does not preclude drastic exposure reductions when they are justified by an analysis of the risks and costs. Yet, although the bias of quantitative risk analysis is to overestimate risks, there is always a small chance that an underestimate of the risk will occur and lead to an overly lax standard. But this small chance must be balanced against the underregulation that occurs routinely as a result of highly protective standards.

Studies to reduce the uncertainty about the impact of a policy of regulating less strictly and more extensively deserve high priority. Chapter 4 marshaled the available evidence to show that it was highly plausible that such a policy would be more cost-effective and could be more effective. On the basis of the existing evidence, this policy is the best bet. But further research on the magnitude of existing exposures to toxic substances, their dose-response relationships, and the marginal costs of abatement will be needed to reach a more definitive conclusion.

The other kind of uncertainty involves the consequences of changing political institutions. The story of this book is not the "soberly optimistic Madisonian story about checks and balances, the slow sifting of policy solutions over a period of years, the creative functions of conflict and disorder, and the inevitability of compromise." [12] The compromise that has emerged—strict, infrequent rule making—is anything but creative. Nor is the story the populist tale of agency capture by industry, the Chicago economists' variant about domination by rent-seeking cartels, or the neoconservative's claim about the ascendancy of an anti-business "new class."

Vogel has given a good account of the historical roots of the current problem. The strong populist strain in American society has frequently looked at big business for the enemy that all populist movements require. Business, in turn, has invited mistrust by traditionally refusing to acknowledge social responsibility or to follow the lead offered by public officials.[13]

The heightened awareness of environmental problems in the 1960s and 1970s occurred throughout the Western democracies. It reflected a new appreciation of the potential harm from pollution and toxic substances and led to a greater willingness to take political action. In the United States these developments were inextricably linked with new attacks on corporate misconduct and criticisms of governmental failures. New statutes tried to limit the discretion of regulators and to prod them toward protective policies. The ability to claim credit for protecting citizens while placing the costs on the corporate sector made the establishment of these programs (although not always their enforcement) appealing to legislators.

In other nations corporatist bargaining is one tool for making the parties sensitive to the opportunity costs of regulatory programs. A government with extensive nationalized industry is also likely to become more sensitive to costs because they have to pass through a budget at some point. Although analysis and evidence play a uniquely important role in the American rule-making process, mistrust of public agencies and the entrepreneurial opportunities for American politicians guarantee that popular values play at least as important a role as scientific expertise.

Other nations do not rely as heavily on analysis in the regulatory process in large part because it is not needed as a legitimating device.[14] In Europe the fact that the parties have agreed on a rule is often taken as sufficient evidence of its legitimacy. In the United States outsiders require analysis in order to compel the agency to address issues that it might otherwise overlook and, in some cases, to provide a basis for challenging its findings. The agencies carry out the analysis in order to try to convince the outside reviewers that their procedures are thorough and their conclusions well supported. Yet reasonableness is inevitably in part a question of substance, of outcomes, and not merely of procedures. The US agenices face statutes and a political environment that make it difficult to produce rules that are substantively reasonable. This difficulty exacerbates the problem of conferring legitimacy on the agency's decisions. The result is increased difficulty in making rules.

Because regulation is an unusually important policy instrument in the United States, the stalemate of the rule-making process poses a serious dilemma. The solution to it is likely to require a mix of the approaches that have been discussed. These include more reliance on strategies that do not rely on hazard-by-hazard rule making or that do not rely on rule making at all. Rules requiring that more information be provided to workers are an example of the first; laws facilitating tort awards for diseases caused by workplace exposures are an example of the second. To the extent that information strategies reduce hazards, they will tend to do so in an efficient manner, but their effectiveness remains hard to predict.

Regulatory negotiation can potentially avoid some of the rigid and inefficient position taking that characterizes current rule making. However, either statutory reform or greater judicial deference to the bargains that are reached through this process will be a necessary condition for its growth. So long as the statute still requires that all standards—including negotiated ones—must be strict and the courts demand evidence of significant human harm, the contribution of negotiations will be limited.

Some form of a regulatory budget could shift agency incentives somewhat in the direction of greater cost-effectiveness. A true regulatory budget remains politically unlikely for the near future. Even if enacted, it would not be especially well suited to address the problem of underregulation.

Thus the proposals developed in this chapter are needed to help remedy the current defects in rule making. These proposals also face significant political obstacles, but there are opportunities as well. Some environmental groups have downplayed confrontational tactics to work with industry and government to solve problems.[15] Compared to environmental groups, unions have more incentive to acknowledge the trade-offs involved. Because they are not single-issue organizations, unions are not required to foster conflict on this *particular* issue. Membership interests can be their guiding concern. At the least, those interests may conflict with and constrain ideological motivations.

Yet the perspective of organized labor may be too narrow. Most new health standards have dealt with hazards faced primarily by unionized workers, yet the best evidence indicates that health hazards confront as many nonunion as union workers. Thus nonunionized workers have suffered disproportionately from underregulation. Although unions have shown concern for workers outside their fold, it would be too much to expect them to be impartial in setting their priorities.[16] Legislators have an important role to play in developing a policy that will deal with a broader set of risks. When the OSH Act was being written, legislators working with associates of Ralph Nader played an important role in demanding provisions both to uphold workers' rights and to require strict and timely responses by policymakers. What is required now is a more sophisticated entrepreneurship that shows awareness that the popular view that strictness is always better is a poor guide to protective policies in the long run. Legislators and others who try to develop this policy will ultimately need support from within the union movement, but they can provide a spur to action.

Thus the political entrepreneurship that, in the past, contributed to the regulatory dilemma by forcing the incorporation of simplistic, blunt policy measures and popular shibboleths against valuing the prevention of death could contribute to a resolution. The strategy cannot be to confront those shibboleths head on but to circumvent them with a new definition of the problem. The literature on regulatory reform emphasizes the critical role that new ideas have played in allowing reforms to occur.[17]

A fruitful resolution is most likely to require employment of more than one of the tools in the portfolio of reforms I have discussed. But unless the portfolio includes fundamental reforms in the statute that structures the program, substantial problems will remain. It is hard to believe that the advocates of the OSH Act fully understood the impact of strictness on underregulation when they designed this program or that the nation is well served by the results.

Appendix A
Variable Definitions in Regression

TOXPROB — Value = 1 for all workers who said they faced a "sizable" or "great" prolem from exposures to either "dangerous chemicals; radiation" or "air pollution from smoke, dust, fumes, fibers, etc."

Union — Value = 1 for all union members and those covered by contracts.

Bigsize — Value = 1 if more than 500 workers employed at work site.

Experience — Value = years worked since age 16.

Tenure — Value = years worked with present employer

Education — Value = years of education.

Too fast — Value = 1 for workers who agreed or agreed strongly that the pace of their work was too fast.

Repetitive — Value = 1 for workers who agreed or agreed strongly that their job was repetitive.

No Control — Value = 1 for workers who agreed or agreed strongly that they lacked control over what they did at work.

Bad Health — Value = 1 for workers who said that their health problems impaired to a sizable or great extent their ability.

Appendix B
Retrospective Studies of the Costs of Standards

Asbestos

A 1974 reanalysis by a university-based economist suggested that OSHA's consultant had roughly doubled the true cost of compliance with OSHA's 2-fiber standard because the consultant had assumed that exposures were considerably higher than they really were. The reanalysis estimated that the annualized compliance costs for the manufacturing and insulation sectors totaled about $75 million (in 1970 dollars, discounting at 10 percent over a fifty-year period).[1] A careful retrospective study of the manufacturing sector in 1980 estimated costs that were in line with this earlier estimate.[2]

Vinyl Chloride

This standard provided the most blatant overestimates of compliance costs. OSHA's consultant estimated that meeting a PEL in the range of 2 to 5 ppm in the vinyl chloride monomer sector would cost about $22 million a year. Meeting a 10–15-ppm exposure limit in the polyvinyl chloride sector would cost about $87 million a year. Although the consultants argued that the 1-ppm PEL proposed by OSHA simply could not be attained, they cited one firm's estimate that the costs of compliance with that level would be several times higher.[3] OSHA's 1974 standard did set a PEL of 1 ppm, but several years later a review by researchers from the Wharton School of Business estimated that the total compliance costs for both sectors had been about $20 million a year.[4] The Wharton researchers gathered data from firms with over 70 percent of the industry's capacity. Unfortunately, the study did not pay close enough attention to the issue of whether the costs were all really attributable to OSHA. The researchers appear to have followed a rule of attributing costs to OSHA if the company mentioned OSHA. Because it is doubtful that firms would have pursued an exposure level close to 1 ppm in the absence of OSHA, that bias may be minor. However, the standard did generate several productivity-enhancing measures, and the study failed to consider the joint costs problem. But because some other cost items were ignored, the $20 million figure ($40 million in 1985 dollars) may be roughly right.[5]

Coke Oven Emissions

The Council on Wage-Price Stability estimated the cost of the coke oven standard at $160 million in 1975 dollars, well below the range of $200 million to over $1 billion (1975 dollars) that OSHA's contractor had suggested. In 1985 dollars the figure is $293 million. Table 2.1 uses a range of $200–$400 million. Although there is substantial uncertainty about the actual costs, a little evidence is available that suggests that the high end of the contractor's estimate was indeed too high.

Although no retrospective study was performed specifically on coke oven emissions, we can make use of data from the most systematic attempt to derive estimates of the overall costs of regulatory programs. The Business Roundtable commissioned the accounting firm of Arthur Anderson to survey a sample of forty-eight large firms about the total costs they incurred during 1977 as a result of the requirements of several regulatory agencies, including OSHA. The three steel firms in the sample reported spending between $5 million and $7 million in 1977 to comply with the coke oven standard, which had been promulgated in December 1976.[6] Only $1 million to $2 million was for capital expenditures. OSHA's consultant had estimated compliance costs for each firm; for these three, it had estimated capital costs of $93 million and annual operating costs of $34 million to comply with the standard, which became effective in 1977.[7]

The disparity between these figures is doubtless due in large part to the incomplete status of compliance at the end of 1977. Indeed, even in the mid-1980s a large percentage of coke workers are still exposed above the PEL. However, the finding that only relatively minor expenditures were made in the first year is important because delays reduce the present value of the costs. If a firm can delay an "unproductive" investment for five years, it (and society) gains all of the returns it will earn by investing it productively for that period. (Of course, society also loses whatever health benefits are lost as a result of the delay.) The consultant had assumed that the capital investments would be undertaken rapidly, contributing to an overestimate of the real social costs. The size of the overestimate depends on how long the delay lasted.

Cotton Dust

OSHA's economic consultant estimated in 1976 that compliance with OSHA's proposed PEL of 0.2 mg/m^3 would require annualized costs of almost $700 million. The standard OSHA actually promulgated in 1978 allowed higher PELs in some sectors. OSHA claimed that the annualized costs would be $205 million; however, critics complained that the OSHA figures had little credibility.[8] A careful, new study, conducted in 1982 after the Reagan administration had called for a reappraisal of the standard, estimated that the ultimate compliance costs would be $83 million a year. The textile industry experienced a major spurt in capital expenditures after 1978 and a major issue in this study was deciding what proportion to attribute to OSHA compliance.[9] The figure of $95 million used in table 2.1 reflects an adjustment to 1985 dollars.

Lead

Assessing cost estimates for the 1978 lead standard is extremely difficult. First, the cost study for that standard assumed that the compliance goal was a PEL of 0.100 mg/m^3, whereas the final standard adopted a PEL of 0.050 mg. Second, even though the standard allowed up to ten years for engineering compliance in some industries, it has become clear that in some sectors engineering compliance will not be feasible. Third, different studies were done at different times for different industries. In large part OSHA took estimates of the cost of complying with a 0.100-mg PEL and used them as its estimate of the cost of meeting a 0.050 PEL.[10] Nevertheless, more recent studies seem to indicate that the resulting figures are roughly right and that a number around $500 million a year is plausible.[11] In table 2.1 a range of $400–$600 million is adjusted to 1985 dollars.

It is useful to distinguish the steps of identifying hazards and of quantifying the risk they pose, although in practice the two are closely related. For most of its history OSHA ignored the issue of *how many* diseases would be prevented by its standards and asked only whether there was evidence that current exposures could be harmful. Because most of the hazards being addressed were suspect carcinogens, that question became whether there was good evidence that they were carcinogens.

Industry spokespeople have been consistent in their views about the need for caution in identifying chemicals as carcinogens. They have claimed that OSHA relies far too heavily on shoddy studies, incomplete data, and a kind of scientific Murphy's law that assumes that any chemical that might possibly be hazardous is. OSHA's retort was that the OSH Act commanded it to use the "best *available* evidence" and to pursue the overriding objective of worker protection.

In contrast, when it came to *quantifying* the diseases that standards would prevent, industry (at least until the 1980 Supreme Court decision in the benzene case) called for the use of the best available evidence, even if the evidence was not very good. Now it was OSHA's turn to complain that these risk assessments relied on such inadequate data and such a long string of tenuous assumptions that the results were meaningless.

OSHA's leaders wanted to use criteria for identifying hazards that would facilitate its efforts to regulate. But once that decision had been made, they feared that estimating the magnitude of risks could hand OSHA's enemies a stick to beat it with. If the numbers were small, critics could raise the specter of cost-benefit analysis and question whether the costs were justified. Ignorance about the magnitude of the effects precluded that challenge and helped to maintain the agency's autonomy in carrying out its protective mission.

The Supreme Court's benzene decision mandated some sort of quantitative risk assessment. Once OSHA acceded to the Court's ruling and began to offer its own estimates, the industry focus shifted from a simple call for making estimates to an insistence that assessments use reliable data and that they not make assumptions that lead to unreasonable overstatements of risk.[1] Now that risk assessment was required, industry stood to gain by the delays that insistence on additional data would bring. And when the assessment was conducted, the use of "best estimates" rather than extrapolation form the 95 percent upper confidence interval would help to prevent the risks from being systematically overstated.

To capture the flavor of this debate, consider the following hypothetical pre-1981 dialogue between a COWPS economist and an OSHA spokesman on the issue of risk assessment:

OSHA: A quick glance at the uncertainties affecting estimates of the risks posed by acrylonitrile (shown in table 3.2) should suffice to show that the attempt to quantify health effects quickly degenerates into a sheer guessing game.

COWPS: Perhaps, but how does a confession of ignorance help us to make a decision about what exposure levels to permit? And don't tell me that we should keep exposures as low as "feasible"; that approach totally ignores the question of whether the health gains justify the costs.

OSHA: Well, "feasibility" is the criterion cited in the statute, but I agree it's vague. Maybe a more workable criterion is that OSHA should minimize the probability of catastrophic outcomes. Suppose, for example, that it seemed possible, although unlikely, that failing to lower the acrylonitrile exposure level from 2 ppm to 1 ppm would result in 200 extra deaths a year. Even a small possibility of that outcome would justify the stricter standard.

COWPS: How small: one in a million, one in ten? You can't just ignore what the size of the probability is. And you can't ignore the costs.

OSHA: This is hypothetical, because you can't estimate the risks, but I would say that any terrible outcome with more than a 1 percent or maybe 5 percent probability of occurring should trigger the strictest standard.

COWPS: What do you mean by "terrible," and how did you arrive at those figures? I object to your adoption of such extreme risk aversion. Most people just aren't that pessimistic or traumatized by unlikely threats. But I want to get back to your equating great uncertainties with total ignorance. We're not totally ignorant. As in the case of acrylonitrile, we do have a basis for estimates of risk. It's irresponsible to ignore the best available evidence.

OSHA: It's irresponsible to act as if the evidence allows greater precision than it does. Point estimates are deceiving. Almost every variable needs to be expressed as a distribution. You would need to conduct a sensitivity analysis to see how the answers vary as you choose different points in the distribution.

COWPS: Fine.

OSHA: Hold it! I should add that we really don't know what the distributions look like. Many probably look more like upside-down pie plates than bells, with broad plateaus where a wide range of figures are equally probable.

COWPS: But you're admitting that estimates can be made. For each variable we can carry out the process you describe. For example, how much of a difference could cigarette smoking make in our calculation of the cost per life saved? Of course, since we don't know whether workers exposed to acrylonitrile smoked more or less than other Du Pont workers, the expected effect is zero. Studies show that the smoking history of the sample generally has to be dramatically different from the population to significantly change the estimate of excess deaths. A dramatic difference seems unlikely. If there had been unusual rules forbidding smoking at these jobs, we probably would know about them. Thus the possible impact of smoking history on our estimate is probably small; perhaps there's a 20 percent chance that it could result in adding or subtracting one excess death to our estimate of four excess deaths. In this manner we sketch a rough distribution. Multiplying these distributions will give us a final distribution of the probabilities of different numbers of excess deaths.

I grant that some of these results won't be worth very much, but some will help us focus on what the crucial uncertainties are and should guide efforts to develop better data and better tools for making estimates. After all, when we're talking about spending hundreds of millions of dollars for each regulation, the payoff from better estimates could be a bonanza.

OSHA: The problem with this whole exercise is that the computed estimates will cover such a wide range that they won't be useful. At best, you will proudly conclude that there's a 50 percent chance that the cost per life saved is between $100,000 and $6 million, with only a 10 percent chance that it is less than $20,000 or more than $12 million. So what?

COWPS: I'll tell you "so what." We could conclude that on this criterion this standard is quite likely to be superior to one where there's a 50 percent chance that the cost per life saved is between $8 million and $20 million. But I don't think we will know how useful estimates will be until we start making them. And the more effort we devote, the better the estimates will become. Why don't you start trying before you judge the attempt a failure?

OSHA: You may recall that on one of our earliest standards, the economic impact consultant surveyed medical experts to derive an estimate of the health effects of different exposures to asbestos. The survey revealed a near consensus on what we now believe to be a substantial underestimate of the risks. The experts may not know the answers.

COWPS: But again, what is the alternative to relying on the best available evidence?

OSHA: That sounds nice, but what does it mean in practice? For most hazards, we don't have any human evidence at all. Scanty as the evidence is on acrylonitrile, we have a flood of it compared with what we have in most cases.

COWPS: That's true if you look at the universe of toxic substances but not if you look at the hazards that OSHA has actually addressed. Some evidence on human effects was usually available.

OSHA: But in the future that will usually not be the case.

COWPS: You may be right, but there will still be opportunities to use animal tests and short-term tests (for mutagenicity) to glean some insight about the cancer threat to humans. Almost without exception, substances known to cause human cancers also cause animal cancers, although the site of the tumors is not always the same. Moreover, in most of the six cases in which fairly solid estimates of dose-response curves for carcinogens in humans have been established, there is a rough correlation between potency in rodents and in people. Given the enormous range of biological potencies of carcinogens possible (over a millionfold), this rough correlation is quite significant.

OSHA: Your willingness to base policy on a string of highly tenuous quantifications amazes me.

COWPS: No more than your disregard of the magnitude of health effects astonishes me.

When the uncertainties are acknowledged, the policy implications are often murkier than COWPS suggests. However, OSHA deserved to be criticized for failing to examine even what range of effects was plausible. The debate was ultimately resolved by the Supreme Court in its 1980 decision overturning OSHA's benzene standard because the agency had failed to show that it addressed a "significant risk." [2]

At least since early 1972 union and and public health advocates have publicized a NIOSH statement that "based on limited analysis of violent/non-violent mortality in several industries, there may be as many as 100,000 deaths per year from occupationally caused diseases." [1] An extrapolation from three epidemiological studies of small populations in England, this conclusion deserved to be treated as no more than a wild guess. But despite its humble origins, it helped to legitimize a strong regulatory effort and became one of the "mythical numbers" in the occupational health field. [2] One hundred thousand amounts to 5 percent of all deaths or 10 percent of male deaths if all were assigned to them.

Several studies published in 1976 and 1977 tried to estimate the proportion of the 400,000 annual cancer deaths caused by occupational exposures. They arrived at figures such as 1 to 3 percent of all cancers (Higginson and Muir), 4 percent of male cancers and 2 percent of female cancers (Wynder and Gori), and less than 15 percent for men and 5 percent for women (Cole). [3]

In September 1978 a controversial new estimate appeared that stated that "occupationally related cancers may comprise as much as 20% or more of total cancer mortality in forthcoming decades. Asbestos alone will probably contribute up to 13%–18% and the data [on five other carcinogens] suggest at least 10%–20% more. These data do not include effects of radiation, nor effects of a number of other known chemical carcinogens." [4]

The paper in which these conclusions were presented, entitled "Estimates of the Fraction of Cancer in the United States Related to Occupational Factors," was given as testimony in OSHA's 1978 hearings on its proposal for a "generic" carcinogen standard. (See chapter 5 for a discussion of the Cancer Policy.) OSHA's proposal drew heavy fire from industry spokespeople and many scientists for resolving virtually every issue in the most protective fashion. Yet, although it went beyond it on some issues, the proposal largely hewed to the consensus that had emerged among federal scientific and regulatory agencies. The severity of the attack on the OSHA policy alarmed many of the scientists who had helped to forge that consensus. The paper appeared with eight names under the title, including the directors of the National Cancer Institute and the National Institute of Environmental Health Sciences and senior scientists from those bodies and from NIOSH. Their intent was to counter the earlier analyses that had indicated that occupational exposures were not a major contributor to cancer and, more broadly, to support the view that strong government measures in response were needed. As one of the signers later explained: "We knew that Selikoff [the leading asbestos researcher] had stated that asbestos might be causing 50,000 deaths a year. We wanted to see if we could find a way to support that figure." [5] Even before the testimony was presented, HEW Secretary Joseph Califano cited the results in a speech before the AFL-CIO supporting tough cancer regulation.

The Cancer Policy had spurred industry to set up a new organization, the American Industrial Health Council (AIHC), whose role was to monitor and evaluate the scientific basis of regulatory policy. The AIHC quickly turned out a critique of the "Estimates" paper that helped to discredit the reasoning behind the high estimate.[6] In its review of the controversy, *Science* stated that "the rebuttal ... necessitates the conclusion that [the "Estimates" paper] predictions are invalid." [7] (I analyze why these figures are overestimates later.) Nevertheless, the figure of 38 percent (18 percent for asbestos plus 20 percent for other hazards) quickly became cited with approval by other federal agencies (most prominently the Toxic Substances Strategy Committee and OSHA) and by labor organizations in the United States and Europe. The TSSC, an interagency group established by President Carter, gave credibility to both unsupported figures in its 1980 statement that "more than 100,000 workers are believed to die each year as a result of physical and chemical hazards at work, but the magnitude of the long-term health effects of occupational conditions is unknown. Occupational exposure to carcinogens is a factor in an estimated 20 to 38 percent of all cases of cancer." [8]

By 1981, the debate among scientists had lost some of its acrimony. A conference brought together many of the protagonists.[9] Although the method of several of the report's critics had relied essentially on informed judgment rather than on any new data, their lower range of 2 to 10 percent was not seriously challenged. The absence of a challenge, however, did not mean that everyone accepted that range but rather that all agreed that the currently available evidence could not support a higher estimate. One scientist who had both signed the "Estimates" document and undermined it with his own analysis of asbestos-caused diseases wryly observed: "In hindsight, the DHEW scientists would have been less subject to criticism if they had simply stated that the 20 percent figure was suggested by their collective intuition, which is basically the approach that most other investigators seem to have employed in such attempts." [10]

The Fallacies in the "Estimates" Paper

The easiest way to understand the nature of the fallacies in the "Estimates" paper is to look at the methodology it used for the five hazards other than asbestos (arsenic, benzene, chromium, nickel, and petroleum distillates). Its first step was to review epidemiological studies to get a "risk ratio" (the rate at which exposed workers get the diease compared to the rate at which unexposed workers do). Thus for arsenic the risk ratio for respiratory tract cancer was between 3 and 8. The next step was to multiply that range (actually, the relative risk minus one, in order to get the excess risk) times the age-adjusted incidence of respiratory cancer per 100,000 males (131 per 100,000 for lung cancer). Finally, that product was multiplied by the number of workers currently exposed to the hazard. The exposure figures were drawn from a NIOSH National Occupational Hazard Survey conducted in 1972 through 1974.[11] For arsenic the number said to be exposed was 1.5 million workers. The number of arsenic-induced deaths expected annually from this methodology was 3900 to 14,000.

The major reason that future diseases were overestimated by this procedure is that the epidemiological studies on which the relative risk calculations were based involved workers whose exposures mostly occurred in the 1930s and 1940s at levels far in excess of those prevalent today, whereas the NIOSH survey greatly exaggerates the number of workers with significant levels of exposure (as opposed to any possible exposure). For example, in contrast to the NIOSH estimate of 1.5 million workers, OSHA's economic contractor in 1976 identified only 1700 workers exposed to arsenic at levels above 0.010 mg/m^3 (a level below that of the most lightly exposed smelter workers just two decades before), and another 5600 workers exposed above 0.004 mg/m^3.[12] In its critique the AIHC estimated a maximum of fourteen cancers a year from current exposure levels, about 500 times fewer than the figure in the "Estimates" paper. Shortly thereafter OSHA agreed that this lower range was correct.[13]

The asbestos estimates were not exaggerated to the same degree. A more careful 1981 study indicated that excess cancer deaths resulting from asbestos would peak in the 1980s at about 3 percent of the annual cancer death toll, with a range of 1.4 to 4.4 percent.[14] Another major study appearing in 1981 criticized the "Estimates" paper sharply in the course of its attempt to apportion the causes of current US cancers. Written by Richard Doll, dean of British epidemiologists, and Richard Peto, it argued that occupation probably accounted for about 4 percent of cancer deaths, although the range could run from 2 to 10 percent.[15]

Asbestos

Exposure figures are from Research Triangle Institute, "Asbestos Dust: Technological and Feasibility Assessment and Economic Impact Analysis of the Proposed Occupational Standard" (September 1978). The risk assessment is based on Julian Peto's suggestion that "3% of textile workers exposed for 20 years at 1 fiber/cm^3 would die of asbestos-related disease." See his article "Dose-Response Relationships for Asbestos-Related Disease: Implications for Hygiene Standards: Mortality," *The Annals of the New York Academy of Science* (1979), 330: 195–204. Peto also observes that, although asbestos can cause other fatal diseases besides bronchial cancer and mesothelioma, "it is probably reasonable to ignore mortality due to both gastrointestinal cancer and asbestosis in any formal prediction of the effects of low dust levels" (p. 200).

Arsenic

Both the exposure estimates and the risk assessment are drawn from the testimony of OSHA staff scientist Kenneth Chu in his affidavit to the Ninth Circuit Court in *ASARCO et al. v. OSHA*, 78–1959, and in Appendix B, "Risk Assessment for Inorganic Arsenic." The risk assessments are based on a linear, one-hit model, prepared by Chu and dated January 14, 1981.

Ethylene Oxide

Exposure figures for directly exposed workers and the results of various risk assessment models are presented in Departments of Labor, Health and Human Services, Education, and Related Agencies, *Appropriations for 1984 Hearings before a Subcommittee of the Committee on Appropriations*, 98th Cong., 1st sess., 19–784 (Washington, D.C.: Government Printing Office, 1983), pp. 716, 718. I used the multistage model in table 4.8; the differences for five of the six models presented there are within a factor of 3.

Chromium

Estimates of exposure to hexavalent chromium are taken from the extensive analysis by Centaur Associates, "Technological and Economic Impact

Study of OSHA Standards for Chromium" (1980), mimeo, Exhibit 3.1.
The estimate of chromium's potency is found in EPA Environmental
Criteria and Assessment Office, *Health Assessment Document for Chromium* EPA-600/8-83-014A (July 1983), pp. 7–76. It has been adjusted to
workplace exposure time.

Benzene

Exposure estimates by Arthur D. Little, Inc., "Economic Impact Study for
Proposed Benzene Standard" (1976), estimated that 36,000 workers were
exposed to over 1 ppm. The risk assessment used here was developed by
Mary C. White, Peter F. Infinte, and Kenneth C. Chu in "A Quantitative
Estimate of Leukemia Mortality Associated with Occupational Exposure
to Benzene," *Risk Analysis* (September 1982), 2(3):145–204. They used a
linear one-hit model.

Perchloroethylene and Trichloroethylene

Exposure estimates are based on Arthur D. Little, Inc., "Technology
Assessment and Economic Impact Study of OSHA Regulations: Perchloroethylene, Trichloroethylene, and Methyl Chloroform" (October 1977),
Table 4-6. The study estimated the number of workers in different exposure categories. For example, for perchloroethylene there were 152,000
workers exposed to less than 170 mg/m^3; 40,000 exposed to between 170
and 340 mg; 8200 exposed to between 340 and 680 mg; and 1100 exposed to
between 680 and 1020 mg. For calculations I used the midpoint of these
exposure ranges. In addition, 555 workers were exposed above 1020 mg in
one industry (I assumed an exposure of 1200 mg/m^3) and 6300 exposed between 340 and 3400 mg in another (I assumed 600). For perchloroethylene
the risk of cancer per microgram of lifetime exposure was 2.4×10^{-5}. For
workplace exposure this was divided by 7 (8 hours a day, 260 days a year,
for 45 to 70 years) to get a risk of 3.4×10^{-6}.

Formaldehyde

Estimates of the distribution of exposures and of the dose-response curve
were made for OSHA by Clement Associates in a report to OSHA. The
EPA Carcinogenic Assessment Group's risk estimate differs from the
figures used by Clement by less than 50 percent.

Coke Oven Emissions

The risk estimates, based on work by Charles E. Land, are reported in Carol K. Redmond, "Cancer Mortality among Coke Oven Workers," *Environmental Health Perspectives* (1983), 52:67–73. The number of workers exposed at different levels is not known. The table assumes that the decline in the steel industry has reduced the number employed in coke plants from about 22,000 in 1975 to about 15,000. Because a large number of workers are known to be exposed above the PEL, the current average exposure was estimated to be in the range of 100 to 150 μg/m^3.

To buttress the general argument that strict standards work to retard the pace of standard setting, it is helpful to examine the mechanisms through which this occurs. They include restricting the flow of information needed by regulators, increasing the probability of court challenges, increasing the probability that courts will overturn the standards brought before them, increasing the delays that White House reviewers can impose, and increasing the general perception that regulation is costly and inefficient and decreasing support for measures to expand its scope.

The Information That Firms Provide to Regulators

In general, firms have an incentive to withhold the information that regulators need to develop standards that will withstand judicial challenges. If the regulators cannot make a persuasive case, they are more likely to delay promulgating a standard; or, if they do promulgate one, the courts are more likely to overturn it. In either case the typical firm is better off than if a standard is issued quickly and permanently. Information from industry is needed by the regulators, because firms almost always know more about the technical feasibility of standards and their financial impact than the agency does and they often have important information about the health effects as well.

The more costly a firm expects the standard to be, the more benefits they will get from delaying or killing it. In the most simple model, therefore, greater strictness reduces the flow of information and impedes the pace of standard setting. The simple model does overlook several factors, however. First, in some cases firms or whole industries may believe that they can moderate the regulation by providing information showing that a low PEL is not needed. The stricter the expected regulatory action, the stronger they may feel that "education" of the agency is necessary. At the same time, of course, they are building a record for reviewing courts to use in questioning the standard. The agency may be pursuing a strategy of proposing a strict standard precisely in order to "smoke out" this type of information from firms. In general, the firm will provide evidence against the standard and withhold evidence that would favor it.

The second complication arises because of divisions among firms; some may benefit from the standard and others may lose. We have seen that, when splits within an industry are sharp, OSHA is likely to benefit from a greater flow of information from the advantaged firms. Is there any relationship between the strictness of a standard and the likelihood of divisions within an industry? The stricter the standard, the more likely it becomes that *all* firms in the industry will incur costs to comply. In addition, it becomes more likely that firms will view the standard as unreasonable on scientific and ideological grounds as well as self-interest. However, the effect of stricter standards on variations in the *absolute* costs of compliance is more difficult to predict.[1] These cost differences may be the more accurate predictor of whether firms take opposing positions on standards. Thus, although there is some reason to believe that stricter standards reduce industry splits (and therefore restrict the flow of information), the matter remains uncertain.

The Probability of Court Challenges

The second mechanism is that appeals of agency actions are more likely when standards are stricter. This assertion might be questioned on the grounds that, because appeals are likely to save them money, many firms in an industry will have a strong incentive to appeal *regardless* of the strictness of standards. The assumption underlying this skepticism is that the expected benefits from these two sources are so far in excess of the expected costs of appealing (that is, of the lawsuit) that even fairly large reductions in compliance costs are unlikely to tip the calculus in favor of accepting the standard. The expected benefits of appealing come from the prospect that the appeal will delay the compliance costs, reducing their present value; and the prospect that the standard will be overturned in whole or in part, eliminating all or part of the costs it would impose.[2]

A few facts about appeals help us to see that the issues are not quite as simple as this calculation suggests. Firms cannot always be certain that appeals will delay compliance costs. In some cases the courts have granted a stay of the engineering control requirements of the standards, but in other cases they have not. Even if they do grant a stay, the impact may be minor because the standards themselves frequently allow several years before compliance through engineering controls is required.

Nevertheless, on balance, the argument that the expected benefits of appealing are likely to outweigh the expected costs even for less strict standards remains plausible. However, its plausibility is a function of the model of firm or industry decision making that we employ. These models, presented in an order that makes the argument increasingly less plausible, are outlined in the following:

1. Decisions are made by a profit-maximizing unitary actor.

2. Decisions are made by many profit-maximizing actors, but all of them share the same interests. The new problem here is organizing collective action toward a common goal.

3. Decisions are made by many profit-maximizing actors, some of whom have opposing interests. The new factor here is that, although the standard imposes net costs on some firms, it confers net benefits on others.

4. Decisions are made by actors whose decisions are not made on the basis of weighing litigation costs against compliance costs for individual standards.

In the first model a firm that is a monopolist or a trade association that dominates the firms comprising it makes the decisions. Even if we assumed that the legal costs of the appeal came to $1 million (probably two or three times the real costs), it is hard to make the calculations show that appealing is a bad strategy. Even for the DBCP standard, whose compliance costs had an estimated present value of only $36.5 million, even a 5 percent chance of winning the challenge would confer total benefits of almost $2 million, at least twice the costs. A serious caveat to this analysis (one that applies to the other models as well) is that the compliance costs will often not be a good measure of the actual financial costs that will enter the firms' calculations. For example, an industry that faces an inelastic demand curve that will allow it to pass along higher costs without suffering a significant drop in sales will tend to be less anxious to appeal than one that faces an elastic demand curve.

The second model makes appeals less likely in a limited set of circumstances. For example, if a hundred firms are affected by the standard and each of them faces costs of $500,000, no single firm may be willing to finance the challenge on its own even though collectively they stand to gain up to $50 million. This result can usually be prevented if either of two conditions are met: (1) At least one firm has expected savings in excess of the litigation costs; or (2) the firms have previously overcome the barriers to organization and have established a system for financing collective action. Whether the first condition is met depends on the scope and stringency of the standard and the structure of the industry. Almost certainly, the condition was met in all of OSHA's health standards except possibly DBCP. The maximum total compliance costs for a single firm probably did not exceed $2 million. The gains from a year or two delay in compliance would not have been enough to justify litigation. A firm would also have had to expect a reasonably high probability of overturning the standard.

Of course, the plethora of trade associations in Washington testifies to the success with which the second condition has been satisfied. However, difficulties may arise because their memberships may be overinclusive or underinclusive with respect to the particular standard being challenged. Some members may not want their dues spent on fighting a regulation that does not affect them. In other cases, new alliances may have to be formed across organizations.

The third model takes into account that different firms and industries can have opposing interests. Some firms may believe that they gain a competitive advantage over others within their industry. Or firms in the industry that produces a chemical may favor a standard that imposes controls on the downstream industries that might misuse their product, especially if those industries cannot easily find substitutes. Conflict within an industry may make it impossible for the trade association to take a position. In that event the costs of collective action escalate as firms must create a new ad hoc coalition. The alternative is for an individual firm to assume the burden.

The fourth model raises the most important reasons why appeals may not be automatic. Earlier I mentioned that one external benefit of appealing from the perspective of firms was the possible intimidating effect it could have on regulators: They better be prepared for appeals on future standards as well. However, at some point a reputation for toughness can turn into a reputation for unreasonableness, and that can be costly for a firm or industry. That conclusion seems especially apt if they are constantly dealing with regulatory agencies on a broad series of fronts. The chemical industry is an obvious case. A reputation for unreasonableness is likely to play poorly not only with regulators, who may mistrust the industry and harass it, but also with political leaders and media who have helped to create a pervasive system of chemical regulation. In addition, that reputation may impose internal strains on the firms involved. The tobacco industry may be able to get its employees to accept its claims that the evidence linking cigarettes to cancer is unconvincing, but it seems less likely that science-based firms such as Monsanto, Dow, and Du Pont could parade such disreputable views for long. I am not implying that industry scientists will not tend to interpret data in ways favorable to their firms; only that there are limits to how far the interpretations can be stretched.

I am arguing that the probability that standards will be appealed varies with their strictness. In fact, we saw that not all OSHA health standards were appealed, including the final standards for acrylonitrile and DBCP. In addition, we saw that industry did not appeal all of the ETSs that OSHA issued, letting those for asbestos, vinyl chloride, and DBCP go unchallenged. We have seen that the issuance of an ETS does speed up the promulgation of a permanent standard. Thus, although the industries did eventually challenge the final standards for the first two of these hazards, they did not pursue a strategy of seeking every possible delay.

In both of these cases the need for some reduction in the exposure limits was so compelling and the emergency PEL sufficiently moderate (5 fibers for asbestos versus the final PEL of 2 fibers; and 25 ppm for vinyl chloride versus the final PEL of 1 ppm) that the industry decided not to mount a challenge.

In this discussion of appeals I have not mentioned appeals by labor unions. Yet, if less strict standards would be less likely to be appealed by industry, wouldn't they be more likely to be appealed by unions? I think that the answer is yes, but I do not believe that the union increase would fully offset the industry decrease. The first reason is that the unions have fewer resources to devote to litigation. The more important reason is that they have nothing to win by litigating except a principle. If the litigation delays the implementation of a standard or overturns it, the result is that workers will be less well protected. If the agency does try to develop a revised standard after it is overturned, some other standard will get a lower priority. These concerns give OSHA some room to maneuver before unions decide that an appeal is worthwhile. We saw that this perspective dominated the union strategy on challenging the vinyl chloride standard. Of course, principles do matter; they determine longer run policies. Labor has challenged some OSHA standards, although in all of those cases industry had also appealed. Some union appeals will certainly continue to be made, especially if the agency strays too far from protective norms.

The Probability That Courts Will Overturn the Standard

Given the protective language found in risk-regulation statutes, agency attempts to set lax standards run a high risk of being overturned by the courts. Many judicial decisions reiterate the especially prized value accorded to protecting the public's health. Yet I have argued that beyond a certain point greater strictness also entails increasing jeopardy from judicial review. Thus the relationship between the strictness of a standard and the probability of its being overturned is U-shaped. My argument is based on the assumption that most agencies are operating on the upward sloping part of the curve, that is, where greater strictness increases the risk.

The Supreme Court's decision in the benzene case was, I argued, a vote on the reasonableness of that standard as well as a reflection of the Court's general mistrust of OSHA. Although perhaps not actually the most stringent OSHA standard, on the basis of cost per death prevented, the risk assessments presented to the Court certainly depicted it as outrageously costly. The "significant risk" test was invented by the Court to provide a method for the Court to strike down this standard while requiring OSHA to quantify its estimates of benefits. I argued that the purpose of the test, to show that rules are needed, would logically require showing that the risk exists not only at the current PEL but also at the levels down to the proposed PEL. In the benzene case, however, the Supreme Court appeared to limit its application to whether OSHA had shown that such a risk existed at the preexisting PEL. Once OSHA has shown that it does, there is no restriction on how low the PEL can be reduced; indeed, the cotton dust decision required that it be set as low as feasible. Yet if the real concern of the courts is with reasonableness, they will find methods to express it to the agency.

The most handy tool is the substantial evidence test, which can be applied to all facets of the standard, including the significance of the risks addressed, the economic and technical feasibility of the controls, and the justification for provisions for monitoring and medical exams. The knowledge that courts will scrutinize strict standards more carefully makes regulators less certain of a successful outcome and encourages them to put extra time and effort into preparing their case.

Oversight by OMB Regulatory Reviewers

Reagan's enhancement of the OMB's regulatory review powers, including the authority to shape agencies' priorities and delay rules it does not like, may be modified by his successors; but they are unlikely to scrap it. The dominant value of the reviewers is economic efficiency. In addition, the executive office is the prime conduit for the complaints of major corporations. To an extent that is difficult to ascertain, the OMB decisions sometimes reflect these interests even when they are not coincident with efficiency.

The combined result of OMB norms and White House pressures is likely to be that standards that are viewed as unreasonably strict and not cost-effective and those that industry opposes most strongly will generate the biggest fights and the longest delays.

Broader Perceptions of Agency Reasonableness

Perceptions of how well an agency carries out its task influence the success of its efforts to get more resources or to streamline its procedures to work more expeditiously. The reaction of key figures—cabinet officers, OMB budget officials, the congressional appropriations committee members, editorial writers and judges—will depend on whether they think that expanding the agency's activities will make matters better or worse.

Support for highly protective regulation remains a popular political position. Political leaders are also quick to criticize agencies for falling behind in the pace of regulating. But what they have rarely been willing to do is either supply the bureaucracy with enough resources to speed the pace or cut the Gordian knot by establishing standards themselves. One explanation for this pattern of events focuses on the incentives of the legislators. They benefit from championing the protection of public health. They benefit from riding herd on foot-dragging bureaucrats. They would not benefit from a system of setting standards less strictly but more extensively. The main reason is that it is harder to claim the symbolic mantle of protector when each individual standard reflects an attempt to reconcile other values with protectiveness.

This analysis has considerable merit. However, we should not focus so much on legislative incentives that we ignore the interests of the organized groups. After all, those groups supply many of the carrots and sticks that shape these incentives. If organized labor and the chemical industry agreed to support a shift to less strict and more extensive regulation, many legislators would support them.

Dates of Completed OSHA Rules for Health Standards

OSHA Regulation[a]	NIOSH recommendation (criteria document)	Advisory committee (first meeting)	Emergency temporary standard (ETS)[b]	Advance NPRM
Asbestos	Jan. 21, 1972	Feb. 3, 1972	Dec. 7, 1971	none
14 Carcinogens	none	June 25, 1973	May 3, 1973	none
Vinyl chloride	Mar. 11, 1974	none	Apr. 5, 1974	none
Coke oven emissions	Feb. 28, 1973	Nov. 8, 1974	none	none
Benzene	July 24, 1974	none	May 3, 1977	none
DBCP[f]	Sept. 2, 1977	none	Sept. 9, 1977	none
Arsenic (inorganic)	Nov. 8, 1974	none	none	none
Cotton dust	Sept. 26, 1974	none	none	Dec. 27, 1974
Acrylonitrile	Sept. 29, 1977	none	Jan. 17, 1978	none
Lead	Jan. 5, 1973	none	none	none
Cancer Policy	none	none	none	none
Access to employee exposure and medical records	none	none	none	none

NPRM	Hearings begin	Final standard (*Federal Register* (date, vol.: page))	Section 6(f) legal challenge to final rule (court and date of decision)[c]	Formal reconsideration
Dec. 12, 1972	none	June 7, 1972 37:3155	D.C. Circuit, Apr. 15, 1974	(d)
July 16, 1973	Sept. 1973	Jan. 29, 1974 39:3756	3rd Circuit, Aug. 26, 1974; 3rd Circuit, Dec. 17, 1974	MOCA[e] standard deleted Aug. 20, 1976
May 10, 1974	June 25, 1974	Oct. 4, 1974 39:35890	2nd Circuit, Jan. 31, 1975	none
July 31, 1975	Nov. 4, 1975	Oct. 22, 1976 41:46742	2nd Circuit, Mar. 28, 1978	none
May 27, 1977	July 19, 1977	Feb. 10, 1978 43:5918	5th Circuit, Oct. 5, 1978; Supreme Court, July 2, 1980	standard deleted June 19, 1981; request for information July 8, 1983
Nov. 1, 1977	Dec. 13, 1977	Mar. 17, 1978 43:11514	none	none
Jan. 21, 1975	Apr. 8, 1975	May 5, 1978 43:19584	9th Circuit, Sept. 13, 1984	supplemental statement (risk assessment) Jan. 14, 1983
Dec. 28, 1976	Apr. 5, 1977	June 23, 1978 43:27350	D.C. Circuit, Oct. 24, 1979; Supreme Court, June 17, 1981	(g)
Jan. 17, 1978	Mar. 21, 1978	Oct. 3, 1978 43:45762	none	none
Oct. 3, 1975	Mar. 15, 1977	Nov. 14, 1978 43:52952	D.C. Circuit, Aug. 15, 1980	(h); see also lead, reconsideration
Oct. 4, 1977	May 16, 1978	Jan. 22, 1980 45:5001	5th Circuit, pending	Advance NPRM published Jan. 5, 1982; administrative stay of candidate list Jan. 4 1983
July 21, 1978	Dec. 5, 1978	May 23, 1980 45:35212	5th Circuit, May 16, 1984	proposal to modify rule July 13, 1982

(continued)

OSHA Regulation[a]	NIOSH recommendation (criteria document)	Advisory committee (first meeting)	Emergency temporary standard (ETS)[b]	Advance NPRM
Occupational noise exposure hearing conservation amendment	Aug. 14, 1972	Feb. 21, 1974	none	none
Lead, reconsideration of respirator fit-testing requirements	none	none	none	none
Coal tar pitch, modification of interpretation[j]	Sept. 1977	none	none	none
Hearing conservation, reconsideration	–	–	none	none
Hazard communication (labeling)	1974	Sept. 19, 1974	none	Jan. 28, 1977
Ethylene oxide	(1)	none	none	Jan. 26, 1981

Source: U.S. Congress, Office of Technology Assessment, *Preventing Injury and Illness in the Workplace*, p. 363.

a. Generally, these regulations are standards issued after rule making under the authority of section 6(b) of the OSH Act. In 1982 OSHA also issued a regulation authorizing OSHA compliance officers to use personal sampling devices during workplace inspections. Because this applies only to OSHA's inspection authority, it is not included in this table. See *Federal Register* (December 10, 1982), 47:55478.

b. In addition to those listed, OSHA also issued an ETS for a group of twenty-one pesticides on May 1, 1973. The emergency standards for the fourteen carcinogens, benzene, acrylonitrile, pesticides, and asbestos (1983) were the subjects of legal challenges. See appendix H for the citations to these cases. The emergency standards for asbestos (1971), vinyl chloride, and DBCP were not challenged.

c. See appendix H for complete citations to these cases.

d. OSHA first proposed to revise the asbestos standard on October 9, 1975. On November 4, 1983, it issued an ETS, but this was vacated by the Fifth Circuit Court of Appeals on March 7, 1984. OSHA published a new proposal on April 10, 1984, and hearings on this began in June 1984.

e. 4,4-methylene-bis(2-chloroaniline).

f. 1,2-dibromo-3-chloropropane.

g. Court decisions on the cotton dust standard also include the Supreme Court (October 6, 1980), affecting the warehousing industry; and the Fifth Circuit (November 14, 1980), affecting the cotton ginning industry. Administrative stays have been issued for waste processing and utilization (September 1, 1978), warehousing and classing (July 29, 1980), and knitting industries (February 4, 1983). The D.C. Circuit vacated the standard for the cotton seed oil industry. Formal reconsiderations on the cotton dust standard include deleted standard for cotton ginning (June 10, 1981), Advance NPRM (February 9, 1982), and proposed rule (June 10, 1983).

h. Lead, formal reconsideration: Supplemental Statement of Reason (January 21, 1981); Advance NPRM (April 21, 1981); Revised Supplemental Statement of Reasons and Amendment of Standard (December 11, 1981). In addition, in 1981 OSHA had on several

NPRM	Hearings begin	Final standard (*Federal Register* (date, vol.: page))	Section 6(f) legal challenge to final rule (court and date of decision)[e]	Formal reconsideration
Oct. 24, 1974	June 23, 1975	Jan. 16, 1981 46:4078	4th Circuit, Nov. 7, 1984	(i); also see hearing con- servation re- consideration
May 19, 1981	Sept. 22, 1981	Nov. 12, 1982 47:51110	none	none
none	May 28, 1982	Jan 21, 1983 48:2764	none	none
Aug. 21, 1981	Mar. 23, 1982	Mar. 8, 1983 48:9738	4th Circuit, Nov. 7, 1984	none
Mar. 19, 1982[k]	June 15, 1982	Jan. 25, 1983 48:53280	3rd Circuit, pending	none
Apr. 26, 1981	July 19, 1983	June 22, 1984 49:25734	D.C. Circuit, pending	none

occasions delayed implementation of several provisions of the lead standard, particularly those involving the trigger levels for medical removal protection.

i. OSHA deferred the effective date of the hearing conservation amendment from April 15, 1981, to August 21, 1981, when major portions of the standard went into effect. The administrative stay was continued on other provisions to allow reconsideration. See Hearing Conservation, Reconsideration, in this table.

j. In 1972 OSHA adopted an interpretation of the coal tar pitch volatile standard (November 21, 1972). In 1982 OSHA modified this interpretation to exclude petroleum asphalt from coverage.

k. The first proposal for hazard communication was published on January 16, 1981, and then was withdrawn on February 12, 1981.

l. No criteria document, but NIOSH issued a "Special Occupational Hazard Review" in 1977 and a "Current Intelligence Bulletin" in 1981.

The source of this appendix is US Congress, Office of Technology Assessment, *Preventing Injury and Illness in the Workplace*, p. 365.

Access to Employee Exposure and Medical Records

Louisiana Chemical Association et al. v. Bingham et al.: The Fifth Circuit Court of Appeals remanded this case to the US District Court for the Western District of Louisiana, 657 F. 2d 777 (Fifth Circuit, 1981). The district court affirmed the standard, 550 F. Supp. 1136 (1982); The Fifth Circuit Court of Appeals affirmed without opinion the decision of the district court (May 16, 1984).

Acrylonitrile

Vistron v. OSHA (Sixth Circuit, March 28, 1978): The ETS was contested, and a request for a stay of standard was denied, 6 OSCH 1483. The petition for review was then withdrawn.

Arsenic (Inorganic)

ASARCO Inc. et al. v. OSHA, 746 F. 2d 483 (Ninth Circuit, September 13, 1984): The court remanded the arsenic standard to OSHA (April 7, 1981). After OSHA developed a risk assessment to comply with the Supreme Court's ruling in the benzene case, the Ninth Circuit Court of Appeals affirmed the arsenic standard.

Asbestos

Industrial Union Department, AFL-CIO v. Hodgson, 499 F. 2d 467 (D.C. Circuit, April 15, 1974): Affirmed OSHA's 1972 asbestos standard.

Asbestos

Asbestos Information Association/North America v. OSHA, 727 F. 2d 415 (Fifth Circuit, March 7, 1984): Vacated the ETS issued on November 4, 1983.

Benzene

American Petroleum Institute v. OSHA, 581 F. 2d 493 (Fifth Circuit, October 5, 1978); Industrial Union Department, AFL-CIO v. American Petroleum Institute, 448 U.S. 607 (Supreme Court, July 2, 1980): Both the Fifth Circuit Court of Appeals and the Supreme Court vacated the OSHA benzene standard, although for different reasons.

Cancer Policy

American Petroleum Institute et al. v. OSHA et al., nos. 80-3018 et al. (Fifth Circuit, pending).

Coke Oven Emissions

American Iron and Steel Institute v. OSHA, 577 F. 2d 825 (Third Circuit, March 28, 1978): The Third Circuit Court of Appeals largely affirmed the coke oven emissions standard. The Supreme Court agreed to review this decision, but the request for review was withdrawn before the case could be heard, 448 U.S. 917 (1980).

Cotton Dust

AFL-CIO v. Marshall, 617 F. 2d 636 (D.C. Circuit, October 10, 1979); American Textile Manufacturers' institute Inc. v. Donovan, 452 U.S. 490 (June 17, 1981): Both the D.C. Circuit Court of Appeals and the Supreme Court upheld the major requirements of the cotton dust standard as applied to the textile industry.

Cotton Dust

Cotton Warehouse Association v. Marshall, 449 U.S. 809 (October 6, 1980): The Supreme Court granted a petition for review and vacated the decision of the court of appeals with respect to the warehousing and classing segments of the industry.

Cotton Dust

Texas Independent Ginners Association v. Marshall, 630 F. 2d 398 (Fifth Circuit, November 14, 1980): Vacated cotton dust standard as applied to cotton ginning operations.

Ethylene Oxide

Public Citizen Health Research Group et al. v. Auchter, 554 F. Supp. 242 (D.C. Circuit, January 5, 1983); Public Citizen's Health Research et al. v. Auchter et al., 702 F. 2d 1150 (D.C. Circuit, March 15, 1983): Public Citizen requested a court order compelling OSHA to issue an ETS. The district court decided to issue such an order. The case was appealed to the D.C. Circuit Court of Appeals, which refused to order that an ETS be issued but did order OSHA to expedite its section 6(b) rule.

Fourteen Carcinogens

Dry Color Manufacturing Association v. Department of Labor, 486 F. 2d 98 (Third Circuit, October 4, 1973): Vacated the ETS for two of the fourteen carcinogens.

Fourteen Carcinogens

Synthetic Organic Chemical Manufacturers Association v. Brennan, 503 F. 2d 1155 (Third Circuit, August 26, 1974): Affirmed standard for ethyleneimine under the 14 carcinogens standard (SOCMA I). A petition for rehearing was denied on October 6, 1975. The Supreme Court denied a request for review, 420 U.S. 973 (March 17, 1975).

Fourteen Carcinogens

Synthetic Organic Chemical Manufacturers Association V. Brennan, 506 F. 2d 385 (Third Circuit, December 17, 1974): The Third Circuit Court of Appeals vacated the standard for MOCA (one of the fourteen carcinogens) (SOCMA II). The Supreme Court denied a request for review. Oil, Chemical and Atomic Workers International Union, AFL-CIO v. Dunlop, 423 U.S. 830 (October 6, 1975).

Hazard Communication (Labeling)

United Steelworkers of America, Public Citizen, State of Massachusetts, Fragrance Materials Association, People of the State of Illinois, Flavor and Extract Manufacturing Association, State of New York v. Auchter, nos. 83-3554, 83-3561, 83-3565, 84-3066, 84-3087, 84-3093, 84-3117, 84-3128 (Third Circuit, pending).

Occupational Noise Exposure/Hearing Conservation Amendment

Forging Industry Association v. Secretary of Labor, no. 83-1232 (Fourth Circuit, November 7, 1984): The Fourth Circuit Court of Appeals vacated the Hearing Conservation Amendment.

Lead

United Steelworkers of America v. Marshall, 647 F. 2d 1189 (D.C. Circuit, August 15, 1980): The D.C. Circuit Court of Appeals affirmed the lead standard in part but directed OSHA to determine the feasibility of engineering controls for thirty-eight industries and occupations. The Supreme Court denied a request for review, Lead Industries Association, Inc. v. Donovan, 453 U.S. 913 (1981).

Pesticides

Florida Peach Growers Association, Inc. v. Department of Labor, 489 F. 2d 120 (Fifth Circuit, January 9, 1974): The Fifth Circuit Court of Appeals vacated the ETS for pesticides.

Vinyl Chloride

Society of the Plastics Industry, Inc. v. OSHA, 509 F. 2d 1301 (Second Circuit, January 31, 1975): The Second Circuit court of Appeals affirmed the vinyl chloride standard. The Supreme Court denied a request for review, Firestone Plastics Co. v. US Department of Labor, 421 U.S. 992 (May 27, 1975).

Notes

Chapter 1

1. For two accounts of these developments, see Bruce Ackerman and William Hassler, *Clean Coal, Dirty Air* (New Haven: Yale University Press, 1981); and Shep Melnick, *Regulation and the Courts* (Washington, D.C.: Brookings Institution, 1983), chap. 1.

2. The chief successes of the deregulation efforts of the Reagan administration were in slowing down the pace of new rule making and in weakening the enforcement of existing rules.

3. For the cost figure on ozone, see Lawrence J. White, *Reforming Regulation* (Englewood Cliffs, N.J.: Prentice-Hall, 1981), p. 62. The EPA argued that the costs were only half as much. Estimates of the costs of OSHA standards are provided by Ivy E. Broder and John Morrall, III, "The Economic Basis for OSHA's and EPA's Generic Carcinogen Regulations," in *What Role for Government? Lessons from Policy Research*, Richard J. Zeckhauser and Derek Leebaert, eds. (Durham, N.C.: Duke University Press, 1983), pp. 242–254.

4. For an earlier, briefer statement of the argument, see my article "Does Overregulation Cause Underregulation? The Case of Toxic Substances," *Regulation* (September–October 1981), 5:47–52.

5. David Vogel, *National Styles of Regulation* (Ithaca, N.Y.: Cornell University Press, 1985), p. 192. However, as noted later, Vogel argues that only a small part of the cross-national difference in the degree of conflict over regulations can be attributed to differences in their costs.

6. Lester Lave, ed., *Quantitative Risk Assessment in Regulation* (Washington, D.C.: Brookings Institution, 1982), p. 8.

7. For a review of the theory and evidence for this approach, see Robert S. Smith, "Compensating Wage Differential and Public Policy: A Review," *Industrial and Labor Relations Review* (April 1979), 32(3):339–352.

8. John D. Graham and James W. Vaupel, "The Value of a Life: What Difference Does it Make?" *Risk Analysis* (March 1981), 1(1):89–95.

9. John A. Haigh, David Harrison, Jr., and Albert L. Nichols, "Benefit-Cost Analysis of Environmental Regulation: Case Studies of Hazardous Air Pollutants," *Harvard Environmental Law Review* (1984), 8(2):395–434.

10. Broder and Morrall, "The Economic Basis."

11. This broader view of the regulatory problem can be usefully analogized to the analysis of the cost-minimizing trade-off between errors in testing. In cancer testing, for example, a false-positive error occurs when we label a chemical a carcinogen when it really is not; a false-negative error occurs when we label a chemical a noncarcinogen when it really is a carcinogen. For a given investment in information we can have fewer of one type of error only by accepting more of the other. At the extremes we could be sure to eliminate false positives only by never regulating; we could eliminate false negatives only by regulating everything. The mix of errors that minimizes the cost to society depends on the relative expected costs of false positives and false negatives. If we expect false positives to be much more costly, we would minimize our total cost by altering our standard of proof so that we accepted fewer of them and more false negatives.

   In some senses false positives are analagous to overregulation; false negatives, to underregulation. Uncertainties about costs and effects mean that we will always regulate too severely in some cases and too lightly in others. However, the important difference between regulation and cancer testing is that it is possible to choose a point where we could simultaneously have both less overregulation and less underregulation. As with cancer testing, better information can help make that shift; unlike cancer testing, the more fundamental prerequisite is political change.

For an excellent discussion of false-positive and false-negative errors in the context of risk regulation, see Talbot Page, "A Framework for Unreasonable Risk in the Toxic Substances Control Act (TSCA)," in *Management of Assessed Risk for Carcinogens*, W. J. Nicholson, ed. (New York Academy of Sciences, 1981), pp. 145–166.

12. For a rich discussion of the differences between screening and standard setting, on which I have drawn heavily, see Peter Huber, "The Old-New Division in Risk Regulation," *Virginia Law Review* (1983), 69:1024–1107.

13. In contrast, several commentators have observed that American regulators have been *more* willing than their European counterparts to regulate on the basis of a single animal test. See Ronald Brickman, Sheila Jasanoff, and Thomas Ilgen, *Controlling Chemicals: The Politics of Regulation in Europe and the United States* (Ithaca, N.Y.: Cornell University Press, 1985), p. 203. Although true for some programs (for example, the FDA's review of existing food additives), this policy has not characterized OSHA's or the EPA's regulation of hazardous air pollutants.

14. A third possibility is that strictness and pace are positively related. Some factors do lead to a positive correlation. I point out in chapter 5 that a strongly protective policy is more likely to attract zealots. Zealots are likely to include higher-quality staff than the agency is usually able to recruit. High-quality staff, in turn, do facilitate the difficult task of churning out standards.

15. Thus Brickman et al. write:

The absence of chemical-related litigation in France and Britain and the infrequency of such lawsuits in Germany must be explained partly in light of factors that lie outside the preserve of law.... What can be easily verified ... is that all three European governments go to considerable lengths to protect the accommodations they reach with industry, using the institutional and procedural devices described .... For example, significant prior consultation with industry (Britain, France, and Germany), voluntary safety requirements (Britain), and low reliance on ambient workplace standards (Britain and France) can all be regarded as "pro-industry" practices that reduce the probability of litigation. After winning most of what can be won during administrative deliberations, industry stands to gain little more from taking the agencies to court. (*Controlling Chemicals*, p. 126)

16. Robert Leone, *Who Profits: Winners, Losers, and Government Regulation* (New York: Basic Books, 1986).

17. Roger Noll, "The Political Foundations of Regulatory Policy," *Journal of Institutional and Theoretical Economics* (1983), 139:380.

18. National Academy of Sciences, *Toxicity Testing: Strategies to Determine Needs and Priorities* (Washington, D.C.: National Academy Press, 1984).

19. The conflict can be seen in the development of the NHTSA's most important rule, passive restraints. In the face of industry opposition to air bags, the secretary of transportation under President Ford had called in 1975 for a large-scale pilot program in order to test their safety and efficacy and, at least as important, to fortify public support for them. His successor in the Carter administration canceled this plan because he wanted to issue a passive restraint standard without a long delay. Four years later the Reagan administration repealed the Carter rules before they could be implemented. Then the Supreme Court voided the revocation of the standard. The new Department of Transportation timetable calls for all new cars to come

equipped with passive restraints in 1990, unless a sufficient number of states enact compulsory seat belt use laws, in which case the requirement will be rescinded.

The lesson appears to be that, when standards require technological changes with lead times of several years or more, a solid political consensus is a prerequisite for their timely development.

For an account of passive restraints policy through 1980, see John Mendeloff, "Passive Restraints and Auto Safety: Another Look," in *Reforming Social Regulation*, LeRoy Graymer and Frederick Thompson, eds. (Beverly Hills, Calif.: Sage, 1982), pp. 93–110. For an account of the 1984 Department of Transportation decision, see John D. Graham, "Secretary Dole and the Future of Automobile Airbags," *The Brookings Review* (1985), 3:10–15.

20. For a discussion of this point, see W. Kip Viscusi and Richard Zeckhauser, "Optimal Standards with Incomplete Enforcement," *Public Policy* (Fall 1979) 27:437–456. Carol Jones has shown that enforcement is either not sufficiently strict or sufficiently targeted on the sectors for which compliance is costly to force their compliance rates up to the levels that other sectors attain. (A concern with efficiency might lead us to applaud this result, for it is a step in the direction of equalizing the marginal costs of compliance across sectors.) See her "Models of Regulatory Enforcement and Compliance, with an Application to the OSHA Asbestos Standard," Ph.D. dissertation, Economics Department, Harvard University (1982). On the problems of reasonableness of enforcing standards, see Eugene Bardach and Robert Kagan, *Going by the Book: The Problem of Regulatory Unreasonableness* (Philadelphia, Penn.: Temple University Press, 1982).

21. Anthony Robbins and Talbot Page, "Cost-Benefit Analysis," in *Recent Advances in Occupational Health*, Corbett McDonald, ed. (London: Churchill Livingston, 1981), p. 277.

22. Officials may vary, however, in their assessment of how great those risks are or in their willingness to take chances. Some examples of these differences are presented in chapter 5.

23. In American Textile Manufacturers Institute v. Donovan, 452 U.S. 490 (1981), the Supreme Court ruled that OSHA had to set standards for toxic substances at the lowest level feasible. In Industrial Union Department v. American Petroleum Institute, 448 U.S. 607 (1980), it stated that a prerequisite for upholding an OSHA standard was a showing that existing exposures to the hazard constituted a "significant risk." These cases are examined in chapters 5 and 7.

24. Florence Heffron with Neil McFeeley, *The Administrative Regulatory Process* (New York: Longman, 1983), p. 229.

25. This term was coined by Alvin M. Weinberg, "Science and Trans-Science," *Minerva* (1972), 10:202–222.

26. For a review of this model, see Bruce Ackerman and William Hassler, *Clean Coal, Dirty Air*.

27. Heffron, *Administrative Regulatory Process*, p. 244.

28. Martin Shapiro, "On Predicting the Future of Administrative Law," *Regulation* (May–June 1982), 6:23.

29. Terrence M. Scanlon and R. A. Rogowsky, "Back-Door Rulemaking: A View from the CPSC," *Regulation* (July–August 1984), 8:27.

30. The same reason has been given as an *explanation* (as well as a justification) for Congress's preference for delegating. The adequacy of the explanation has been questioned by those who note that Congress has not delegated all complicated issues and that the political incentives facing legislators must be a factor in their decisions about what to delegate and what to decide themselves. See Morris Fiorina, "Group Concentration and the Delegation of Legislative Authority," in *Regulatory Policy and the Social Sciences*, Roger Noll, ed. (Berkeley, Calif.:

University of California Press, 1985), pp. 175–197. See also Matthew D. McCubbins and Talbot Page, "A Theory of the Choice of Regulatory Reform," paper presented at the Midwest Political Science Association meeting, Chicago, Ill., April 20–23, 1983.

31. Steven Kelman, *Regulating America, Regulating Sweden* (Cambridge, Mass: MIT Press, 1981), and David Vogel, "The 'New' Social Regulation in Historical and Comparative Perspective," in *Regulation in Perspective*, Thomas McCraw, ed. (Cambridge, Mass.: Harvard University Press, 1981), pp. 155–185.

32. For a discussion of negotiating standards, see chapter 8. The science court proposal has been championed by Arthur kantrowitz, "Controlling Technology Democratically," *American Scientist* (September–October 1975), 63:505.

33. A sampling of the search for alternatives to standard setting includes Michael S. Baram, *Alternatives to Regulation* (Lexington, Mass.: D. C. Heath, 1982); Robert W. Poole, Jr., ed., *Instead of Regulation* (Lexington, Mass.: D. C. Heath, 1982); and Eugene Bardach and Robert A. Kagan, eds., *Social Regulations: Strategies for Reform* (San Francisco, Calif.: Institute for Contemporary Studies, 1982).

34. Vogel, *National Styles of Regulation.*

Chapter 2

1. For a discussion of these conflicts, see Guido Calabresi and Philip Bobbitt, *Tragic Choices* (New York: Norton, 1978). In this book I use the term "saving lives" for the sake of convenience. But lives are only extended, not saved, by risk reduction measures. The difference is especially relevant for distinguishing policies that "save" young people from those that "save" old people.

2. Economists' discussions usually point out how high these figures are in comparison with other risk-reduction programs and how they exceed estimates of how much the people at risk would pay to reduce risks, but unambiguous statements that the costs are excessive apply to figures considerably above those shown in table 2.1. For example, in his discussion of the OSHA arsenic standard, Kip Viscusi said that the cost of $68 million per death, the estimated average cost of the extra deaths prevented by tightening the PEL from 0.050 to 0.004 mg/m³, "dwarfs any realistic estimate of the value of life." In fact, however, the 0.004-mg PEL was not adopted. See W. Kip Viscusi, *Risk by Choice* (Cambridge, Mass.: Harvard University Press, 1983), p. 124. In a discussion of OSHA's benzene standard, Lester and Judith Lave note that "although there is uncertainty about the proper dollar value to be attached to averting a premature death, no one believes the estimate is remotely close to $100,000,000" "Decision Frameworks to Enhance Occupational Health and Safety Regulation," in *Preventing injury and Illness in the Workplace*, Working Paper OTA-H-256, Congress, Office of Technology Assessment (Washington, D.C.: Office of Technology and Assessment, April 1985), p. 60; available from the National Technical Information Service).

Martin J. Bailey has argued that the proper amounts to spend will usually be under one million (1985) dollars. See his *Reducing Risks to Life: Measurement of the Benefits* (Washington, D.C.: American Enterprise Institute, 1980).

3. For a fuller discussion of the issues in the text, see John Mendeloff, "Problems in Valuing Health," *Journal of Health Politics, Policy, and Law* (Fall 1983), 8:554–580.

4. For a discussion of the 100,000 figure, see appendix D.

5. Although, as I stated, explicit statements on this point are rare, the general warning is that agencies that, like OSHA, refuse to temper their protective mission with a concern for costs will end up with standards that make society worse off. In addition to the works cited in note 2,

see Robert Stewart Smith, *The Occupational Safety and Health Act: Its Goals and Its Achievements* (Washington, D.C.: American Enterprise Institute, 1976); and Ivy E. Broder and John F. Morrall, III, "The Economic Basis of OSHA's and EPA's Generic Carcinogen Regulations," in *What Role for Government?* Richard Zeckhauser and Derek Leebaert, eds. (Durham, N.C.: Duke University Press, 1983), pp. 242–254.

6. Unlike earlier studies, this one used on-the-job occupational death rates rather than on-the-job industry deaths rates or actuarial occupational death rates. Industry rates are much less precise measures of risk than occupational rates. The particular job that a person does is a better indicator of the risk he faces than is the industry in which he works. Actuarial rates, for reasons discussed later in the text, may also be misleading measures of perceived job risk.

7. Another argument is that the desirability of a given policy can never be assessed because all policies are political currency. The approval of a bad policy may have been the sine qua non of the approval of a good policy. Because we are never likely to know what the exchanges were, we can never properly assess any individual policy choice. Although there is surely some truth in this argument, it does not obviate the need for analyses that will tell the political bargain markers the worth of the policies they are getting and giving up in the process.

8. Yet the analysis is more complicated, as recent arguments that "richer is safer" have tried to remind us. Those arguments point out that the trade-off is not simply "lives" versus economic output. One of the benefits of greater wealth is often greater protection. Thus the comparison is not between increased protection (P_1) and greater wealth, but between P_1 and greater wealth plus some increased protection (P_2). In concept, if we want to compare the trade-off between protection and wealth, we should subtract P_2 from P_1 and compare the remainder with the foregone gain in wealth.

The general argument that richer is safer seems valid. Most of the health gains of the last century have been a function of measures—sanitation, better diet, better medical care—that in turn depend on greater societal wealth. Greater wealth enables us to pay for more "failsafe" safety features. Yet the general argument hardly provides a basis for rejecting specific safety measures on the grounds that they will slow economic growth. An analysis of each measure is required.

A cross-sectional study by J. Hadley and A. Osei ("Does Income Affect Mortality?" *Medical Care* (September 1982), 20:901) found that a 1 percent increase in income led to a reduction in mortality rates of 0.05 percent. Based on this relation, Huber claims that a 15 percent increase in income for a 45-year-old man would have the same risk-reducing value as eliminating *all* on-the-job mortality risks (that is, accident risks) faced by the average worker in manufacturing. Huber multiplies the overall risk of death faced by the average 45-year-old male (0.01) times 0.0075 (0.05 percent times 15) to get a risk reduction of 0.000075. (The average manufacturing worker faces an annual risk of death of roughly 0.0001 or 0.0002.) See Peter Huber, "The Market for Risk," *Regulation* (March–April 1984), 5:47–52. The implication is that, if we just give workers a few thousand dollars instead of forcing their employers to spend it on safety measures, they would benefit much more.

One of the problems with this analysis is that we do not fully understand the reasons for the cross-sectional findings on which it is based. Indeed, the Hadley and Osei study is unusual in finding a clear relation between income and mortality in the United States. However, any relation that does exist is probably due in large part to health practices that are rooted in the social class and educational level of the individual and his family. Thus it would be farfetched to think that a 15 percent increase in income for workers would have anywhere near as large as effect on their mortality as Huber calculates. The effect on the next generation might be larger than the effect on the first. See also Aaron Wildavsky, "Wealthier Is Healthier," *Regulation* (January–February 1980), 4:10–12, 55.

Nevertheless, the "richer is safer" analysis is provocative and deserves further study.

9. W. Kip Viscusi, *Risk By Choice*, pp. 110–112.

10. Mendeloff, "Problems in Valuing Health," p. 564. For an attempt to make empirical estimates of the valuation of third parties, see Lionel Needleman, "Valuing other People's Lives," *Manchester School of Economic and Social Studies* (December 1976), 44: 309–342.

11. Using his risk premium estimate of $2 million (in 1979 dollars), Viscusi estimated that total annual payments for risk premiums equaled $69 billion. Viscusi, *Risk by Choice*, p. 44. He relied on National Safety Council estimates that the number of workplace deaths was 15,000. However, the best estimate of the number of known deaths is around 6000. See the 1985 Office of Technology Assessment report, *Preventing Injury and Illness*, pp. 30–31. In addition, Viscusi's work and others' have found risk premiums only among unionized blue-collar workers. Risks faced by other workers may be more poorly compensated, reducing the total compensation payments.

The other $40 billion came from assuming that workers receive premiums of about $20,000 for each of the two million disabling accidents that occur each year. Because other analysts have failed to detect any premiums for nonfatal accidents, this valuation seems less reliable. Nevertheless, the point that the market generates large premiums is plausible if not certain.

12. We do have evidence that risk premiums appear to be lower for workers in riskier jobs, which suggests that self-selection occurs as more risk-averse workers choose safer jobs. However, that finding does not tell us whether the same person values risk reductions differently in different contexts. See Viscusi, "Labor Market Valuations of Life and Limb: Empirical Evidence and Policy Implications," *Public Policy*. (1978), 26(3): 359–386.

13. For evidence about differentials in "acceptable risk," see Baruch Fischhoff, Paul Slovic, and Sarah Lichtenstein, "How Safe Is Safe Enough?" *Policy Sciences* (1978), 9: 127–152.

14. See John Mendeloff and Robert M. Kaplan, "Are Twenty-Fold Differences in 'Life-Saving' Costs Justified? A Psychometric Study of the Relative Value Placed on Preventing Deaths from Programs Addressing Different Hazards," Proceedings of the Society for Risk Analysis Conference, Paolo Ricci, ed. (New York: Plenum, forthcoming).

15. Paul Slovic, Sarah Lichtenstein, and Baruch Fischhoff, "Images of Disaster: Perception and Acceptance of Risks from Nuclear Power," in *Energy Risk Management*, G. Goodman and W. Rowe, eds. (London: Academic Press, 1979), pp. 223–245; and Stephen D. Beggs, "Diverse Risks and the Relative Worth of Government Health and Safety Programs: An Experimental Survey," EPA Report 230-04-85-005, US Environmental Protection Agency, Environmental Benefits Analysis Series, (Washington, D.C.: Environmental Protection Agency, June 1984). In Beggs's study, which included only fifteen respondents, the median willingness to pay for preventing deaths from "job cancer, where workers were uninformed about the risk," was one of the highest of sixty-one risks, but only 6 percent higher than the willingness to pay for law-abiding auto drivers. The Slovic et al. study did not have comparable programs.

16. W. Kip Viscusi, "Labor Market Valuations of Life and Limb."

17. W. Kip Viscusi, *Risk By Choice*, ch. 6.

18. The preliminary nature of this conclusion should be emphasized. One important caveat is that my discussion assumed that the responses to the questions were disinterested. This may not be correct. Individuals may give higher ratings to the programs that reduce risks that they personally face or that people close to them face. To the extent that this is true, the disinterested quality of the judgments is diluted. The ratings would reflect the number of people facing each hazard as well as the ethical judgments; hazards that confront more people would get higher ratings, holding the ethical judgments constant. If this were true, use of the methodology would show that the more people who face a risk, the bigger the benefit from preventing a single premature death from that cause.

19. In a well-functioning market the price also reflects the cost of the last unit produced (that is, price equals marginal cost). Thus the value that consumers place on it will just equal the value of the resources that are used to produce it. However, when the project being assessed is large, the use of prices, which are based on marginal valuations and costs, may be inappropriate.

20. The difference in property values is a rough measure of the capitalized value that people place on achieving that reduction in noise levels. For a review of these studies and their shortcomings, see David Harrison, Jr., "The Problem of Aircraft Noise," in *Incentives for Environmental Protection*, Thomas Schelling, ed. (Cambridge, Mass.: MIT Press, 1983), ch. 2.

21. Yet it can also be argued that, precisely because these are areas where there are strong beliefs and litttle analysis, the potential contribution from applying systematic analysis can be great. In an analagous way, Charles Schultze has pointed out the dilemma that the areas that would benefit most from analysis are precisely those that, because the policies are guarded by powerful interests, will not get it. See his *Politics and Economics of Public Spending* (Washington, D.C.: Brookings Institutions, 1968). For an example of what analysis can contribute to an understanding of such a fundamental value as liberty, see the provocative and entertaining paper by James W. Vaupel and Philip J. Cook, "Life, Liberty, and the Pursuit of Self-Hazardous Behavior," Working Paper 8781, Institute of Policy Sciences and Public Affairs, Duke University (Durham, N.C.: Duke University, August 1978).

22. D. MacLean and M. Sagoff, "A Critique of Cost-Benefit Analysis as a Technique for Determining Health Standards under the Occupational Safety and Health Act," OTA Working Paper 7 for the study, *Preventing Injury and Illness in the Workplace*, Office and Technology Assessment, Washington, D.C., April 1983, mimeo, p. 9.

23. MacLean and Sagoff, "Critique of Cost-Benefit Analysis," p. 15.

24. One issue raised by some who are skeptical of the efficiency of competitive forces in the labor market is that compensation depends on institutional factors, such as the presence of unions. Another institution, the job evaluation techniques used by large firms, often incorporates wage premiums for hazards. Thus premiums may not result from direct market forces and may reflect preferences that are somewhat different from those a competitive market would reflect. I return to this issue in the discussion of information in chapter 8.

25. For interesting discussions of this issue, see Thomas Schelling, "The Intimate Contest for Self-Control," *The Public Interest* (Summer 1980), 60:94–118. and Richard H. Thaler and H. M. Shefrin, "An Economic Theory of Self-Control," *Journal of Political Economy* (April 1981), 89(2):392–406.

26. Does the right to a healthful job environment take precedence over the right not to lose your job? In a review of OSHA's asbestos standard, the D.C. Court of Appeals said that the legality of a standard became questionable if it forced major portions of an industry to shut down but not if only a few firms closed. It is not clear what logic led the Court to decide that rights to health took precedence in one case and rights to jobs in the other. See the discussion of *IUD v. Hodgson* in chapter 7.

27. Arthur Okun, *Equality and Efficiency: The Big Trade-Off* (Washington, D.C.: Brookings Institution, 1976).

28. Section 2(b) of the OSH Act.

29. James V. DeLong, "Defending Cost-Benefit Analysis: Replies to Steven Kelman," *Regulation* (March–April 1981), 5:39–40.

30. Viscusi, *Risk By Choice*, ch. 6.

31. For an exposition of this point and an attempt to distinguish the ethical from the efficiency

issues, see Thomas Schelling, "Economic Reasoning and the Ethics of Policy," *The Public Interest* (Spring 1981), 63:37–61.

32. For a good review of the difficulties, see Robert S. Smith, "Compensating Wage Differentials and Public Policy: A Review," *Industrial and Labor Relations Review* (April 1979), 32:339–352.

33. Alan Marin and George Psacharopoulos, "The Reward for Risk in the Labor Market: Evidence from the United Kingdom and Reconciliation with Other Studies," *Journal of Political Economy* (1982), 90(4):827–853.

34. See Dorothy Nelkin and Michael S. Brown, *Workers at Risk: Voices from the Workplace* (Chicago, Ill.: University of Chicago Press, 1984); and Paul Brodeur, *Expendable Americans* (New York: Viking, 1974).

35. One reason why workers might place a low value on preventing certain perceived disease risks is that self-selection could induce the least risk-averse workers to take the jobs with the greatest toxic risks. In the case of safety, Viscusi has shown that risk premiums paid in the most risky quartile of industries are lower than those paid in other industries, most likely because of such self-selection.

36. Marin and Psacharopoulos, "The Reward for Risk."

37. W. Kip Viscusi and Charles O'Connor, "Are Workers Bayesians? Adaptive Responses to Job Hazard Information," *American Economic Review* (1984), 74:942–956.

38. The data used are from the 1977 Quality of Employment Survey, made available by the Inter-University Consortium for Social and Political Research. Viscusi used the 1970 version of that survey. In studies of safety hazards, researchers have found that most if not all of the premiums are paid in the unionized sector. The union-toxic interaction term tests whether that result applies for health hazards as well. Apparently, it does not. A related hypothesis is that the premiums are paid in larger firms, where formal job evaluation programs are more common. The last column indicates that just the opposite is true; at larger plants, workers actually appear to lose money for working in risky jobs, whereas workers in smaller plants get large premiums. The role of unions is taken up again in chapter 8.

39. The other hazards dealt with "working outside in bad weather," "extremes of temperature or humidity indoors," "too much noise," "dangerous tools, machinery, or equipment," "risk of catching disease," "dirty or badly maintained areas," "risk of traffic accidents," "risk of personal attack," and "dangerous work methods." Interestingly, none of them was statistically significant at the .10 level and most had negative coefficients. The only one with a coefficient larger than its standard error was the disease variable. Its negative coefficient was significant at the .13 level. It is unclear whether the "risk of catching diseases" was perceived by workers as pertaining to toxic hazards. If so, it would raise questions about our interpretation of the positive coefficient on TOXPROB.

The failure of any of the other coefficients for unpleasant job traits to have negative signs certainly raises more general questions about the theory of compensating differentials.

40. This finding is consistent with Viscusi's finding for his broader measure of health hazards.

41. W. Kip Viscusi, *Employment Hazards* (Cambridge: Harvard University Press, 1979), p. 233.

42. In an extensive analysis of the 1977 Quality of Employment Survey, James Robinson estimated that the annual premium for blue-collar workers facing one or more hazards (safety or health) was $606, with a standard error of $403. See his table 4.4. On an hourly basis (assuming 2000 hours), this is almost exactly the same as the 31-cent estimate in table 2.3. See James Robinson, "Work and Health: An Economic and Policy Analysis," Ph.D dissertation, University of California, Berkeley, Department of Economics (1984).

43. For an eloquent and persuasive case for emphasizing the prevention of early death, see James W. Vaupel, "Early Death: An American Tragedy," *Law and Contemporary Problems* (Autumn 1976), 40:73–121.

44. The argument that discounting is a psychological frailty and should not be undertaken is made by Robert Goodin in "Discounting Discounting," *Journal of Public Policy* (1984), 2(1):53–71. The argument for using the same discount rate for costs and benefits is made by Milton C. Weinstein and William B. Stason, "Foundations of Cost-Effectiveness Analysis for Health and Medical Practices," *New England Journal of Medicine* (1977), 296:716–721. For a defense of discounting life years but a critique of the proposal that both life years and resource costs should be discounted at the same rate, see John Mendeloff, "Problems in Valuing Health." In "Psychological Considerations in Valuing Health Risk Reductions" (*Natural Resources Journal* (July 1983), 23(3):659–673), Weinstein and Robert J. Quinn investigate "to what extent the contextual and psychological attributes of a risky decision have sufficient *normative* status to justify their formal inclusion in methods for valuing risk" (p. 662).

45. Thaler and Shefrin, "An Economic Theory."

46. John Morrall, III, has concluded that, at a 10 percent discount rate, even OSHA's 1972 asbestos standard had a cost per death prevented of $7.4 million (in 1984 dollars). The figure for the ethylene oxide standard was $25.6 million. See his "A Review of the Record," *Regulation* (1986), 10:25–34.

47. R. Thaler and W. Gould ("Public Policy toward Life Saving: Should Consumer Preferences Rule?" *Journal of Policy Analysis and Management* (Winter 1982), (2):223–242) have shown that willingness to pay more for a treatment program than for a prevention program, for a given increment in the probability of survival, is rational if we assume that an individual values an increment more the lower his initial probability of survival. In other words, the conclusion depends on the assumption that health, like other good things, is subject to declining marginal utility. Of course, individuals who require expensive medical treatment tend to have relatively low survival probabilities. With a normal economic good, say automobiles, the extra utility from the second car is less than the utility from the first. Consumers do not spend all their money on just one or two types of goods. Although the assumption of declining marginal utility is often presented as an empirical generalization, the conditions under which it is true are often not discussed. In the case of health one might argue that good health is a prerequisite for the enjoyment of other goods. However, life unfortunately presents many examples of poor people who forgo medical care because they do not want to forgo other consumption that also contributes to their utility. See also Milton Weinstein, Donald Shepard, and Joseph Pliskin, "The Economic Value of Changing Mortality Probabilities: A Decision Theoretic Approach," *Quarterly Journal of Economics* (1980), 94:373–396.

48. See Leslie I. Boden and Carol Adaire Jones, "Occupational Disease Remedies: The Asbestos Experience," paper presented at the National Science Foundation–Carnegie-Mellon University Conference, Regulation at the Crossroads, Airlie House, Virginia,, September 12–14, 1985.

Chapter 3

1. Given the existing structure of penalties for violations, a larger number of inspections would be needed to ensure 100 percent compliance with the new PEL, at least in cases (such as the lead standard) where the number of affected workplaces is quite large.

2. Productivity refers to a measure of output per unit of input; often the input measure is hours of labor, and thus we speak of labor productivity. In addition to studies of individual standards, there have been attempts to examine the impact of regulation in a more aggregate

fashion. Most of this literature concludes that EPA and OSHA regulation (often the only kinds studied) did reduce productivity, although the size of the reduction was small. The best known of these studies is by Edward F. Denison, *Accounting for Slower Economic Growth: The United States in the 1970s* (Washington, D.C.: Brookings Institution, 1979). A more recent study by Wayne Gray found a larger effect, estimating that OSHA alone caused as much as a 0.3 percent per year decline in total factor productivity between 1973 and 1978. Gray's study used a measure of OSHA's inspection activity at the 4-digit SIC level as a proxy for OSHA's impact on each industry. Whatever the validity of his conclusion, it is not possible to infer what portion of the impact was attributable to new health standards. See Wayne B. Gray, "The Impact of OSHA and EPA Regulation on Productivity," NBER Working Paper 1405, (Cambridge, Mass.: National Bureau of Economic Research, July 1984).

3. Another possible impact of regulation is a change in industry structure as a result of the relatively large burden that regulations may place on smaller firms within an industry. Most of the economic impact analyses of new OSHA health standards did predict such effects. However, an aggregate study of the impact of the EPA and OSHA on industry structure found that, although the EPA appeared to have contributed to the disappearance of small plants, there was no evidence that OSHA had. See B. Peter Pashigian, "How Large and Small Plants Fare under Environmental Regulation," *Regulation* (September-October 1983), 7:19–23.

4. My guess is that there will be less criticism for ignoring this category of highly uncertain costs than there would be for ignoring a category of similarly uncertain benefits. If true, that asymmetry reflects a more general pattern of leaning in the direction of protectiveness. That pattern emerges in stronger form in the practice of estimating health effects, discussed later.

5. For a more detailed discussion of these issues, see the Office of Technology Assessment, "Assessment of Technologies for Determining Cancer Risks From the Environment," OTA-H-138 (Washington, D.C.: Office of Technology Assessment, 1981). See also Lester Lave, ed., *Quantitative Risk Assessment in Regulation* (Washington, D.C.: Brookings Institution, 1982) and *The Strategy of Social Regulation* (Washington, D.C.: Brookings Institution, 1981).

6. Structural activity relationship analysis relies on the assumption that chemicals with similar chemical structures will have similar toxic qualities. Unfortunately, to date, this type of analysis has proven to be a crude guide because scientists do not know enough about which similarities and which differences are crucial.

Short-term tests got their name to distinguish them from bioassays, which take several years to conduct. Many of them are based on the knowledge that many carcinogens cause mutations in the DNA within cells. One widely used test exposes bacteria to a chemical and examines whether a large number of mutations occur. The only method to validate the results of such tests is to compare them with what we have learned from bioassays and epidemiology. Most, although by no means all, of the chemicals found positive in bioassays have also tested positive in short-term tests. One reason why no single test is likely to be adequate is that there are many processes leading to cancer and not all of them are initiated by mutations in the DNA. The current role of short-term tests is still one of raising suspicions or perhaps supporting other, more substantial evidence, rather than of providing sufficient evidence by themselves to trigger regulatory action.

OSHA's 1980 Cancer Policy (discussed in chapter 5) would, however, have given a much larger role to short-term tests in future decisions. Implementation of the key parts of that policy has been stayed by the Reagan administration.

7. In testimony during OSHA's hearing on its Cancer Policy, Dr. Robert Hoover of the National Cancer Institute noted that the

lowest excess cancer risk that I know of that is directly observable in a group of exposed individuals that is generally accepted as being due to that exposure and not to some other factor, is the 30% excess risk of childhood leukemia among children who were exposed to radiation in utero in the last trimester of pregnancy. Indeed, it has taken us some 20 years to be reasonably convinced of this 30% excess risk. (OSHA, "Identification, Classification, and Regulation of Potential Occupational Carcinogens," *Federal Register* (January 22, 1980), 45:5040)

8. Philip E. Enterline, "Epidemiologic Basis for the Asbestos Standard," *Environmental Health Perspectives* (1983), 52:96. Enterline shows the populations that would be needed for studying workers with fifty years of exposure for six different models. For five of them the numbers range from 4000 to 220,000; for the other, it is 110. If we look instead at workers exposed for twenty-five years, a more likely period, the required sample sizes would roughly quadruple.

9. The average number of years of exposure given the twenty-year latency assumption is 3.75. Dividing 4 excess deaths by 470 workers and then by 3.75 years gives an excess mortality risk from cancer of 0.00227 per person per year of exposure. Assuming that 3400 workers are exposed at 20 ppm is convenient, because this is the level of exposure that COWPS assumed had prevailed at the Du Pont plant. Multiplying 3400 by 0.00227 gives 8 deaths.

10. M. O'Berg, J. L. Chen, C. A. Burke, J. Walrath, and S. Pell, "Epidemiological Study of Workers Exposed to Acrylonitrile: An Update," *Journal of Occupational Medicine* (November 1985), 27(11):835–840.

11. The large growth in the number of bioassays will inevitably identify new hazards and new candidates for regulation. The impact may be greatest in screening programs because, as we have seen, agencies usually require less evidence to block the introduction of new hazards than they do to remove existing ones. However, standard-setting programs will feel some impact too. (I argue in chapter 10 that OSHA should be much more willing to regulate on the basis of bioassays, if it regulates moderately.)

One interesting sign of the change is that in the EPA's implementation of section 8 of the Toxic Substances Control Act, which allows it to require research on suspected hazards, it has eschewed epidemiology and chosen to rely solely on bioassays for both identifying hazards and quantitatively estimating risks (remarks of Joseph Merenda before the National Academy of Sciences panel on Occupational Safety and Health Statistics, December 5, 1985).

12. Low doses cannot be used with small sample sizes because such experiments would be too likely to fail to detect evidence of harm. For example, suppose that a certain level of exposure to a toxic substance doubles the number of cancers from three to six among fifty rats. With that sample size, the increase would not be statistically significant at the .05 level and the test would have failed to detect a "true positive."

For any given test, the number of these false negatives (that is, carcinogens falsely identified as noncarcinogens) can be reduced only by increasing the number of false positives (that is, noncarcinogens falsely identified as carcinogens). The problem of false positives is also not trivial, largely because bioassays routinely search for tumors in about thirty different organs in four sex-species groups. Chance alone may cause some of the tumor rates to be elevated. One analysis reports that accepting only a 0.05 false-positive rate at each site can lead to a false-positive rate of 40 to 50 percent for the experiment as a whole, although the rate will depend on the spontaneous tumor rate. (See J. K. Haseman, "A Re-examination of False-Positive Rates for Carcinogencity Bioassays," *Fundamental and Applied Toxicology* (1983), 3:334–339.) The proper balance of false-positive and false-negative rates depends on the costs of making each type of mistake, but in practice these costs are rarely considered.

13. Office of Technology Assessment, *Assessment of Technologies for Determining Risks*, pp. 167–168.

14. Office of Technology Assessment, *Assessment of Technologies for Determining Risks*, p. 170.

15. For example, a reanalysis of the tumor slides from the MIT study that found evidence that nitrates were carcinogenic showed that there was not an excess number of tumors. See William Havender, "The Abuse of Science in Public Policy," *Journal of Contemporary Issues* (Summer 1981), 4:5–20.

16. John Higginson, former director of the International Agency for Research on Cancer, in US Congress, House, Committee on Science and Technology, *Formaldehyde: Review of Scientific Basis of EPA's Risk Assessment*, 97th Cong., 2d sess., 1982, H-165, p. 122.

17. "The Welfare Economics of Occupational Safety and Health Standards," Ph.D dissertation, University of Wisconsin, Department of Economics, 1974.

18. See Julian Peto, "Dose-Response Relationships for Asbestos-Related Disease: Implications for Hygiene Standards, II. Mortality," in *Health Hazards of Asbestos Exposure*, Irving J. Selikoff and E. Cuyler Hammond, eds. (New York: New York Academy of Sciences, 1979), vol. 330, pp. 202–203.

19. Herbert R. Northrup, Richard L. Rowan, and Charles R. Perry, *The Impact of OSHA* (Philadelphia, Penn.: University of Pennsylvania, 1978), pp. 403–405.

20. Joseph Wagoner, "The Toxicity of Vinyl Chloride and Poly (Vinyl Chloride): A Critical Review," *Environomental Health Perspectives* (1983), 52:61–66.

21. The EPA estimate appears in table 17 of "Updated Mutagenicity and Carcinogenicity Assessment of Cadmium," EPA-600/8-83-025A, (Washington, D.C.: Environmental Protection Agency, 1983), mimeo, p. 127. I adjusted to occupational exposure by dividing the lifetime risk by a factor of 8 to account for the reduced exposure (45 years instead of 70; 2000 hours a year instead of 8760). One part per million of vinyl chloride is equivalent to 2 mg/m^3. Exposure information is from Foster Snell Division of Booz-Allen, *Economic Impact Study of Proposed Vinyl Chloride Standard*, (New York, 1984), pp. 147, 150.

22. Land's study is reported in C. K. Redmond, "Cancer Mortality among Coke Oven Workers," *Environmental Health Perspectives* (1983), 52:67–73.

23. Redmond, "Cancer Mortality," p. 72.

24. Richard Wilson, testimony before the US Department of Labor regarding "Proposed Regulations for Identification, Classification, and Regulation of Toxic Substances Posing a Potential Occupational Carcinogen Risk," OSHA Docket H-090, p. 51.

25. Mary C. White, Peter F. Infante, and Kenneth C. Chu, "A Quantitative Estimate of Leukemia Mortality Associated with Occupational Exposure to Benzene," *Risk Analysis* (1982), 2:195–201.

26. Criticisms of the White et al. study appear in *Risk Analysis* (1984), 4:1–13. For a good review of the epidemiological studies and the risk estimates, see Thomas R. Bartman, "Regulating Benzene," in *Quantitative Risk Assessment in Regulation*, Lester B. Lave, ed. (Washington, D.C.: Brookings Institution, 1982), pp. 99–134.

27. See Kenneth C. Chu, "Risk Assessment for Inorganic Arsenic" Occupational Safety and Health Administration (n.d.), mimeo.

28. See OSHA, "Preliminary Regulatory Impact and Regulatory Flexibility Assessment of the Proposed Standard for Ethylene Oxide," Occupational Safety and Health Administration (April 14, 1983), Executive Summary, mimeo.

29. OSHA, "Preliminary Regulatory Impact," ch. 4, p. 21.

30. This criticism was frequently aired in testimony at the hearings on OSHA's proposed Cancer Policy and taken up by the American Industrial Health Council, which was formed to oppose that policy and has continued to serve as a forum for scientific criticism.

31. In the first few years of the Reagan administration, top regulators talked about radical changes in the presumptions for assessing evidence about carcinogenicity, including the relevance of animal tests to human risks. However, the agencies deferred changes until the Office of Science and Technology Policy (OSTP) had developed a position. Released in May 1984, the document disappointed some industry leaders because, despite its more moderate tone, it upheld many of the key presumptions that undergird protective regulatory policy, including the no-threshold assumption and the use of animal tests. The OSTP document appears in the *Federal Register* (May 22, 1984). For one criticism see "Revision without Revolution in Cancer Policy," *Regulation* (July-August 1984), 8:5–7.

32. Lave, *Strategy of Social Regulation*, p. 36.

33. Lave *Strategy of Social Regulation*, p. 35. See also Albert L. Nichols and Richard J. Zeckhauser, "The Perils of Prudence," *Regulation* (1986), 10:13–24.

34. Paul Slovic, Sarah Lichtenstein, and Baruch Fischhoff, "Modeling the Societal Impact of Fatal Accidents," *Management Science* (1984), 30(4):464–474. See also Baruch Fischhoff, Paul Slovic, and Sarah Lichtenstein, "How Safe Is Safe Enough?" *Policy Sciences* (1978), 9:127–152.

Slovic et al. asked subjects to choose between preventing 30 single-fatality accidents and reducing the probability of a 300-fatality accident from .01 to .001 (with an expected reduction of 27 deaths). Thirty percent chose the latter. When the problem was presented as a much more uncertain option (that is, the number saved could be fewer or greater), 43 percent chose the latter.

Chapter 4

1. See Emmett B. Keeler, John C. Bailar, and David Atkins, "Changes in Voluntary Industrial Health Standards," paper presented at the Research Conference of the Association of Public Policy Analysis and Management, Minneapolis, October 22–24, 1982, mimeo, p. 29.

2. Of course, attitudes toward risk reduction are not simply or even primarily a function of a rational calculation of economic costs and benefits. Measures of health status and longevity show that Americans have never had it so good, but polls show that the public believes that life is getting riskier. In 1980, 78 percent of the public agreed that "people are exposed to more risk today than they were 20 years ago"; only 6 percent thought there was less risk. In addition, 55 percent felt that "the risks to society stemming from various scientific and technological advances will be somewhat greater 20 years from now than they are today," and only 18 percent thought they would be somewhat less. This is a Louis Harris and Associates poll, reported in National Research Council, Committee on Risk and Decision Making, *Risk and Decision Making: Perspectives and Research* (Washington, D.C.: National Academy Press, 1982), p. 2.

The opposite trends in health status and perceptions of risk are not necessarily contradictory, but they are intriguing and have spawned several attempts to explain why perceptions have changed. Some focus on social and political factors. The threat of nuclear war is one, although there is no evidence that people believe that the threat is any greater than it was twenty years ago. On a somewhat less cataclysmic level, we do know that people express less confidence than they once did in government and business, the traditional institutions for managing risks (National Research Council, *Risk and Decision Making*, p. 13). Some claim that environmental groups, in their struggle for organizational survival, have exploited this mistrust and exaggerated the perils that industry and technology pose to health. See Mary Douglas and Aaron Wildavsky, *Risk and Culture* (Berkeley, Calif.: University of California Press, 1982), chs. 7 and 8.

3. In contrast, we can imagine a system of "tiered" information development, in which a large list of candidates for regulation is winnowed through a succession of increasingly comprehensive studies; only the better candadates proceed to the next rounds. Adoption of such a system, however, presumes that the basis for setting priorities is analytical. One reason that OSHA has not developed it, as we will see in chapter 6, is that there are more political benefits and fewer political costs from letting outside interests set the agenda. See Milton Weinstein, "Decision Making for Toxic Substances Control," *Public Policy* (1978), 27(3): 333–383. See also National Research Council, *Toxicity Testing: Strategies to Determine Needs and Priorities* (Washington, D.C.: National Academy Press, 1984).

4. An interesting account of this debate is given in Edith Efron's polemical work *The Apocalyptics* (New York: Simon and Schuster, 1984), pp. 437–448. A particularly good example of the debate appeared in the pages of *Nature*. See Richard Peto, "Distorting the Epidemiology of Cancer: The Need for a More Balanced Overview," *Nature* (March 27, 1980) 284: 297–300; and Samuel S. Epstein and Joel B. Swartz, "Fallacies of Lifestyle Cancer Theories," *Nature* (January 15, 1981), 289: 127–130. The basic documents discussed are Kenneth Bridbord, Arthur Upton, David Rall, et al., "Estimates of the Fraction of Cancer in the United States Related to Occupational Factors" (September 15, 1978), mimeo, prepared by eight authors from the National Cancer Institute, the National Institute of Environmental Health Sciences, and the National Institute of Occupational Safety and Health; and the reply from the American Industrial Health Council, dated October 23, 1978. The AIHC also sponsored "A Critical Review," by Reuel Stallones and Thomas Downs (n.d.), mimeo. This review largely accepted the conclusions of the "Estimates" paper, a result of accepting its assumptions about the data and simply performing the calculations a bit differently. Pro-labor groups claimed that the AIHC withheld this report.

5. For a good review of these inadequacies, see Harvey J. Hilaski and Chao Ling Wang, "How Valid Are Estimates of Occupational Illness?" *Monthly Labor Review* (August 1982), 105: 27–35. In 1983 the Bureau of Labor Statistics survey reported 106,000 cases of occupational disease; 40,000 were dermatitis; only 1700 were "dust diseases of the lungs" and 7900 were "respiratory conditions due to toxic agents" (Bureau of Labor Statistics, *Occupational Injuries and Illnesses in the United States by Industry, 1983*, Bulletin 2236 (Washington, D.C.: Government Printing Office, 1985), p. 39).

Although estimates of disease based on exposures are the primary method for determining the scale of public health problems, other methods have been pursued. Surveys of those aged 20 to 64 in 1972 found that of about 15 million people who said they were totally or partially disabled, 11.7 percent (1,657,000) said that their condition was caused by an occupational illness; another 5.2 percent said an occupational injury was the cause. The validity of self-reported measures of disease causation seems highly suspect because most people probably tend to search for causes that will absolve themselves; dust at work rather than cigarette smoking will be blamed. But, whatever the validity of the measure, it is politically significant that a large number of people believe that occupational illnesses caused their disabilities. See US Department of Labor, *An Interim Report to Congress on Occupational Diseases*, (Washington, D.C.: Government Printing Offices, 1980), 43–49.

More information about the perceived seriousness of health hazards comes from the 1977 Quality of Employment Survey (QES) that I discussed in chapter 2. It asked workers whether their jobs exposed them to various hazards and whether these presented "no problem at all," a "slight problem," a "sizable problem," or a "great problem." Over 20 percent claimed that either chemicals or "fumes and dust" constituted a "sizable" or "great" problem. Thus whatever the effects of current toxic exposures on disease, we do have evidence that a large number of disabled and currently employed workers believe that they constitute a major problem.

6. Fred Hoerger, "Indicators of Exposure Trends," in *Quantification of Occupational Cancer*, Banbury Report 9, Richard Peto and Marvin Schneiderman, eds. (Cold Spring Harbor, Mass.: Cold Spring Laboratory, 1981), pp. 435–453.

7. These trends should not, however, be taken to invalidate the charges that firms often hide evidence of illness and refuse to abate hazards. In the short run (which may become painfully long), firms may often have both economic and psychological incentives to deny that exposures are causing harm. But the costs of reducing exposures decline over time as control measures can be incorporated in new plants or as substitute processes, chemicals, or products can be developed. In addition, as noted, increasing worker wealth can be expected to increase employee demand for safer worker conditions.

8. OSHA Management Information System.

9. The figure of 53,000 comes from the National Research Council study on *Toxicity Testing*, p. 3. For fiscal 1986 and 1985, the EPA announced that the number of premanufacture notifications of new chemicals totaled 1670 and 1700, respectively. See *Pesticide and Toxic Chemical News*, (September 24, 1986), p. 9. An earlier figure of 500 new chemicals a year came from the National Toxicology Program, *Annual Plan* Fiscal Year 1980, as cited in Office of Technology Assessment, *Assessment of Technologies for Determining Cancer Risks from the Environment* (Washington, D.C.: Office of Technology Assessment, 1981), p. 131.

10. National Research Council, *Toxicity Testing*, pp. 13–14. The NRC study looked at a subsample of one hundred chemicals. Some industry groups have claimed that this conclusion about the paucity of testing data ignored substantial proprietary data in industry hands.

11. US Congress, Office of Technology Assessment, *Information Content of Premanufacture Notices*, OTA-BP-H-17 12. Fred Hoerger, William H. Beamer, and James S. Hanson, (Washington, D.C.: Government Printing Office, April 1983), pp. 6–7. "Cumulative Impact of Health, Environmental, and Safety Concerns on the Chemical Industry during the Seventies," *Law and Contemporary Problems* (Summer 1983), 46(3):79.

13. The most sophisticated treatment of the latter issue is found in Talbot Page, "A Framework for Unreasonable Risk in the Toxic Substances Control Act (TSCA)," in *Management of Assessed Risk for Carcinogens*, W. J. Nicholson, ed. (New York: New York Academy of Sciences, 1981), pp. 145–166.

14. OSHA does not conduct its health inspections in a random fashion. One particular reason why OSHA inspection data may not provide a good measure of the relative frequency of overexposures is that agency priorities may dictate relatively more attention to certain hazards. For example, during the period covered by table 4.2, OSHA was putting a heavy effort into checking compliance with the newly issued lead standard. However, lead remains at or near the top of the list in other periods as well. In a study for OSHA I compared the inspection data on the number of overexposed workers with the comparable figures from the handful of studies performed for OSHA as part of its regulatory analysis procedure. For hazards with a relatively large number of inspections, the rank order was quite similar. See John Mendeloff, "Estimating Worker Exposures to Toxic Substances" (1984), mimeo.

15. With a linear dose-response curve, the disease reduction would be proportional to the reduction in dose. The OSHA penalties, small to begin with, would make a small drop to zero if the firm can avoid being cited for a violation. Major penalties would be incurred only if the firm were cited but blatantly refused to abate the violation. The evidence here is consistent with the theoretical expectations or W. Kip Viscusi and Richard Zeckhauser, "Optimal Standards with Incomplete Enforcement," *Public Policy* (Fall 1979), 27:437–456.

16. James H. Sterner, "Determining Margins of Safety: Criteria for Defining a 'Harmful' Exposure," *Industrial Medicine* (1943), 12:514–518, esp. p. 517.

17. For the early history of the ACGIH, see John J. Bloomfield, "What the ACGIH Has Done for Industrial Hygiene," *American Industrial Hygiene Association Journal* (1958), 19:338–344; William G. Frederick, "The Birth of the ACGIH Threshold Limit Committees and Its Influence on the Development of Industrial Hygiene," *Transactions of the Thirtieth Annual Meeting of the ACGIH*, (Cincinnati, Ohio: ACGIH, 1968), pp. 40–43; and Anna Baetjer, "The Early Days of Industrial Hygiene: Their Contributions to Current Problems," *Transactions of the Forty-second Annual Meeting of the ACGIH*, (Cincinnati, Ohio: ACGIH, 1980), pp. 10–19.

18. Ernest Mastromatteo, "Background and Interpretation of Threshold Limit Values," paper presented to the Mining Section, National Safety Council, October 26, 1971; reprinted in *Threshold Limit Values: Discussion and Thirty-Five Year Index with Recommendations*, Marshall E. LaNier, ed. (Cincinnati: ACGIH, 1984), 207–213.

19. Section 6(a) of the OSH Act. For a more extended discussion of OSHA's response to this provision, as it applied to safety, see Mendeloff, *Regulating Safety* (Cambridge, Mass.: MIT Press, 1979), pp. 36–41.

20. Herbert Stokinger, "Threshold Limit Values," in *Threshold Limit Values*, Marshall E. LaNier, ed., p. 280.

21. Charles Lindblom, "The Science of 'Muddling Through,'" *Public Administration Review* (1959), 19:79–88.

22. ACGIH, *Threshold Limit Values for Chemical Substances and Physical Agents in the Workroom Environment with Intended Changes for 1981* (Cincinnati, Ohio: ACGIH, 1981), p. 2.

23. Herbert E. Stokinger, "Criteria and Procedures for Assessing the Toxic Responses to Industrial Chemicals," in *Threshold Limit Values*, Marshall E. LaNier, ed., p. 155.

24. Mastromatteo, "Threshold Limit Values," pp. 208–209. At the time, Mastromatteo was the Director of Environmental Health Services for the Province of Ontario.

25. The first discussion of carcinogens came in a 1962 appendix to the TLV list. The policy of considering potency was first stated in the 1976 report.

26. For example, the ACGIH states that "no substance is to be considered an occupational carcinogen of any practical significance which reacts ... by the gastrointestinal route at or above 500 mg/kg/d for a lifetime." This dosage explicitly excluded trichloroethylene from consideration as a carcinogen because the relevant study involved exposures of 900 mg/kg/d in mice. However, the ACGIH did announce a 50 percent reduction in the TLV for trichloroethylene in 1979. See ACGIH, "Threshold Limit Values," p. 41.

27. Keeler et al., "Voluntary Industrial Health Standards," p. 31.

28. Personal communication with Melvin First, Professor of Industrial Hygiene, Harvard School of Public Health. This rule of thumb appears less valid for comparing the costs of reductions that begin at different exposure levels. For example, even a 90 percent reduction from a 1-ppm exposure might cost more than a 99 percent reduction from 1000 ppm. The data in table 4.3, which show that noncompliance increases for hazards with lower PELs, suggest that the absolute level of the exposure limit affects the marginal costs.

29. Note that the higher marginal costs to achieve lower exposure levels are not simply a result of the rising marginal cost curve for reducing exposures for a specific operation. As the exposure limit is dropped, more and more different operations must be controlled and more workers protected. Plants that already met the higher exposure limit now will have to undertake expenditures to meet the lower limit. There is no way to distinguish which of the expenditures are due to the cost function for particular operations and which are due to the

extra number of operations that must be controlled. For the purposes of this argument, however, the distinction is not critical.

30. See Herbert Stokinger, "Modus Operandi of Threshold Limit Committee of ACGIH," *American Industrial Hygiene Association Journal* (1964), 25:589–594.

31. Stokinger, "Criteria and Procedures," pp. 157–158.

32. Keeler et al., "Voluntary Industrial Health Standards," pp. 18–21.

33. For a discussion of the general duty clause, see Donald L. Morgan and Mark N. Duvall, "OSHA's General Duty Clause: An Analysis of Its Use and Abuse," *Industrial Relations Law Journal* (1983), 5:283–321.

34. My review of the ACGIH changes identified 148 substances for which exposure limits were introduced for the first time, the time-weighted average exposure limit was reduced by more than 25 percent, or, in the case of substances with no time-weighted exposure limit, the ceiling exposure limit was reduced. I excluded substances with time-weighted average changes where the only change was a reduction in the ceiling value. (A ceiling value is a limit that may not be exceeded for any period regardless of the average exposure over an eight-hour day.) For a review of biases in reporting to the OSHA Management Information System, see John Mendeloff, "An Analysis of OSHA Health Inspection Data," background paper for the Office of Technology Assessment's *Occupational Safety and Health Control Technology*; the paper is available from the National Technical Information System.

35. The nine were acetone (1000 to 750), formaldehyde (3 to 2), ammonia (50 to 25), styrene (100 to 50), toluene (200 to 100), calcium oxide (5 to 2), propylene oxide (100 to 20), 1,2-dichloroethane (50 to 10), and ethylene glycol (0.2 to 0.02).

36. Hoerger et al., "Cumulative Impact," p. 87.

37. That is, 60,000 to 52; 130,000 to 9; and 20,000 to 20.

38. Centaur Associates, "Technological and Economic Impact of OSHA Standards for Chromium" (1980), mimeo, Exhibit 3-1. The EPA estimates of chromium's carcinogenic potency are found in EPA, Environmental Criteria and Assessment Office, "Health Assessment Document for Chromium" EPA-600/8-83-014A (Washington, D.C.: Environmental Protection Agency, July 1983), mimeo, pp. 7–76.

39. Both the potency estimates in the figures and the IARC (International Agency for Research on Cancer) evidence categories come from EPA, "Health Assessment Document for Tetrachloroethylene," Final Report, EPA/600/8-82/005F (Washington, D.C.: Environmental Protection Agency, July 1985), mimeo, Table 9–11.

40. Taking the $\log_{10}$ of the PEL and the potency is a useful way of comparing the two variables. The meaning of that transformation for the PEL is that 0 means a PEL of 1 mg/m^3; +1 means a PEL of 10 mg/m$_3$; +2 means a PEL of 100 mg/m^3.

41. Office of Technology Assessment, *Technologies for Determining Cancer Risks from the Environment* (Washington, D.C.: Government Printing Office, 1981), pp. 127–128, 140.

42. Thus, when the "potency" variable is dropped from the equation, the "animal" coefficient does take on the expected sign (moving from +0.31 to −0.32), but its t-statistic remains between 0.5 and 0.6.

43. The coefficient for animal evidence turned from positive to negative but was still quite insignificant. However, the larger coefficient for potency again picks up some of that effect.

44. This conclusion might not be correct if the administrative costs of rule making are large enough. For example, suppose that the most desirable rule for a particular hazard would have social net benefits of $1 million. If the process of establishing the rule costs more than this amount, then the most efficient choice would be to ignore it.

45. This statement is plausible under the no-threshold hypothesis. For example, several thousand workers are exposed to levels of vinyl chloride below the PEL of 1 ppm. We do not know the number exposed above the PEL, but it is probably not more than two hundred, perhaps with an average exposure of 2 ppm. If 4000 workers have an average exposure of 0.4 ppm, then, under the linear no-threshold hypothesis, the aggregate number of diseases resulting from their exposures will be 4 times greater than the number resulting from the exposures of the 200 workers exposed above the PEL (4000 × 0.4 ppm = 1600 ppm; 200 × 2 ppm = 400 ppm).

46. The reader may wonder why I did not try to present similar estimates for diseases caused by exposures above the PELs. The reason is that the studies of worker exposures by OSHA consultants rarely presented their findings in a way that would allow isolating that group. For a discussion of these studies, see my study "Estimating Worker Exposures."

47. This limitation is likely to cause significant errors only for arsenic and coke oven emissions, where a large number of workers are exposed above the PEL; presumably, many of them wear respirators.

48. For the suggestion that trichloroethylene and perchloroethylene are "apparently non-genotoxic," see Bruce N. Ames, Renae Magaw, and Lois Swirsky Gold, "Ranking Possible Carcinogenic Hazards," *Science* (April 17, 1987), 236:271–280.

Chapter 5

1. For an example of the pejorative assumption, see US Senate Committee on Governmental Affairs, *Study on Federal Regulation*, Volume IV, *Delay in the Regulatory Process* (Washington, D.C.: Government Printing Office, 1977). The first sentence of the report states that "delay is a fundamental impediment to the effective functioning of regulatory agencies" (p. ix).

2. For discussions of OSHA's activities, including some that focus on standard setting, see Joseph A. Page and Mary-Win O'Brien, *Bitter Wages* (New York: Grossman, 1973); Nicholas Ashford, *Crisis in the Workplace* (Cambridge, Mass.: MIT Press, 1976); John Mendeloff, *Regulating Safety* (Cambridge, Mass.: MIT Press, 1979); Steven Kelman, *Regulating America, Regulating Sweden* (Cambridge, Mass.: MIT Press, 1981); David P. McCaffrey, *OSHA and the Politics of Health Regulation* (New York: Plenum, 1982); Ted Greenwood, *Knowledge and Discretion in Government Regulation* (New York: Praeger, 1984); Graham K. Wilson, *The Politics of Safety and Health* (New York: Clarendon Press, 1985); Charles Noble, *Liberalism at Work* (Philadephia, Penn.: Temple University Press, 1986).

3. Section 6(b)5 of the OSH Act.

4. Section 6(f) of the OSH Act.

5. See Industrial Union Department, AFL-CIO v. American Petroleum Institute, 448 U.S. 607 (July 2, 1980) for benzene; and American Textile Manufacturers Institute, Inc. v. Donovan, 452 U.S. 490 (June 17, 1981) for cotton dust.

6. See Mendeloff, *Regulating Safety*.

7. Quoted in Kelman, *Regulating America, Regulating Sweden* (Cambridge, Mass.: MIT Press, 1981), p. 29.

8. Forging Industry Association v. Secretary of Labor, 83-1232 (Fourth Circuit, November 7, 1984).

9. *Federal Register* (October 3, 1978), 43:45781.

10. *Federal Register* (November 4, 1983), 48:51098.

11. The nine ETSs include the five shown in table 5.1, plus one for pesticides and one for "14 Carcinogens" in 1973, for commerical diving in 1976, and a second asbestos ETS in 1983.

12. Interview with Daniel Jacoby, Deputy Associate Solicitor for Standards (1982).

13. David Doniger, *The Law and Policy of Toxic Substances Control* (Baltimore: Johns Hopkins University Press, 1978), p. 52. Doniger is reporting the observations of the director of health and safety for the Industrial Union Department of the AFL-CIO.

14. Wrenn, interview (1982).

15. Wrenn, interview (1982).

16. These figures were reported by Assistant Secretary Thorne Auchter, while testifying before the Senate Labor Committee in 1981.

17. The staff of the AFL-CIO and its Industrial Union Department *do* have a broader range of concerns with health standards, but they must contend with the priorities of the stronger member unions.

18. Greenwood, *Knowledge and Discretion*, p. 136.

19. Vance, Interview (1982).

20. Corn, interview (1983).

21. Hutt, interview (1981).

22. Nicholas Ashford, who was the chair of OSHA's formal National Advisory Committee on Occupational Safety and Health during this period and a forceful proponent of strict regulation, also headed the Center for Policy Alternatives at MIT, a group that performed several key analyses for OSHA, including the relationship between air-lead levels and blood-lead levels. Ashford's initial work on OSHA in the early 1970s had been sponsored by the Ford Foundation. His project officer at the foundation had been Basil Whiting, who later became Bingham's deputy assistant secretary at OSHA.

23. Benjamin W. Mintz, *OSHA: History, Law, and Policy* (Washington, D.C.: Bureau of National Affairs, 1984), p. 251.

24. The exception is the view championed by Justice Rehnquist in both the benzene and cotton dust decisions that the vague guidance in the OSH Act about the role of feasibility considerations constituted an unconstitutional delegation of authority by Congress. For Rehnquist's statement, see the discussion of those decisions in the text.

25. Section 6(f) of the OSH Act. This requirement that agency decisions be backed by "substantial evidence" generates, in theory, more intense judicial scrutiny than the "arbitrary and capricious" test that is part of the Administrative Procedure Act's general requirements. In fact, most observers have trouble detecting differences in judicial responses.

26. In 1979 the D.C. Circuit Court of Appeals voided the applicability of the cotton dust standard to the cottonseed oil industry because OSHA had not shown substantial evidence that the standard was feasible there. In 1981 the Supreme Court further held that OSHA had failed to show that the income replacement measures in that standard were "reasonably necessary" to protect workers' health. The D.C. Circuit ruling on the lead standard upheld the agency with respect to the major provisions and industries but remanded thirty-seven industries to OSHA for further study of feasibilty.

The bulk of the lead standard was upheld on a 2-1 vote. The majority acknowledged that the rule "was something less than a masterpiece of administrative procedure." One of the chief themes of the dissent was that OSHA had failed to give adequate notice (as required by the OSH Act as well as by the Administrative Procedure Act) to allow interested parties to participate effectively in the proceeding. The 1975 NPRM had set out a PEL of 0.10 mg/m^3.

Most of the debate as well as the studies of the feasibility of the standard focused on that PEL, but OSHA chose a PEL of 0.05 mg/m^3 in the final standard. The majority was willing to accept OSHA's argument that the lower PEL was a "logical outgrowth" of the higher one, but the vigorous dissent showed that OSHA was treading on thin legal ice. In the same rule making, fear of violating the notice requirement had convinced OSHA to hold a new set of hearings after it decided to add a provision for guaranteeing the wages of workers getting medical transfers. Finally, the Supreme Court's benzene decision, discussed in the text later, essentially mandated the use of some type of quantitative risk assessment, a requirement that the Fifth Circuit later used to overturn OSHA's standard for the cotton ginning industry. For a discussion of the procedural aspects of these cases, see Mintz, *OSHA*, pp. 233–240, 251.

27. S. Goldman and T. P. Jahinge, *The Federal Courts in a Political System* (New York: Harper and Row, 1976), p. 164. The importance of judges' policy preferences is usually downplayed in the law review literature, the usual aim of which is to find or invent legal principles to explain their decisions. Nevertheless, some recent reviews have both cited and championed decisions that have tested an agency's fidelity to the statute by assessing whether its regulations were unreasonable in light of the evidence and the statute. See Merrick B. Garland, "Deregulation and Judicial Review," *Harvard Law Review* (January 1985), 98(3): 553–555.

Political scientists also express some ambivalence about the role of policy preferences, especially for courts below the Supreme Court. R. Shep Melnick states:

While one must be attentive to the possibility that judges have policy preferences that they express in their opinions, one should not exaggerate the idiosyncratic nature of judicial decisionmaking. Judges must explain their decisions in written opinions that can be reviewed by higher courts. This both inhibits them from simply voting their policy preferences and produces legal doctrines that help *to* reveal the patterns of judicial action. (*Regulation and the Courts* (Washington, D.C.: Brookings Institution, 1983), p. 62)

Yet, as Melnick stresses, the new administrative law is based precisely on a judicial perception that the other branches of government have failed to protect the public against well-organized business interests and that

the role of the court is to enfranchise those groups disenfranchised by other institutions. While proponents of judicial modesty consider this argument a convenient veil for the imposition of judges' and law professors' upper-middle class conservation ethic, others see such judicial activism as a necessary step toward the development of a new environmental ethos. (p. 70)

28. Section 3(8).

29. American Petroleum Institute v. OSHA, 581 F. 2d 493 (Fifth Circuit, 1978).

30. *Federal Register* (February 10, 1978), 43: 5946.

31. Just as the Fifth circuit had paid no attention to the decisions of other circuits, the lawyers argued that the other courts would be free to ignore its benzene decision. An appeal to the Supreme Court, in contrast, threatened to spread the damage, not limit it. During the deliberations about whether to appeal, Bingham took the highly unusual step of asking lawyers for the unions to come to present the argument in favor. Her political strength prevailed and OSHA appealed (interview with Ben Mintz, 1985).

32. Interview with Basil Whiting, Deputy Assistant Secretary for OSH (1980).

33. Viscusi, who was reviewing regulations as deputy director of the Council on Wage-Price Stability at the time, concurs that "the moratorium on new health risk regulations during the final three yeasrs of the Carter Administration can be traced to the uncertainties raised by the benzene case and related court tests of OSHA's authority" (*Risk by Choice* (Cambridge, Mass.: Harvard University Press, 1983) p. 14).

The most important other factor contributing to the moratorium was that most of what had been in the pipeline when Bingham took office had been sent through. However, new standards for several harzards, including asbestos, cadmium, and chromium, had been under consideration for some time. A second factor was that important standards that used a generic approach—hazard labeling, access to medical information, the generic carcinogen rule—were being developed.

34. Industrial Union Department v. American Petroleum Institute, 448 U.S. 607 (1980).

35. Industrial Union Department, AFL-CIO v. American Petroleum Institute.

36. Industrial Union Department, AFL-CIO v. American Petroleum Institute.

37. See, for example, Howard A. Laitin, "The 'Significance' of Toxic Health Risks: An Essay on Legal Decisionmaking Under Uncertainty," *Ecology Law Quarterly* (1982) 10(3):339–395.

38. Industrial Union Department v. American Petroleum Institute, p. 45.

39. Industrial Union Department v. American Petroleum Insitute.

40. The EPA's Carcinogenic Assessment Group (CAG) has used the upper 95 percent confidence interval in its quantitative risk assessments.

41. The D.C. Circuit had no trouble accepting that the cotton dust standard addressed a significant risk. In that case OSHA had presented estimates of the number of cases of byssinosis at different exposure levels. A tougher hurdle was passed with the same court's acceptance of the lead standard. In that case OSHA estimated the number of workers whose blood lead levels would decline by various amounts because of the standard. However, the agency had no data on the number of illnesses or so-called subclinical effects that would be prevented as a result of this reduction.

42. By mid-1986 OSHA had conducted five formal QRAs. For three of them (asbestos, arsenic, and benzene), the calculations used epidemiological data. For two (ethylene oxide and formaldehyde), bioassay data were used for the calculations.

43. Interviews with Grover Wrenn (1982) and Ben Mintz (1982).

44. Interview with Grover Wrenn (1982).

45. George C. Eads and Michael Fix, *Relief or Reform: Reagan's Regulatory Dilemma* (Washington, D.C.: Urban Institute Press, 1984), pp. 49–50.

46. Quoted in Bureau of National Affairs, *Occupational Safety and Health Reporter* (April 2, 1981), 11:1386.

47. US General Accounting Office, "Improved Quality, Adequate Resources, and Consistent Oversight Needed If Regulatory Analysis Is to Help Control Costs of Government Regulation," GAO/PAD83-6 Washington, D.C.: Government Accounting Office, (November 2, 1982), Although the report concluded that "OMB review under E.O. 12291 has not in general directly resulted in increased delays in the regulatory process," that conclusion largely reflects the fact that only about 2 percent of all rules qualified as major rules subject to OMB review. For these major rules the effects were often significant. See pp. 50–51 of the GAD report. See also George C. Eads and Michael Fix, *Relief or Reform*, ch. 6.

48. Morton Corn, "Report on OSHA Prepared by Outgoing Assistant Secretary Morton Corn and Submitted to Labor Secretary W. J. Usery," reprinted in the Bureau of National Affairs, *Occupational Safety and Health Reporter* (January 14, 1977), p. 1098.

49. This account of the standard relies on Kelman, *Regulating America*, pp. 54–61.

50. Interview with Grover Wrenn, Director of Health Standards (1981).

51. Quoted in "The First of 400," in *Job Safety and Health* (Washington, D.C.: OSHA, June 1975), p. 5.

52. "The First of 400," p. 7.

53. Corn, "Report on OSHA," p. 1098.

54. OSHA, "Access to Employee Exposure and Medical Records: Final Rules," *Federal Register* (May 23, 1980), 45:35214.

55. For example, in response to industry requests, the final regulation spelled out more specifically the criteria that industry would have to meet to rebut the presumptions that OSHA would use; however, as noted in the text, these presumptions were so difficult to meet that this was a Pyrrhic victory. The final regulation also included provisions for regular amendments to the Cancer Policy and for the introduction of new evidence in specific rules.

56. 29 CFR 1990.144(a) in *Federal Register* (January 22, 1980), 45:5287.

57. 29 CFR 1990.144(b) in *Federal Register* (January 22, 1980), 45:5287.

58. 29 CFR 1990.112 in *Federal Register* (January 22, 1980), 45:5284.

59. 29 CFR 1990.147 in *Federal Register* (January 22, 1980), 45:5288–5289.

60. In one case (coke oven emissions), OSHA began counting earlier than the first *Federal Register* notice, reaching back to the first meeting of the Advisory Committee on that standard. In several cases the first published notice concerned OSHA's request for information about a hazard; in other cases it was the announcement of an ETS. At the other end of the process, OSHA kept the clock running until the denial of certiorari by the Supreme Court.

61. *Federal Register* (January 22, 1980), 45:5012.

62. EDF v. EPA, 598 F. 2d 62 (1978). OSHA cited this case in the preamble to the Cancer Policy *Federal Register* (January 22, 1980), 45:5014.

63. For an enthusiast, see Thomas O. McGarity, "Substantive and Procedural Discretion in Administrative Resolution of Science Policy Questions," *Georgetown Law Journal* (February 1979), 67:729–810.

64. Regulatory Analysis Review Group, "Occupational Safety and Health Administration's Proposal for the Identification, Classification and Regulation of Toxic Substances Posing a Potential Occupational Carcinogenic Risk" (October 24, 1978), mimeo, p. 12. The RARG was analyzing a report submitted by the AIHC, which included three scenarios: a low scenario involving the regulation of thirty-eight high-volume substances; a medium scenario involving 1970 substances categorized in an NIOSH survey; and a high scenario involving 2415 substances listed as suspected carcinogens. The $20 billion cost estimate was from the AIHC report for the medium scenario with a 1-ppm PEL. An obvious question, not addressed in the RARG report, is the time period during which this quantity of standard setting is supposed to occur. The RARG expressed skepticism about the validity of the AIHC cost estimates, but it did not question the assumption that considerable additional standard setting would occur.

65. Interviews with Anson Keller and Grover Wrenn (1983).

66. For a thoughtful discussion of the Cancer Policy that gives more emphasis to the issues of scientific legitimacy, see Sheila Jasanoff, "Science and the Limits of Administrative Rule-Making: Lessons from the OSHA Cancer Policy," *Osgoode Hall Law Journal* (1982), 20(3):536–561. She concludes that the policy failed on two counts: "It failed to accommodate crucial differences between administrative and scientific criteria of legitimacy and it paid insufficient heed to the political aspects of the scientific controversies uncovered during the rule-making process" (p. 538).

67. Synthetic Organic Chemical Manufacturers Association (SOCMA), "Proposal of the Synthetic Organic Chemical Manufacturers Association for Appropriate Amendments to the Z-Tables of 29 C.F.R 1910.1000" (February 2, 1983), mimeo, p. 2.

68. SOCMA, "Proposal for Amendments," p. 8.

69. John Graham, "The Failure of Agency-Forcing: The Regulation of Airborne Carcinogens under Section 112 of the Clean Air Act," *Duke Law Journal* (1985), 85(1): 100–150.

70. Graham, "Failure of Agency-Forcing," p. 118.

71. David Doniger, *Law and Policy*, p. 67. Doniger is an attorney with the Natural Resources Defense Council.

72. Doniger writes that the "EPA, however, has never been comfortable with the apparent policy of section 112 to minimize the risk of death or serious injury from air pollutants regardless of cost. The agency has been reluctant to act under the hazardous air pollutant section since its enactment in 1970" (*Law and Policy*, p. 72). Graham observes that "the perception that section 112 might require extremely strict emission limits appears to have had a counterproductive effect—the EPA has been reluctant to list pollutants and to promulgate emission standards" ("Failure of Agency-Forcing," p. 131).

73. Quoted in Graham, "Failure of Agency-Forcing," p. 131.

74. Doniger, *Law and Policy*, p. 159, note 891.

75. For a discussion of the issues in this paragraph, see Graham, "Failure of Agency-Forcing," pp. 123–127.

76. For two good treatments of this point, see Kelman's *Regulating America* and David Vogel's *National Styles of Regulation* (Ithaca, N.Y.: Cornell University Press, 1986).

Chapter 6

1. The only condition on which this result appears dependent is that the marginal cost curves are sloping upward.

2. Ted Greenwood provides a good discussion of the different methods in *Knowledge and Discretion in Government Regulation* (New York: Praeger, 1984), pp. 83–86.

3. Section 6(g) of the OSH Act.

4. Sections 6(b)(1) and 6(g) of the OSH Act.

5. The only other period in which OSHA relied heavily on NIOSH indicated again the flaw in that strategy. There was a rash of proposals in late 1975—including lead, ammonia, beryllium, sulfur dioxide, toluene, toluene di-isocyanate, and trichloroethylene—all flowing from NIOSH recommendations. This veritable gusher had a simple source. Labor Secretary Dunlop, upset with the slow pace of standard setting, was concerned that the new Ford administration requirements for Inflationary Impact Statements would delay the process further. He negotiated an agreement with the White House to allow all proposals issued before November 1975 to omit those analyses. That led to frenzied activity, with staff picking the hazards largely from the NIOSH list on a "first-in, first-out" basis, regardless of the merits of regulation or the political support they enjoyed. The result was that none of those proposals, except lead, ever was followed by a permanent standard. Interview with Anson Keller, former Special Assistant for Regulatory Affairs (1982).

6. Benjamin W. Mintz, *OSHA: History, Law, and Policy* (Washington, D.C.: Bureau of National Affairs, 1984), p. 197.

7. Interviews with Grover Wrenn, Director of Health Standards (1981), and John Froines, Chief of the Office of Toxic Substances (1981).

8. Mintz, *OSHA*, p. 687.

9. Mintz, *OSHA*, p. 697.

10. Albert Gore and Barney Frank—two smart and media-conscious legislators who headed

subcommittees outside the usual labor network—held six hearings on OSHA during 1981 and 1982. OSHA's (and the EPA's) failure to respond to new evidence on the carcinogenicity of formaldehyde was a major point of contention.

11. Ronald Brownstein and Nina Easton, *Reagan's Ruling Class* (Washington, D.C.: Presidential Accountability Group, 1982), p. 297.

12. National Congress of Hispanic American Citizens v. Usery, 554 F. 2d 1196 (1977).

13. National Congress of Hispanic American Citizens v. Marshall, 626 F. 2d 882 (1979).

14. Public Citizen Health Research Group v. Auchter, 554 F. Supp. 242 (D.D.C., 1983), p. 251.

15. Public Citizen Health Research Group v. Auchter, 702 F. 2d 1150 (D.C. Circuit, 1983).

16. In 1985 President Reagan created a new regulatory planning program in Executive Order 12498, which called for OMB approval of an agency's intended regulatory actions for the coming year. See chapter 8 for a discussion of this program.

17. See Richard W. Lowerre, "Statutory Deadlines for Environmental Decisions," in the National Research Council's *Decision Making in the Environmental Protection Agency*, Vol. IIb (Washington, D.C.: National Academy of Sciences, 1977), pp. 264–285. He notes that, until the emergence of environmental statutes with their pervasive timetables, "few courts found that an agency's delay was an abuse of discretion" (p. 269).

18. Interview with George Cohen (1981), who headed the unions' legal team in the benzene and cotton dust cases as well as in many other OSHA cases.

19. Given the OMB's critical stance toward regulation, it may prefer referrals to OSHA precisely because it believes that the likelihood of OSHA's actually producing a rule is lower than the EPA's.

20. Milton C. Weinstein, "Decision Making for Toxic Substances Control: Cost-Effective Information Development for the Control of Environmental Carcinogens," *Public Policy* (Summer 1979), 26(3): 333–383. Weinstein also argues for a system of "parallel" rather than "serial" testing. All data elements (for example, health effects and costs) would be considered at each tier, rather than considering only one (say, health effects) and bringing in the other factors at a later stage.

21. NIOSH does conduct periodic surveys of "exposures"; however, these do not sample actual exposure levels but provide only crude estimates of the number of workers "exposed" to any amount of a chemical. Because of this fundamental defect, these surveys are not used by OSHA.

22. The number of inspections required would depend on the diversity of industries in which exposures occur. A review of OSHA's past rule makings indicates that twenty inspections would have been quite adequate in most of them. Data from OSHA's inspections would not be the only source of information.

23. Interview with Peg Seminario, Director of Health and Safety, AFL-CIO (1986).

Chapter 7

1. See David Vogel, *National Styles of Regulation: Environmental Policy in Great Britain and the United States* (Ithaca, N.Y.: Cornell University Press, 1986).

2. For the weakness of the White House regulatory review program from 1974 to 1980, see Christopher DeMuth, "Constraining Regulatory Costs, Part I. The White House Review Programs," *Regulation* (January-February 1980), 4: 13–26. On the absence of White House influence, see Richard Nathan, *The Administrative Presidency* (New York: Wiley, 1983);

G. Calvin Mackenzie, *The Politics of Presidential Appointments* (New York: Free Press, 1981); and US Senate, Committee on Government Operations, *Study on Federal Regulation. Volume 1. The Regulatory Appointments Process* (Washington, D.C.: Government Printing Office, 1977).

Paul Quirk's study of the FDA found that it "operates quite independently of HEW and the Presidential Administration." See his chapter, "The Food and Drug Administration," in James Q. Wilson's *The Politics of Regulation* (New York: Basic Books, 1980), pp. 191–235. Herbert Kaufman portrays the same scene: All of the Executive Office agencies "were relatively distant figures in the day-to-day life of the bureaus" he studied. See his *Administrative Behavior of Federal Bureau Chiefs* (Washington, D.C.: Brookings Institution, 1981), p. 58. Steve Kelman reached the same conclusion in his study of OSHA, *Regulating America, Regulating Sweden* (Cambridge: MIT Press, 1981).

In one of the few quantitative studies of the impact of administration on regulatory agencies, Terry Moe found that the NLRB decisions tilted clearly in the labor direction with Democratic appointees and back with Republican. The results for the FTC and the SEC were ambiguous, although both the measures of performance and the theory underlying the predictions were weak. Moe actually argues that the behavior of all three agencies shifted with changes in administration. However, for the FTC and the SEC his measures of performance—number of complaints issued and cases filed—may not be valid indicators of regulatory stringency, as he acknowledges. Moreover, contrary to his predictions, stringency for those agencies was greater under Eisenhower. Moe suggests that Democrats needed to show that they were not anti-business. Although possibly correct, this ex post explanation is inconsistent with the finding for the NLRB, for which he has a much more valid measure of stringency. See Terry Moe, "Regulatory Performance and Presidential Administration," *American Journal of Political Science* (May 1982), 26(2): 197–224.

3. Interview with Grover Wrenn (1982). The chance to avoid a challenge appealed to Wrenn. He was the same official who, four years earlier, had pressed for a questionably feasible 1 ppm for vinyl chloride. That standard had been upheld. Now, with a stronger case, he held back. Four years before it had seemed important to establish the principle of highly protective OSHA regulation. In 1978, with controversial rules on arsenic, benzene, and cotton dust already issued and a major standard on lead about to be issued, the problem was the overloading of the agency's capabilities and the depletion of its political capital. Nevertheless, if Bingham, who was much more of an ideologue than Wrenn, had been more actively involved, a decision to reduce the PEL below 2 ppm would have been much more likely.

4. John Mendeloff, "Reducing Occupational Health Risks," *Technology Review* (May 1980), 82: 66–78.

5. I am indebted to James Robinson for this observation (personal communication, 1984).

6. The Lead Industry Association (LIA), suspicious of the consultants (who had close ties to organized labor) and their equations relating air-lead levels to blood-lead levels, believed that OSHA had cooked the numbers to achieve this result. The LIA argued that the relationship was highly uncertain and that blood-lead levels were more heavily influenced by matters of personal hygiene than by the level of airborne lead.

7. See John Mendeloff, *Regulating Safety* (Cambridge, Mass.: MIT Press, 1979), p. 77.

8. Interview with Mary Win O'Brien, associate counsel, and Michael Wright, industrial hygienist, United Steelworkers of America (1983).

9. The trade association spokesperson who provided this information in 1981 requested anonymity.

10. George J. Stigler, "The Theory of Economic Regulation," *Bell Journal of Economics and Management* (Spring 1971), 2(1): 3–21.

11. On differences among firms in compliance costs, see Robert Leone, ed., *Environmental Controls: The Impact on Industry* (Lexington, Mass.: Heath, 1976), and Robert Leone and John Jackson, "The Political Economy of Federal Regulatory Activity: The Case of Water-Pollution Controls," in *Studies in Public Regulation*, Gary Fromm, ed. (Cambridge, Mass.: MIT Press, 1981), pp. 231–271. Arguments about the role of regional conflicts in air pollution are presented by Robert Crandall in his *Controlling Air Pollution* (Washington, D.C.: Brookings Institution, 1983), ch. 7; Peter Pashigian, "The Political Economy of the Clean Air Act" (St. Louis, Mo.: Washington University Center for the Study of American Business, 1982); and Bruce Ackerman and Curtis Hassler, "Beyond the New Deal: Coal and the Clean Air Act," *Yale Law Journal* (July 1980), 89(8): 1466–1571. In "How Large and small Firms Fare under Environmental Regulation" (*Regulation* (September–October 1983) 7: 19–23), Pashigian argued that the market share of small firms had declined in industries with heavy costs to comply with EPA regulations. He found no effect for OSHA rules; however, most of the economic impact studies of OSHA standards indicate that small firms will tend to be at a disadvantage.

12. Michael T. Maloney and Robert E. McCormick, "A Positive Theory of Environmental Quality Regulation," *Journal of Law and Economics* (April 1982), 25: 108.

13. John S. Hughes, Wesley A. Magat, and William E. Ricks, "The Economic Consequences of the OSHA Cotton Dust Standards: An Analysis of Stock Price Behavior," *Journal of Law and Economics* (April 1986), 24: 29–59.

14. Interview with Dr. Harold Imbus, former medical director of Burlington Industries (1983).

15. Harold R. Imbus, "The Development of a Cotton Dust Standard," *Journal of Occupational Medicine* (August 1974), 16(8): 547–551.

16. Interview with Dr. Harold Imbus (1983).

17. Interview with Dr. Harold Imbus (1983).

18. One reason for this conclusion is that a model of firm behavior driven only by profit-maximizing concerns is probably wrong. Firms' reactions to standards must be developed, in large part, by their health experts. These professionals complain about OSHA standards, in good part because they view them as scientifically unsupported and therefore unreasonable. Thus, for reasons of internal decision making, strategic concerns will often not dominate a firm's response.

19. Section 6(b)(5).

20. I base this statement on a meeting I attended the month after the passage of the OSH Act with the legislative directors of the Steelworkers and the Oil, Chemical, and Atomic Workers unions and the director of the AFL-CIO's Health and Safety Department.

21. This view may seem farfetched in light of more recent evidence, but at the time it was a credible position. The role of scientific evidence is discussed later in this chapter.

22. Benjamin W. Mintz, *OSHA: History, Law, and Policy* (Washington, D.C.: Bureau of National Affairs, 1984), p. 172.

23. Industrial Union Department v. Hodgson, 449 F. 2d 467 (D.C. Circuit, 1974).

24. Industrial Union Department, AFL-CIO v. Hodgson.

25. Industrial Union Department, AFL-CIO v. Hodgson.

26. Industrial Union Department, AFL-CIO v. Hodgson, pp. 477–478.

27. Industrial Union Department, AFL-CIO v. Hodgson, pp. 477–478.

28. An often-noted feature of social regulation is the adoption of lofty, technology-forcing standards, followed by enforcement processes that give much more weight to the losses that will be imposed on firms. See, for example, R. Shep Melnick, *Regulation and the Courts*

(Washington, D.C.: Brookings Institution, 1983), ch. 7, on the Clean Air Act. The function of regulation in slowing change is presented in Bruce M. Owen and Ronald Braeutigam, *The Regulation Game* (Cambridge, Mass.: Ballinger, 1978).

29. *Federal Register* (October 4, 1974), 39 : 35892.

30. Society of the Plastics Industry v. OSHA, 509 F. 2d 1301 (Second Circuit, 1975).

31. AFL-CIO v. Brennan, 530 F. 2d 109 (Third Circuit, 1975).

32. 617 F. 2d 636 (D.C. Circuit, 1979).

33. *Federal Register* (February 17, 1981), 46 : 13193

34. American Textile Manufacturers Institute v. Donovan, 452 U.S. 490 (1981).

35. The Supreme Court's decision had two parts. The Court unanimously agreed that the NHTSA's failure even to consider relying on air bags instead of automatic belts was "arbitrary and capricious." In addition, by a 5-4 margin, the Court ruled that the agency had failed to justify adequately its conclusion that detachable automatic belts would not substantially reduce deaths. It is this part of the decision that I am criticizing in the text. See Motor Vehicle Manufacturers Association v. State Farm Mutual Auto Insurance, 103 S. Ct. 2856 (1983); and Merrick Garland, "Deregulation and Judicial Review," *Harvard Law Review* (January 1985), 98 : 505–591.

36. Interviews with Daniel Jacoby, Deputy Associate Solicitor for Standards (1983), and Dennis Kade, Deputy Associate Solicitor for Appellate Review (1983).

37. See Charles Lindblom, "The Science of 'Muddling Through,'" *Public Administration Review* (1959), 19 : 79–88.

38. Interviews with Robert Nagle and Daniel Krivit (1975).

39. The Supreme Court did not expressly prohibit the use of benefit-cost analysis, although its decision has been interpreted to do that.

40. Chevron, U.S.A., Inc. v. National Resources Defense Council, Inc., 104 S. Ct. 2778 (1984).

41. See Judge Patricia Wald, "The Realpolitik of Judicial Review in a Deregulation Era," *Journal of Policy Analysis and Management* (Spring 1986), 5(3) : 540.

42. Ted Greenwood, *Knowledge and Discretion in Government Regulation* (New York: Praeger, 1984), p. 100.

43. Arthur D. Little, Inc., *Estimated Compliance Costs of OSHA Asbestos Standard: Report to the Department of Labor* (April 1972), pp. 1–2.

44. *Federal Register* (June 7, 1972), 37 : 3157.

45. Nathan Karch, "Explicit Criteria and Principles for Identifying Carcinogens: A Focus on the Controversy at the Environmental Protection Agency," in the National Research Council's *Decision Making in the Environmental Protection Agency*, Vol. IIa (Washington, D.C.: National Academy of Sciences, 1977), pp. 119–206.

46. Greenwood, *Knowledge and Discretion*, p. 229. The report endorsing thresholds was the National Research Council, Committee on Biological Effects of Atmospheric Pollutants, *Asbestos* (Washington, D.C.: National Academy Press, 1971). An example of the no-threshold view was a report to the Surgeon General from the Ad-Hoc Committee on the Evaluation of Low Levels of Environmental Chemical Carcinogens, "The Evaluation of Environmental Carcinogenesis" (April 22, 1970), mimeo.

47. In both cases the agency largely dismissed qualms about feasibility and adhered closely to a PEL recommended primarily on the basis of health criteria. Yet with asbestos no one doubted that exposures to 12 fibers were dangerous, whereas the vinyl chloride industry claimed that all of the cancer deaths caused by vinyl chloride had involved exposures greater than 200 ppm.

The difference between 200 ppm and the OSHA PEL of 1 ppm is far greater than the difference between the 12-fiber limit for asbestos and the 2-fiber PEL OSHA established. In addition, the qualms about the ability to achieve the PEL were greater in the case of vinyl chloride.

48. Linda E. Demkovich, "Labor Report: OSHA Launches Dual Effort to Reduce Job Health Hazards," *National Journal* (December 7, 1974), 6:1839.

49. A good example of scientific "flexibility" came in OSHA's flip-flop in interpreting data about whether the harm from cotton dust exposures varied depending on the stage of processing.

When Morton Corn proposed the cotton dust standard in December 1976, he called for a uniform 0.200-mg/m^3 PEL for all cotton processing industries, excluding only cotton harvesting at the front end and garment manufacturing at the back. Although the exact etiology of byssinosis remains uncertain, the chief study that OSHA relied on had shown that later stages of manufacturing were associated with less disease for any given level of dust, apparently because the biologically active material is diluted before the yarn reaches the weaving stage. Yet in its 1976 proposal OSHA concluded that

there is a lack of data indicating that exposure to cotton dust affects workers differently in the various industries affected, specifically, that workers react in a manner dissimilar to that of the textile workers. Indeed, the evidence that is available supports the view that exposure to cotton dust, regardless of the stage of processing in which the dust is encountered, results in byssinosis and other respiratory diseases. (*Federal Register* (December 28, 1976), 41:56503)

At that time Corn had expressed his view that it would not be acceptable for OSHA to set different PELs, although he acknowledged that allowing different amounts of time to comply with them would be.

A little more than twelve months later, OSHA decided to establish different PELs, ranging from 0.200 mg to 0.750 mg for various industry sectors. This new standard would, according to OSHA, impose annual costs of $550 million a year, well under half of what a uniform 0.200-mg PEL would have cost. In the final standard, OSHA used the findings of differential disease impact, which it had discounted earlier, to justify this step.

OSHA gave many reasons for its change of mind, including qualms about the technical and economic feasibility of a 0.200-mg/m^3 PEL in some sectors. But the preamble to the 1978 standard clearly acknowledges that, given the high cost and uncertain success of engineering controls for weaving processes, "optimal worker protection would be served by concentrating resources on achieving 0.200 mg in yarn manufacturing as rapidly as feasible rather than diverting substantial resources to eliminating dust exposures in weaving" (*Federal Register* (June 23, 1978), 43:27360). It was clear in this case that OSHA had become more sensitive to cost arguments than it had been in earlier rule makings; although the change was limited. OSHA still could not accept bald cost-effectiveness arguments, and would incorporate them only to the extent that they could be neatly meshed with its more traditional positions. Nevertheless, it is likely that, if OSHA had tried to adopt its original, much more costly 0.200-mg proposal, Carter's regulatory review process would have succeeded in shooting it down.

50. US Congress Office of Technology Assessment, *Preventing Illness and Injury in the Workplace*, OTA-H-256 (Washington, D.C.: Government Printing Office, April 1985), p. 182. The cost of engineering controls is sensitive to the choice of the PEL, whereas the cost of a respirator approach is not. For example, in this case, achieving a 0.2-fiber PEL would add another $36 million to the cost of engineering controls but only $2 million to the cost of protective equipment.

51. *Federal Register* (May 22, 1980) 45:5223.

52. One study at General Motors has shown that ear muffs and ear plugs could provide more protection than engineering controls that just get exposures below the PEL. See James C.

Miller, III, and Thomas F. Walton, "Protecting Workers' Hearing: An Economic Test for OSHA Initiatives," *Regulation* (September–October 1980), 4:31–37.

53. Kelman, *Regulating America*, p. 91.

54. Cited in Office of Technology Assessment, Preventing Illness and Injury, p. 183.

55. Interviews with OSHA staff (1983).

56. Alvin Weinberg, "Science and Trans-Science," *Minerva* (1972), 10:202–222.

57. John D. Graham and James W. Vaupel, "The Value of a Life: What Difference Does it Make?" *Risk Analysis* (1981), 1:89–95.

58. For a review of seven possible explanations for differences between OSHA and the NHTSA, see John D. Graham, "Some Explanations for Disparities in Lifesaving Investments," *Policy Studies Review* (May 1982), 1(4):692–704.

59. Kelman, *Regulating America*, p. 62.

60. For a good study of the politics of this period, see Graham K. Wilson, *The Politics of Regulation*.

61. Ronald Brickman, Sheila Jasanoff, and Thomas Ilgen, *Controlling Chemicals: The Politics of Regulation in Europe and the United States* (Ithaca, N.Y.: Cornell University Press, 1985), p. 49.

62. Kelman, *Regulating America*, p. 76.

63. Kelman, *Regulating America*, p. 79.

64. See Vogel, *National Styles of Regulation*, pp. 196–209.

65. Vogel, *National Styles of Regulation*, pp. 253–254.

66. Congressional Quarterly, *Environment and Health* (Washington, D.C: CQ Press, 1981). Paul Quirk reports a similar finding in his study of the diverse regulatory activities of the Food and Drug Administration: "Except for those issues on which agency issues affect agriculture, the only actions seen as bearing a risk of budgetary damage were those that led to *public* protest and opposition" ("The Food and Drug Administration," in *The Politics of Regulation*, James Q. Wilson, ed. (New York: Basic Books, 1980), p. 214).

67. Others have noted an apparent paradox in many of the activities of Ralph Nader and other like-minded critics of government regulation: Despite their fears that government regulators will be captured, their solutions always involve more government regulation. Yet this paradox disappears if one believes that there are no nonregulatory solutions and that public vigilance can prevent capture from occurring.

Chapter 8

1. Robert Reich, "Warring Critiques of Regulation," *Regulation* (January–February 1979), 3:37–42. See also Colin S. Diver, "Policymaking Paradigms in Administrative Law," *Harvard Law Review* (December 1981), 95:393–434.

2. Robert Litan and William Nordhaus, *Reforming Federal Regulation* (New Haven, Conn.: Yale University Press, 1983), p. 3.

3. For a recent critique of the view that agencies are out of control, see Barry Weingast and Mark Moran, "Bureaucratic Discretion or Congressional Control: Regulatory Policymaking by the Federal Trade Commission," *Journal of Political Economy* (1983), 91:756–801. For a view that stresses agency autonomy, see James Q. Wilson, *The Politics of Regulation* (New York: Basic Books, 1980), pp. 357–394.

4. The classification of the legistlative veto, although moot because of the Supreme Court's recent decision invalidating it, is less certain.

5. George Eads and Michael Fix, *Relief or Reform: Reagan's Regulatory Dilemma* (Washington, D.C.: Urban Institute Press, 1984), chs. 3 and 4.

6. Christopher DeMuth, "The White House Review Programs," *Regulation* (January–February 1980), 4:13–26.

7. Eads and Fix, *Relief or Reform*, chs. 6–8; and John Mendeloff, "OSHA and Regulatory Theory," paper presented at the Conference on the Political Economy of Public Policy, Standard University, Stanford, California, March 15–17, 1984.

8. Of course, there is an irony about DeMuth's comment about the "unpromising ideas" of centralizing decision making because he later headed the OMB unit that tried to move from being "Kibitzers to superregulators."

9. Hearings in 1980 on the regulatory budget elicited admiration from Robert Crandall, Christopher DeMuth, Lester Lave, and James C. Miller, III. U.S. Congress, Joint Economic Committee, *Hearings on Regulatory Budgeting and the Need for Cost-Effectiveness in the Regulatory Process*, (August 1, 1979), 96th Cong., 1st sess.

10. Christopher DeMuth, "The Regulatory Budget," *Regulation* (March–April 1980), 4:29–39, 42–44.

11. For example, in his testimony before the Joint Economic Committee, Crandall proposed OSHA as a candidate for an experiment. A similar proposal appears in John Schmitz, "OSHA after *American Petroleum Institute*: A Proposed Regulatory Budget," *Stanford Law Review* (1981), 33:917–935.

12. Benefit-cost analysis is not strictly symmetric. As we have seen, the assumption of an upward sloping marginal cost curve, underestimates costs more than benefits.

13. Litan and Nordhaus, *Reforming Federal Regulation*, ch. 7.

14. Litan and Nordhaus, *Reforming Federal Regulation*, p. 169.

15. Ted Greenwood, *Knowledge and Discretion in Government Regulation Policy* (New York: Praeger 1984).

16. Litan and Nordhaus, *Reforming Federal Regulation*, p. 169.

17. Litan and Nordhaus, *Reforming Federal Regulation*, p. 169.

18. This discussion of politics of the regulatory budget benefited from conversations with Gary Jacobson and Heather Campbell (1983)

19. Allen Schick, *Congress and Money* (Washington, D.C.: Urban Institute Press, 1980), p. 43.

20. Schick, *Congress and Money*, Schick, p. 73.

21. Phillip Harter, "Negotiating Regulations: A Cure for Malaise," *Georgetown Law Journal* (1982), 71(1):17.

22. Harter, "Negotiating Regulations," p. 17.

23. Harter, "Negotiating Regulations," p. 19.

24. Harter, "Negotiating Regulations," p. 20.

25. Harter, "Negotiating Regulations," pp. 45–51.

26. Harter, "Negotiating Regulations," p. 103.

27. Harter, "Negotiating Regulations," p. 107.

28. Harter, "Negotiating Regulations," p. 109.

29. US Congress, Senate, *Joint Hearings before the Select Committee on Small Business and the*

Subcommittee on Oversight of Government Management of the Committee on Governmental Affairs, United States Senate, Regulatory Negotiation, 96th Cong., 2nd sess.

30. The following account of the benzene negotiation is based on an interview with Phillip Harter (September 1984). More recently, OSHA has initiated another regulatory negotiation addressing methylene dianiline (MDA).

31. Peter Schuck, "Litigation, Bargaining, and Regulation," *Regulation* (July–August 1979), 3:34.

32. See, for example, W. Kip Viscusi, "Presidential Oversight: Controlling the Regulators," *Journal of Policy Analysis and Management* (Winter 1983), 2:157–173.

33. For example, in 1983 the D.C. Court of Appeals ordered OSHA to issue a proposal to regulate ethylene oxide, citing section 555(b) of the Administrative Procedure Act and section 6(g) of the OSH Act. Public Citizen Research Group v. Auchter et al., 83-1071, March 15, 1983.

34. For a thoughtful and extended discussion of Reagan's use of the OMB through 1983, see Eads and Fix, *Relief or Reform*, ch. 6.

35. W. Kip Viscusi, *Risk by Choice: Regulating Health and Safety in the Workplace* (Cambridge, Mass.: Harvard University Press, 1983), pp. 150, 164.

36. National Research Council, *Risk Assessment in the Federal Government: Managing the Process* (Washington, D.C.: National Academy Press, 1983).

Chapter 9

1. To a degree, the paucity of epidemiological studies of injuries are the cause of this shortcoming. However, workplace hazards (such as slippery floors) will often be so situationally specific that research findings may not be applicable.

2. OSHA, "Draft Regulatory Impact Analysis and Regulatory Flexibility Analysis of the Hazard Communication Proposal" (March 1982), mimeo, p. I-6.

3. See the testimony by the heads of OSHA and NIOSH on HR 1309, the High Risk Occupational Disease Notification and Prevention Act of 1985, before the Subcommittee on Health and Safety of the House Committee on Education and Labor, (November 20, 1985).

4. Philip J. Harter and George C. Eads, "Policy Instruments, Institutions, and Objectives: An Analytical Framework for Assessing 'Alternatives' to Regulation," *Administrative Law Review* (Summer 1985), 37(3):252–253.

5. Harter and Eads, "Policy Instruments," pp. 255–256.

6. Viscusi, *Risk by Choice*, pp. 157, 160.

7. W. Kip Viscusi, "Analysis of OMB and OSHA Evaluations of the Hazard Communication Proposal" (March 1982), mimeo; included as Appendix E in OSHA's "Draft Regulatory Impact Analysis," p. E-4.

8. In the past, proposals for education and information campaigns were rarely subjected to regulatory analysis and were adopted without any evidence that their benefits would justify their costs. More recently, proposals such as OSHA's hazard communication standard have been subjected to analysis. See Robert S. Adler and R. David Pittle, "Cajolery or Command: Are Educational Campaigns an Adequate Substitute for Regulation?" *Yale Journal of Regulation* (1984), 1(2):159–193.

9. OSHA, "Draft Regulatory Impact Analysis," p. I-7.

10. See chapter 4.

11. Viscusi, "Analysis of Evaluations," p. E-13.

12. Viscusi, *Risk by Choice*, p. 159. Viscusi's desire for OSHA to experiment with informational strategies and assess their impacts is laudable. My only point in this paragraph is that assessments will be difficult and that this is a drawback of a strategy that relies heavily on information.

13. It also ignores the heterogeneity of firms in the costs of compliance. I believe that reasonably set standards should reflect cost differences among industries.

14. Viscusi, *Risk by Choice*, p. 80.

15. Viscusi, *Risk by Choice*, p. 55.

16. Based on an analysis I did of the 1977 Quality of Employment Survey. The survey was carried out by the Institute for Social Research, University of Michigan.

17. Other interpretations of these findings are possible. For example, workers who are skeptical of their employers' concern for their welfare may therefore be more likely to believe that they face serious hazards.

18. Anthony Mazzochi of the Oil, Chemical, and Atomic Workers Union, quoted by Paul Brodeur in *Outrageous Misconduct: The Asbestos Industry on Trial* (New York: Pantheon, 1985), p. 350.

19. Brodeur, *Outrageous Misconduct*, p. 5.

20. Leslie I. Boden and Carol. Jones, "Occupational Disease Remedies: The Asbestos Experience," paper presented at the NSF-CMU Conference, Regulation at the Crossroads, Airlie House, Virginia, September 12–14, 1985.

21. When the discounting issue has been raised, writers usually assume that it causes a "problem"—underinvestment in prevention. But this is true only if the discount rate is too high, that is, higher than the rate that would best secure society's broader interests. Unless the rate is higher than we think the firm should use, discounting is not a source of inefficiency despite its impact on prevention. Workers themselves often seem to use a high discount rate, both for health-related decisions and others.

Some claim that American firms have, at least recently, been overestimating the returns that they could earn on alternative investments and thus, even by their own criteria, use too high a discount rate. As I noted in chapter 2, the proper criteria for choosing a rate are in dispute. Even if we choose to look at "society's preferences" regarding the appropriate discount rate for occupational disease costs, we face an intractable empirical problem. Nevertheless, there appears to be a widespread belief that the rates typically used for firms' decisions are indeed too high. If this is true, then there is indeed underprevention resulting from discounting. However, precisely because of the discrepancy between corporate and social discount rates, this is not a problem that can be easily remedied through reform of the tort or compensation systems.

22. Eugene Bardach and Robert A. Kagan, "Liability Law and Social Regulation," in their *Social Regulation: Strategies for Reform* (San Francisco, Calif.: Institute for Contemporary Studies, 1982), p. 385.

23. George Eads and Peter Reuter, *Designing Safer Products* (Santa Monica, Calif.: Rand Corporation, 1983), p. 108.

24. The Manville policy is quoted in Carol Jones, "Models of Regulatory Enforcement and Compliance, with an Application to the Occupational Safety and Health Administration Asbestos Standard," Ph.D. dissertation, Department of Economics, Harvard University (July 1982), pp. 142–143.

25. The one study that has reported on changes in wages for asbestos workers estimated that

they had achieved about a 5 percent premium by 1971 but that it was unchanged for at least the following six years. See Peter S. Barth, "Compensation for Asbestos-Associated Disease: A Survey of Asbestos Insulation Workers in the United States and Canada," in *Disability Compensation for Asbestos-Associated Disease in the United States*, Irving J. Selikoff, ed. (New York: New York Academy of Sciences, 1983), pp. 213–282.

26. Boden and Jones, "Occupational Disease Remedies," p. 31, Table 4.

27. Jones, "Models of Regulatory Enforcement," p. 141.

28. W. Curtiss Priest and Sohail Bengali ("A Microeconomic Study on Productivity: Impact of OSHA Regulation on the Asbestos Industry" (Cambridge, Mass.: Center for Policy Alternatives, MIT, November 1981 mimeo) estimated that firms manufacturing asbestos products incurred capital expenditures of $28 million and annual expenditures of $13 million to comply with OSHA's 1972 standard. This estimate does not include any labor market effects (for example, higher wages or higher quit rates); however, the study does not indicate that such effects were prominent.

29. For example, from 1973 to 1979, of ninety-two OSHA inspections that were followups to earlier asbestos violations and that sampled for asbestos, only seven cited violations of overexposure to asbestos (OSHA Management Information System). Although citations usually lead to compliance, weaknesses in enforcement have frequently been identified by General Accounting Office studies. See General Accounting Office, *Sporadic Workplace Inspections for Lethal and Other Serious Health Hazards*, HRD-77-143 (Washington, D.C.: Government Printing Office, April 5, 1978), and General Accounting Office, *Workplace Inspection Program Weak in Detecting and Correcting Serious Hazards*, HRD-78-34 (Washington, D.C.: Government Printing Office, May 19, 1978).

30. Priest and Bengali, "Microeconomic Study on Productivity."

31. Jones, "Models of Regulatory Enforcement," p. 142.

32. Brodeur, *Outrageous Misconduct*, p. 81.

33. Because OSHA does not inspect a random sample of firms, inspection findings may not provide a valid measure of changes over time. However, Jones has employed corrections for sample selection bias that generate estimates within the range given in the text. See Jones, "Models of Regulatory Enforcement," Table 3.9.

34. In concept, higher judgments could be levied when someone is at fault, but the "excess" could go to the state rather than to the victim.

35. The proposals were culled from various sources, including US Department of Labor, *An Interim Report to Congress on Occupational Disease* (Washington, D.C.: Government Printing Office, June 1980), ch. 3; W. Kip Viscusi, "Structuring an Effective Occupational Disease Policy: Victim Compensation and Risk Regulation," *Yale Journal on Regulation* (1984), 2(1):53–81; Peter Huber, "Safety and the Second Best," *Columbia Law Review* (1985), 85:277–377; Stephen M. Soble, "A Proposal for the Administrative Compensation of Victims of Toxic Substances Pollution: A Model Act," *Harvard Journal of Legislation* (1977), 14:683–769; and Eugene Bardach and Robert A. Kagan, "Liability Law." The assessments of these proposals were also influenced by these sources.

36. Soble, "Proposal for the Administrative Compensation."

37. See James R. Chelius, *Workplace Safety and Health: The Role of Workers' Compensation* (Washington D.C.: American Enterprise Institute, 1977), and Robert S. Smith, "Protecting Workers Safety and Health," in *Instead of Regulation: Alternatives to Federal Regulatory Agencies*, Robert W. Poole, Jr., ed. (Lexington, Mass.: Heath, 1982), pp. 311–338.

38. See Peter Huber, "Safety." He argues convincingly that, when public agencies are already addressing categories of risk, the courts' ad hoc interventions can cause much mischief. A key

example is liability awards for harm caused by the side-effects of vaccines. The FDA already regulates the safety of vaccines, but these awards have threatened the availability of some vaccines. However, Huber's point is weakened to the extent that underregulation exists. If an agency, such as OSHA, is incapable of adequately addressing the risks posed by the category of hazards it is responsible for, then there is no reason to assume that tort actions will be upsetting rationally made public policy.

39. The chief case of substitution is the information strategy and the proposal in chapter 10 for adoption of a large number of rules. To exaggerate, "if no exposures are allowed, then there is little role for information to play." But of course, exposures will be allowed; moreover, worker information is a complement in the sense that better-informed workers will increase the likelihood that exposure limits are observed by employers.

Chapter 10

1. Talbot Page, "A Framework for Unreasonable Risk in the Toxic Substances Control Act (TSCA)," in *Management of Assessed Risk for Carcinogens*, W. J. Nicholson, ed. (New York: New York Academy of Sciences, 1981), pp. 145–166.

2. Some would argue that we should eschew expected cost minimization in favor of a more risk-averse strategy. I am not opposed to introducing some moderate degree of risk aversion so long as it remains sensitive to the available data and does not go to the extreme of adopting strategies like minimax regret.

3. The discussion of standard setting and screening draws heavily on Peter Huber, "The Old-New Division in Risk Regulation," *Virginia Law Review* (1983), 69:1024–1107.

4. Huber, "The Old-New Division," argues that regulating new risks more strictly than old risks will generally be efficient, although he wants agencies to compare the risks of old and new products in order to identify the cases in which retarding the introduction of the new activity would increase risks. However, I do not think that Huber's broader claim of efficiency is persuasive in light of the economic critique presented in the text. The chief reason to regulate newer risks differently is not that the costs will be lower but rather that these risks will never be addressed unless there is a two-track system. See the text for this argument.

5. Huber notes that the situation in screening programs is reversed. Although "small risks" tend to be ignored in standard-setting programs, they bear the major brunt of screening programs. For example, a drug company faced with a $50 million fixed cost to get regulatory approval for a new drug will proceed only with those that it expects to be big sellers.

6. Huber, "The Old-New Division," pp. 1069–1070.

7. John D. Graham, "The Failure of Agency-Forcing: The Regulation of Airborne Carcinogens under Section 112 of the Clean Air Act," *Duke Law Journal* (1985), 85:100–150.

8. A strategy of relying on private organizations to speed the regulatory process is not limited to OSHA. In his discussion of section 112, for example, Graham suggests that, instead of Congress determining which chemicals are hazardous enough to be "listed," the EPA could rely on the classifications of carcinogens that the International Agency for Research on Cancer has published. See Graham, "The Failure of Agency-Forcing."

9. W. Kip Viscusi, "The Status of OSHA Reform: A Comment on Mendeloff's Proposals," *Journal of Policy Analysis and Management* (Spring 1986), 5(3):469–475.

10. Viscusi, "Status of OSHA Reform," p. 473. As I argued in chapter 7, firms' strategic uses of the regulatory process do not appear to have played a dominant role in standard setting. The only OSHA evidence cited by Viscusi is the study by McCormick and Maloney. As we saw, their conclusions have been contradicted by a more recent and rigorous study.

11. This implication assumes that the issues are confined to the ones in the figure. Of course, it is possible that new bargains and possible agreements could be created by introducing additional policy issues, for example, on import restrictions or restrictions on anti-union activity by employers.

12. Gene Bardach, personal correspondence (1986).

13. David Vogel, *National Styles of Regulation* (Ithaca, N.Y.: Cornell Unversity Press, 1986), p. 242.

14. Ronald Brickman, Sheila Jasanoff, and Thomas Ilgen make this point in *Controlling Chemicals* (Ithaca, N.Y.: Cornell University Press, 1985), pp. 168–186.

15. See Robert A. Jones, "'3rd Wave' Alters course of Environmental Movement," *Los Angeles Times* (November 22, 1986), pp. 1, 3, 35.

16. Although we saw in chapter 7 that most of OSHA's new health standards addressed hazards found disproportionately among unionized workers, unions may have an interest in pushing for standards in other circumstances as well. In a partially organized industry (such as textiles), a standard may be especially important to avoid putting unionized plants at a competitive disadvantage if the unions push for safety and health improvements.

The extent to which union's priorities may ignore the interests of the unorganized depends on the extent to which particular unaddressed hazards cut across industries with low and high unionization. Data to examine this relationship are available but have not yet been explored.

17. See Martha Derthick and Paul Quirk, *The Politics of Deregulation* (Washington, D.C.: Brookings Institution, 1985); Michael Levine, "Revisionism Revisited? Airline Deregulation and the Public Interest," *Law and Contemporary Problems* (1981), 44:179–195; Roger Noll and Bruce Owen, *The Political Economy of Deregulation* (Washington, D.C.: American Enterprise Institute, 1983); and James Q. Wilson, "'Policy Intellectuals' and Public Policy," *The Public Interest* (Summer 1981), 64:31–46.

Appendix B

1. Russell Settle, "The Welfare Economics of Occupational Safety and Health Standards," Ph.D. dissertation, Department of Economics, University of Wisconsin, 1974. See pp. 130–135 and Appendix F to chapter 4.

2. See W. Curtiss Priest and Sohail Bengali, "A Microeconomic Study on Productivity: Impact of OSHA Regulation on the Asbestos Industry" (November 1981), mimeo. This report was prepared by the Center for Policy Alternatives at MIT for the US Department of Labor and is available from the National Technical Information Service. From data on sixteen plants the study extrapolated costs to this sector of $28 million in capital expenditures and $13 million in annual operating costs.

3. See the report by the Foster Snell Division of Booz, Allen, Hamilton, "Economic Impact Analysis of Proposed Vinyl Chloride Standard." More specifically, the estimate for the vinyl chloride monomer sector was for a 10-ppm ceiling and a time-weighted average of 2–5 ppm. The estimated capital costs were $27 million, plus a one-time productivity loss of $7 million. Capital costs were amortized over a ten-year period at a 12 percent rate (see Exhibit V-15). For the polyvinyl chloride industry, the estimate was for a ceiling of 15–25 ppm and a time-weighted average of 10–15 ppm. Capital costs were $151 million, and the one-time productivity loss was $78 million (see Exhibit V-16). Footnote 5 to that exhibit explains that one firm had estimated that attainment of "no detectable level" of exposure (which is close to 1 ppm) would cost $856 million in capital expenditures in that sector.

4. Herbert R. Northrup, Richard L. Rowan, and Charles R. Perry, *The Impact of OSHA* (Philadelphia, Penn.: Industrial Research Unit, Wharton School, University of Pennsylvania, 1978), pp. 383–389.

5. Northrup et al., pp., *Impact of OSHA*, 371–381. For example, negative impacts on operating productivity because of the use of air-line respirators were not included. Nor was the time top management officials spent on implementing the standard in the first year.

6. Arthur Andersen and Co., *Cost of Government Regulation Study, Appendix* (March 1979). The survey showed that firms in SIC 33 (which includes the steel industry) anticipated spending an extra $11 million in 1977 as a result of OSHA standards for toxic substances (appendix 5–29). Page 8-14 of the main study says "most of the $11 million was reported by steel companies and 80% of their costs was for coke oven emissions." This suggests spending in the $5–7 million range for the three firms.

7. David Burton Associates, "Economic Impact of Proposed Standard on Coke Oven Emissions" (1976), mimeo, p. 23.

8. For example, see Justice Brennan's dissent in the OSHA cotton dust case, where he charges that OSHA failed to show that the standard was feasible. American Textile Manufacturers' Institute v. Donovan, 452 U.S. 490 (June 17, 1981).

9. Centaur Associates, Inc., "Technical and Economic Analysis of Regulating Occupational Exposure to Cotton Dust" (January 1983), mimeo, p. I-8. The study assumed that 17.5 percent of capital expenditures for production equipment were attributable to the standard.

10. OSHA explains some of the difficulties with the studies in Attachment D to the lead standard. *Federal Register* (November 21, 1978), 43: 54473–54509.

11. One 1983 study of primary smelters, secondary smelters, and battery plants estimated annualized costs (in 1982 dollars) of about $180 million. See Robert Goble, (Dale Hattis, Mary Ballew, and Deborah Thurston, "Implementation of the Occupational Lead Exposure Standard," Working Paper 16 for the Office of Technology Assessment's study *Preventing Injury and Illness in the Workplace* (1983), mimeo. This study used data collected by Charles River Associates. Another study of nine other industries estimated costs of about $320 million. This figure included almost $120 million for shipbuilding and repair to reach the 0.200-mg level, which was judged the lowest attainable level with engineering controls. We should probably not count this cost toward the total cost of OSHA's reduction in the PEL from the preexisting level of 0.200 to the new level of 0.050 mg. See Jaca Corporation, "Summary of the Total Compliance Costs for the Remand Industries: Current OSHA Standard for Lead" (November 19, 1982), mimeo.

Appendix C

1. See the press release of the American Industrial Health Council, the industry umbrella group overseeing "scientific quality" (May 1983). Industry won a victory in 1983 in the Fifth Circuit Court of Appeals. It overturned a Consumer Product Safety Commission standard on formaldehyde, in part because it had relied on a risk assessment using only the set of experimental data that resulted in the highest estimate of risk and then extrapolated the results using the linearized 95 percent upper confidence interval of a multistage model. The court ruled that the agency had to look at all sets of data and use several models, not just the ones that gave the highest risk estimates (Gulf South Insulation. v Consumer Product Safety Commission, 701 F. 2d 1137 (1983)).

2. See chapter 7 for a discussion of the benzene decision.

Appendix D

1. Report of the Secretary of Health, Education, and Welfare, in *The President's Report on Occupational Safety and Health* (Washington D.C.: Government Printing Office, May 1972), p. 111.

2. Max Singer, "The Vitality of Mythical Numbers," *The Public Interest* (Spring 1971), 23:3–9.

3. J. Higginson and C. S. Muir, "The Role of Epidemiology in Elucidating the Importance of Environmental Factors in Human Cancer," *Cancer Detection and Prevention* (1976), 1:79–105; E. L. Wynder and G. B. Gori, "Contribution of the Environment to Cancer Incidence: An Epidemiological Exercise," *Journal of the National Cancer Institute* (1977), 58:825–832; P. Cole, "Cancer and Occupation: Status and Needs of Epidemiologic Research," *Cancer* (1977), 39:1788–1791.

4. Kenneth Bridbord, Arthur Upton, David Rall, et al., "Estimates of the Fraction of Cancer in the United States Related to Occupational Factors" (September 15, 1978), mimeo.

5. Interview with Marvin Schneiderman, former deputy director of the National Cancer Institute (1982).

6. See AIHC, "Reply" (October 23, 1978). See chapter 4, note 4.

7. Thomas H. Maugh, I, "Industry Council Challenges HEW on Cancer in the Workplace," *Science* (November 10, 1978), 202:602–604.

8. Toxic Substances Coordinating Committee, "Toxic Chemicals and Public Protection" (May 1980), mimeo, p. 4.

9. The papers were published in Richard Peto and Marvin Schneiderman, eds., *Quantification of Occupational Cancer* (Cold Spring Harbor, Mass.: Cold Spring Laboratory, 1981).

10. David G. Hoel, Review of *Quantification of Occupational Cancer, Science* (November 5, 1982), 28(4572):560. The review of this controversy provides reasons for both pessimism and optimism about the role of science in public policy debates. The "Estimates" document is an example, in Richard Peto's phrase of how "a group of reasonable men can collectively generate an unreasonable report," and its uncritical reception by many informed organizations shows how politically motivated the use of evidence can be. But it also shows that scientific peer pressures still can serve to discredit demonstrably false arguments.

11. NIOSH, Department of Health, Education, and Welfare, *National Occupational Hazard Survey, Volume 3* (Washington, D.C.: Government Printing Office, 1976).

12. Arthur Young and Co., "Economic Impact of OSHA Arsenic Standard" (April 1976), mimeo.

13. In a risk assessment submitted to the Ninth Circuit Court in January 1981, OSHA estimated that current exposures to arsenic were causing eight to twenty-eight cancer deaths a year. See Kenneth Chu, Affidavit to the 9th Circuit Court in ASARCO et al. v. OSHA, 78-1959.

14. Michael D. Hogan and David G. Hoel, "Estimated Cancer Risk Associated with Occupational Asbestos Exposure," *Risk Analysis* (March 1981), 1(1):67–76.

15. Richard Doll and Richard Peto, *The Causes of Cancer: Quantitative Estimates of Avoidable Risks of Cancer in the United States Today* (New York: Oxford University Press, 1981).

Appendix F

1. The difference in absolute costs depends on the distribution of costs among firms and the shapes of the marginal costs curves they face. For example, if two firms with the same marginal cost curve have different exposure levels, the difference in compliance costs will increase until the PEL equals the exposure level at the plant with better controls. Beyond that point the compliance costs grow equally for both firms. In contrast, if the firm with the lower exposure level has a less steeply sloping marginal cost curve (a plausible assumption), then further decreases in the PEL will increase the absolute difference in compliance costs.

2. A third benefit that challenging standards can provide to industry comes from the effect that it has on OSHA. Each challenge reinforces the expectation that future standards will be challenged, including OSHA to try to make elaborate defenses of its standards and to avoid promulgating ones that will be vulnerable in court. However, this benefit is likely to be perceived as an *external* benefit by many industries, accruing to others who will come later and not to themselves. As in other cases, the chemical industry may see itself as a frequent enough player to take this benefit into account. However, as I describe in the text, most of the externalities faced by the chemical industry seem likely to encourage cooperation rather than conflict.

Index

Page numbers in *italics* indicate tables.